Family Constellations in Contemporary Ibero-American and Slavic Literatures

Family Constellations in Contemporary Ibero-American and Slavic Literatures

Historical Imaginary, Transnationality, Narrative Form

Edited by
Anna Artwińska, Ángela Calderón, and Jobst Welge

DE GRUYTER

We acknowledge financial support for the publication of the open access book by the Sächsisches Staatsministerium für Wissenschaft, Kultur und Tourismus. We also want to thank the Fritz Thyssen Foundation for their extremely generous financial support of this publication. We would like to thank Matteo Colombi for his inspired suggestion of Paul Klee's painting "Family of Flowers V" for the cover art. Furthermore, our sincere thanks go to Juliana Błaszczyk for her indefatigable work with the preparation of the final manuscript.

UNIVERSITÄT LEIPZIG

Fritz Thyssen Stiftung für Wissenschaftsförderung

ISBN 978-3-11-120776-6
e-ISBN (PDF) 978-3-11-120866-4
e-ISBN (EPUB) 978-3-11-120947-0
DOI https://doi.org/10.1515/9783111208664

Library of Congress Control Number: 2024939648

Bibliographic information published by the Deutsche Nationalbibliothek
The Deutsche Nationalbibliothek lists this publication in the Deutsche Nationalbibliografie; detailed bibliographic data are available on the internet at http://dnb.dnb.de.

Cover image: bpk/The Solomon R. Guggenheim Foundation/Art Resource, NY.
Typesetting: Integra Software Services Pvt. Ltd.

www.degruyter.com

Contents

Introductory Matter

Introductory Matter

Anna Artwińska, Ángela Calderón, and Jobst Welge

Family Constellations in Contemporary Ibero-American and Slavic Literatures

1 Familial Relations, Imagined Bonds, and Literary Form

Since the nineteenth century, the family novel, or family saga has been an important sub-genre of the novel, which, through the depiction of a narrative line that spans several generations, has frequently been used to represent crises and transformations of national histories and identities (Weigel 2006; Welge 2015). Such allegorical or synecdochic tendencies characterize also well-known examples of this form, such as Thomas Mann's *Buddenbrooks* (1901), Maria Dąbrowska's *Noce i dnie* (1932–1934) [Nights and Days] or Gabriel García Márquez's *Cien años de soledad* (1967) [*One Hundred Years of Solitude* (1970)]. In such classical texts, families are typically decadent, yet this appears against a patriarchal framework, and the form of these novels is often characterized by an epic sweep and by a (post-)naturalist understanding of genealogical causes. While familial relations continue to play a significant role in contemporary literature, these novels – or at least the novels we are interested in – are no longer 'family novels' in the sense outlined above, nor are the families conceived as extended genealogies or organic micro-unities. Because of their commemorative function and transgenerational perspective, they share similarities with the recent German 'family and generational novels' (see Eichenberg 2009; Costagli and Galli 2010), but go beyond this pattern in terms of content and structure. Instead, we see a marked difference in the ways 'family' is conceived of, both generally and in its narrative representation through literary form.

The term we have adopted here, 'family constellations,' acknowledges these different possibilities of construing narratives around the relationship between individual family members, both present and absent ones, but also of non-blood relations conceived of as 'family.' And although the deconstruction of notions such as 'blood ties' or 'kinship' has long been the focus of cultural studies dealing with family issues,[1] the literary texts we will discuss are challenging, because they do not so

1 Biological descent as the basis of kinship was questioned by Claude Lévi-Strauss: "There is no doubt that the biological family exists and persists in human society. But what gives kinship its character as a social fact is not what it must retain from nature: it is the essential step by which

Anna Artwińska, Ángela Calderón, Jobst Welge, Leipzig University

https://doi.org/10.1515/9783111208664-001

much redefine the semantic fields of family and generation on a theoretical level, but rather test the boundaries of these fields through plot, storyline and character constellation. For this reason, in most of these texts, the sources of genealogical knowledge, such as the family tree, are treated in a non-canonical, subversive way. In literature, as in life, a family is constituted in a performative praxis, which allows us to draw parallels with the production of gender. In contemporary family novels one can observe the strategy of "doing family" (see Schier and Jurczyk 2007, 10). This implies not necessarily a radical departure from the idea of the family as "well-founded fiction" (Bourdieu 1996, 20), but rather refers to the exploration of different family constellations in their relation to the respective (homodiegetic) narrator, as is the case in many of the novels discussed in this volume.

Furthermore, and especially in relation to the perspectival representation of autofictional forms, family constellations continue to function in a vertical way, for instance as narratives of filiation (Viart 2019, 18), where typically a first-person narrator embarks on an 'archaeological' quest for family secrets and histories. Yet some autofictional works also emphasize the horizontal dimension. For instance, the autosociobiographical novel *El viaje a pie de Johann Sebastian Bach* (2014) [Johann Sebastian's Journey on Foot] by the Spanish author Carlos Pardo constantly emphasizes the communal dimension of his narrative, speaking about his family – and especially his siblings – in the first-person plural. This tendency, to see the self as part of a group, applies not only to the social class of the family, in this case a rather poor lower-middle class family, but also to the age cohort of the generation, which, as a temporal frame and a structuring principle of narrative, has experienced a certain come-back in recent times, in order to supply a broader pattern of meaning and cohesion, after the demise of the *grands récits* (Weigel 2006, 108).

A reconfiguration of family narratives may also be realized through the hovering presence of such figures as a half-brother or surrogate mother, or through the subversive use of such motifs as 'origin,' or the 'family album,' in which narrative is generated through the intermedial relation of words and images (Venzon

it separates itself from it. A system of kinship does not consist in the objective ties of descent or consanguinity between individuals; it exists only in the consciousness of men, it is an arbitrary system of ideas, not the spontaneous development of a factual situation" (1963, 66). That the equation of kinship with consanguinity occurs primarily in Western cultures can be found in Christina von Braun: "The majority of people in the world do not assume that kinship is constituted by blood ties. Rather, family is defined by characteristics such as: living together, sharing food, feeding from the same soil, working together, suffering together, sharing memories, taking responsibility for each other" (2017, 22).

2024). Thus, it is not so much a matter of writing a 'family history' as of thinking about the *possibilities* of writing a family history, based on the particular case study one is trying to convey. The reasons for this distanced attitude toward the possibility of a linear, coherent, and complete family narrative are complex. One important reason certainly lies in the condition of the global present. Secondly, the aftermath of the violent history of the twentieth century continues to exert its influence: after the Shoah, after the Second World War, after the era of totalitarianism and military dictatorships in Europe and beyond, family history can only be recounted piecemeal, in a fragmentary way, since one very often has too little knowledge about what had truly occurred and one is confronted with speculation and gaps as well as the deliberate silence of older generations. The third reason is generated by the meta-reflection on the old genre of the family novel: many authors attempt to incorporate their reflections about writing in the molds of this genre within the story they are trying to tell. The new 'family histories' thus become spaces for exploring the ways in which a twenty-first-century family novel can be constructed in terms of both content and form.

An example of vertical, autofictional and meta-poetic storytelling is *Książka* (2011) [Book] by Polish writer Mikołaj Łoziński. It consists of eleven very short chapters with the following titles: "Drawer," "Telephone," "Hair Clippers," "Coffee Maker," "Notebook," "Ring," "Key," "Sign," "Glasses," "Package" and "Cigarette Holder." Each chapter recounts a scene, story or anecdote from the author's Polish-Jewish family history, with the titular object acting as a trigger for the narrative, a reminder or signature of past events. The scenes, stories or anecdotes are brief and focus on small, almost impressionist details. The objects remind the narrator of certain situations or encounters with his family, evoke childhood memories, point to the phantomatic and mysterious in his family's history. The chapters are separated by black pages documenting the conversations the narrator had with his parents and brother about writing the book. They have plain titles such as "Mother," "Father," "Older Brother." Leafing through the book, the black pages look like they have been taken from a photo album: the printed word replaces the photographs. The conversations are mostly very short: they provide information about the process of making the book and at the same time show the affective involvement of each family member in the family history that had just been sketched out. Let us look at a conversation with the father as an example:

> "My son, there's one more thing I don't want you to write about."
> "Oh no, what is it?"
> "It's my father's party card. In 1968 they took him in for questioning. He destroyed the guy who interrogated him. He looked down on the bastard and, by the end of the interrogation, was mocking him. But why didn't he hand in his party card? [...] I can't understand that. That's why I have an alternative version that I tell everyone: When they asked him about

> his nationality, Dad got up, threw his party card on the table and walked out. Let's keep this version in. It's the one he deserves more [...]."
>
> ["Synku, jest jeszcze jeden przedmiot, o którym masz nie pisać".
> "O nie, jaki?"
> "Legitymacja partyjna mojego taty. W 1968 wezwali go na przesłuchanie. Zniszczył faceta, który go przesłuchiwał. Potraktował gnoja z góry, a na końcu wyśmiał. Ale czemu nie oddał wtedy legitymacji? [...] Nie jestem w stanie tego zrozumieć. Dlatego mam alternatywną wersję, którą wszystkim opowiadam. Kiedy spytali, jakiej jest narodowości, tata wstał, rzucił książeczkę partyjną na stół i wyszedł. Niech ta wersja zostanie. Po prostu bardziej mu się należy [...]" (Łoziński 2011, 125).

This quote shows that the narrator does not conform to his family's expectations. The party card is introduced *ex negativo* into the collection of family objects. The first-person narrator gives himself the freedom to decide which items will be best to capture and tell the family story. His choice is emotionally charged: There is almost always an affective connection between an object and a family member – though not always a positive one. The hair clippers, for example, remind the mother of her post-war childhood and of living with her irascible father, who once cut off almost all of her long hair in a fit of rage. The objects in the book have a strong presence: most are ordinary items that are an integral part of everyday life. The writer describes their origin, appearance and, in some cases, their movement from one place to another. This approach is intended to give the impression that things, like people, can have a biography and a past. At the same time, the process conveys an impression of materiality: while family history is often incomplete and difficult to grasp, memory can crystallize in objects. The materiality emphasized in the text is, of course, conveyed by narrative means. As the handbook *Literature & Material Culture* puts it: "Literary texts thus become, in a special way, a medium for the reflection of materiality, corporeality, spatiality, texture and perception itself. [...] [A]lthough the material side of things is lost – the irritating ambivalence of the symbolic and at the same time non-symbolic nature of things becomes recognizable" (Kimmich 2018, 21).

Mikołaj Łoziński constantly shifts between "the irritating ambivalence of the symbolic and non-symbolic nature of things." The non-existent thingness of things in the text is overcome by the final product: Writing has created an object that you can actually hold in your hands. His book, entitled *Book*, can be seen as a collection of imaginary items. At the same time, it is a modern family album in which some pages are missing and some photographs have faded. Instead of a 'real,' linear and coherent text, Łoziński's narrative album presents the results of a long and complex creative process.

The novels being examined in this collection may also in other ways be related to questions of memory, inheritance, transgenerational trauma, etc., which is in turn reflected in their fragmentary or essayistic form. As Astrid Erll has written, family memory is a typical mode of inter-generational memory: "a kind of collective memory that is constituted through ongoing social interaction and communication between children, parents, and grandparents" (2011, 306). With respect to the disruptive and traumatic experiences of violent history, Marianne Hirsch (1997) has coined the term postmemory, taken up by several essays in this volume. In those post-memorial novels, genealogy becomes, in the spirit of Michel Foucault, a network of problematic connections and tangled destinies. Blood relations have no intrinsic value, nor are they obvious: in these stories, one's descent is never certain:

> [T]o follow the complex course of descent is to maintain passing events in their proper dispersion; it is to identify the accidents, the minute deviations or conversely, the complete reversal – the errors, the false appraisals, and the faulty calculations that gave birth to those things that continue to exist and have value for us; it is to discover that truth or being do not lie at the root of what we know and what we are, but the exteriority of accidents (Foucault 1993, 146).

This tendency can be seen in Sergei Lebedev's novel *Predjel zabvjenia* (2013) [*Oblivion*], one of the first Russian novels of the twenty-first century to explore the legacy of the Soviet gulag system in a transgenerational perspective, and a book about the power and danger of family secrets passed down to, or perhaps silenced for, successive generations (see Artwińska 2016). Its narrator and protagonist is a young student, the author's alter ego, who tells the story of his childhood, growing up between Moscow and a summer house somewhere in the provinces where he spent his holidays. The central figure in his family constellation is the so-called "Grandfather II" – an elderly, blind neighbour who acts as family confidant and friend. The relationship between him and the narrator seems to resemble the classic grandfather-grandson relationship, although the boy experiences a strange tension and fear of the old man. Feeling that his blind neighbour's life is full of gaps and half-truths, the narrator attempts to reconstruct his life's story. In the course of this process, it soon becomes clear that this story is inextricably linked to the history of twentieth-century Russia. As a young man, the neighbour was in charge of a Siberian labour camp, responsible for the deaths of countless prisoners and a staunch supporter of Stalinist terror. An ensuing visit to a labour camp has no therapeutic function: becoming aware of the camps makes it possible for the narrator to unravel his family's secrets and free himself from the tormenting feeling of a permanent unknown, but at the same time it irredeemably changes his identity. Once he realizes that the figurines and toys his other grandfather keeps in his drawer were made by slave laborers, and were almost certainly made from fragments of human and animal skin, he is no longer the same person. For him, the past becomes a stigma, made all the more difficult to bear by the fact that perpetrator trauma and its aftermath are still taboo in Russian culture.

Lebedev also plays with the idea of non-blood relations and defines family as an assortment of random affinities. When the narrator is hospitalised after an accident and needs blood transfusion, "Grandfather II" becomes his donor, dying in the process but saving his "grandson's" life. Thus, the cultural bond becomes intertwined with a physical bond, which the narrator experiences as a kind of imprint: "Thus my existence coincided with his, and I was never just myself again – Grandfather II's blood, which saved me, circulated in me [...] I grew up branded by the inestimable sacrifice made by Grandfather II; I grew like a graft on old wood." (Lebedev 2016, 60) ["Так мое существование совместилось с его существованием; я уже никогда не был до конца самим собой – во мне обращалась кровь Второго деда, спасшая меня; [...] я рос под знаком неоценимой жертвы, которую Второй дед принес ради меня; рос как черенок, привитый на старое дерево" (Lebedev 2011, 42)].

2 Historical Imagination

Given the essential relevance of the personal and public past, we have to ask how this comparative dimension has been linked to the question of the historical imagination. For this purpose, we will first introduce some ideas discussed by Kaisa Kaakinen in her study *Comparative Literature and the Historical Imagination* (2017). The first point made by Kaakinen is to address the very notion of the contemporary, namely by highlighting its intrinsic heterogeneity: "the present has a particularly uncertain status between the other temporal modes of the past and the future, and the 'contemporary' assumes a unity of heterogeneous experiences" (2017, 10). This implies, for instance, that the contemporary is no longer understood within a logic of progressive development and linear chronology, as it had underwritten, to a large extent, the regime of Western modernity. Of course, this is hardly controversial; yet Kaakinen highlights how this situation fosters the "coming together of different historical trajectories in the same present" (2017, 15), including the present(s) of heterogeneous contemporary readers in a global context of reading. A comparative dimension is thus introduced, as Rebecca Walkowitz (2017) has put it, when literary fiction is "born translated," which is to say, when it already implies and projects its (possible) relations to multiple places and languages. Furthermore, as Kaakinen proposes, such spatial and temporal multiplications may be concretely analyzed on the level of narrative. For instance, there arises the question of how larger units of narrative are linked to each other, how they suggest analogy and juxtaposition, how their relation is possibly left undetermined, in the form of *parataxis*, or what Kaakinen calls weak analogy: "While hypotaxis emphasizes hierarchy and causality, parataxis is a mode of linkage that does not determine the evoked relationships in terms of cause or subordination" (2017, 19). Such an undetermined relation may take on the shape of a specific form of untimeliness, namely a posttraumatic temporality. In other words, we may ask how such narratives may generate historical linkages and juxtapositions across temporal, geographical and medial gaps. At stake, then, is not just the question of "multidirectional memory" (Rothberg 2009), but an analysis of the "structures of asymmetrical address in transnational literary texts" (Kaakinen 2017, 23).

The narrative imagination also allows for the exploration of a given historical context as a space of possibilities (Meretoja, 2017), so that "different historical experiences and orientations come into contact and conflict" (Kaakinen 2017, 38). By addressing the question of divergent readerly positions, Kaakinen provides a productive model for the analysis of a historical imaginary that is engendered by simultaneous and heterogeneous constellations. A recent novel by the Puerto Rican author Marta Aponte Alsina, *La muerte feliz de William Carlos Williams* (2022) [The Happy Death of William Carlos Williams], exemplifies how the historical imaginary connects family relations across time and space. The bio-fictional narrative of the famous North American modernist poet is traced back to the history of his father, a perfume merchant working in Latin America as well as his mother, an important painter in nineteenth-century Puerto Rico, who traveled to Paris. At the same time, this biographical narrative is linked to the author's own family history, thus creating a network of historical juxtapositions, connections or comparisons, and effects of simultaneity.

Historical relationality of the paratactic kind, the constant juxtaposition of autobiographical memory with a hypothetically reconstructed family memory may certainly be observed in Maria Stepanova's widely translated work *Pamjati pamjati romans* (2019) [*In Memory of Memory*], which correlates family memories with excerpts of letters and description of photos or objects. Like Kaakinen, Stepanova, in this highly self-conscious novel, insists on the undoing of the causal chain of narrative as an effect of the present regime of temporality: "Digital storage gives us a whole range of possibilities, and it affects how we see things: history, biography, one's own or another's text – nothing is seen as a linear text unrolling in time, glued with the wallpaper paste of cause and effect" (Stepanova 2021, 90) ["Веер возможностей, которые предоставляют новые носители, меняет способы восприятия: ни история, ни биография, ни свой текст, ни чужой больше не воспринимаются как цепочка – как события, разворачивающиеся во времени, скрепленные клеем причин и следствий." (Stepanova 2019, 80)]. Stepanova's book mirrors the history of her own family in a plethora of testimonies, artworks, and allegories, suggesting a sense of universal interconnection, but also highlighting moments of a-synchronicity, of a daily life that almost paradoxically has existed alongside the catastrophes of the twentieth century. Reflecting on the hypertrophy of postmemory (she cites Hirsch explicitly; 76) during this epoch, she sees the past as overpowering the present: "A story about myself became a story about my ancestors" (Stepanova 2021, 77) ["Рассказ о себе оказывается рассказом о предках." (Stepanova 2019, 69)].

3 Transnationality

What strikes us when looking at contemporary 'family novels' is that they very often tell a transnational story, that is, a story that cannot be confined to a clearly defined cultural space but one that meanders between different nations, cultures, languages, and memories. Our comparative perspective on Ibero-American and Slavic literatures makes this case for the two cultural areas, respectively, yet we will also consider concrete 'entanglements' *between* the two cultural (linguistic, geographical) fields, thus making some attempts to transcend our respective disciplinary, philological boundaries (Hudzik et al. 2024). This tendency can be explained by the coordinates of the contemporary hybrid and globalized world: due to the processes of migration, cultural translation, and mobility, there is an increasing awareness of the hybrid nature of cultures that can no longer be described as homogenous, since the homogeneity of territory, language, history, and ethnicity is considered to no longer exist. Many contemporary authors of family novels lead transnational lives themselves – their literary texts may therefore be categorized as transnational when the authors' own biographies elude national localization. As a result, in many texts not only the present of the narrative but also the familial past is presented through a transnational prism, as a heterogeneous, multicultural past that cannot be ascribed to a national paradigm. Moreover, the critique of essentialist thinking that is (rightly) characteristic of our present leads to a situation in which the category of the nation is no longer perceived as a fixed entity. While in modern family novels, as Aleida Assmann has shown, the relationship between nation and family was organized around the principle of analogy, the contemporary family novel tends to assume that 'nation' and 'family' are no longer analogous and that other reference points are needed for the narrative construction of a family story. "In the new family novel," writes Assmann, "there are no analogies and mirroring relationships as in the older family sagas. The family has ceased to represent the whole of society and its culture" (2009, 51). In addition, the formerly rigid or 'organic' concepts of 'nation' and 'family' have been consistently deconstructed in recent years, both in research and in literary practice. The idea of the nation as an 'imagined community,' to use Benedict Anderson's term, corresponds to the notion of family as an 'elective kinship' in which traditional figures of thought and concepts of genealogy, such as blood ties or family tree (see Weigel 2006), are no longer considered central to the concept of 'family.'

An interesting example for such a sort of transnational writing and perspective is the novel *Chmurdalia* (2010) [Cloudalia] by Polish author Joanna Bator. It is a sequel to Bator's family saga, *Piaskowa góra* (2009) [Sandy Mountain], which tells the story of the Chmura family living in the People's Republic of Poland, with flashbacks to the Second World War. In *Chmurdalia*, the story focuses on the character of Dominika Chmura, a representative of the generation born in the late socialist era but whose adult life began to unfold after the political changes of 1989. Unlike her parents, Dominika does not feel that she belongs anywhere in particular and does not want to spend her life in a (post)socialist settlement in the south-western Polish city of Wałbrzych or in Poland in general. As a nomad, she constantly moves between countries and cultures – she has lived in Germany, in the USA and on a Greek island, and she speaks several different languages and defies categorization in terms of nationality, gender, and sexual orientation. Despite the physical and mental distance, Dominika cannot completely separate herself from her family's history.[2] Unlike her mother, Jadwiga, who clings to the glorious family myth about her Polish father, who supposedly died in the Second World War, Dominika is not afraid to be confronted with her actual Polish-Jewish origins. Since national affinity is not significant for her, she does not feel obliged to perpetuate the ideas of a 'good,' i.e. purely ethnic Polish background, which are still very important for Jadwiga. On the contrary, her Jewish ancestors help her to understand certain aspects of herself or her personality. At the same time, she is not obsessed with her family history, nor is she obsessed with writing it down. Much more important to Dominika are her chosen

2 Without wanting to negate the transnational perspective of texts like *Chmurdalia*, when analyzing them one must always consider the role that the national plays in the transnational – also as a possibly negative plane of reference. Indeed, the relationship between the earlier family novels, which intertwined the categories of family and nation as analogous, and the more recent ones, which dispense with this principle, need not be construed as one of substitution: "[I]n a so-called post-national age, 'the national' as a framework for identity and memory-making is still a powerful one, indeed one that may be reinforced in response to calls for new types of confederation and integration." (de Cesari and Rigney 2014, 25) This is indeed an important point, since the new transnational family novels do not emerge out of a void. Even when they are detached from their respective national contexts, they are still connected to them.

relatives and friends she meets in the course of her nomadic life, and the resulting family-like constellations. In the words of literary critic Przemysław Czapliński: "Characters do not appear [in *Chmurdalia* – A.A.] because they belong to the family, but because of chance encounters. The novel thus has the structure of a genealogical bush – a tangle that resembles gossip rather than a chronicle" (2010). In *Chmurdalia*, Bator adopts this plot device to ironically comment on the ubiquity of family narratives in Polish culture, especially those created by the intelligentsia and used as a class distinction. In *Piaskowa góra*, she already playfully dealt with genealogical motifs – for example, by having Dominika's grandmother fill a German family album found in a house formerly inhabited by Germans with her own family photographs – and in *Chmurdalia* this tendency is intensified. Thus, the story of Dominika Chmura is interwoven with an internal narrative about "Napoleon's Chamber Pot," an object that symbolically unites the Polish-Jewish-American family history of Dominika and her African-American friend Sara, and at the same time ironically reveals the dangers presented by family myths as such.

Bator's project thus exemplifies what we see as a characteristic tendency of contemporary literature, namely a more flexible interpretation of, and correlation between, the terms 'family' and 'nation.' Transnational movements and migrations are prominent in many novels by authors of Jewish descent, as is the case also for the autofictional novel *A Resistência* (2016) [Resistance] by the Brazilian writer Julián Fuks, about his relation to a brother that his parents had adopted before fleeing the dictatorial regime in Argentina for Brazil. The transnational aspects of contemporary family narratives are therefore indicative of how these texts make claims toward specific (national) locations while simultaneously engaging with other geographical and cultural orientations. This deeply relational practice means that the novels produce tensions and "analogies between past and present, between places and dislocations" (Ekelund 2022, 21). The possible move from concrete, inhabited places to broader entanglements and imaginary reconfigurations of space – including world literary space – is evident in many of the novels considered in this volume.

Bibliography

Aponte Alsina, Marta. *La muerte feliz de William Carlos Williams*. Barcelona: Candaya, 2022.

Artwińska, Anna. "Transfer międzypokoleniowy, epigenetyka i 'więzy krwi.' O *Małej Zagładzie* Anny Janko i *Granicy zapomnienia* Siergieja Lebiediewa." *Teksty Drugie* 1 (2016): 13–29.

Assmann, Aleida. "Unbewältigte Erbschaften. Fakten und Fiktionen im zeitgenössischen Familienroman." Eds. Andreas Kraft/Mark Weißhaupt. *Generationen: Erfahrung – Erzählung – Identität*, Konstanz: UVK, 2009. 49–71.

Bator, Joanna. *Chmurdalia.* Warszawa: WAB, 2010.

Bourdieu, Pierre. "On the Family as a Realized Category." *Theory, Culture & Society* 13.3 (August 1996): 19–26.

Costagli, Simone, and Matteo Galli. *Deutsche Familienromane: Literarische Genealogien und internationaler Kontext*. München: Fink, 2010. 1–28.

Czapliński, Przemysław. "Not in English Yet: Cloudalia." *Beweekly. link with culture*. https://www.biweekly.pl/article/1253-not-in-english-yetcloudalia.html (February 22, 2024).

De Cesari, Chiara, and Ann Rigney. Eds. "Introduction." *Transnational memory*. Berlin/Boston: De Gruyter, 2014. 1–25.

Eichenberg, Ariane. *Familie-Ich-Nation. Narrative Analysen zeitgenössischer Generationenromane.* Göttingen: V&R unipress, 2009.

Ekelund, Bo G. "Land, language, literature: Cosmopolitan and vernacular claims to place." *Claiming Space. Locations and Orientations in World Literature*. Eds. Bo G. Ekelund/Adnan Mahmutović/Helena Wulff. New York: Bloomsbury Academic, 2022. 1–27.

Erll, Astrid. "Locating family in cultural studies." *Journal of Comparative Family Studies* 42.3 (2011): 303–318.

Foucault, Michel. "Nietzsche, Genealogy, History." *Language, Counter-Memory Practice. Selected Essays and Interviews*. Ed. Donald F. Bouchard. Trans. Sherry Simon. Ithaca/New York: Cornell UP, 1993. 139–166.

Fuks, Julián. *A Resistência*. São Paulo: Companhia das Letras, 2018.

Hirsch, Marianne. *Family Frames: Photography, Narrative, and Postmemory*. Cambridge, MA: Harvard UP, 1997.

Hudzik, Agnieszka Helena, Joanna Moszczyńska, and Patricia A. Gwozdz. Eds. *Elective Affinities. Rethinking Entanglements between Latin America and East Central Europe*. Berlin: De Gruyter, 2024.

Kaakinen, Kaisa. *Comparative Literature and the Historical Imagination. Reading Conrad, Weiss, Sebald.* Cham: Palgrave Macmillan, 2018.

Kimmich, Dorothee. "Dinge in Texten." *Handbuch Literatur & Materielle Kultur*. Eds. Susanne Scholz/Ulrike Vedder. Berlin/Boston: De Gruyter, 2018. 21–29.

Lebedev, Sergej. *Oblivion.* Transl. Antonina W. Bouis. London: Head of Zeus, 2022 [e-book].

Lebedev, Sergej. *Predjel zabvjenija*. Moskva: Pervoe sentjabrja, 2011.

Lévi-Strauss, Claude. "Language and kinship." *Structural Anthropology*. Transl. C. Jacobson/B. G. Schoepf. New York: Basis Book, 1963. 31–80.

Łoziński, Mikołaj. *Książka*. Kraków: Wydawnictwo Literackie, 2011.

Meretoja, Hanna. *Ethics of Storytelling. Narrative Hermeneutics, History, and the Possible*. Oxford: Oxford UP, 2018.

Pardo, Carlos. *El viaje a pie de Johann Sebastian Bach*. Cáceres: Periférica, 2014.

Rothberg, Michael. *Multidirectional Memory. Remembering the Holocaust in the Age of Decolonization.* Stanford: Stanford UP, 2009.

Schier, Michaela, and Karin Jurczyk. "Familie als Herstellungsleistung in Zeiten der Entgrenzung." *Aus Politik und Zeitgeschichte* 34 (2007): 10–17.
Stepanova, Maria. *In Memory of Memory.* Transl. Sasha Dugdale. New York: New Directions, 2021.
Stepanova, Maria. *Pamjati pamjati: romans.* Moskva: Novoe izdatel'stvo, 2019.
Venzon, Ruben. *Revelaciones. Álbum familiar y fototextualidad autobiográfica en la narrativa española del siglo XXI.* Madrid/Frankfurt a. M.: Iberoamericana Vervuert, 2024.
Viart, Dominique. "Les récits de filiation. Naissance, raisons et évolutions d'une forme littéraire." *Cahiers ERTA* 19 (2019): 9–40.
von Braun, Christina. "Rote Tinte. Ohne Schrift keine Blutslinien." *Die Familie. Ein Archiv.* Ed. Ellen Strittmatter. *Marbacher Katalog* 70 (2018): 22–40.
Walkowitz, Rebecca. *Born Translated: The Contemporary Novel in an Age of World Literature.* New York: Columbia UP, 2017.
Weigel, Sigrid. "Familie und Generation." *Genea-Logik. Generation, Tradition und Evolution zwischen Kultur- und Naturwissenschaften.* Ed. Sigrid Weigel. München: Fink, 2006. 87–138.
Welge, Jobst. *Genealogical Fictions. Cultural Periphery and Historical Change in the Modern Novel.* Baltimore: Johns Hopkins Press, 2015.
White, Nicholas. "Family Histories and Family Plots." *The Cambridge Companion to Emile Zola.* Ed. Brian Nelson. Cambridge: Cambridge UP, 2007. 19–38.

Anna Artwińska, Ángela Calderón, and Jobst Welge

Overview of the Volume

This volume examines Ibero-American as well as Slavic literatures of the twenty-first century and studies how historical imaginaries are functionalized for individual, collective, and (post)national identities. The volume as a whole – but also on the level of some of its individual contributions – proposes a matrix of *comparative* constellations among the areas of contemporary Slavic and Ibero-American literatures. In fact, this project was born from our intuition that one can identify certain family resemblances, *Familienähnlichkeiten* (Ludwig Wittgenstein) among the works of these different literatures – namely with respect to how these texts relate historical experiences via the narrative presentations of family constellations. Additionally, this comparative dimension is also a vital principle or symptom *within* many examples of contemporary family narratives.

Furthermore, these novels are often grounded in transgenerational memories, with regard to historical events, catastrophes, and traumas that have shaped the individual and collective experiences of the twentieth century – and which continue to reverberate and to be represented in the literature of the twenty-first century. They are written by members of a generation that, as a rule, did not directly experience these historical events. It is also significant that these narratives are no longer conceived as representing national identities, but paradigmatically speak for a collective that defines itself in regional, ethnic, religious or ideological terms. Moreover, many, if not most of the representative examples considered here are to varying degrees conceived as transnational with respect to their depiction of familial stories and experiences. Furthermore, while typically grounded in (trans)national experiences and local positionings, these works of contemporary literature often are more or less directly conceived for an international readership, just as they are participating in global literary trends. It seems, therefore, that these narratives of family constellations are in need of more flexible typological rubrics and interpretive frameworks. Intended as a sustained comparative study of such family narratives, this volume is a contribution to understanding how historical caesura, experiences, and their literary representation work on the self-understanding of the present. This volume is based on a conference which we organized at Leipzig University in November 2022 and which served to foster and deepen the kind of

Anna Artwińska, Ángela Calderón, Jobst Welge, Leipzig University

https://doi.org/10.1515/9783111208664-002

cross-area and comparative perspectives reflected in the essays. We hope that they might inspire more comparative and collaborative research in these fields.

We have divided the volume into three different clusters to suggest formal and thematic proximities and resonances between different case studies, yet these constellations are far from rigid, and we invite readers to combine them in different ways.

1 Transnational Relations/Constellations

The collaborative analysis by **Anne Brüske** and **Karoline Thaidigsmann** shows how the transnational constellation of our volume is here enacted in the context of a single, comparative essay, with respect to a specific literary-artistic medium: the graphic narrative. In this essay, the authors propose a comparative analysis of two contemporary graphic narratives, from Cuba and Poland, respectively. In both cases the medium serves to represent the autobiographic experience of growing up in a socialist country from a retrospective, diasporic perspective, involving questions of the relations to family, (trans)nationality, as well as the relation between micro- and macro-history. The combination of visual and textual elements, often not only complementing but contradicting each other, the authors argue, puts the reader in a position to trace and imagine the interconnectedness of spatial and temporal dimensions. The two near-contemporary works being closely analyzed here, *"Notes for a journey... to Germany..."* [*"Apuntes para un viaje... a Alemania..."* (2016)], by Carlos Aguilera and Aldo Damián Menéndez, and *Totally Not Nostalgia. Memoir* [*Totalnie nie nostalgia. Memuar* (2017)], by Wanda Hagedorn and Jacek Frąś, are both remarkable for their complex integration of cultural and global references into their 'private,' temporally layered narratives. While in the Cuban example the family narrative is subsumed by a broader reflection on life in totalitarian or repressive societies, the Polish example uses the family narrative to reflect on such broader issues from a post-socialist perspective. The Cuban example shows – in a way that is also echoed by the contribution by Rodríguez-Alfonso – how the social and affective institution of the family is replaced by the ideological program of state collectivization, and how this program is aesthetically realized through state propaganda. The essay argues that the travel narrative and the displacement to Germany foster a multi-directional approach with respect, for instance, to the practice of ideological indoctrination in both socialist Cuba and Nazi Germany. The Polish example portrays the memory of a dysfunctional, patriarchal family during the 1960s–1970s and its analogies with broader structures of power, both experienced as forms of alienation.

Although a somewhat more conventional narrative, the essay demonstrates how *Totally not Nostalgia* marshals a visual, implicit allusion to a self-portrait by Mexican artist Frida Kahlo as a sign for female empowerment. Despite the different approaches taken by the two graphic novels, including the different strategies to dismantle the structure of the family, or to imagine alternatives to the notion of the patriarchal and nuclear family, both examples demonstrate how the visual/verbal interface of this medium can make an important contribution to the cultural imaginary of post-socialist societies – and their family relations.

In her article, **Anna Artwińska** compares the novel *K.* (2011) by Brazilian author Bernardo Kucinski with the novel *The House with the Two Towers* [*Dom z dwiema wieżami* (2018)] by Polish-Swedish journalist Maciej Zaremba Bielawski. Both works are based on violent and traumatic events that happened to the real-life authors: The kidnapping of a sister by the security forces in Brazil (Kucinski) and the 'discovery' of Jewish origins and subsequent migration to Sweden (Zarem-ba Bielawski). In both cases, however, the autofictional mode and the narrative role reversal both alienate and universalize their own family history, making it exemplary for the 'big History' in Brazil and Poland respectively, as well as for Jewish history in general. What Kucinski and Zaremba Bielawski have in common is their focus on a selected family constellation (between father and daughter in *K.* and between son and mother in *The House with the Two Towers*), which determines the dynamics of the plot. Artwińska argues that comparative reading highlights central characteristics of contemporary family novels, such as transnationality, cultural translation, the affiliation with different cultures of memory, and an experimental approach to form.

In her contribution, **Maria de Fátima Marinho** considers a broad arch of the recent history of the Portuguese novel. While the novels of the 1980s and 1990s explored the repercussions of History on the lives of individual families, the more recent novels of the new century, Marinho argues, are built on a more indirect relation between historical change and domestic life, as represented through individual focalization, often dwelling especially on the experience of women. Surveying this recent production in a synthetic fashion, Marinho identifies three general tendencies, as illustrated by representative examples. Firstly, there are novels that focus on a personal past and entertain only a tenuous relationship to the external world, such as Teolinda Gersão's novel from 2021, *Julia Mann's Return to Paraty* (2021) [*O Regresso de Júlia Mann a Paraty*]. Secondly, there are novels dealing with a personal present that can only be explained by means of the past (such as Lídia Jorge's *The Memorables* [*Os Memoráveis*] from 2014). Finally, there are novels that feature personal focalizations of specific historical facts, which Marinho exemplifies with Maria Cardoso's *The Return* (2016) [*O Retorno* (2011)], a novel which uses a first person, adolescent male narrator to reflect on how the independence of Angola is experienced by a family subsequently moving 'back' to Portugal. Marinho's essay suggests a general panorama of how the narrative techniques of these novels reflect in oblique ways the interpenetration of private and public events and identities.

In her contribution, **Serena Cianciotto** explores Portuguese writer José Luís Peixoto's use of the multigenerational model in the novel *Book* [*Livro* (2010)]. The circular parabola that sees the book object pass through the hands of three generations of the same family, finally arriving at the eponymous narrator Livro, becomes a metaphor for the transmission of traumatic memory, from the twentieth century to the present, and across national borders, from those who experienced the events directly to the generation of post-memory. The transnational and transgenerational dimensions of the text touch on themes of dictatorship, poverty, emigration and return, as well as violence in both the public and the private domain. Through innovative narrative techniques and a strong autofictional and referential dimension, the novel affirms the necessity of memory as the only means of analyzing and questioning History and historical narratives. In her analysis of the novel, Cianciotto argues that the circle of eternal repetition and violence can only be broken through the establishment, within the memorial network, of 'oblique' familial relations, that is, relations not based on direct consanguinity or cohabitation, but rather on affective proximity and the transmission of knowledge.

2 Transgenerational/Transtemporal Relations

In her contribution, **Tamara Hundorova** shows how the confrontation with the Soviet past is linked to a critique of the figure of the mother and motherhood in contemporary Ukrainian literature. The symbolic equation of mother and nation, which can also be found in other postcolonial cultures, leads to the mother being held responsible for historical traumas on both an individual and a collective level, and serves as a projection screen for coming to terms with one's own colonial status. Based on novels by authors such as Maria Matios (*Sweet Darusya. A Tale of Two Villages* [*Солодка Даруся. Драма три життя* (2004); *Solodka Darusia. Drama na try zhyttia*]), Oksana Zabuzhko (*Fieldwork in Ukrainian Sex* [*Польові дослідження з українського сексу* (1996); *Polovi doslidzhennia z ukrainskoho seksu*]) and Evgenia Kononenko (*Nostalgia* [*Ностальгия* (2002); *Nostalhiia*]), Hundorova analyzes the strategies of dealing with the mother figure and her role in the respective family constellations before and after the collapse of the Soviet Union. It becomes clear that dissatisfaction with one's own collective identity in Ukraine leads to a kind of mother phobia, and that this dissatisfaction encompasses not only the political sphere, but also the maternal world of the family and home. An interesting variant of the criticism of the mother figure can be found in the texts of the post-2000 generation, in which the main character is often portrayed as a fatherless loser with a disturbed relationship to his own mother. Hundorova argues that such constellations, which can be found, for instance, in Sashko Ushkalov's story *BZhD. Crazynovel* [*БЖД. Crazynovel* (2008)], should be understood as manifestations of postcolonial traumas.

In his chapter **Michael Karrer** addresses questions of the family archive in a post-dictatorial context and with regard to the documentary, non-fictional film *Papirosen* (2011), by the Argentine filmmaker Gastón Solnicki. Invoking concepts from the critic Josefina Ludmer, and situating his analysis in a broader perspective of Argentinian 'microhistorical' documentaries, Karrer argues that the notion of family serves to form connections between different temporalities, and that the micro-historical approach, often incorporating photographs or home videos, provides an important corrective to official historical accounts. Being anchored in the flight of the filmmaker's Jewish grandparents from Nazi-occupied Poland, as well as in the story of his father's past life in Poland and Czechoslovakia, the film illustrates not only transgenerational relations (three generations) and family conflicts, but also the historical entanglements between Eastern Europe and Latin America. Karrer's detailed analysis of the audiovisual elements of the film highlights the ambivalent role of the filmmaker (as both implicated family member and exterior analyst) as well as the heterogeneous temporalities inscribed in the filmic material (the sophisticated montage of archival material and present recordings).

In his chapter, **Matteo Colombi** analyses the novel *With Baťa in the Jungle* [*S Baťou v džungli* (2017)] by the Czech writer Markéta Pilátová, whose life and work are closely linked to South America. The novel tells the story of a section of the Baťa family, the world-famous Czech shoe entrepreneurs who left the country for Brazil during the Second World War to escape Nazi rule, only to be forced into permanent exile by the socialist regime after the war. The novel is a work of both factual reconstruction of the Baťas' story, based on written documents and oral testimonies, and fiction. The textual analysis focuses on three aspects: firstly, the relationship between the family history and the violent past; secondly, the transgenerational and transnational representation of the family; and thirdly, the elements of *realismo mágico* [magic realism] that Pilátová has introduced into the text to show the tension between life and fiction. As Colombi argues, *With Baťa in the Jungle* aims to show the complexity of reconstructing the past by highlighting the different perspectives from which different family members remember and represent it. In the last part of the article, Colombi discusses an important aspect of the novel, the doubt about human agency, which can be seen as an element of the postmodern world.

The traumatic temporality discussed by Karrer in his analysis of a Jewish-Argentine family is similarly evident in the essay by **Jobst Welge**. He discusses the literary work by the Guatemalan-born author Eduardo Halfon in light of its autofictional, memorial, and transnational dimensions. The short novels and short stories of this writer, such as *The Polish Boxer* [*El boxeador polaco* (2008)], *Monastery* [*Monasterio* (2014)], or *Canción* [*Canción* (2021)], explore questions of Jewish identity and post-memory, of dislocation and belonging, in a transgenerational perspective. While a central role is accorded to the Polish past of the paternal grandfather of the author, a survivor of Auschwitz, the individual texts focus on various episodes and family relations differently located in space and time. The (auto)fictions of Halfon, in focusing each on specific familial constellations (brother/sister; brother/brother; grandson/grandfather), form also a literary constellation of texts, in which references and themes reoccur not only on the level of individual texts, but also between different texts. This diversified and fragmentary form of writing is a persuasive equivalent for the sense of fractured and multiple identity, experienced by the self in its relation to family and transnational frameworks. As Welge further argues, the personal/familial experiences are mobilized by the narrative to connect with other experiences in an intersubjective and multi-directional sense.

Anja Tippner discusses in her chapter Ol'ga Lavrent'eva's graphic novel *Survilo* [*Сурвило* (2019); *Survilo*] as a particular example of a multi-temporal and multi-directional family constellation and an interesting example of the 'non-fiction turn' or fact-based comic literature. While the post-war Soviet generations were confronted with a formalized culture of remembrance of the Second World War, the Lavrent'ev generation uses its family history to deal with the Russian past in a different way, often focusing on the specific experiences of ethnic groups such as Russian Germans, Tatars or Jews. In *Survilo*, the author tells the story of her maternal grandmother, Valentina Survilo, which echoes the terror, especially Stalinist repression and the blockade of Leningrad. As Tippner shows, Lavrent'eva's graphic novel creates a specific visual poetics that uses the graphic novel as a medium to retell the violent Soviet past and reconfigure the transnational, Polish-Belarussian-Russian family history.

3 Imagined Bonds, New Formations

Basing himself on the psychoanalytic tradition as well as on classical myth, **Pablo Valdivia Orozco** shows in his contribution that family narratives are frequently not only about violence, but that they point to the violent, determinant aspects of the very structure of sequential narrative. First, Valdivia argues that in the paradigmatic Colombian family saga of *One Hundred Years of Solitude* [*Cien años de soledad* (1967)] by Gabriel García Márquez the repeated constellation of near-incest of members of the apparently thoroughly patriarchal Buendía family and the principle of repetition generally present an alternative model to the violence of the law, teleological models of historical development, and the idea of the proper family as desired by the nation state. Secondly, the essay briefly indicates how two more contemporary Latin American writers, the Chilean-born Roberto Bolaño and the Colombian Héctor Abad Faciolince, confront in their own works the 'father' image of García Márquez, through their more concrete indictments of Latin American violence. Finally, the essay proposes a detailed interpretation of Colombian writer Patricia Quintana's novel *The Bitch* [*La perra* (2017)], about the relation between an Afro-Colombian woman and a female dog, highlighting its critical subversion of conventional images of motherhood as well as of the sequential logics of a plot. The interspecies relation turns into an *ersatz* for motherhood and family, yet it also projects the disturbing, traumatic image of a 'bad motherhood,' in a patriarchal context of persistent violence. According to Valdivia, Quintana's novel, if read against the background of the male-centered Latin American family novel, shows us how the familial function of motherhood can work both as an agent and as symptomatic victim of repressive violence, and that it is here where any vision of social change must first be enacted.

The article by **Anna Gaidash** examines the transnational aspects of Ukrainian writer Sofia Andrukhovych's short prose texts in the context of historical and temporal dimensions of family stories in the early twenty-first century. Through experimentation with content and form, Andrukhovych challenges literary canons, reflecting a highly transcultural situation in her writing. The family constellations in Andruchovych's imagery are built with the help of continuity and the pronounced interaction between the generations. In *Old People* [*Старі люди* (2008); *Stari Ludy*], through the characters of Marta and Luka, Andrukhovych presents a hedonistic vision of age, emphasizing joy, self-discovery, and transgenerational connections. The continuity indicative of family constellations in *Stari Ludy* tackles time and timelessness as both an affirmation of Ukrainian national identity and Ukraine's belonging to a Western past and present. The novella *Summer of Milena* [*Літо Мілени* (2002); *Lito Mileny*] incorporates elements of magical realism, contributing to a transcultural imagery with universal appeal. Andrukhovych's narratives highlight the positive role of elderly characters, challenging discriminatory practices and emphasizing the importance of family relaions in transcultural and transgenerational contexts. As Gaidash shows, by blurring conventional dichotomies and exploring themes of migration and identity, Andrukhovych's work contributes to a nuanced understanding of Ukrainian national identity within a global context.

In her contribution to this volume **Adriana Rodríguez-Alfonso** discusses how recent novels by diasporic Cuban authors (in conjunction with autobiographical and testimonial texts) have responded to the dissolution of the Soviet Union, by looking back to the era of the Cold War, by depicting characters that undertake journeys through countries of the former Eastern Bloc. In these diasporic wanderings, Rodríguez-Alfonso shows, the characters find transnational contacts and social communities that might be understood as 'families,' alternatives not only to the traditional unit of the family, but also to the metaphorical rhetoric of family employed by authorities and socialist state propaganda. The first major example considered is *Manuel's Four Escapes* [*Las cuatro fugas de Manuel* (2002)] by Jesús Diaz. The protagonist Manuel, a Cuban physics student, experiences the last months of the Soviet Union in Kharkiv, Ukraine, and he embarks on many visits to cities in Western and Eastern Europe, eventually meeting the author's son in Berlin. As Rodríguez-Alfonso argues, the experience of dislocation, exile, and the subjection to state control, produces the longing for a social network of friends and lovers, of various ideological persuasions: the narrator's 'family.' Similarly, the second example considered, the (autofictional) *Stoic and Frugal* [*Estoico y frugal* (2019)], by Pedro Juan Gutiérrez, follows the (train) journeys of Pedro Juan, a Cuban writer, across various European countries. The novel engages the memory of Cuban cold war narratives on multiple, intersected geographical and temporal planes, and the narrator's ephemeral contacts with other people, mostly women, encountered on his journeys, form, again, an alternative sort of family. In spite of its opposition to the idea of the traditional family and Fidel Castro's 'Cuban family,' the metaphor of the family persists in these exilic formations of interpersonal relationships.

Ángela Calderón's contribution approaches Sara Mesa's recent novel *The Family* [*La familia* (2022)] from a discourse-theoretical perspective. She examines the extent to which discursive patterns can also be part of a heritage that is experienced as violent. This violence is centered on the father figure, Damián. His communicative violence is flanked by his wife Laura, who – although seemingly subordinate, as she only stands for a small proportion of the spoken words within this novel – participates in this form of violent communication. Discursive superiority, combined with complicit silence, characterizes the central family constellations in this novel. This comprises also the two children, Damián and Rosa, who suffer from that discursive violence and prove to be linguistically powerless. Both constellations, that of the parents and that of the children, are each complemented by family members who expand the petty-bourgeois family cosmos: Aquilino, the third child, and Martina, an adopted child, as well as Uncle Óscar, Laura's brother. They may be categorized as 'figures of the third,' insofar as it is through them that the violence and coercion that are at work in this seemingly conflict-free family become recognizable. This is demonstrated with the help of R. Guénon's conceptualization of the 'ternaire.'

1 Transnational Relations/Constellations

Anne Brüske and Karoline Thaidigsmann

Horror, not Nostalgia. Socialism, Diaspora and Family in Cuban and Polish Post-Millennium Graphic Novels

1 Introduction

Looking at Cuban and Polish literature of the twenty-first century, one can see an interesting parallel emerge. In both, autobiographical graphic narratives serve to renegotiate individual experiences of socialism through the prism of childhood, family, and diaspora intertwining family history, national history, and world history. From the (retro-)perspective of the adult (post)socialist *I*, the graphic tales create a cosmos at the interface of micro- and macro-history.

By connecting autobiographical and historical accounts with graphic storytelling, Cuban and Polish (diaspora) literatures have been following an international trend. In the twenty-first century, graphic narratives have become a prominent form for the telling of one's own family history, making the autobiographical graphic novel a subgenre in its own right (Kuhlman 2017). Many of those "autographic narratives" (Whitlock 2006) link family history with the broader context of local, national, world or global history.[1] Following Gillian Whitlock's definition, the appeal of autographic narratives for the representation and retrospective reflection of autobiographically experienced history, trauma, and migration lies in its "biocularity," that is, the entanglement of verbal and visual strands of narration and representation, "asking us to read back and forth between images and words" (Hirsch 2004, 12–13), thus giving the reader more liberty regarding the order of reception than a words-only narrative.[2] The organization of the panels in graphic narratives and their multiple ways of combining visual contents and textual discourse (speech bubbles, captions, onomatopoeia) provide a particularly wide range of possibilities to produce different, at times overlapping layers of time, spatiality, and perspective. Thus, at the core of graphic narrative analysis lies the relationship between its visual and its verbal

1 Most prominently in Art Spiegelman's landmark comic *Maus* (1986; 1991), or Marjane Satrapi's graphic novel *Persepolis* (2000–2003).
2 On the narrative modes in graphic narratives see e.g. Whitlock (2006).

Anne Brüske, University of Regensburg
Karoline Thaidigsmann, Heidelberg University

https://doi.org/10.1515/9783111208664-003

planes, prompting questions about their mutual complementarity or contradiction, about whether they pursue their own agendas and possibly distinct semantics.

The comparative analysis of two graphic narratives from the Ibero-American and the Slavic context, *"Apuntes para un viaje… a Alemania…"* (2016) ["Notes for a journey… to Germany…"] by Carlos Aguilera and Aldo Damián Menéndez and *Totalnie nie nostalgia. Memuar* (2017) [Totally Not Nostalgia. Memoir] by Wanda Hagedorn and Jacek Frąś – dating almost from the same year – allows us to consider the genre's wide range of visual-verbal possibilities regarding the reflection of socialism, autobiography, and family history. At one end of the scale, we find an experimental photo-text collage (Aguilera and Menéndez), at the other a delicately drawn graphic memoir obsessed with detail (Hagedorn and Frąś). What links the two books on a formal level is their broad integration of cultural and textual references. In both cases, these serve to underpin the texts' intellectual and ideological agendas, which display some remarkable structural similarities. Both texts superimpose what we may call a global pattern on the protagonists' autobiographical experience in a socialist system and thus situate it in a broader political, cultural, or social context. While for Aguilera and Menéndez Cuban socialism is regarded as one particular example of totalitarianism destroying humanity by alienation, Hagedorn and Frąś consider childhood in socialist Poland as one particular example of patriarchy alienating the individual from family and society. The authors and illustrators create a suffocating cosmos highlighting the family resemblances between these totalitarian or patriarchal systems. They also renegotiate the nostalgic 'touch' of narratives about the socialist past and, in the Cuban case, a socialist childhood and young adulthood often disrupted by migration outside Cuba. The role of the autobiographical family narrative, however, follows opposite principles in the two books, thus emphasizing different focal points. While in *"Apuntes para un viaje… a Alemania…"* the family narrative almost disappears beneath a global take on totalitarianism and a fundamental reflection on aesthetics in repressive political systems, in *Totalnie nie nostalgia* the global perspective – patriarchy – serves as an echo chamber for the individual family narrative. The authors' visual and verbal reworkings of the past contribute – in a risky way – to understanding the present as they provide an overarching model in which to integrate different past, present, and future experiences. This is all the more significant as both texts are written from the perspective of diaspora and exile, adding yet another level of reflection on the complicated relation of socialism and family to their narratives.

Adopting a comparative and transversal perspective (Derichs et al. 2020) that takes into account specific local, national, and regional contexts, in the following we will examine how the two diasporic graphic narratives negotiate the legacy of socialism and which (post)socialist structural similarities and differences they display. Due to the texts' fundamentally different aesthetics, the subsequent analyses will follow a similar but not strictly analogous structure, concentrating on the intertwining of global patterns of argumentation and autobiographical family narratives, on aesthetic and poetic reflection, as well as on diasporic perspectives.

2 Totalitarianism – Socialism – (No) Family: *"Apuntes para un viaje… a Alemania…"*

Aguilera and Menéndez' avant-gardist project *"Apuntes para un viaje… a Alemania…": El cómix* (2016) casts a satirical eye on the arrival of a freshly exiled Cuban writer in reunified Germany in 2002. This bizarre and at times very drastic autographic composition is based on a nearly eponymous short text that Aguilera first published in 2006 and in which he recounts his arrival and his first travel experiences in Germany.[3] Aguilera (*1970) at that time was a Cuban dissident writer, the co-publisher of the well-known underground journal *Diáspora(s)* (1997–2002) and a representative of the Cuban current of *novísima narrativa.* He had been able to leave Cuba, under socialist rule since the "triumph of the Revolution" in 1959, thanks to a scholarship by the German branch of the PEN club, who put pressure on the Cuban government to give him a travel permit.[4] The visual artist Menéndez (*1971), one of the members of the critical Havana artist collective *ArteCalle* (1986–1988) had already left the island in 1991. After stops in Miami (*La Clínica del Arte*) and Madrid (*Fuera de Serie, Fusión Gráfica*), he settled on the Spanish Canary Islands, from where he continues publishing his poignant anti-socialist satirical blog *Castor Jabao* on Cuban politics, the title being an anagram of the programmatic dissident outcry "Down with Castro" ["Castro abajo"].[5]

In 2016, Aguilera and Menéndez, both highly critical of their home country's political regime and the social, cultural, and economic hardship it inflicts on the island's population, jointly published a comic version of the original literary text. The short 2006 text was inserted in its full length mostly via captions or speech bubbles into collages of black-and-white photographs of different times and places,

3 See Aguilera (2006): "Apuntes para un viaje a Alemania," published in the Cuban-Spanish journal *Encuentro de la cultura cubana* and Aguilera's 2017 publication in a volume co-edited with Idalia Morejón Arnaiz: "Apuntes sobre el movimiento de los trenes en A."

4 After numerous scholarships in German and Austrian cities, Aguilera has settled in Prague where he works as a literary journalist (*Nuevo Heraldo*), writer, and Spanish instructor while being part of the socio-literary project *InCubadora.* See "Carlos Aguilera *1970."

5 For biographical information on Menéndez see his blog profile; for his blog "Castor Jabao."

sporting subjects from Central and East European contexts, from Castro's Cuba, or from globalized popular culture ranging from silent movies from the 1920s to the Star Wars trilogy from the late 1970s and 1980s. Both regarding its verbal and its visual texts, *"Apuntes"* is different from other Cuban autographic narratives published outside Cuba, such as *Cuba. My Revolution* (2010) by Inverna Lockpez and Dean Haspiel or *Adiós mi Habana* (2017) by Anna Veltfort, which feature a more classical illustrative visual style and follow typical patterns of fact-driven writing on Cuban diaspora life. To be sure, the autobiographical text refers to Aguilera's departure to Germany with his family in 2002, dubbing it an "Operetta destiny" ["destino de opereta" (Aguilera and Menéndez 2016, 14)] that Aguilera and his family must face.[6] It mentions important stations of their first journeys within Germany: Düsseldorf, Bonn, and, of course, Berlin (Espinoza Domínguez 2017; Pérez Hernández 2019; Aguilera and Morejón 2017). However, rather than emphasizing a family, a travel, or a coming-of-age narrative, the verbal text primarily traces an episode in the author's inner life that makes the autobiographical I renounce the search for "the [one] truth" ["la verdad" (Aguilera and Menéndez 2016, 7)] and, more generally, reject state totalitarianism and repressive socialist regimes. The underlying travel narrative of the family is superseded by a reflection on totalitarian aesthetics and on the common features of (post)socialisms. The verbal discourse is characterized by a myriad of references to works by European and American artists, all directly or indirectly reflecting fascism and the Holocaust: Hungarian-Jewish writer Imre Kertész, German painter and sculptor Anselm Kiefer, East German writer Uwe Johnson (a member of the West German Group 47), German-Jewish philosopher Hannah Arendt, Cuban playwright Virgilio Piñera, NS film director Leni Riefenstahl, and German-Jewish scholar Victor Klemperer. On a visual level, with their style of photo-collages Aguilera and Menéndez make use of Central and Eastern Europe as a "grand archive of totalitarianism" ["un gran archivo de totalitarismo" (Rojas quoted in Espinoza Domínguez 2017)][7] and especially of images from national socialist Germany and the German Democratic Republic (Pérez

6 All English translations from *"Apuntes para un viaje… a Alemania…"* (Aguilera and Menéndez 2016) are mine [A. B.]. All citations from this text are reproduced in normal typography while the original exclusively uses capital letters.

7 In 2017, Carlos Espinoza Domínguez wrote with reference to Aguilera's oeuvre, quoting Cuban literary critic Rafael Rojas: In this book "a comment Rafael Rojas made regarding the novella *Clausewitz y yo* becomes clear: 'Central Europe functions, in the narrative of Carlos A. Aguilera, as a sort of grand archive of totalitarianism, from which it is possible to derive any literary representation of terror.'" ["En [sus libros] se pone de manifiesto algo que Rafael Rojas comentó a propósito de la noveleta *Clausewitz y yo*: 'Europa central funciona, en la narrativa de Carlos A. Aguilera, como una suerte de gran archivo del totalitarismo, del que es posible derivar cualquier representación literaria del terror'." (Espinoza Domínguez 2017)].

Hernández 2019, 7), in order to expose communist Cuba as a space of socialist alienation where the family as a social institution is replaced by state collectivization (Garbatzky 2016).[8] The combination of the verbal and graphic planes gives birth to quite a drastic poetics of horror and (anti-)nostalgia that materializes both visually and verbally through three aspects of entanglement: firstly, the global patterns of the intertwinement of macro- and micro-history, secondly, the aesthetics of kitsch and horror by which socialist regimes intend to forcefully produce a stable image of the past and the present, and finally, the meta-reflection stemming from the text's analysis of post-socialist and post-totalitarian conditions.

2.1 Global Patterns: Intertwining Micro- and Macro-History

Right from the cover page, the autographic narrative immerses its readership in a strange universe where Aguilera's individual life story and world history are intertwined by means of the interplay between verbal and visual discourses. This universe discloses the underlying global pattern of *"Apuntes para un viaje... a Alemania..."* as a graphic narrative that triangulates the micro-history of the narrating I, Cuban national history, and the macro-history of global totalitarianisms. But how is this specific universe produced aesthetically? Starting with the cover page, the graphic narrative arranges crops of black-and-white photographs from the first half of the twentieth century in irregular but most often neatly defined panels. While the cover page sports collages of Aguilera and Menéndez represented as babies in the upper half, the lower half shows photographs of Fritz Lang's 1927 film *Metropolis*. Blue and red bubbles are splashed over this and the following pages and the verbal discourse of the first-person narrator appears in speech bubbles, text boxes, or is integrated in the illustration. This verbal discourse begins with Aguilera's individual knowledge of Germany upon his arrival in the early 2000s, namely the idea of Germany as a tube through which trains pass (Aguilera and Menéndez 2016, 1), as the home of silent movie actors from the 1920s, and as the so-called *"Reich"* ["imperio" (Aguilera and Menéndez 2016, 2)]. By introducing the verbal image of trains as the leitmotiv of Aguilera's journey and encounters with East Germans, the text grounds Aguilera's imagination in world history, and more precisely in the history of the Holocaust. Indeed, on an associative level it refers to the deportation of the Jewish population of Europe to extermination camps via *Reichsbahn* trains while Aguilera explicitly mentions his

8 See also the contribution by Rodríguez-Alfonso in this volume.

readings of Uwe Johnson as being the primary source of inspiration for this episode, rendered in the comic in a speech bubble (Aguilera and Menéndez 2016, 3).

Paralleling the verbal element, the first page of *"Apuntes para un viaje... a Alemania..."* displays at its top a photograph of an old MRI tube as a panel (Ill. 1). In the panel, a nurse closes the flap of the tube over the patient, Aguilera, recognizable by a photo of his head which is pasted into the original picture. This collage refers to, and at the same time ironically displaces, the idea of Germany as a tube. The lower panel complements the idea of the tube by showing a detail of the futuristic scene in Lang's *Metropolis* in which the female protagonist Maria is put into a glass sarcophagus and transformed into a villainous android machine. On the next double page, seven panels illustrate Aguilera's arrival in what seems to be his imaginary Germany.

Ill. 1: © Carlos A. Aguilera and Damián Aldo Menéndez. Aguilera and Menéndez 2016, 2–3.

The left page incorporates portions of a well-known photograph of the Auschwitz extermination camp, probably from the 1940s, which shows the camp and the train tracks leading up to its entrance. Shots of the twentieth-century Havana waterfront, the Malecón, are superimposed with increasing intensity on variations of this photograph in several panels. While the photograph taken in Poland refers to Germany, the visual representation of the Malecón serves as a stand-in for Cuba's tropical insularity and its connection to the North American continent. Indeed, Florida, the main destination of Cuban rafters in the 1990s and a well-known bastion of Cuban exile and diaspora communities, is only 90 miles away from the Malecón.[9] This may be interpreted as a reference to the autobiographical subject's migration to Germany on the verbal plane and his subsequent mental production of space, in which stereotypical images of Cuba and an imagined Germany overlap: sea water washes around the railroad tracks, and the Castillo del Moro, one of Havana's landmarks, appears next to the camp's entrance gate. Here, the visual discourse connects Auschwitz as the apotheosis of German fascism on a political level with socialist Cuba, represented by its iconic waterfront. The continuity of the autobiographical narrative is established visually by inserting the figure of the author Aguilera – but also the head of the illustrator Menéndez – into the photographs. From a visual point of view, Aguilera's family, though mentioned early in the verbal discourse, is not given any importance. It is depicted later in the style of an old family portrait and in an alienated manner that underscores the dissolution of family structures in totalitarian regimes: the postcard-style, edited photograph of a large family shows, amongst others, Aguilera and Menéndez' heads pasted onto the original family members, sporting the inscription "we got off at Düsseldorf" ["bajamos a Düsseldorf" (Aguilera and Menéndez 2016, 14)], drawn from the original autobiographical text.

Using similar techniques, the double page following the composite image of the Auschwitz entrance and the Malecón (Aguilera and Menéndez 2016, 5–6) unveils Cuba and Nazi Germany as ideologically dominated spaces. Leaping from an individual to a collective perspective, the visual discourse accentuates the *Gleichschaltung* of society both in German Nazism and Cuban socialism. The visual discourse again superimposes photographs, organized in the three horizontal panels on the left, to visualize the analogies between the two totalitarian regimes. This time it employs images of the ideological indoctrination of children in Nazi and Cuban classrooms (panels above and below), with the middle panel showing a hybrid between Nazi Germany and communist Cuba, while the page on the right shows a 1960s photograph of Fidel Castro in conversation with young Cuban pioneers (above) and a march of the Hitler Youth through a German town (below), respectively. Through the analogous visual construction, the similar motif, and the red coloring of details of the national socialist and the Cuban flags highlighting the swastika and the

9 In 1980, for instance, more than a hundred thousand Cubans left the island by boat from the harbor of Mariel after the Cuban government granted the right to leave.

Cuban star, respectively, the visual discourse heavily suggests ideological resemblance, diminishing the distance in time. The verbal discourse, in return, added in speech bubbles burgeoning from Aguilera's or Menéndez' mouth, refers to Aguilera's wish to follow in Uwe Johnson's footsteps and visit Berlin, a city which he believes to stand for the whole of Europe, both in the sense of being the former capital of fascism and of representing a zone of contact between the socialist and capitalist world order of the cold war: "I wanted to see Berlin – for me of the same dimension as the whole of Europe – and take a trip like Johnson's to any place" ["Tuve deseo de conocer Berlín – para mí del mismo tamaño de toda Europa – y hacer un viaje parecido al de Johnson por cualquier lugar" (Aguilera and Menéndez 2016, 5)].

Reading these introductory pages of Aguilera's and Menéndez' co-production through a biocular lens allows us to work out the general pattern of argumentation in the graphic narrative *"Apuntes para un viaje… a Alemania…"*. Firstly, these pages are exemplary of how the verbal discourse transports the first-person narrator's individual imagination and knowledge clearly embedded in history while, secondly, the visual discourse highlights even more the importance of global history and of the related collective imaginaries. It also emphasizes the efforts of collectivization and *Gleichschaltung* of civil society behind which the family threatens to disappear while the individual is left to him- or herself. Thirdly, and most importantly, drawing on iconic photographs of Nazism, its emblematic chronotopes, and its mass phenomena, the visual discourse dramatically insists on the parallels between political systems that the graphic narrative denounces as totalitarian, namely Nazi Germany and revolutionary Cuba, and their horrors.

2.2 Aesthetics (of Kitsch) and Horror: Reflections on the Production of the Past and the Present

In line with this general pattern of argumentation, *"Apuntes para un viaje… a Alemania…"* as an autographic narrative also generates a deeper reflection on aesthetics as a political means. For one, parting from the drastic critique of the Cuban Revolution's iconic aesthetics, the narrative ponders explicitly the commonalities of socialist (and other totalitarian) aesthetics and their inadvertent ridiculing of the past and the present. Moreover, the graphic narrative's own poetics may be deduced by analyzing its handling of seemingly nostalgic elements such as the reference to children's television series. This poetics is centered around the critical (re)production of a totalitarian indoctrinating past and the analysis of a post-socialist present, advocating implicitly a future without repressive political systems and their long-lasting psychological burden for the populations concerned.

In its capacity as medium of graphic narrative art, *"Apuntes para un viaje... a Alemania..."* emphasizes the political role of aesthetics and visual culture for socialism and, more generally, forms of totalitarianism. It offers its readership an explicit reflection on socialist aesthetics. This reflection is triggered by the narrator's first trip to Berlin where he sees the residues of the German Democratic Republic and of the Berlin Wall, as we can read in the speech bubbles and text captions (Aguilera and Menéndez 2016, 43–45, also for the following quotations). What strikes the narrating I is the commodification of these remnants of the Cold War, their being turned into postcards. Drawing parallels between these residues of German Cold War socialism transformed into commodified items of pop culture and Cuban visual culture, the verbal discourse refers to Cuba as "a country with a high potential for ideological kitsch" ["un país con alto potencial kitsch ideológico"]. Artists and intellectuals should therefore do a "piecework reading of aesthetics under socialism" ["una lectura a destajo de la estética bajo el socialismo"]. Instead of showing those postcards and sellable visual items of GDR culture and thus corroborating the verbal discourse, the visual strand of the text uses photographs of Fidel Castro, Ernesto Guevara, but also Hitler and Leni Riefenstahl and her *Olympia* movies (1938), widening the perspective from the GDR context to other totalitarian regimes: Cuba and Nazi Germany. Yet, when it comes to the critique of the "bad epic" of socialism in Cuba, the visual and the verbal discourse rejoin. According to the verbal discourse this "bad epic" ["la mala épica"] culminates in the murals of the Cuban revolution, whose heroes the narrator's discourse considers to be victims of the "triumph of the [aesthetic] stereotype" ["el triunfo del estereotipo"] instead of being agents of the proverbial "triumph of the Revolution."[10] In line with this, the graphic narrative presents

10 Distributed over four pages, the text reads as follows: "For someone like me, coming from a country with a high potential for ideological kitsch, all the postcards sold on Unter den Linden are more than interesting. There is the famous reproduction in which Brezhnev kisses Honneker [sic] and which provoked interpretations and mockery in many places; there are those that show pieces of the Wall and views of Checkpoint Charlie | I am convinced that all those 'pendants' would serve – more than others – to make a piecework of reading of the aesthetics under socialism. Research that if done would also have to consider the murals that have been painted during more than forty years of Revolution in Cuba ... and the different ways in which they show the 'triumph of the stereotype,' the bad epic" ["Para alguien proveniente como yo de un país con alto potencial kitsch ideológico, todas las postalitas que se venden en Unter den Linden resultan más que interesantes. Allí está la famosa reproducción en la que Brézhniev se besa con Honneker [sic] y suscitó interpretaciones y burlas en muchos sitios, las que muestran pedazos del muro y vistas del Checkpoint Charlie [...] | Estoy convencido de que todos esos 'colgantes' servirán – más

four panels that reproduce photographs of worn political murals, showing either the triumvirate of Fidel Castro, Ernesto Guevara, and Camilo Cienfuegos, or individual mural portraits of Guevara subtitled with recurrent slogans of the Revolution such as: "until the final victory," or "Che, paradigm of the exceptional man" ["¡Hasta la victoria! [sic] siempre" or "Che, paradigma de hombre excepcional" (Aguilera and Menéndez 2016, 46–47)]. The verbal discourse explicitly mentions one of the representations of Che Guevara in old Havana that it considers to correspond to a mix between the Phantom of the Opera and a caricature of Kim Il Sung (Aguilera and Menéndez 2016, 47). The visual discourse does not exactly reproduce this comparison; instead, the readers are shown a photomontage of Che Guevara and the extraterrestrial character Chewbacca from the space epos *Star Wars* sitting side by side in individual armchairs (Ill. 2).

By replacing the verbal reference to the North Korean dictator with this visual reference to US popular culture, the graphic narrative conveys yet another layer of meaning: it not only highlights the idea of totalitarian aesthetics (and of totalitarianism menacing the "good," just as in the science fiction epos by George Lucas) but also ironically points to Cuba's tense relation with U.S.-dominated consumer capitalism while adding humoristic undertones. In the speech bubbles issuing from Guevara and Chewbacca's mouths, the original name of Chewbacca is transformed into "Che" and "waka," meaning literally "Che" and "cow," thus drawing one of the most important heroes of the Cuban Revolution into the semantic field of bovines. In doing so, the narrative aims at exposing the ridiculousness of Cuban socialist iconography. Indeed, it interprets the mural as an allegory of the failure of the Revolution, which, through an exaggerated cult of personality and subsequent kitsch representations, inadvertently ridicules its past heroes in the public space and, thus, can only keep control over Cuba's population by transforming itself into a repressive monster (Aguilera and Menéndez 2016, 48).[11] In other words, socialist aesthetics fails to produce a palatable version of its own past that inspires the population and, therefore, the political elites must fall back on more ideology and terror in order to realize a socialist present.

que otros – para hacer una lectura a destajo de la estética bajo el socialismo. Investigación que si se hace tendría que asumir también los murales que se han pintado durante más de cuarenta años de Revolución en Cuba ... y las diferentes maneras que tienen de mostrar el 'triunfo del estereotipo', la mala épica" (Aguilera and Menéndez 2016, 42–46; Aguilera 2006, 67)].

11 "A state that ridicules its own heroes in this way is a state that lives outside all reality, a state that needs to turn itself into a monster in order to continue to exist" ["Un estado que ridiculiza de esa manera a sus propios héroes es un estado que vive fuera de toda realidad, un estado que necesita convertirse a sí mismo en monstruo para perpetuarse" (Aguilera and Menéndez 2016, 48)].

Ill. 2: © Carlos A. Aguilera and Damián Aldo Menéndez. Aguilera and Menéndez 2016, 47.

The graphic narrative definitely exposes this type of aesthetics as absurd. Moreover, it also develops an interesting critique of the principles of socialist visual aesthetics and propaganda as it illustrates their (failed) effort to produce and reproduce over and over again a heroic past and to conjure an ideal socialist present through an avalanche of stereotypical images of men, i.e., that of Guevara's 'new man,' 'hombre nuevo.' By including representations of Riefenstahl's photographs of 'Aryan' athletes from the 1930s but also of the African Nuba people published in *Die Nuba* (1973), the visual discourse once again exceeds the verbal discourse, pointing to the structural analogies of visual propaganda and aesthetics in different totalitarian regimes (Aguilera and Menéndez 2016, 45; 59; 61, 62).

2.3 (Post-)Socialist Poetics of Non-Nostalgia and Horror

However, *"Apuntes para un viaje... a Alemania..."* insists especially on the absurd as the most salient common denominator between different historic experiences of socialism. This feeling of living in an alienating world in which nothing seems to make sense is unveiled by the verbal discourse as a direct consequence of socialist states that ridicule their own heroes (Aguilera and Menéndez 2016, 49). Therefore, according to the narrating I, it is the structurally similar past and the shared legacy of socialism that enables him, the Cuban, and "los ossis," the East Germans, to connect easily as they both have experienced socialist despotism and "ideological horror" ["horror ideológico" (Aguilera and Menéndez 2016, 50)] "in their own flesh" ["en carne propia" (Aguilera and Menéndez 2016, 49)]. On the visual level, the common experience of the absurd is echoed by the recurrent motif of the train and the altered photograph of an overcrowded Cuban bus into which Aguilera and Menéndez' avatars have been pasted (Aguilera and Menéndez 2016, 49). But more importantly, through the interplay between verbal and visual discourse, the autographic narrative (Aguilera and Menéndez 2016, 50–51) then reconsiders possibly nostalgic interpretations of a common socialist past, unveiling trans-socialist strategies of cultural uniformization. The visual composition of the following page shows in its upper half two identical, photoshopped versions of Stalin who is transformed into a young girl with long braids (Ill. 3). The two Stalin-girls escort an elderly Castro in a wheelchair between the two of them. The lower half of the image quotes a trans-socialist cultural artifact, the Polish animation series *Bolek i Lolek* (1963–1986) that was dubbed into Spanish and widely broadcast in Cuba from the 1960s on. Whereas the representations of Stalin and the aging Castro stand for the repressive and simultaneously fragile side of state socialism, *Lolek y Bolek*, also affectively known in Cuba as the "Russian puppets" ["muñequitos rusos"], could represent a more nostalgic view of Cuban children and youth cultures, as numerous Cuban diaspora internet pages on this and other imported animation series from Russia and Eastern Europe attest (see e.g., Darias Alfonso 2015; Puñales-Alpízar 2015).[12]

The dynamic interplay between verbal and visual discourse, however, forbids an all too nostalgic interpretation, for, in an autoreferential gesture, one of the cartoon characters reports that the "way in which [Cubans and East Germans] were exposed thousands of miles away to the same ideological horror" "to the point of watching the same television shows" has led to identical forms of fear and to a "kind of idiocy" that can only be hidden behind a "long hysterical giggle" (Aguilera and Menéndez 2016, 50).[13] Hence, even the possibly nostalgic memory of children's culture visualized in the seemingly cute cartoon characters is verbally unmasked as an instrument of ideological brainwashing. Indeed, the verbal and visual discourses move along in tension with one another, characterized by relative proximity, ostensible dissonance, and ironic displacement. While the dictators

12 See also "Muñequitos rusos en Cuba. ¿Trauma o nostalgia?".

13 "[L]a manera en la que el horror ideológico nos había cruzado a miles de kilómetros," "habíamos visto hasta idénticos programas de televisión," "una suerte de idiotez," "una risita larga, histérica" (Aguilera and Menéndez 2016, 50)].

Ill. 3: © Carlos A. Aguilera and Damián Aldo Menéndez. Aguilera and Menéndez 2016, 50–51.

Castro and Stalin are not mentioned in the text, they nevertheless appear in photomontages, and while the visualized cartoon children might evoke a milder view of the past, in a speech bubble they literally accuse themselves of being part of the ideological apparatus. To be sure, these verbal-visual dissonances as well as the alienation of iconic images from both their original form and contexts also allow for a humorous reception. Yet, despite their postmodern aesthetics and their iconography of horror, conveyed through photos of Holocaust mass murders, they push for a serious post-socialist reading emphasizing the transcultural regularities of the socialist experience (e.g., Aguilera and Menéndez 2016, 61). From a Cuban perspective, however, this critical reading is only possible from outside Cuba, from an inner or outer diaspora, or from a postmodernist distance that Aguilera and Menéndez also develop in other works, such as Aguilera's *Teoría del alma china* (2006) or Menéndez' video poem *Mao* (2015), an adaptation of Aguilera's eponymous poem.

2.4 Family Resemblances and Diaspora: Creating One's Own Totalitarian Pasts

Finally, *"Apuntes para un viaje… a Alemania…"* as an artistic autographic narrative produces its own vision of both the past and the present by confronting its audience with an overwhelming flood of iconic images, placing them in new visual or political contexts and alienating them. The past is created through the purposeful selection and recontextualization of sometimes distressing photographs pertaining mostly to macro-history. They show elements of popular culture and scenes of totalitarian and socialist regimes, ranging from pictures of everyday life via portraits of political leaders to images of state repression, human rights violations, and genocide. What they have in common is, apart from occasional humorous undertones, the omnipresent sense of horror, socialist depression, and therefore the total absence of nostalgia that emanates from them both visually and verbally. The past, i.e. a European socialist or totalitarian past, depicted from a negative angle and brought into line with the Holocaust, appears as dark and menacing as it protrudes into the present.[14] Against this backdrop of contagion, Cuba's socialist present can only be overcome by leaving the island, as the last panels of the autographic narrative may suggest, where statues of iconic communist thinkers are shown to crumble and Aguilera and Menéndez' avatars leave town in a colorful car towards a brighter future, possibly in exile or diaspora (Aguilera and Menéndez 2016, 71–73). In light of Aguilera's and Menéndez' diasporic and dissident background, *"Apuntes para un viaje… a Alemania…"* and its poetics of horror certainly create a conscious counter-ideological and pessimistic gaze on the past and on the present, pushing for a future without socialism or totalitarianism, either achieved on an individual level by exiting the repressive system or by destroying it. Considering *"Apuntes para un viaje… a Alemania…"* as a genuine piece of biocular autographic art, we may observe that the tension between written anxiety and at times drastic, at times humorous visualization is always accompanied by a distancing and self-ironic reflection. Its primary purpose,

14 But the narrative also invokes individual events, pertaining to the realm of micro-history but reconnected to macro patterns. For instance, the verbal narratives quote the true story of a woman in the East Berlin neighborhood of Prenzlauer Berg who conducted horrific medical experiments on young children. While the verbal strand makes the narrating I's association between this crime of infanticide and the GDR's political morbidity explicit, the visual discourse illustrates the words of horror with more innocent photographs of a nurse looking over Aguilera and Menéndez' avatars here represented as babies (see Aguilera and Menéndez 2016, 22). The Holocaust as a global historical fact and central turning point for humankind is reflected upon in the verbal discourse by means of numerous intertextual references, e.g. to Kertész, Arendt, Kiefer, etc., while it is visualized using images of deportation, mass executions, and images of NS officials (e.g., Aguilera and Menéndez 2016, 14; 44; 61).

then, is not to highlight the destiny of an individual person or a particular family but to make global patterns of interaction between micro- and macro-history recognizable. While family and family constellations are indeed mentioned, the occasional verbal references to Aguilera's family (e.g., Aguilera and Menéndez 2016, 14) serve foremost as echo chambers for the narrating I who is caught up between individual experience and the absorption of the individual by the collectivizing political system which is visualized by photographs of Nazi Germany's and socialist Cuba's youth organizations and schools. Again, in the visual discourse, the question of the family as a social and affective unit is displaced by the flood of images and the narrative's urge to carve out family resemblances between different types of totalitarianism and socialism – and between the populations suffering from them.

3 Patriarchy – Socialism – Family: *Totalnie nie nostalgia. Memuar*

Totalnie nie nostalgia. Memuar by Wanda Hagedorn (*1958; text) and Jacek Frąś (*1977; illustrations) was first published in 2016 in a French translation under the title *Pas de retour en ostalgie*. The original Polish version came out one year later.[15] It was not the first graphic narrative about childhood in socialist Poland or other socialist Eastern European countries, but unlike most of them it stretched the time frame further in two directions, namely, the pre-socialist and the post-socialist period, and intertwined the childhood recollection explicitly with intellectual discourse on the narrative level. Moreover, it focused on childhood in the 1960s and early 1970s instead of the more frequently depicted period of the late 1970s and the 1980s.[16] In comparison to Aguilera's and Menéndez' experimental collage-like book, *Totalnie nie nostalgia* – praised

15 In an interview (Pstrągowski and Frąś s.a.) the authors state that, for them, the Polish version was the more elaborate. After handing in the French version, they had time to polish the book for the Polish publication. I will therefore refer to the Polish version in the following.

I would like to thank Wanda Hagedorn for the free reproductions from *Totalnie nie nostalgia* in this chapter and Jacek Frąś for his willingness to participate in an online meeting with German and Polish students in spring 2023, which offered interesting insights into his graphic art.

16 The most popular Polish graphic narrative about childhood in socialist Poland is the book series *Marzi* (2004–2017) by Marzena Sowa (text) and Sylvain Savoia (illustrations). Just like Hagedorn, Sowa emigrated from Poland as an adult and has been living in France ever since, where *Marzi* was originally published. Further graphic narratives about childhood in socialist Eastern Europe that came out earlier than *Totalnie nie Nostalgia* are Jacek Frąś's *Stan – autobiograficzna historia dziejąca się w Polsce, w stanie wojennym* (2006) [*The State – an Autobiographical Story*

as the first Polish graphic memoir (Stańczyk 2020, 203) –[17] is a more classical graphic narrative based on Wanda Hagedorn's childhood memories, combining autobiographical verbal discourse and detailed graphics that either illustrate or complement the verbal text. But just like *"Apuntes para un viaje... a Alemania..."*, the book links the personal life story to a larger historical perspective. By embedding her experience of a dysfunctional family in the Polish People's Republic into an overarching pattern of patriarchy, Hagedorn adopts an explicitly feminist stand.[18]

3.1 The Global Pattern: Intertwining Micro- and Macro-History

The global perspective opens up right at the beginning of the graphic narrative and then gradually narrows down to the context of socialist Poland and the microperspective of the individual family history, thus creating a line of analogies. In the prologue, we see the author Wanda Hagedorn at home in Australia, to where she emigrated in 1986 at the age of twenty-eight. The panels depict her on her way to work while she is reflecting on a recent sexism scandal in the Australian government, and at work for an NGO, where she is responsible for an intercultural project on the prevention of violence against women and their children. By concluding (in a thought bubble), "misogyny, sexism, day by day ... it's up for a global mantra!"[19] ["mizoginia, seksizm, dzień w dzień ... to się nadaje na globalną mantrę!" (Hagedorn and Frąś, 2017, 12)], she sets the tone for the following narrative and links times, spaces, and political systems. The actual beginning of Hagedorn's retrospective childhood narrative in chapter one focuses on an overgeneralized Polish and socialist perspective: "The first 11 years of my life I spent in Regained-for-the-Motherland-Szczecin" ["Pierwsze 11 lat życia spędziłam w Odzyskanym-dla-macierzy-Szczecinie"]; "It was a Catholic, patriarchal and people's-republic-of-Poland-type

Taking Place in Poland, under Martial Law], about the time of martial law in Poland, Peter Sís' *The Wall. Growing Up Behind the Iron Curtain* (2007) about growing up in communist Czechoslovakia and Mawil's *Kinderland* (2014) about a childhood in the GDR. Apart from Sís' book (which starts in the 1950s), these narratives depict the late 1970s and the 1980s.

17 Pstrągowski (2015) locates the beginning of autobiographical comics in Poland at the transition from the twentieth to the twenty-first century. Stańczyk (2020) emphasizes that it is precisely the autobiographical graphic narrative that in Poland has contributed to comics and graphic novels breaking free from their niche in the twenty-first century and being read by a wider audience and appreciated by critics.

18 Olsza (2021) and Stańczyk (2020) both stress *Totalnie nie nostalgia*'s relevance for the development of feminist comics in Poland.

19 All translations from *Totalnie nie nostagia* are mine [K. T.].

childhood, that is, a depressive-oppressive-repressive one, quite banal at that time" ["Było to dzieciństwo katolickie, patriarchalne i pe-er-el-owskie, czyli depresyjno-opresyjno-represyjne, całkiem banalne w tamtym czasie" (Hagedorn and Frąś, 2017, 17)]. From this point on, the narrative shifts heavily to the individual situation of Hagedorn's family, dominated by an abusive father, who takes out his aggressions, frustrations, (failed) aspirations and misogyny on his wife and four daughters. However, the family story, Polish society and the socialist state remain symbolically intertwined on the verbal as well as on the visual plane of the narrative. Patriarchal structures and dysfunctionality characterize all three dimensions. Hagedorn thus refers to the classic family novel as a mirror of society.

Emblematic of the analogy between individual and collective history, between the private and the public sphere, is an accident during a military parade in the Polish city of Szczecin in 1962 – the only historical event that is presented in detail in *Totalnie nie nostalgia*. Set against the backdrop of growing tensions between the United States and the Soviet Union, which culminated in the Cuban Missile Crisis shortly after, the Soviet Union, the German Democratic Republic and Poland carried out joint military exercises in order to demonstrate the strength of the Warsaw Pact Alliance. These exercises were to end with a grand military parade in Szczecin on October, 9 – five days before the Soviet Union deployed missiles on Cuban territory. However, a tragic accident occurred during the parade, which was attended by cheering schoolchildren and citizens lining the streets. A Polish tank lost control and drove into the crowd, killing at least seven schoolchildren and seriously injuring another forty people. The incident is part of Hagedorn's biography since she was a student at the primary school most affected by the tragedy. Yet the event also takes on a symbolic quality in the graphic narrative, revealing parallels between family and state structures. Seen from this perspective, the incident shows the Polish state brutally rolling over its children just as the violence of Hagedorn's father rolls over his daughters' life.[20]

It is the illustrations by Jacek Frąś that comment on this intertwining of state and patriarchal violence in the family in a subtle manner.

---

20 Hagedorn herself affirms this metaporic reading in an interview: "This was an incident I remember very well from my childhood. At the time I didn't yet notice the irony in it. This scene is a metaphor for what happened later in my family, and generally how children were treated in the People's Republic of Poland. We were symbolically run over by various tanks – of patriarchy, of hypocrisy, of pretence. And we had to deal with it somehow" ["To było wydarzenie, które bardzo dobrze zapamiętałam z dzieciństwa. Wtedy jeszcze nie dostrzegałam w nim ironii. [...] Ta scena to metafora tego, co się działo później w mojej rodzinie, i generalnie tego, jak dzieci były traktowane w PRL-u. Byłyśmy symbolicznie przejeżdżane przez różne czołgi – patriarchatu, hipokryzji, pozorów. I musiałyśmy jakoś sobie z tym radzić" (Jabłońska 2017)].

Ill. 4: © Wanda Hagedorn. Hagedorn and Frąś 2017, 27.

The first two panels on page 27 (Ill. 4) show the moment before the accident happens. The tank approaches and drives along the street lined by the cheering crowd. On the right margin of the illustration we see an advertising column with the reproduction of an original propaganda poster that depicts the figure of a man (his head is not visible on the poster) holding a little girl by the hand. The poster's text reads: "Father, beware of an accident – my fate is in your hand" ["Ojcze, strzeż się wypadku – mój los w twym ręku" (Hagedorn and Frąś 2017, 27)]. Read against the backdrop of the tank accident and Hagedorn's abusive childhood, the poster suggests that both incarnations of paternal protection – the socialist state as well as the biological father – instead of being guardians are themselves the threat from which the little girl on the poster must be protected.[21]

21 On the paternalistic nature of the socialist state see Thaidigsmann (2022, 66–68); on the patriarchal character of the Polish People's Republic see Olsza (2021, 221). The fact that the poster by Czesław Wielhorski dates back to 1936 and thus to the pre-socialist era (even though it was still in use during socialism) broadens the perspective beyond the socialist period. The word "Circus" ["Cyrk"], that adorns the column, underlines the situation's bitter irony.

While other historical events that took place in socialist Poland, like the bloodily suppressed workers' strikes of 1970 and 1976 or the imposition of martial law in 1981, have become icons of Polish collective memory,[22] the Szczecin tank accident is scarcely remembered, and it is to Hagedorn's credit that she returns it to Polish post-socialist memory. The tank accident was tabooed in the Polish Peoples' Republic. Only one newspaper mentioned it at the margin of a double spread article celebrating the success of the parade (replicated in its entirety by Hagedorn and Frąś 2017, 31). The responsibility for the accident was transferred to the spectators of the parade and the parents of the children, while the state denied any responsibility.[23] State politics follow the same principle as family politics. Both realms are subject to what Hagedorn calls the "principle of the façade." Covering up the accident is similar to Wanda's mom drawing the curtains in her home: "Remember, don't you ever tell anybody about what's going on. Family business stays in the family" ["Pamiętaj, masz nigdy nikomu nie mówić o tych awanturach! Domowych spraw nie wynosi się poza dom" (Hagedorn and Frąś 2017, 169)].[24]

By drawing an analogy between the system of the socialist state and the patriarchal family system, *Totalnie nie nostalgia* makes it clear that family does not provide a counterspace to the socialist state nor even a realm of withdrawal and refuge (neither does the state provide a counterspace to the family). The Polish state, society, and her family become spaces of alienation for the heroine and lead her into an inner diaspora – visualized by the Kafkaesque metamorphoses she undergoes in the graphic memoir (see Hagedorn and Frąś 2017, 198; 226–227). However, Hagedorn's wider family constellation suggests that state, society, and family might not necessarily have to reflect each other but could also offer an alternative to each other. The suffocating atmosphere of a world dominated by the oppressive (state/biological) 'father' is counterbalanced by the protagonist's relationship with her grandmother, who plays a major role in both Hagedorn's

22 The imposition of martial law became emblematic of the experience of the last socialist generation of children in Poland (born in the 1970s). On the so-called "martial law generation" see Vassileva-Karagyozova (2015).

23 For more information on the tank accident and its public taboo in Socialist Poland see Miedziński (2015) and Zadworny (2014). In 1993 the journalist Krystyna Pohl published the first-ever article on the accident in the magazine *Morze i Ziemia* [Sea and Land]. In 1996 Iwona Bartólewska shot her documentary film ... *i wjechał czołg* [... and a tank drove in] on the subject (see Zadworny 2014).

24 The double page spread on pages 160–161 takes the image of the façade one step further by showing the exterior of a typical socialist apartment block; it shows the flats' prison-like windows from which speech bubbles emanate, testifying that patriarchal power structures become a metaphor for the country as a whole.

childhood and the graphic narrative. In order to emphasize her argument, Hagedorn idealizes her grandmother in the book, while in an overgeneralizing gesture not showing a single positive male character.[25] With her unconventional lifestyle as a bisexual woman who does not care for regulations and promotes women's need for financial independence, the grandmother departs from society's norms. She becomes an icon of resistance and an emotional refuge for her granddaughter, introducing her to erotic literature and feminist thinking. When later on the grandmother begins to display symptoms of dementia, she – then a bisexual, elderly and ill woman – becomes the epitome of intersectional marginalization. "In our family," Hagedorn comments in the caption with regard to her grandmother, "uniqueness was always interpreted in a negative way" – a statement that not only describes Hagedorn's family but also the collectivist idea of socialist society as such. The grandmother's marginalization in society and her idealized representation in the graphic memoir points to the fact that the model of alternative familial and societal relations she embodies is more of a utopian vision than lived reality. Hagedorn circumvents and invalidates a narrative that at first glance one might think she is serving here: the anti-communist narrative that postulates that Polish society indeed lived in a socialist system, but internally remained untouched by it, because its actual life took place in circles of family, friends and like-minded people that represented a counter-reality to the system.

In order to tell Hagedorn's childhood and to connect the individual story of oppression and gradual empowerment with an overarching national and global perspective, *Totalnie nie nostalgia* uses verbal and visual strategies that show the potential of biocular narratives and inscribe the individual experience in intercultural contexts and transcultural discourses.[26]

3.2 Visual Strategies: Between Illustration and Graphic Metaphor

While Frąś' skillful and delicate drawings often provide a very detailed illustration of the verbal narrative, the graphic memoir becomes most rewarding in those passages where the visual narrative goes beyond the purely illustrative function and initiates a discourse of its own or transforms a motif into a multifaceted metaphor. One of the best examples is a full-page portrait of Hagedorn's ill grandmother (Ill. 5).

---

25 In an interview Hagedorn herself points to the fact that she idealizes her grandmother (Jabłońska 2017).

26 On transnationalism in Eastern European graphic narratives, see Kuhlman and Alaniz (2020, 14–18).

Ill. 5: © Wanda Hagedorn. Hagedorn and Frąś 2017, 125.

The template for this image is a self-portrait by Frida Kahlo from 1940 titled "Self-Portrait with Thorn Necklace and Hummingbird".[27] By referring to Kahlo's self-portrait, the authors allude not only to one of the most impressive artists regarding the expression of personal pain and anguish but also to an international icon of resistance against the patriarchal tradition, which Kahlo considered not to have been overcome in her own country by the Mexican revolution. In her art, Kahlo reflects the cultural and political via the most personal and intimate. She supported the Mexican revolution and socialism but was increasingly frustrated by the movement's narrow image of womanhood, limited to selflessness and martyrdom and undermining the idea of equality[28] – aspects that Hagedorn and Frąś highlight in their graphic narrative with regard to the perception of women in socialist Poland. The superimposition of the portraits of Frida Kahlo and Hagedorn's grandmother

27 Instead of a monkey and a cat on her shoulders as in Kahlo's self-portrait, in the illustration of Wanda's grandmother we see the grandmother's two sisters in the background (introduced to the reader in a portrait of the three women two pages later) (Hagedorn and Frąś 2017, 127).

28 Pankl and Blake (2012, 5–6). On the role of women during and after the Mexican Revolution see Olcott (2005).

places the significance of the latter's story and her symbolic meaning in the graphic narrative in a context that transcends the individual and the national.

The name Frida Kahlo is not mentioned once in *Totalnie nie nostalgia*. The authors leave it to the readership's attentiveness to recognize the artwork underlying Frąś' portrait of Wanda's grandmother and to read along with it. Once one has recognized the portrait's template, various pieces of biographical information about Hagedorn's grandmother given in the graphic memoir gain a second meaning, linking the Polish grandmother to the Mexican artist: they share the same year of birth, 1907 (Hagedorn and Frąś 2017, 126), health issues (after giving birth to Hagedorn's mother, the grandmother cannot give birth anymore) and the rebellious stylization as a flapper (Hagedorn and Frąś 2017, 127).[29]

A second example from *Totalnie nie nostalgia* shows how the book's visual discourse transforms a cultural motif into a multidimensional metaphor that links Hagedorn's childhood experience with the meta-discourse of writing. One of the intertextual references alluded to in *Totalnie nie nostalgia* is Kafka's novella *The Metamorphosis*. In contrast to the Kahlo portrait, this reference is part of the verbal as well as of the visual plane. We learn that Hagedorn's adolescent self has read Kafka's story. In the illustration we then see Hagedorn identifying with Kafka's protagonist Gregor Samsa (in his state as an insect), who like her feels alienated from his family. In a dreamlike sequence Hagedorn's father is depicted throwing apples at his child, just like Gregor Samsa's father did.[30] But unlike Kafka's protagonist, Hagedorn's adolescent self does not surrender to the violence but in an act of empowerment throws the apple out of the window – and out of the panel – into the graphic memoir's last panel some pages later (Ill. 6, 7, 8), where the father is depicted alone in his allotment – his private paradise garden (thus the biblical motif underlying Kafka's story is taken up). The autobiographical experience is transformed into a metaphorical vision of oppression and liberation, and the transgression of the panel's boundaries signals the heroine's stepping over the boundaries set by her father.

29 According to Pankl and Blake (2012, 7) as a young woman Kahlo fashioned herself in the American flapper style of the 1920s.

30 Olsza (2021, 232) convincingly argues that Hagedorn and Frąś transform an earlier scene, where Wanda is hit in the face by her father (Hagedorn and Frąś 2017, 224–225) into this metaphorical scene, and through this transformative repetition illustrate Wanda's process of empowerment.

Ill. 6, 7, 8: © Wanda Hagedorn. Hagedorn and Frąś 2017, 226–227; 234.

The motif of the apple is stretched even further on the visual level, connecting the book's first page with the epilogue and Wanda's childhood experience with the adult author's writing process. On the graphic narrative's inner title page (Ill. 9) the child-protagonist is depicted sitting on a pile of books and biting into an apple (the expulsion from childhood paradise and at the same time the recognition of good and evil). In the epilogue we then see Hagedorn writing her memoir on an Apple computer (Ill. 10). Taken together with the Kafkaesque scenes discussed earlier, the symbolically rich apple scenes can be read as an abridged synopsis of the graphic memoir, visualizing a gradual process of emancipation, knowledge and self-awareness. The impact of the graphic memoir is also enhanced by creating a certain tension between illustration, visual effect, and verbal narrative. This is primarily achieved by applying a sepia-colored filter to the illustrations, giving them a nostalgic touch that is at odds with the omnipresent violence depicted and described in the graphic memoir.

Ill. 9, 10: © Wanda Hagedorn. Hagedorn and Frąś 2017, n. pag.; 231.

Totalnie nie nostalgia's visual discourse supports the verbal discourse while adding its own emphases and stressing the supra-individual dimension of the narrative.

But who is in charge of the visual design? This question is not as trivial as it may seem because, after all, the author of the book hired an illustrator to transform her autobiographical script and artistic vision into a graphic narrative. To put it somewhat drastically, when talking about the relationship between the visual and verbal plane of *Totalnie nie nostalgia* we talk about a creative battlefield. This conclusion can be drawn from interviews with Hagedorn[31] and Frąś[32] but also from a paratext at the margins of the book which may easily be overlooked: On the inside of the book cover we find snippets from Hagedorn's and Frąś' mutual correspondence during their working process. It turns out that *Totalnie nie nostalgia*, which appears to be an organic image-word narrative, is the result of a lengthy and tough negotiation process between author and illustrator, revolving mainly around the question of authority in the creative process. Hagedorn's biographically motivated demand for accuracy and detail contrasts with Frąś' artistic aspirations and the conventions of the comic genre that aim at avoiding a doubling of information in the visual and the verbal discourse. Hagedorn and Frąś decided to reveal this creative and conflictive process to the readership by making it part of the book. The confrontation between author and illustrator forms the backdrop for a central feature of the graphic narrative: its total perspective, reflecting one single mind. The title *Totally not nostalgia* thus gains an additional meaning. This radical subjectivity is reflected by the genre of the memoir, as the book is explicitly labeled in its subtitle. Even though the graphic narrative provides a global perspective, we are made aware of

31 "Our collaboration was a complex and dynamic process. My vision often collided with Jacek Frąs'. I guess I can compare our dialogue to the collaboration between a director and a cinematographer. Our discussions were valuable and led to good solutions. Jacek told me at the end that artistic collisions were the soul of our collaboration" ["Nasza współpraca to był złożony i dynamiczny proces. Moja wizja często ścierała się z wizją Jacka. Myślę, że mogę porównać nasz dialog do współpracy reżyserki z operatorem. [...] Nasze dyskusje były cenne, prowadziły do dobrych rozwiązań. Jacek powiedział mi na koniec, że artystyczne ścieranie się było duszą naszej współpracy" (Jabłońska 2017)]. On the gender aspect of this cooperation see Olsza (2021, 236). One might also take into account the age difference between the authors. Even though both grew up in socialist Poland, the conditions in the 1960s and the 1980s varied remarkably.

32 "Wanda sent descriptions of every frame, every detail, specific shots. I had a problem with the duplication of messages – in Wanda's vision many things resounded twice: both in the verbal narrative and in the graphic narrative. In my opinion, readers are much smarter than we think, and they don't need to be lectured twice" ["[Wanda] przysyłała opisy każdego kadru, każdego detalu, konkretnych ujęć. [...] Miewałem problem z duplikującymi się komunikatami – w wizji Wandy wiele rzeczy wybrzmiewało dwa razy: i w narracji słownej, i w narracji rysunkowej. Stoję na stanowisku, że czytelnicy są dużo inteligentniejsi, niż się nam wydaje, i nie trzeba im nic wykładać dwa razy" (Pstrągowski and Frąś s.a.)].

the fact that this macro-perspective is filtered through the lens of one specific individual – the author Wanda Hagedorn.[33]

3.3 Verbal Strategies: Intellectual Discourse and the Polish Void

While *Totalnie nie nostalgia* offers a chronological account of Hagedorn's childhood, at the same time the retrospective process of writing is permanently kept present in the book. On the verbal as well as on the visual plane fragments from books and studies are implemented that put the individual life story into a broader historical, cultural, psychological, and literary framework, helping Hagedorn to better understand and frame her personal experience while writing her memoir, and to situate it in more comprehensive structures. Two literary strategies can be distinguished in the memoir.

Hagedorn's first strategy is to confront her childhood and teenage experiences of the 1960s and 1970s with the critical feminist awareness emerging at that time in Western countries, to which she as a child and Polish society as a whole, however, did not have access: "At that time, feminism had not yet arrived in Poland. The socio-political context was not favorable to the cause" ["Do Polski nie dotarł jeszcze wtedy feminizm: Socjo-polityczny kontekst nie sprzyjał" (Hagedorn and Frąś 2017, 159)].[34] Thus, Hagedorn's first rebellion against her father in the late 1960s is juxtaposed with the simultaneous emergence of the Redstockings Women's Liberation Movement in the United States and the iconic slogan, attributed to Carol Hanisch, that the personal is political.[35] Hagedorn uses this strategy also when talking about her grandmother's Alzheimer's disease. She points out that at the time her grandmother moved in with them Simone de Beauvoir published her book on ageing in French society (*La vieillesse*) and a little later the American geriatrician Robert Neil Butler coined the term ageism for discrimination against the elderly. Hagedorn comments: "Ageism was also practiced en masse in Poland, but nobody wrote about it or stigmatized it" ["W Polsce również

33 Interestingly enough, the main characteristic of Frąś' earlier comic on childhood in Socialist Poland *Stan* (2006) [The State], written and illustrated by himself, is its multi-perspectivity. For more on Frąś' acclaimed pseudo-autobiographical comic, see Thaidigsmann (2022).

34 For a more nuanced picture of female emancipation and activism in socialist Poland argue Mrozik (2011) and Grabowska (2018).

35 For more information on the differences between Eastern and Western European feminism and the merely apparent equality of women in the Eastern European socialist states, see Olsza (2021).

masowo uprawiało się ageism, ale nikt o tym nie pisał ani piętował" (Hagedorn and Frąś 2017, 138)].

Hagedorn's second strategy is to draw on recent studies and literary works – that is, on the knowledge available at the time when she was writing her memoir. Two things stand out in the author's extensive selection of literature stemming from the time after the fall of communism. On the one hand, there is a lack of studies that focus specifically on Polish history and society or even on socialism. On the other hand, there is an overall lack of references to intellectual contributions by Polish authors. In an interview, Hagedorn states that all books that had inspired her while writing *Totalnie nie nostalgia* were mentioned in the graphic memoir (Czoska 2017, 53). The titles named or cited are written by internationally renowned publicists and authors – predominantly working on feminist subjects – like Kate Zambreno, Nancy Friday, bell hooks or Alison Bechdel. It is, however, not true that there was no feminist discourse in Poland after 1989 as Hagedorn's book selection suggests. Although developing belatedly, it evolved continuously from the 1990s onwards and became an indispensable voice of public discourse in post-socialist Poland. Thus, contributions by Polish women writers and gender specialists such as Agnieszka Graff, Maria Janion, Kazimierza Szczuka, Sławomira Walczewska or Inga Iwasiów would have provided Hagedorn's analysis of Polish society with additional points of view. But in the graphic memoir, post-socialist Poland appears as an intellectual void.

What is most striking is the absence of one particular Polish book on Hagedorn's bookshelf that immediately comes to mind when reading *Totalnie nie nostalgia*: Izabela Filipiak's novel *Absolutna amnezja* [Absolute Amnesia] from 1995. Filipiak's then widely and controversially discussed novel about a girl's childhood in the Polish People's Republic introduced a gendered perspective into the discussion of the socialist past in Poland. Twenty years earlier than Hagedorn, Filipiak had noticed that life in communist Poland and within the communist system was not equally repressive for all parts of the population, but that it affected women far more, since it was established on the foundation of an older, preexisting repressive system, namely, patriarchy. On the grounds of this model even the anti-communist part of the (male) population was in compliance with the ruling political system. As for Hagedorn, also for Filipiak the People's Republic of Poland appears as just another historical embodiment of the basic model of male dominance. Hagedorn's personal intellectual journey is thus predated by Polish intellectual and feminist discourse and affirms it.

The two books are (coincidentally?) even linked by their titles that refer to memory and connect it to the formation of identity: While the title *Absolutna amnezja* refers to the systematic annihilation of the individual by the structures of the socialist state, the equally uncompromising title *Totalnie nie nostalgia* rebels against a retrospective annihilation of the individual by erasing unpleasant memories and nostalgically remembering the past – a feature not uncommon in post-socialist narratives about socialism written from a child's perspective (see Nowacki 2000).[36] In *Totalnie nie nostalgia*, family, society and memory are also connected by applying the concept of "dysfunctionality" to all three elements and relating them to each other. The father as patriarchal head of "the dysfunctional "family" ["rodzin[a] dysfunkcjonaln[a]" (Hagedorn and Frąś 2017, 155)] represents the "reality of the dysfunctional dictatorship of the proletariat" ["Realność dyktatury dysfunkcyjnego proletariatu" (Hagedorn and Frąś 2017, 40)], and the dysfunctionality of the grandmother's memory is reflected in the context of scientific hypotheses about the influence of personal or historical trauma on the development of dementia (Hagedorn and Frąś 2017, 125): "We both had problems – my grandmother struggled with a dysfunctional memory, I struggled with a dysfunctional father" ["Obie miałyśmy problemy – babcia walczyła z dysfunktionalną pamięcią, ja z dysfunkcjonalnym ojcem" (Hagedorn and Frąś 2017, 131)].

3.4 Alienation and Homemaking: The Diasporic Perspective

Why does Hagedorn not include the Polish public discourse on socialism, patriarchy, and gender in the memoir? The reason might be a purely pragmatic one having to do with her detachment from the intellectual developments in Poland after emigrating to Australia and with the limited access to Polish books. But there may be a more profound reason. Ewa Stańczyk argues "that those omissions are not coincidental. Rather, they are aimed at emphasizing the author's conscious rejection of what she sees as that which stymies her growth as a person" (2020, 207–208): "the critique of Polish patriarchy is undertaken [...] through intertextual references which [...] build upon an intricate network of texts, images and associations that are transcultural and detached from Eastern European experience" (Stańczyk 2020, 203–204).

Undoubtedly the omission of Polish books is a conscious act adding to the book's agenda. But Stańczyk's explanation ignores the global dimension of patriarchy that Hagedorn and Frąś address and emphasize in their memoir. Thus, instead of arguing with the desire for demarcation and detachment from the Polish context, it is worth adopting the opposite perspective and asking about the longing for integration and inclusion in the diasporic context, in other words, it is

36 Hagedorn's rejection of nostalgia is also expressed in the fact that the graphic memoir does not feature typical objects, films or books from socialist children's culture.

worth looking at the tension between alienation and homemaking in *Totalnie nie nostalgia*. The feeling of being alien resonates throughout the graphic memoir on all levels of the family's history. It is present in the grandmother's story – her non-conformist lifestyle and the loss of her home in the former eastern borderlands (Kresy) of Poland; it is present in the marriage of Hagedorn's parents that embodies the dysfunctional relationship between the differing classes in Polish society;[37] it is present in the city of Szczecin, where Wanda and her family live amongst the remaining traces of the former German inhabitants, and it is present in Hagedorn's experience of being rejected by her parents. On her childhood spent in Szczecin, Hagedorn comments: "I developed a severe state of alienation there, i.e., a chronic being-out-of-place, and that's the way it remained" ["Nabawiłam się tam cieżkiego stanu obcości, to znaczy chronicznego bycia-nie-stąd, i tak mi już zostało" (Hagedorn and Frąś 2017, 18)].[38] This statement links Hagedorn's past in Poland to her present-day life in Australia. In the graphic narrative the only connections to present-day Poland are Hagedorn's video calls with her mother and sisters.[39] At the same time, the Polish past makes itself felt in dreams, most notably in the figure of a rhinoceros – an embodiment of Hagedorn's difficulties to write about her past.

Hagedorn's task is not to locate herself in Poland and to make herself feel at home there but to come to terms with her former childhood experience in the diaspora. Hagedorn's strategy for handling this tension between detachment and an involuntary bond to the Polish past seems to be the creation of a real and an imagined community at her new home in Australia that allow her to integrate her childhood experiences at least to some degree in the discourses of her current surroundings. The real community is created through her social and educational activities connected to her work in an international NGO for women's rights. The virtual community is created through her reading of Western feminist literature. While the global pattern of patriarchy resonates in her current overseas surroundings on multiple levels, the particular Polish case may not be of great relevance in the diaspora. This may be one explanation why Hagedorn refers to

37 While the mother comes from an intellectual family of landowners, the father stems from a working-class and peasant background. The different origins also produce different attitudes towards the resettlement in the country's new western territories after World War II. While for the mother it means a loss of status and wealth, for the father it means the chance of social advancement.

38 See also Hagedorn in an interview: "The starting point for this comic was the permanent sense of alienation that I carry within me" ["Punktem wyjścia dla tego komiksu było ciągłe poczucie obcości, które w sobie noszę" (Jabłońska 2017)].

39 In an interview Hagedorn states that she returned to Poland for a visit for the first time 10–12 years after she had emigrated (Jabłońska 2017).

internationally received literature but ignores the Polish discourse.[40] Thus the graphics best illustrating a sense of homemaking and homecoming in the novel might be the ones where Hagedorn sits on the floor of her living room surrounded by books that reflect her own experiences while at the same time making her part of an international (feminist) community (Hagedorn and Frąś 2017, 92–93).

What is specific about *Totalnie nie nostalgia* on both the visual as well as on the verbal plane is its tension-filled connection of an absolutely individualistic-subjective perspective and its broadest possible generalization. The personal family experience shapes the perception of society on a national as well as global scale. This overgeneralization is problematic and at odds with other narratives about childhood under socialism, in which the protagonists' families or the private environment are often depicted as providing an alternative to the political system. At the same time, however, it raises awareness of structural parallels across systems and warns against displacing inconvenient perspectives on the socialist past (which had already been offered by Filipiak in the 1990s) with a "fairy tale narrative" (Nowacki 2000, 51). And finally, *Totalnie nie nostalgia* reminds its readership(s) that it is naive to believe that the end of a certain political system would automatically solve the problems of a patriarchal society.

4 Conclusion

Even though *"Apuntes para un viaje... a Alemania..."* and *Totalnie nie nostalgia* both stem from (post)socialist and diasporic contexts, they undoubtedly differ in myriad ways, probably most ostensibly in their aesthetic approaches and the use of autobiographical experience. Whereas in Aguilera and Menéndez' narrative we observe an overwhelming dominance of the visual, in Hagedorn and Frąs' graphic memoir the relationship between the visual and the verbal is the result of a lengthy negotiation process between author and illustrator. One common feature of the books, however, are the conscious dissonances between the verbal and the visual discourses, which contribute to fulfilling one narrative purpose: stressing the horror of repressive systems and delegitimizing any nostalgia with regard to the personally experienced socialist past. In *"Apuntes para un viaje... a*

40 The authors' geographical position also seems to determine the function they ascribe to the graphic memoir. While Frąś states in an interview that the comic was made by Poles for Poles (Pstrągowski and Frąś s.a.), this may not be the main motivation for Hagedorn. At least Hagedorn's neglection of the Polish discourse and of the Polish reception of the book suggest such a conclusion.

Alemania…" this is achieved by photographs that potentiate the impact of the verbal discourse. *Totalnie nie nostalgia* creates a similar effect by applying a nostalgic color effect to the illustrations which is at odds with the omnipresent terror depicted in the memoir.

The most striking parallel between the two works, though, concerns their argumentative structure: both readily employ overgeneralizing patterns that fit the individual and the national scale into a global framework. Departing from the experience of state-imposed socialism (and in the case of Hagedorn and Frąś, of parental violence), the two autographic narratives read the world of their protagonists through the prism of two different, yet related, paradigms. While *"Apuntes para un viaje… a Alemania…"* insists on totalitarianism as an explanation for the exiled Cuban protagonist's sense of (self-)alienation, the trans-socialist psychic damage he shares with the East German population, as well as, more generally, global destruction, *Totalnie nie nostalgia* posits patriarchy as the root of global repression both within the family and within (Polish socialist) society. To be sure, the tendency to overgeneralize comes with obvious risks and side effects but also with benefits. Focusing on *one* structure of oppression instead of adopting a more differentiated approach bears the risk of overlooking other systemic factors and of downplaying historical and cultural specificities. But in spite of this indispensable critique, the merits of *"Apuntes para un viaje… a Alemania…"* and *Totalnie nie nostalgia* remain evident. By identifying general patters of repression, the two graphic narratives not only make societal structures transparent and reveal their underlying imaginaries but also open the floor for a larger, transregional debate about (post)socialist systems and their sociocultural legacy.

One of the most important social institutions in traditional societies is the family, conceived of as the intergenerational 'glue' which helps to form a community and to hold it together. It is hardly surprising that, in accordance with the prisms they adopt to produce their autobiographically inspired worldview – totalitarianism or patriarchy – *"Apuntes para un viaje… a Alemania…"* and *Totalnie nie nostalgia* also differ regarding their position towards the classical analogy between the family and the (nation) state in nineteenth and twentieth century fiction and its dissolution in contemporary literature (Assmann 2009, 51).[41] Whereas Aguilera and Menéndez show the family resemblance between different totalitarian systems while, indeed, proclaiming the disintegration of the family within totalitarianism, Hagedorn and Frąs expose the family as a basic model underlying differing societies and political systems. Interestingly enough, while in its visual

41 "[T]here are no analogies and mirroring relationships as in the older family sagas. The family has ceased to represent the whole of society and its culture" (Assmann 2009, 51).

discourse *"Apuntes para un viaje... a Alemania..."* emphasizes the disappearance of the family through collectivization and its replacement by the political regime obsessed with control, on a verbal level it accentuates the meaning of elective artistic affinities and seems to dismiss the family as a unit of filiation. *Totalnie nie nostalgia* also offers alternatives to the nuclear family. While in the childhood narrative the grandmother represents a counter-image to the patriarchal family and state structures, later in the diaspora the international feminist community can be considered "a family of choice" for Hagedorn that opposes both the patriarchal family as well as political structures, which are based on the very same anthropological principles, i.e., the domination of women by men.

In both autographic narratives, political and social oppression lead to a sense of alienation, a feeling that all characters share across generations, origins and functions,[42] and that finally culminates in a worldly journey away from (alienated) 'home,' i.e., from Poland and Cuba, to a foreign place. The outer journey into exile and diaspora translates the inner alienation into something physical, allowing one to reflect on one's social and political origins from a (secure) distance. The inner journey, then, induces fundamental changes in the main characters: while in *"Apuntes para un viaje... a Alemania..."* the Cuban protagonist admits the relativity of truth, in the case of *Totalnie nie nostalgia* the Polish-Australian protagonist gains increased (self-)awareness.

It is the diasporic perspective that contributes to the comparability of the two autographic narratives that stem from very different cultural contexts while sharing the experiences of a similar political system. In one case, however, this system is still operating (socialism in Cuba), while in the other it has been overthrown, confronting the society with the problems of a post-socialist society (Poland). Although *"Apuntes para un viaje... a Alemania..."* is driven by a strong activist impetus – an impetus not sensed in *Totalnie nie nostalgia* – in both books the diaspora perspective defines the authors' take on the subject as it allows them to create their narrative from a distance, both in terms of time, geography and lack of direct entanglement with the system of socialism (regardless of whether it is still operating or defeated).

What can be the benefit of the small but burgeoning field of transregional and comparative research on former or present socialist regimes in Latin America and Eastern Europe after the breakdown of communism in Eastern Europe to which this chapter contributes? While there is a small corpus of research on political, economic, and cultural entanglements and looser analogies between Eastern

42 In *"Apuntes para un viaje... a Alemania..."* verbal narrator Aguilera and by analogy also the visual narrator Menéndez, are both represented through their photo-montaged avatars.

Europe (especially the Soviet Union) and the Americas regarding the time before 1989 (e.g. Gorsuch and Koenker 2013; Rupprecht 2015; Kola 2018), little has been published so far on the processes of cultural exchange and distancing, of orientations towards different centers in the arts, visual culture, and fiction regarding the post-1989 period, that is, the period after the fall of communism in Eastern Europe.[43] However, adopting a trans- or post-socialist perspective allows us to study cultural products from after 1989 from a wider angle and to better understand their aesthetic and argumentative structures against a similar, yet by no means identical historical, cultural, and political backdrop. Moreover, considering the historically relevant perspectives of diaspora and exile provides insights on (post)socialist cultures from outside the political system, from outside the social places attached to it, and from a temporal distance. This may be even more important regarding literary genres and art forms, the audiences of which are fluent and changing, as in the case of graphic narratives and, more generally speaking, in the various forms of crossover fiction.

In order to examine on a larger comparative scale how the perception of socialist past(s) contributes to shaping the present, how literature imagines possible futures and, finally, to what extent the (post)socialist present leads to new imaginations of the past, a network of transregional research on the Americas and Eastern Europe is required, building on the cooperation between scholars in Slavic and Romance literary and cultural studies.

Bibliography

Aguilera, Carlos A. "Apuntes sobre el movimiento de los trenes en A." *Escenas del yo flotante. Cuba: escrituras autobiográficas*. Eds. Carlos A. Aguilera/Idalia Morejón Arnaiz. Leiden: bokeh, 2017. 115–126.

Aguilera, Carlos A., and Aldo Damián "Maldito" Menéndez. *"Apuntes para un viaje… a Alemania…" El cómix*. [Prague:] Castor Ediciones/InCubaDora, 2016.

Aguilera, Carlos A. "Apuntes para un viaje a Alemania." *Encuentro de la cultura cubana* 40 (2006): 64–69.

Assmann, Aleida. "Unbewältigte Erbschaften. Fakten und Fiktionen im zeitgenössischen Familienroman." *Generationen: Erfahrung – Erzählung – Identität*. Eds. Andreas Kraft/Mark Weißhaupt. Konstanz: UVK 2009. 49–69.

43 Those studies which treat the Eastern European-Cuban relations after 1989 primarily discuss the Cuban context, where the impact of 1989 has been devastating in many realms. See e.g., Puñales-Alpízar 2012; Loss and Prieto 2013; Loss 2013.

"Carlos A. Aguilera (*1971). El comunismo destruye toda posibilidad de ilusión y eso es muy jodido." *Memory of Nations, Memoria de la Nación Cubana Memory of the Cuban Nation*. s.d. https://www.memoryofnations.eu/es/aguilera-carlos-20200528-0 (October 23, 2023).

Czoska, Agnieszka. "Najtrudniejsze było pionierstwo. Z Wandą Hagedorn i Jacka Frąś rozmawia Agnieszka Czoska." *Fabularie* 2.13 (2017): 51–56.

Darias Alfonso, Iván. "Muñequitos rusos: la nostalgia y su contexto en la diáspora cubana." *KAMCHATKA* 5 (2015): 29–45.

Espinoza Domínguez, Carlos. "La plural fecundidad." *Cuba encuentro* (June 9, 2017). https://www.cubaencuentro.com/cultura/articulos/la-plural-fecundidad-329636 (October 23, 2017).

Garbatzky, Irina. "Teorías del archivo, formas de la huida. Sobre *Teoría del alma china* de Carlos A. Aguilera." *Acta literaria* 53 (2016): 77–93.

Gorsuch, Anne, and Diana Koenker. Eds. *The Socialist Sixties. Crossing Borders in the Second World*. Bloomington: Indiana UP, 2013.

Grabowska, Magdalena. *Zerwana genealogia. Działalność społeczna i polityczna kobiet po 1945 roku a współczesny polski ruch kobiecy*. Warsaw: Scholar, 2018.

Hagedorn, Wanda, and Jacek Frąś. *Totalnie nie nostalgia*. Warsaw: Wydawnictwo komiksowe/kultura gniewu, 2017.

"InCUBAdora. Archivo, Academia & Aceleración de Ideas." s.d. https://in-cubadora.com/ (October 23, 2023).

Jabłońska, Urszula. "Wanda Hagedorn: Komiks o dzieciństwie w PRL-u: 'Totalnie nie nostalgia'." *Wysokie obcasy* (February 25, 2017). https://www.wysokieobcasy.pl/wysokieobcasy/7,53662,21410901,wanda-hageforn-totalnie-nie-ofiara-komiks-o-dziecinstwie-w.html (October 17, 2023).

Kola, Adam. *Socjalistyczny postkolonializm. Rekonsolidacja pamięci*. Toruń: NCU Press, 2018.

Kuhlman, Martha. "The Autobiographical and Biographical Graphic Novel." *The Cambridge Companion to the Graphic Novel*. Ed. Stephen E. Tabachnick. Cambridge: Cambridge UP, 2017. 113–129.

Kuhlman, Martha, and José Alaniz. Eds. *Comics of the New Europe. Reflections and Intersections*. Leuven: Leuven UP, 2020.

Loss, Jacqueline. *Dreaming in Russian, The Cuban Soviet Imaginary*. Austin: University of Texas Press, 2013.

Loss, Jacqueline, and José Manuel Prieto. Eds. *Caviar with Rum. Cuba-USSR and the Post-Soviet Experience*. New York: Palgrave Macmillan 2013.

Menéndez, Aldo Damián "Maldito." "Blog profile maldito menèndez." Castor Jabao s.d. https://www.blogger.com/profile/13241685664595315048 (October 23, 2023).

Menéndez, Aldo Damián "Maldito." "Castor Jabao." s.d. https://malditomenendez.blogspot.com/ (October 23, 2017).

Miedziński, Paweł. "Parada naszej siły." *Gremio – miesięcznik szczecińskich środowisk prawniczych* 11.19 (November 2015): 28–29.

Mrozik, Agnieszka. "Akuszerki transformacji. Stosunek do PRL-u jako element polityki tożsamości polskiego feminizmu po 1989 roku." *Opowiedzieć PRL*. Eds. Katarzyna Chmielewska/Grzegorz Wołowiec. Warsaw: Wydawnictwo IBL PAN, 2011. 145–158.

"Muñequitos rusos en Cuba. ¿Trauma o nostalgia?" *DiMeCuba*, April 3, 2023. https://www.dimecuba.com/revista/cubanos/munequitos-rusos-cuba/ (October 23, 2023).

Nowacki, Dariusz. "Widokówki z tamtego świata." *Znak* 7.LII (2000): 28–52.

Olcott, Jocelyn. *Revolutionary women in postrevolutionary Mexico*. Durham: Duke UP, 2005.

Olsza, Małgorzata. "'After all, we must be our own heroines.' The power of feminism, Fun Home, and form in Wanda Hagedorn's graphic memoir Totalnie Nie Nostalgia: Memuar." *Comic Art and*

Feminism in the Baltic Sea Region. Eds. Kristy Beer Fägersten et al. London: Routledge, 2021. 217–238.

Pankl, Lis, and Kevin Blake. "Made in Her Image: Frida Kahlo as Material Culture." *Material Culture* 44.2 (Fall 2012): 1–20.

Pérez-Hernández, Reinier. "Narrativas de vida cubanas: nuevos espacios para su lectura (Reseña/Review Carlos A. Aguilera, and Idalia Morejón Arnaiz. Eds. *Escenas del yo flotante. Cuba: escrituras autobiográficas*. Fwd. Adriana Kanzepolsky. Leiden: bokeh, 2017)." *A contra corrientes. Una revista de estudios latinoamericanos* 16.2 (Winter 2019): 305–314.

Pstrągowski, Tomasz. "Polski komiks autobiograficzny." *Autobiografia* 2.5 (2015): 33–47.

Pstrągowski, Tomasz, and Jacek Frąś. "Cudze wspomnienia. Rozmowa z Jackiem Frąsiem." s.a. https://www.dwutygodnik.com/artykul/6983-cudze-wspomnienia.html (October 17, 2023).

Puñales-Alpízar, Damaris. "Cuba socialista. De la traducción y sus secuelas." *KAMCHATKA* 5 (2015): 166–186.

Puñales-Alpízar, Damaris. *Escrito en cirílico, El ideal soviético en la cultura cubana posnoventa*. Santiago de Chile: Cuarto Propio, 2012.

Rupprecht, Tobias. *Soviet Internationalism after Stalin. Interaction and Exchange between the USSR and Latin America During the Cold War*. Cambridge: Cambridge UP, 2015.

Stańczyk, Ewa. "Women, Feminism and Polish Comic Books: Frąś/Hagedorn's Totalnie nie nostalgia." *Comics of the New Europe. Reflections and Intersections*. Eds. Martha Kuhlman/José Alaniz. Leuven: Leuven UP, 2020. 201–213.

Thaidigsmann, Karoline. *Poetik der Grenzverschiebung. Kinderliterarische Muster, Crosswriting und kulturelles Selbstverständnis in der polnischen Literatur nach 1989*. Heidelberg: Universitätsverlag Winter, 2022.

Vassileva-Karagyozova, Svetlana. *Coming of Age under Martial Law. The Initiation Novels of Poland's Last Communist Generation*, Rochester: University of Rochester Press, 2015.

Whitlock, Gillian. "Autographics: The Seeing 'I' of the Comics." *Modern Fiction Studies* 52.4 (2006): 965–979.

Wróbel, Olga. "Z szuflady na barykady." *Znak* 745 (2017): 100–105.

Zadworny, Adam. "Ale Historia. Masakra na defiladzie." *Gazeta Wyborcza*, February 28, 2014. https://wyborcza.pl/alehistoria/7,121681,15540896,masakra-na-defiladzie.html (October 17, 2023).

Anna Artwińska

Family Riddles, Entangled Catastrophes, and Cultural Translation in Bernardo Kucinski's *K* and Maciej Zaremba Bielawski's *The House with the Two Towers*

1 A Surprising Development: Kucinski and Zaremba Bielawski as Family Chroniclers

Economic journalist, advisor to Brazilian ex-president Luiz Inácio Lula da Silva and university professor Bernardo Kucinski (*1937, São Paulo) made his debut as a novelist at the age of 74. His 2011 novel *K.*[1] – which was celebrated as a great success both in Brazil and abroad, and which has been translated into several languages[2] – tells the story of K., a Jewish scholar from Poland, who, in Brazil in 1974, sets off in search of his daughter, kidnapped by the security forces together with her husband, and writes a novel about her abduction. The sudden disappearance of the daughter, who was a member of the militant underground movement Ação Libertadora Nacional (ALN) led by Carlos Marighela, prompts the narrator to research the crimes of the military dictatorship and to trace back his own Brazilian-Jewish-Polish family history. The novel is based on true events: In reality, however, it was not the writer's daughter who disappeared, but his sister Ana Rosa, a natural scientist at the University of São Paulo. This change brings to the fore the perspective of the suffering and unhappy father, who only found out about his daughter's involvement in the underground movement, and her marriage

1 In the second edition (2012), the title was expanded: *K. Relato de uma busca* [K. A report of a search].

2 In September 2012, Kucinski was recognized as one of the four finalists in the category "Best Book of the Year – Novel Debut" at the Prêmio São Paulo de Literatura and in November 2012, he received a special award from the jury at the Prêmio Portugal Telecom de Literatura awards ceremony. In the International Literary Competition (Concurso Internacional de Literatura, 2012) organized by the Brazilian Writers' Association, *K.* was awarded second place. The second edition of the novel followed in March 2012 and the third edition in September 2013. The novel has been translated into English, Spanish, German, Polish, Italian, French and Japanese, among other languages. On the international presence of Brazilian literature on the Shoah, especially Jewish-Brazilian literature, see Moszczyńska 2022, 72–75.

Anna Artwińska, Leipzig University

https://doi.org/10.1515/9783111208664-004

to Wilson Silvia, after the couple had been kidnapped. Like the protagonists in the ancient Greek tragedies,[3] K. fights for the right to a funeral, a dignified farewell and, as I will discuss later, the right to remembrance. By using a heterodiegetic narrator to describe the events from the perspective of K. and not of himself as a brother, Kucinski distances himself from his own experience of family tragedy (news of the death of his sister reached him in exile in London) and at the same time engages with the figure of his own father. In *K.*, the heterodiegetic narrative perspective is briefly interrupted at the beginning and at the end of the novel by a homodiegetic first-person perspective, which can be identified as the voice of the writer himself. The autobiographical paratexts give the novel a framework which becomes a setting for the autofictional plot. In addition, there are chapters in which other characters involved in the events present their own perspectives – all speaking in the first person. These include, among others, the inner monologue of the perpetrator, who has kidnapped the couple and is now wondering what to do with their dog, or the story of Jesuína Gonzaga, the lover of the investigator of the secret police, Fleury.

The special, tender and intimate relationship between K. and his daughter lies at the center of the narrative and forms the primary family constellation of the novel. Other family members are subordinate to the father-daughter relationship and only become important when they can help the father in his quest to understand his family's history and what led to Ana's abduction. The novel thus has two main protagonists who share an asymmetrical relationship: One elderly and alive, the other murdered at a young age. One is defined above all by his Jewish origins, the other by her stance of resistance in a military dictatorship. What is also special about the family constellation is the fact that we only learn about them from one side: The reader does not know how the daughter defined her relationship with her father and whether she actually perceived his preoccupation with Jewish culture and history as a burden and obstacle in their communication, as K. suggests. The daughter's perspective is a blank space in the novel; she remains a remembered figure who triggers a survivor's guilt syndrome in the father, just like the one he experienced when he had lost his two sisters in Poland, before emigrating to Brazil. Furthermore, we do not know whether and to what extent the figure of the father himself was modeled on reality, even though there are clear parallels between the father in the novel and the author's father Mejer Kucinski.

---

3 In one of the reviews of the Polish translation of the book, K. is described as a "gray-haired Antigone" (see Stanisławski 2023).

Like many other contemporary family novels originating from Latin America, Kucinski's book uses his own family history to deal with his country's history of violence. However, he is concerned not only with the task of bearing witness and contributing to Brazil's culture of remembrance, but also with interweaving the history of the military dictatorship in Brazil with anti-Semitism, which culminated in the Shoah and subsequently developed further in Europe and Latin America. One of the novel's intentions is to show Jewish history in different national contexts, especially in Poland and Brazil, and in relation to the respective non-Jewish majority society, without focusing on the issue of transgenerational transmission of trauma and Jewish identity (see Welge 2016),[4] which is often discussed in twenty-first century family novels. Similar to the works by Antônio Xerxenesky, Julián Fuks, Carola Saavedra or Milton Hatoum, Kucinski's *K.* is an example of the kind of literature from Latin America that deals with the "discomfort of memory" (Moszczyńska 2022, 175): The military dictatorship is not necessarily the central theme here, but it is an important context for the plot and the novel's constellation of characters (Moszczyńska 2022, 175). The different reception of the novel in and outside Brazil shows how the respective national-historical experiences influence its understanding and that, depending on cultural context, different aspects of the intertwined history of violence become important.[5] Such an interpretation also confirms Kaisa Kaakinen's thesis about the twenty-first century as a time in which one must expect an extremely heterogeneous reading public – today's readers "are increasingly in contact with each other in the same present but operate with vastly different […] historical experiences and orientations" (Kaakinen 2017, 13). This means that Kucinski's novel simultaneously belongs to different cultures of remembrance and can be read as a text about Jewish history, about the afterlife of the Shoah and about the military dictatorship in Brazil.

The problem of cultural translation and intertwined histories of violence links *K.* with the novel *Dom z dwiema wieżami* (2018) (The House with the Two Towers) by the Polish-Jewish-Swedish journalist and writer Maciej Zaremba vs. Maciej Zaremba Bielawski (*1951, Poznań). It was published in Swedish in 2018 with the title

---

4 Welge points out that there are texts in contemporary Argentinian and Brazilian literature that can be assigned to the paradigm of Marianne Hirsch's postmemory (such as the books by Sergio Chejfec and Michel Laub), but which are simultaneously characterized by "the problem of transatlantic discontinuity" (Welge 2016, 269).

5 "If *K.*'s reception in Brazil contributed to shaping the public debate on the recent history of the country, its international reception focused on the history of left-wing Jewish exiles in Brazil in the 1930s" (Gagliardi 2020, 215). Rebecca J. Atencio also pointed out that the book "raises additional questions about the relationship between the testimonial and the literary" (Atencio 2016, 119). In the Polish reviews, the focus was again placed more strongly on the time the narrator spent in Włocławek and in Warsaw before the Second World War. See Kucinski 2020.

Huset med de två tornen and appeared in an authorized Polish translation later that year.[6] Although Zaremba Bielawski had already established himself as an author in the Swedish and Polish literary circles thanks to his journalistic publications uncovering the shortcomings of Swedish politics,[7] the publication of *Dom z dwiema wieżami* was greeted by critics with enthusiasm similar to *K.* In addition to the outstanding quality of writing about an entangled family history, the Swedish reviews emphasized, among other things, the sensitization to such global problems as nationalism and anti-Semitism (see Sommardal 2018; Wirtén 2018; Leandoer 2018). Polish reviewers praised the presentation of Jewish history in the context of the history of Eastern and Central Europe and the intimate style of the narrative about the family past (see Kieżun 2018; Wicha 2018).[8] As with Kucinski's *K.*, it was also surprising in this case that an established journalist and author took on the role of family chronicler and confronted the reading public with his own family history, which was not only very well-written, but also clearly different from the flood of transgenerational Polish-Jewish family novels of the twenty-first century;[9] this was mainly achieved through varied narrative techniques – the main protagonist, Maciej, sometimes speaks about himself in the third person – and the strong integration of Jewish history into the history of Eastern and Central Europe.

Dom z dwiema wieżami focuses on two main topics. The first deals with the family's time in communist Poland (until 1968): It focuses on the author's youth and his perception of family life from this perspective. The second concerns the life stories of his parents, well-known Polish psychiatrists,[10] reconstructed by the author

6 In Poland, Zaremba's books are published under the name Zaremba Bielawski. In this article, I refer to the Polish translation by Mariusz Kalinowski, which also serves as the basis for my translation into English. The Swedish original is used in footnotes for comparison.

7 The following reports were published in Polish: *De rena och de andra: om tvångssteriliseringar, rashygien och arvsynd* (1999) [The Pure and the Others. On Forced Sterilizations, Eugenics and Original Sin]; *Den polske rörmokaren och andra berättelser från Sverige* (2006) [The Polish Plumber and Other Stories from Sweden], *Den polske rörmokaren: fyra pjäser om det nya Europa och solidaritetens gränser* (2007) [The Polish Plumber: Four Plays on the New Europe and the Limits of Solidarity], *Skogen vi ärvde* (2012) [The Forest We Inherited).

8 The Polish edition was awarded the prestigious Ryszard Kapuściński Award in 2019.

9 As in almost all European cultures, a number of family histories have appeared in Poland in the twenty-first century that deal with Jewish family origins and life in the shadow of the Shoah in post-war Poland from the perspective of the children's and grandchildren's generation. See for example: Agata Tuszyńska, *Rodzinna historia lęku* (2005) [*Family History of Fear* (2016)]; Ewa Kuryluk, *Frascati* (2009); Monika Sznajderman, *Fałszerze pieprzu. Historia rodzinna* (2016) [Pepper Counterfeiters. A Family History].

10 Zaremba Bielawski's father, Oskar Bielawski (1891–1973), was one of the founders of reformed psychiatry in Poland. The psychiatric hospital in Kościan in Poland, where Bielawski worked immediately after the war, was named after him.

while already in exile in Sweden. Similar to the main protagonist in *K.*, the narrator in Zaremba Bielawski's novel is also preoccupied with filling in the blanks in his family's history, which is Polish on his father's side and Jewish on his mother's, and uncovering the family's secrets. While in *K.* the daughter concealed her involvement with the underground movement from her father, Zaremba Bielawski's mother remained silent about her Jewish roots and the story of her own survival in the Second World War, until she emigrated to Sweden in 1968. Both women were convinced that silence would protect their families and could be preserved forever, a belief that turned out to be illusory. For both women, breaking the silence led to a turning point, after which a return to the previous situation was no longer possible. The abduction of his daughter, her death and the impossibility of finding out the details of this tragedy destroyed the life of K., whereas emigration to Sweden as a result of the anti-Semitic campaign in Poland in the late 1960s[11] marked a break in the Zaremba Bielawski family. The mother decided to emigrate against her husband's wishes and ended up leaving the country alone with her three sons (and her own mother). The narrator's complicated relationship with his mother is at the forefront of the book and is the most important family constellation on the plot level, even if the father's aristocratic background and biography are given just as much attention in the text. The protagonist reconstructs the family history in order to understand his mother's motives for concealing her Jewish heritage and her almost obsessive striving to be seen to belong to Polish society.

An important feature of the novel is that it places the problem of Jewish origin and the transmission of trauma in the context of cultural translation. Zaremba Bielawski not only wrote down his family history, but also considered how it could be made accessible to the Swedish reading public (see Szostak 2019). The history of socialism, Polish-Jewish relations and 'Polish'[12] anti-Semitism before and after the Shoah presented a particular challenge, as these topics are hardly known in Swedish society. However, various specifics of Polish culture are also explained, such as this rule of Polish spelling: "In Polish, nationality is written with a capital letter, and religion with a lowercase letter"[13] ["Po polsku narodowość pisze się z wielkiej

11 The Polish political crisis of 1968 ("March 1968") culminated in a series of major protests by students, intellectuals and others against the communist party. It was also accompanied by a mass emigration of Polish Jews following an anti-Semitic campaign. As a result of this campaign, approximately 13,000 Jews left Poland forever.

12 Zaremba Bielawski explains that at the beginning of his emigration he struggled when talking about explicit 'Polish' anti-Semitism (in contrast to 'Swedish' anti-Semitism). However, the more he dealt with this topic, the more aware he became that anti-Semitism can also be shaped by national contexts.

13 "På polska stavar man nationalitet med stor bokstav, konfession med liten" (Zaremba 2018, 117).

litery, a wyznanie z małej" (Zaremba Bielawski 2018, 122)] writes the narrator in the context of an article by the poet Antoni Słonimski, in which the word "Jews" was always capitalized, not to question Judaism as a religion, but, according to Zaremba Bielawski, to challenge the image of the Jews as a chosen people (Zaremba Bielawski 2018, 122). *Dom z dwiema wieżami* thus performs important translational work: the author uses his own family constellations to explain the 'great history' of Eastern Europe to a Swedish audience, which he construes both from an internal and an external perspective – as someone who was socialized in Poland but had then left the country. The choice of the Swedish reading public as one of the readers addressed in the novel (including the author's daughter, who does not speak Polish) forces the narrator to deautomatize his perception, as Russian formalism would have it (Viktor Šklovskij) and to present things and facts as if they were not well-known or familiar to him. The role of the cultural mediator becomes particularly important when tackling painful facts and events, as these must also be subordinated to the rules of translatability.

As family chroniclers, Kucinski and Zaremba Bielawski set themselves the task of inscribing their own family histories into larger political and historical contexts without generalizing and de-individualizing them. At the same time, they bear witness – pillorying the dictatorships, totalitarianisms and ideologies of the twentieth century – and write literature that focuses on selected family constellations in order to gain a better understanding of their own biographies.

2 Alienation Effects: Between Autofictional Writing, Narrative Role Reversal and Documentary Impetus

Both novels are based on true events and take each family's history as the starting point for the narrative. While Kucinski reveals the autofictional mode of his own writing right at the beginning: "Everything in this book is invented but almost everything happened" (Kucinski 2011b) ["Tudo neste livro é invenção, mas quase tudo aconteceu" (Kucinski 2011a, 14)], Zaremba Bielawski emphasizes the "truth," with the caveat that it is relative: "Everything in this book is true, but you don't have to believe in anything"[14] ["Wszystko w tej książce jest prawdziwe, ale w nic nie trzeba wierzyć" (Zaremba Bielawski 2018, 15)]. These declarations confirm that

14 "Allt i den här boken är sant, men inget behöver man tro på" (Zaremba 2018, 12).

fiction can play an important role in texts with auto/biographical elements and does not necessarily have to stand in contrast to the 'autobiographical pact' (Philippe Lejeune): "Now, fictionality is seen as an integrative element of the creation of a sense of identity, since identity conceived as a narrative construct involves the projection of possible selves which are open to revision" (Löschnigg 2019, 108). For Kucinski and Zaremba Bielawski, autofiction is used not only when the narrators cannot rely on verifiable knowledge about the past, but it becomes a basic mode of literary communication.[15] As such, it must be seen as a distancing strategy and procedure that enables the narrators to emotionally detach themselves from their own family history. In *K.*, "imaginative reworking" (Atentio 2019, 120) and the reliance on autofiction help to report on the disappearance and death of Ana Rosa as if a tragedy similar in consequences had happened to a literary protagonist and not to the author himself. This is further supported by the abandonment of the first-person perspective. At the same time, Kucinski distances himself from any idealization of literary writing: In the chapter "Giving up literature" (Kucinski 2011b) ["O abandono da literatura" (Kucinski 2011a, 131–135)], he even declares an "end" to literature. In this strongly autoreflexive section, the narrator reports on countless attempts to write a literary text about his daughter in Yiddish. He describes in detail the preparations for the work process and the writing stages themselves, which were abandoned after the realization that this story is not suitable as literary material – it can only be entrusted to another family member. For this reason, instead of a book, the narrator in *K.* opts for a letter (in Hebrew) that he sends to his granddaughter. This chapter shows the differences between the true events and their literarization, because, in reality, Kucinski has not given up on literature and has written his first literary text about the cruelty of the Brazilian military dictatorship which claimed the life of his sister. Zaremba Bielawski also distanced himself from the healing power of the narrative: In an interview with Polish journalist Anna Bikont, he said that writing the book brought him no relief: "I thought that when I

15 "Then, adopting story-telling techniques, I put these memories into imaginary situations. I brought together incidents that had happened at different times. Other incidents I made up almost entirely" (Kucinski 2011b). This quotation does not appear in the original edition. It can be found in the last chapter of the English edition, entitled "To the reader."

Zaremba Bielawski does not make any declarations of this kind, but his depictions of the past, e.g. the passages about his mother hiding on the 'Aryan side,' must also be described as imaginative work, despite his thorough research on the topic. At this point, it should be briefly mentioned that Zaremba Bielawski's works belong to the genre of literary reportage. This genuinely Polish genre, whose most important representatives include Ryszard Kapuściński and Hanna Krall, lies in an overlapping area between literature and journalism, fact and fiction. A literary reportage attempts to make the other and the foreign comprehensible by making room for the perspective of the writer, despite its predominantly documentary mode.

finished the book, I would let go of any regrets. But I didn't" ["Myślałem, że jak skończę książkę, to wyrzucę z siebie żal. Jednak nie wyrzuciłem" (Bikont 2019)].

In *Dom z dwiema wieżami,* writing about oneself alternately in the first and third person (as well as the choice to write in Swedish) fulfills a function comparable to the authorial narration and description of events from the perspective of K. in Kucinski's book. This approach allows for the emotional coldness of the mother and the distancing from the young version of one's own self, namely by narrating it as if the family and those experiences belonged to someone else. Let us look at two striking examples: 1) "They should have walked through Auschwitz embracing each other. But they each walk separately, like two strangers. In front of a mountain of cut women's hair, he cries alone" ["Powinni byli przejść przez Oświęcim objęci. Ale idą każde osobno, jak dwoje obcych. Przed górą ściętych kobiecych włosów on płacze sam" (Zaremba Bielawski 2018, 26)].[16] 2) "What can you say that's true about him, who is now walking along the Poniatowski Bridge [...] Five months later, in a second, he will make a decision that will change his life. Does he know what he is doing? Or is there something that knows it for him? I remember what I saw and what I felt" ["Co można powiedzieć prawdziwego o nim, który teraz idzie mostem Poniatowskiego [...] Pięć miesięcy później w ciągu sekundy podejmie decyzję, która zmieni jego życie. Czy wie, co robi? Czy może jest coś, co wie to za niego? Pamiętam, co widziałem i co czułem" (Zaremba Bielawski 2018, 82)].[17] Passages like these confirm that the decision to use the autofictional mode can help to abstract from one's own experiences so that they appear simultaneously as one's own and as belonging to others. In the words of Claudia Gronemann: "Autofiction reveals existential motives for writing [...] The referential self conceives of itself [...] as part of a fiction, because no author can claim to know the real meaning of his or her own story" (2019, 245). Nevertheless, there is no doubt that the main protagonists of both novels are wounded, even traumatised characters, and that there is a connection between them and the real-life authors. The suffering they experience as a result of their respective family constellations is very much present in both texts.

Common to both narrators is the belief that their own families are somehow defective; in both cases it seems to be, to use Freud's words, an *Unbehagen.* It does not arise from violence or abuse, but from the many secrets, bad decisions

---

16 "De borde ha gått omfamnade genom Auschwitz. Men de går var för sig som två främlingar. Inför berget av avklippt kvinnohår får han gråta ensam" (Zaremba 2018, 23).

17 "Vad kan man säga sanningsenligt om honom som nu går över Poniatowskibron med en banan i handen? Fem månader senare kommer han på en sekund fatta ett beslut som ändrar hans liv. Vet han vad han gör? Eller är det något som vet det åt honom? Jag minns vad jag såg och vad jag kände" (Zaremba 2018, 79).

or disrupted communication. The protagonist in *K.* regrets his unhappy (second) marriage to a "German Jewess" and accuses himself of having neglected the present and the life of his own daughter by studying Jewish culture and tradition. After he became aware of his daughter's death, he no longer felt alive himself. His intensive search efforts – he had sought help from the Red Cross in Switzerland, Amnesty International in London, the Human Rights Commission of the Organization of American States and the American Jewish Committee in New York, among others – ended in failure: "The father searching for his disappeared daughter stops searching, defeated by exhaustion and indifference. He no longer holds up the photograph. He is no longer an icon. He is no longer anything. He is the useless trunk of a dried-up tree" (Kucinski 2011b) ["O pai que procurava a filha desaparecida já nada procura, vencido pela exaustão e pela indiferença. Já não empunha o mastro com a fotografia. Deixa de ser um ícone. Já não é mais nada. É o tronco inútil de uma árvore seca" (Kucinski 2011a, 91)]. This reference to a family tree makes the loss and decay of the family clear: A withered tree can only grow with difficulty. It is no coincidence that *K.* ends with the death of the main protagonist.

In *Dom z dwiema wieżami*, the family is described as strange, even eerie, because the narrator's father had to separate from his then wife and their children in order to start his new family: "The man betrays his tribe for the sake of a foreign woman and becomes an outcast. Now the two have only each other and the children who may come. Our family becomes a very lonely caravan, a clan without ancestors, a family without blood ties" ["Mężczyzna zdradza swoje plemię dla obcej kobiety i zostaje wyrzutkiem. Teraz ci dwoje mają tylko siebie i dzieci, które może się urodzą. Tak więc nasza rodzina staje się bardzo małą karawaną, klanem bez pobratymców, rodem bez więzów krwi" (Zaremba Bielawski 2019, 264–265)].[18] The missing blood ties, which are the foundation of every newly founded family, are a metaphor for the incommensurability between the Polish fate of the father and the Jewish fate of the mother, which also becomes the narrator's undoing:

> I didn't understand that before – that when these two meet, they are at the opposite ends of the Polish war experience. [...] But who is he to her, a gentleman with a monocle and pumps who acts as if the catastrophe had never happened? Does she see him as an innocent who has been spared by fate an advanced course in the knowledge of human nature? Yes: she sees a man whom she does not want to infect with her fear. With him, she might just be able to forget.

18 "Mannen förråder sin stam för den främmande kvinnans skull och blir utstött. Nu har de två bara varandra och barn som kanske kommer. Så blir vår familj en mycket ensam karavan, en stam utan förvanter, en släkt utan blodsband" (Zaremba 2018, 253–254).

> [Nie rozumiałem tego wcześniej – że kiedy spotykają się ci dwoje, są na przeciwnych krańcach polskiego doświadczenia wojny. [...] Ale kim on jest dla niej, dżentelmen z monoklem i w pumpach, zachowujący się, jak gdyby katastrofy nigdy nie było? Widzi w nim niewinnego, któremu los oszczędził wyższego kursu wiedzy o ludzkiej naturze? Tak: widzi mężczyznę, którego nie zarazi swoim lękiem. Przy nim być może uda się jej zapomnieć. (Zaremba Bielawski 2018, 281)][19]

Both authors use a whole host of heterogeneous material in their texts: archival documents, academic studies, letters and diaries of family members,[20] photographs and illustrations. The book by Zaremba Bielawski includes a bibliographical note, and the German translation of *K.* an appendix with explanations of terms, historical persons and places that appear in the book. This documentary impetus in texts that display their partly imaginative character can at first be surprising. However, it is intended to reinforce the authenticity of the narrated (albeit literary) story and, it also shows that both authors remain committed to the journalistic tradition from which they hail, even as family chroniclers. The way in which the two novels deal with facts and fiction makes them exciting and confirms that family stories in the twenty-first century are both authentic reports and imaginative re-figurations. Nevertheless, a difference can be observed in the treatment of sources in the two novels. The focus in *K.* is on the investigation of Ana Rosa's abduction: Sources are consulted in order to reconstruct the timeline and course of the abduction and to form a picture of the last days of K.'s daughter's life. The narrator follows every lead and even lets the perpetrators have their say, because everything that can shed light on Ana Rosa and her husband's fate is relevant to him. In contrast, *Dom z dwiema wieżami* is not only about learning about the parents' past, but also about understanding the complicated Polish-Jewish history of the twentieth century, Polish anti-Semitism and the Polish class system (Maciej's father came from the nobility and taught his son to be proud of his aristocratic origins). The thorough research thus helps the authors to learn more about the larger historical, political and social contexts of their families' histories. Although Kucinski's *K.* touches on the history of military dictatorship in Brazil through the daughter's story, the narrator primarily wants to secure knowledge about the individual fate of a missing family member.

---

19 "Jag har inte förstått det tidigare – att när de två möts är deras sinnen så fjärran från varandra som två människor kunde vara våren 1946. Men vem är han för henne, gentlemannen med monokel och knäbyxor som uppför sig som om katastrofen inte varit? Ser hon en aningslös som förskonats från överkursen i menniskans natur? Ja: hon ser en man som hon inte lär kunna smitta med sin rädsla. Hos honom kan hon kanske glömma" (Zaremba 2018, 271).

20 Zaremba Bielawski uses the diary that his mother left behind, while Kucinski adds a letter that his daughter wrote to a friend.

Both the photographs added to the text in Zaremba Bielawski's book, some of which come from his family album and some from various museums and archives, and the descriptions of Ana Rosa's photographs in Kucinski's *K.*, reinforce the family album-like character of the two novels. The visual material and the ekphrasis contribute to making *K.* and *Dom z dwiema wieżami* seem like intimate family mementoes. This effect is by no means nostalgic,[21] it complements the narrative about the respective family catastrophes. As readers, we know that the photographs and the ekphrases represent past worlds and life stories that have come to an abrupt end or progressed in an unexpected direction due to political circumstances. For the authors, the photographs are material, palpable traces of the past that additionally legitimize the narrative and support the memory work. The father in *K.* only realizes in retrospect that photographs "could provoke such strong feelings" (Kucinski 2011b) ["pudessem suscitar sentimentos assim fortes" (Kucinski 2011a, 114)]; until Ana's death, he paid little attention to this medium. This is one of the reasons why no real album was created for Ana; the remaining pictures of her are arranged loosely and randomly. Among them there is not a single photo of the father with his daughter; Ana can be seen in photos with other family members and friends, but not with K. This makes the father sad and angry; the lack of photos showing them together reinforces his feeling of loss and challenges the belief in the unique bond between him and his daughter. Maciej Zaremba Bielawski, in contrast, was interested in photographic art as a teenager and enjoyed taking photos himself. When his mother broke the news about the emigration to Sweden, he was in the process of developing his photos and – inspired by Michelangelo Antonioni's film *Blow up* (1966) – enlarging them. "If you magnify the image enough, you can discover things that people want to hide" ["Jeśli powiększyć obraz dostatecznie, to można odkryć rzeczy, które ludzie pragną ukryć" (Zaremba Bielawski 2018, 101)],[22] Maciej ponders just before the big revelation. The darkness of the bathroom, in which he tries to remove the new prints from a pane of glass with a razor blade in his hand, forms an equivalent to the equally dark, but in its illuminating function 'bright,' message from his mother.

---

21 Only the photographs from the time before emigration have a nostalgic effect in *K.*: "K. had brought from Europe an album of those blurred sepia pictures that possess a certain magic" (Kucinski 2011b) ["K. trouxera da Europa um álbum de retratos naqueles tons marrons enevoados de sépia que emanavam certa magia" (Kucinski 2011a, 116)].

22 "Om man förstorar en bild väldigt mycket kan man upptäcka sådant som människor velat dölja" (Zaremba 2018, 98).

3 Jewish Origin in a Transnational Setting

In both novels, the Jewish background of the protagonists plays an important role, albeit a different one in each case. The Jewish scholar in Kucinski's *K.* sees himself as a guardian of Judaism and his task as preserving and cultivating Jewish culture and tradition. His preoccupation with Jewish studies therefore has little to do with everyday life in Brazil, as outlined at the beginning of the novel. Only after his daughter has been kidnapped does the Jewish experience – his own in pre-war Poland and that of the Jews who were murdered during the Shoah – become an important point of reference. The daughter's role in the underground movement is compared with his own subversive activities in Włocławek and Warsaw in the 1930s, and the Brazilian military dictatorship is interpreted as a continuation of the history of political and cultural violence against Jews. An equivalence arises between the father and the daughter that could be described, after Ludwig Wittgenstein, as a kind of "family resemblance" (*Familienähnlichkeit*) – i.e. a non-taxonomic resemblance:[23]

> Even though it was a family tradition, he'd been surprised to find out about her political militancy; he'd always seen her as a sensitive person, who read poetry, who loved cinema and didn't care much for politics. But once he learned of her political activism, he understood why she'd been secretive. Basic rules of safety. He'd also behaved like this when he'd been an activist in Poland. (Kucinski 2011b)

> [Surpreendera-o a revelação de sua militância política, embora fosse tradição de família; sempre a vira como a filhinha sensível que lia poemas, que gostava muito de cinema e pouco de política. Mas, uma vez revelado esse ativismo, de modo trágico, entendeu as razões do segredo. Razões elementares de segurança. Ele também adotara esse procedimento nos tempos de sua militância clandestina na Polônia (Kucinski 2011a, 46–47)].

When K. is accused by a general of spreading serious accusations against the military in Jewish circles and it is then insinuated that his daughter had not disappeared but had fled to Buenos Aires with a lover, he recalls the words of a police officer in Poland who claimed at the time that his sister Gita had not died of tuberculosis in a prison cell in Warsaw but had run away to Berlin with a lover. When a rabbi refuses to allow him to place a gravestone for his daughter in the Jewish cemetery because her body is missing, K. replies that there are no bodies under the memorial stone for the victims of the Shoah either and that for him his

---

23 The concept of family resemblances had first appeared in the writings of Arthur Schopenhauer and Friedrich Nietzsche, but only gained significance through Wittgenstein's *Philosophical Investigations* of 1953. See Mittelstraß 2005, 474.

daughter's tragedy is the continuation of the Shoah,[24] without wanting to take away from the uniqueness of that other tragedy. Through such comparisons and contextualizations, it becomes clear that K. associates the violent history of Brazilian military dictatorship with other violent histories that befell him and his family as Jews. Jewish origin always proves to be problematic in different national contexts. For K., his missing daughter Ana Rosa is a victim not only of the Brazilian military dictatorship, but also of the eternal persecution of Jews throughout history in general. Although it is not clear whether Ana Rosa's Jewish origins played a role for her identity and in her death at all, the father interprets her disappearance in the context of his transnational, Brazilian, Jewish and Polish family history.[25] This tendency becomes clear in a scene in which a printer refuses to print K.'s memoir about his daughter because she was a communist. Here Kucinski not only criticises the notion that all opponents of the regime in Brazil are communists, but also alludes to the Polish stereotype of *żydokomuna* ('Jewish Bolshevism'). This stereotype implies a blanket conflation of Jews and communism and is used whenever the responsibility for the introduction of communism in Poland is to be attributed solely to the Jews. It can be assumed that K. was familiar with this stereotype from his work in the Polish left in the 1930s.

The protagonist Maciej in *Dom z dwiema wieżami* only learns of his Jewish origins on his mother's side shortly before emigrating to Sweden. This knowledge proves to be a very important building block in understanding his family's history, especially his mother's actions. The main protagonist now realizes his multiple identities: he is a Pole of noble origin – his ancestors on his father's side can be traced back to the fourteenth century – and a Polish Jew, but increasingly also a Swede with an immigrant background.[26] The anti-Semitic pogroms of 1967–1968, which he witnessed while still in Warsaw, become part of his personal history from the moment of his mother's confession: "I'm going back to my notes to check when I started writing 'they' about the nation I came from. It was after three weeks buried in the archives, following in the footsteps of my mother's father. They. Poles. No longer we" ["Wracam do swoich zapisków, żeby sprawdzić, kiedy zacząłem

24 "K. agreed with this but said that for him his daughter's tragedy was a continuation of the Holocaust" (Kucinski 2011b) ["Com isso K. concordou, mas retrucou que para ele a tragédia da filha era continuação do Holocausto" (Kucinski 2011a, 81)].

25 It should be noted that members of Kucinski's family also live in other countries, including the UK and Israel.

26 Asked by Anna Bikont about his own identity, Zaremba Bielawski replied: "After two weeks in Poland, I feel more and more Swedish and Jewish. It's easier for me to feel Polish in Sweden than in Poland. This order updates itself. If we have a wave of anti-Semitism in Sweden, there is no way around it, I will be more and more Jewish. The same is true in Poland: I definitely feel more Jewish now than under the previous governments" (Bikont 2019).

pisać 'oni' o narodzie, z którego pochodzę. To było po trzech tygodniach w archiwach, śladami ojca mojej mamy. Oni. Polacy. Już nie my" (Zaremba Bielawski 2018, 135)].[27] For Maciej, however, being a Jew means something different than for the protagonist in *K.* For generational reasons alone, he does not see himself as a keeper of Jewish tradition, which, incidentally, he has never dealt with, but as someone who has to understand why his mother's Jewish origins have been completely tabooed in his family. The answer to this question leads him to Tarnów, where his mother's Jewish family lived before the war. Thanks to his research, he learns more about the family's past and also about the complicated Polish-Jewish relations before the Second World War and during the Shoah. The story of "Lila-Liliana-Elżbieta-Iza-Elisabeth Immerdauer-Jarosławska-Imierowska-Bielawska-Drottfors" (Zaremba Bielawski 2018) – the names the mother went by in the course of her life – proves to be a paradigmatic portrayal of a typical Jewish person's life in Poland, characterized by experiences of anti-Semitism, exclusion and fear. As in many other Polish-Jewish family stories – a good basis for comparison would be the book *Fałszerze pieprzu* by Monika Sznajderman –[28] Zaremba Bielawski also reconstructs the individual stages of his Jewish mother's life in the Polish-majority society in great detail. This tells us nothing that we would not already know from the historical works on Polish anti-Semitism,[29] and yet this story sticks with us. In particular, her experience of hiding among the Poles and everything that happened to her during this time is told in a very moving way. As a Shoah survivor, Zaremba Bielawski's mother lived in the shadow of this catastrophe and interpreted the anti-Semitism of the post-war period as its direct continuation. This is why she made the decision to emigrate so quickly: for her, March 1968 was a signal that "this" was beginning again.[30] What changes is the perpetrator-victim constellation: during the war she fled from the Germans, now the threat comes from her Polish neighbors.

---

27 "Jag går tillbaka i anteckningarna för att se när jag började skriva, de om folket som jag kommer från. Det var efter två veckor i arkiven i morfars spår. De. Polackerna." (Zaremba 2018, 130).

28 Monika Sznajderman's family history *Fałszerze pieprzu. Historia rodzinna* from 2016 tells the author's Polish-Jewish family history with a focus on the divergence between Polish and Jewish historical experiences and asks how these asymmetries are stored in the national collective memory. Sznajderman criticizes the Polish intelligentsia as a social class that continued to live in its semiosphere (Jurij Lotman) with its idyllic country life, parties, hunting trips and duels while the Polish Jews were being exterminated.

29 Due to the anti-Semitic laws (*numerus nullus*), her mother was not allowed to study medicine before the war, for example.

30 This attitude can be found in many autobiographical texts written by Polish authors of Jewish origins in context of the anti-Semitic campaign of 1968. See Artwińska 2018.

Kucinski, Bernardo. *K.* Trans. Sue Branford. Rugby: Practical Action Publishing with Latin American Bureau, 2011b [ebook].

Leandoer, Kristoffer. "Bokrecension: Maciej Zaremba sonar sin oskuld." *Dagens Nyheter*, August 24, 2018.

Löschnigg, Martin. "Narratology." *Handbook of Autobiography/Autofiction*. Vol. 1: *Theory and Concepts*. Ed. Martina Wagner-Egelhaaf. Berlin: De Gruyter, 2019. 103–111.

Mittelstraß, Jürgen. Ed. *Enzyklopädie Philosophie und Wissenschaftstheorie*. Vol. 2. Stuttgart: Metzler, 2005.

Moszczyńska, Joanna M. *A memória da Destruição na escrita judaico-brasileira depois de 1985. Por uma literatura pós-Holocausto emergente no Brasil*. Berlin: Peter Lang, 2022.

Nogaś, Michał. "Maciej Zaremba Bielawski. Laureat reporterskiego Nobla." *Gazeta Wyborcza*, May 28, 2019.

Sommardal, Göran. "Granskar sig själv. Göran Sommardal läser grävande journalisten Maciej Zarembas skildring av sina polska rötter." *Aftonbladet*, August 25, 2018.

Stanisławski, Wojciech. "Sieci." https://claroscuro.pl/k_relacja_z_pewnych_poszukiwan_recenzje.php (December 15, 2023).

Szostak, Natalia. "Nagroda Kapuścińskiego 2019. Zaremba Bielawski: Myślałem, że narażę się Polakom. A dotarła do mnie fala ciepła." *Gazeta Wyborcza*, May 25, 2019.

Welge, Jobst. "Transgenerational Memory in Contemporary Argentinean and Brazilian Literature (Sergio Chejfec, Michel Laub)." *Artefrakte: Holocaust and World War II in Experimental Forms of Representation in Literature and Art*. Ed. Esther Kilchmann. Cologne: Böhlau, 2016. 269–282.

Wicha, Marcin. "Mama powiedziała: 'Wyjeżdżamy. Jestem Żydówką'. Nowa książka Zaremby Bielawskiego jest jak operacja na samym sobie." *Gazeta Wyborcza*, December 4, 2018.

Wirtén, Per. "Nationalismen dömde dem till ensamhet." *Expressen*, August 25, 2018.

Wiszniowska, Monika. "*Dom z dwiema wieżami* Macieja Zaremby Bielawskiego jako 'arcypolska opowieść reporterska napisana po szwedzku.'" *Konteksty kultury* 18.3 (2021): 430–447.

Zaremba Bielawski, Maciej. *Dom z dwiema wieżami*. Trans. Mariusz Kalinowski. Kraków: Karakter, 2018.

Zaremba, Maciej. *Huset med de två tornen*. Stockholm: Weyler, 2018.

Maria de Fátima Marinho

Merging Public and Private Identities: Topics in Twenty-First Century Portuguese Novels

1 Introduction

The boundaries between public and private identities can become blurred within a community when its historic heritage plays an undeniable role and when the players in the identity-making process tend to foster interferences between events belonging to a strictly private sphere and events that belong to the wider public sphere and are supposedly separate from personal histories. These boundaries, which must necessarily be considered artificial, since they are impossible to define, present very specific features in the novels of the second half of the twentieth century, when authors seek to interpret and/or view public events through individual focalization. Such perspectives are conditioned not only by external factors but also, and especially, by personal traits and interests which are hardly objectifiable.

It is not too bold to state, as does Hanna Meretoja in her recently published *The Ethics of Storytelling – Narrative Hermeneutics, History and the Possible*, that to (re)interpret "one's life is to interpret it *in medias res*" (2018, 84; emphasis in the original), because each version of history brings with it a new interpretation. The tensions among all these versions exist in separate social contexts, while the sense of the possible is transfigured and takes on a crucial significance (Meretoja 2018, 90). All these arguments combined allow us to maintain that reading is always a means of connecting oneself through storytelling (Meretoja 2018, 117). Stories always end up revealing more than we would expect, helping us rethink the way in which we read literary works, insofar as these can no longer be regarded simply on their own but become part of a (real or virtual) network together with the empirical author's prior readings.

Assumptions of this kind and knowledge obtained through oblique readings and transversal sensations form the basis of hybrid narratives which, through a private focalization, describe historical events and mutual interferences, tangents and intersections.

In the nineteenth century, the historical novel was primarily interested in legitimizing nationalities, which found themselves in a state of fragile balance after the sweeping changes brought about by the French Revolution and Napoleon's

Maria de Fátima Marinho, University of Porto

https://doi.org/10.1515/9783111208664-005

imperialistic policy, less in paying attention to private, subjective views. Even though some novels, such as Eugène Sue's well-known *Mystères du Peuple ou Histoire d'une Famille de prolétaires à travers les âges* (1849–1856) [*The Mysteries of the People or History of a Proletarian Family Across the Ages*], focused on successive generations of the same family, the truth is that the family was just a pretext for narrating external achievements and making them known to readers. In the early twentieth century, however, Thomas Mann's famous novel *Buddenbrooks. Verfall einer Familie* [*Buddenbrooks. The Decline of a Family*], published in 1901, was undoubtedly a prime example of the genre which showed how social and historical processes are played out on the level of family life over three generations.

In the mid-twentieth century, with the theories of the New History and the perception that history can no longer be considered a static science, but rather a dynamic, ever-changing construction necessarily based on different points of view, a new type of novel emerged. These are fictions that represent a given period of time, but they do so almost exclusively by addressing the consequences and repercussions that historical events have in the life of a family. We must keep in mind that historical phenomena that took place in the second half of the twentieth century had a fundamental influence on the perception of public historical developments and their inevitable impact on private households. An example in Portugal is the Revolution of April 25, 1974 and the resulting independence of the former colonies, with the return of settlers to the *metrópole*, as the Portugal territory was then called by those living in the colonies. This event was of decisive importance for the revival of history-based novels and for the (public and private) reading of facts, their consequences as well as the controversial, linear, or orthodox interpretations.

In *O Romance Histórico em Portugal*, I (1999, 150–172) examined some of these novels, drawing attention to a domestic interpretation of history, and the priorities that it generates, including both obvious and less oblique cases, such as the novels by José Saramago, Álvaro Guerra, Helena Marques and Luísa Beltrão, or the more subtle constructions by Maria Isabel Barreno and Mário Cláudio.

There are three other interesting, symptomatic cases (Marinho 2009; 2019; 2020) that can serve as a basis for this essay: two novels by Teolinda Gersão, *A Casa da Cabeça de Cavalo* (1995) [The House of The Horse's Head] and *A Árvore das Palavras* (1997) [*The Word Tree* (2013)], and one by Lobo Antunes, *O Esplendor de Portugal* (1997) [The Splendor of Portugal].

In Gersão's *A Casa da Cabeça de Cavalo*, the former, now deceased inhabitants of a house, discuss political events, such as the French invasions, and produce different versions of the same events stemming from distinct focalizations, since they belong to people whose lives had nothing in common. The family – viewed not in its generational linearity, but as a household comprising masters and servants, power relations that may issue from labor contracts or from family dynamics – negotiates the separate and well-defined male and female spheres. It is there that the underlying conflicts are played out and eventually legitimize the opposing, alternative visions of the external circumstances that affect the family.

This is not very different from the universe of *The Word Tree* where Gita, a white child born in Mozambique, notices the different behaviors of characters driven by opposite focalizations of a single reality. The atmosphere in the colony, the relations between colonizers and colonized cannot be read uniformly or be based on homogeneous groups. Gita's insightful focalization, which is noticeably opposed to her mother's and is closer to the female black servant's, outlines the dysfunctional vision of a family that is seeking itself but becomes shattered in its dissonant perception of reality.

Lobo Antunes's novel is also about a crumbling household, set in the time after Angola's independence, when the children return to Lisbon while the mother remains in Africa. The discovery of fragile identities, the different perceptions of the external events, and the difficulty in situating oneself in a univocal space (the mestizo by definition lacks his/her own, unquestionable space) tend to turn individuals into hesitant, problematic beings who are unable to find a time and a space that may validate their tormented, de-centered, a-social and fragmented existences. Angola's decolonization has profound repercussions on personal and familial experiences, leading to narrative focalizations marked by multiple insecurities.

In the novels published in Portugal after the year 2000 there is no longer a clear insistence on the relations between the external world and the family's private space. This means that references to History, be it contemporary history or decisive moments in the life of the nation, are no longer as pressing a subject as in previous decades, particularly in the 1980s and 1990s. What we see instead is a shift in the understanding of private history, building identities through a subterranean legacy mainly focused on domesticity, within a framework that construes the outside world as a dark place of vertiginous presence-absence.

Speaking about domesticity inevitably means speaking about women. Although usually silenced and forgotten, women often become the drivers of historical developments, even if only subliminally and indirectly, which becomes a privileged way to assimilate external events. In *O Osso do Meio* (2020) [The Middle Bone], Gonçalo M. Tavares highlights this commonly ignored evidence:

> Buzz is the family's female machine, it makes things, it produces, here is the right example: female buzz produces what will later be called the History of the family. There is more buzz than facts in History, in fictive history, but this is the only history there is both in the family and in individual lives; women win; they are the best at assimilating the past.[1]

1 Unless otherwise noted, all translations are my own.

> [O burburinho é a máquina feminina da família, faz coisas, produz, eis o exemplo certo: o burburinho feminino produz aquilo a que mais tarde se chamará História da família. Há mais burburinho que factos na História, na história fictícia, mas esta é a única que existe tanto na família como nas vidas singulares; as mulheres vencem; são as que melhor assimilam o passado. (Tavares 2020, 15)]

Having identified these common traits in contemporary Portuguese novels, I will now seek to determine the main dynamics governing the construction of family identities, as reflected in the interpretation or perception of external, historical data whose influence becomes less clear, although obliquely essential. For this purpose, this essay is divided into three topics: a focus on the personal past with a tenuous relationship to the external world; the presentation of a present that can only be explained through the past; a personal focalization of specific historical facts.

While analyzing the three topics, I will attempt to describe the specificity of Portuguese literature during the last twenty years and its sustained concern with family constellations that produce controversial, maladjusted, distressing, and problematic identities.

2 Focus on the Personal Past with a Tenuous Relationship to the External World

In order to approach our first topic, let us start with António Lobo Antunes' novel *Que Cavalos são aqueles que fazem Sombra no Mar?* [What Horses Are Those Who Shade On The Sea?], published in 2009. Unlike in earlier novels by the same author, in this one there is no clear relationship with the historical past (as in, for instance, *Os Cus de Judas* (1979) [*South of Nowhere.* (1983) or *The Land at the End of the World.* (2012)], or *O Esplendor de Portugal* (1987) [The Splendor of Portugal], where the colonial wars play an important role). Here, the identity crisis resides entirely within the subject and the family, who are gathered together on the occasion of the mother's death. For instance, here we read: "when a photograph which had hitherto remained invisible emerged from the dark or a mirror stained with the mysteries of time duplicated the portraits from a different angle, which was disturbing because it was not them while still being them" ["quando uma fotografia até então invisível surgia do escuro ou um espelho enodoado pelos mistérios do tempo duplicava os retratos num ângulo diferente que assustava porque não eram eles sendo eles" (Antunes 2009, 13)]. Through such a passage we understand how difficult it is to embrace one's identity and to enter into the intricate web of family relationships, which expand into a wider universe, because "a portrait emerged from the promising darkness" ["retrato surgia do escuro esperançoso" (Antunes 2009, 26)] and "were it not for clocks and we would never grow old" ["se não fossem os relógios não envelheceríamos nunca" (Antunes 2009, 155)].

Such allusions to the anguishing passing of time and the inexorable presence of death can also be found in other authors and other novels, such as Gonçalo M. Tavares' *The Middle Bone*, published in 2020, ("Children grow, old people too, and the latter die" ["As crianças crescem, os velhos também, e estes morrem" (Tavares 2020, 48)]) or Lídia Jorge's *Os Memoráveis* (2014) [The Memorables]: "The city must be dark, the streets must be empty, the tramway tracks must look like veins, the Rua Augusta Arch must appear in the background, but the clock's hands must not be there, and its face must be blind." ["A cidade deve ser escura, as ruas devem estar desertas, os carris dos elétricos devem parecer veias, o Arco da Rua Augusta deve surgir ao fundo, mas as agulhas do relógio não devem existir, e o mostrador deve estar cego." (Jorge 2019, 331)]

The challenging attempt to bracket time and death, which is present in so many novels, creates an existential conflict, where the historical past plays an essential role, although it is kept hidden and is only indirectly related to the characters' lives. It is this subterranean relation between private experience and history that José Luís Peixoto intends to portray in his novel *Almoço de Domingo* (2021) [Sunday Lunch]: "The past must constantly prove that it did exist. Things forgotten and things that did not happen occupy the same space. There is so much reality happening out there, fragile, carried by only one person. If this individual vanishes, all that reality will irrevocably vanish as well, there is no way to recover it, it is as if it had never existed." ["O passado tem de provar constantemente que existiu. Aquilo que foi esquecido e o que não existiu ocupam o mesmo lugar. Há muita realidade a passar-se por aí, frágil, transportada apenas por uma pessoa. Se esse indivíduo desaparecer, toda essa realidade desaparece sem apelo, não existe meio de recuperá-la, é como se não tivesse existido." (Peixoto 2021, 14)]

With regard to the relation between history and memory, the premier importance of the latter legitimizes such statements as in Lídia Jorge's *O Vento Assobiando nas Gruas* (2002) [*The Wind Whistling in the Cranes* (2022)]: "Death isn't dying, death is disappearing from people's memories" (Jorge 2022, 498) ["A morte não é morrer, a morte é sair da memória." (Jorge 2002, 529)]. Similarly, in Lobo Antunes' 2009 novel, memory is defined as something disposable and prone to change: "the memory of a pair of gloves on the floor without one being unable to remember whom they belonged to, how strange life is, what can one do, where does one start" ["a memória de um par de luvas no chão sem que recordemos a quem pertenciam, que estranho viver, como se faz, começa-se por onde" (Antunes 2009, 36)]. In a more recent book, *Para Aquela que está sentada no escuro à minha espera* (2016) [For the Girl Sitting in the Dark Waiting for Me], a character speaks of "my memory episodes with no relation one to the other" ["a minha memória episódios sem relação entre si" (Antunes 2016, 209)]; we hear of the fragmentation of images from the past ("I forgot everything but the ponytail" ["esqueci tudo excepto o rabo de cavalo" (Antunes 2016, 127)]), the undoing of all concrete experiences ("they have gradually taken everything from me, words, the past, theatre" ["vão-me tirando tudo, as palavras, o passado, o teatro" (Antunes 2016, 193)], everything leading to the desperate plea, "Help me be myself again" ["Ajudem-me a tornar ser eu" (Antunes 2016, 73)], which shows how difficult it is to build a solid identity.

If we consider that one's language is part of one's identity and that silencing it is a means to annihilate it, we easily understand the extent to which such a limitation or prohibition determines the subject's relations with History and the possibility of a reconciliation with himself/herself. This is what happens to Lillias Fraser, the protagonist of Hélia Correia's novel by the same name (2001), who is forbidden to speak her own language to avoid giving herself away, in order to hide her true identity.

In *O Regresso de Júlia Mann a Paraty* (2021) [Julia Mann's Return to Paraty] by Teolinda Gersão, Sigmund Freud, who is the fictive narrator of one of the chapters, says the following about Thomas Mann: "I came to die on this English island which has welcomed me and to which I am grateful, whose parliamentary monarchy government I approve, but where I still feel like a foreigner. | German is the language in which I shall always continue to write, and most of all, to think." ["Vim morrer nesta ilha inglesa que me acolheu e a que estou grato, cujo governo de monarquia parlamentar aprovo, mas onde não deixo de me sentir estrangeiro. | Será sempre em alemão que continuarei a escrever, e sobretudo a pensar." (Gersão 2021, 8)]

These thoughts by Freud about Thomas Mann legitimise in turn Julia's sense of uprootedness. Julia is Thomas Mann's wife to be, born in Brazil to a Brazilian mother and a German father. She will never be able to feel German or to express herself in her own language, thus making impossible any true communication, either with her father's or her husband's family:

> In the meantime, Julia had left a colored world and was coming into another one where everything was black and white or, on most days, grey. The city was dark, the air was cold, even in summer, and the whole inhospitable *habitat* felt like an aggression to her.
> The language people spoke was unintelligible, and nobody understood hers.
> Interaction with Maria [i.e. her sister] was reduced so that they would not speak Portuguese between them.

Maria de Fátima Marinho

Merging Public and Private Identities: Topics in Twenty-First Century Portuguese Novels

1 Introduction

The boundaries between public and private identities can become blurred within a community when its historic heritage plays an undeniable role and when the players in the identity-making process tend to foster interferences between events belonging to a strictly private sphere and events that belong to the wider public sphere and are supposedly separate from personal histories. These boundaries, which must necessarily be considered artificial, since they are impossible to define, present very specific features in the novels of the second half of the twentieth century, when authors seek to interpret and/or view public events through individual focalization. Such perspectives are conditioned not only by external factors but also, and especially, by personal traits and interests which are hardly objectifiable.

It is not too bold to state, as does Hanna Meretoja in her recently published *The Ethics of Storytelling – Narrative Hermeneutics, History and the Possible*, that to (re)interpret "one's life is to interpret it *in medias res*" (2018, 84; emphasis in the original), because each version of history brings with it a new interpretation. The tensions among all these versions exist in separate social contexts, while the sense of the possible is transfigured and takes on a crucial significance (Meretoja 2018, 90). All these arguments combined allow us to maintain that reading is always a means of connecting oneself through storytelling (Meretoja 2018, 117). Stories always end up revealing more than we would expect, helping us rethink the way in which we read literary works, insofar as these can no longer be regarded simply on their own but become part of a (real or virtual) network together with the empirical author's prior readings.

Assumptions of this kind and knowledge obtained through oblique readings and transversal sensations form the basis of hybrid narratives which, through a private focalization, describe historical events and mutual interferences, tangents and intersections.

In the nineteenth century, the historical novel was primarily interested in legitimizing nationalities, which found themselves in a state of fragile balance after the sweeping changes brought about by the French Revolution and Napoleon's

Maria de Fátima Marinho, University of Porto

https://doi.org/10.1515/9783111208664-005

imperialistic policy, less in paying attention to private, subjective views. Even though some novels, such as Eugène Sue's well-known *Mystères du Peuple ou Histoire d'une Famille de prolétaires à travers les âges* (1849–1856) [*The Mysteries of the People or History of a Proletarian Family Across the Ages*], focused on successive generations of the same family, the truth is that the family was just a pretext for narrating external achievements and making them known to readers. In the early twentieth century, however, Thomas Mann's famous novel *Buddenbrooks. Verfall einer Familie* [*Buddenbrooks. The Decline of a Family*], published in 1901, was undoubtedly a prime example of the genre which showed how social and historical processes are played out on the level of family life over three generations.

In the mid-twentieth century, with the theories of the New History and the perception that history can no longer be considered a static science, but rather a dynamic, ever-changing construction necessarily based on different points of view, a new type of novel emerged. These are fictions that represent a given period of time, but they do so almost exclusively by addressing the consequences and repercussions that historical events have in the life of a family. We must keep in mind that historical phenomena that took place in the second half of the twentieth century had a fundamental influence on the perception of public historical developments and their inevitable impact on private households. An example in Portugal is the Revolution of April 25, 1974 and the resulting independence of the former colonies, with the return of settlers to the *metrópole*, as the Portugal territory was then called by those living in the colonies. This event was of decisive importance for the revival of history-based novels and for the (public and private) reading of facts, their consequences as well as the controversial, linear, or orthodox interpretations.

In *O Romance Histórico em Portugal*, I (1999, 150–172) examined some of these novels, drawing attention to a domestic interpretation of history, and the priorities that it generates, including both obvious and less oblique cases, such as the novels by José Saramago, Álvaro Guerra, Helena Marques and Luísa Beltrão, or the more subtle constructions by Maria Isabel Barreno and Mário Cláudio.

There are three other interesting, symptomatic cases (Marinho 2009; 2019; 2020) that can serve as a basis for this essay: two novels by Teolinda Gersão, *A Casa da Cabeça de Cavalo* (1995) [The House of The Horse's Head] and *A Árvore das Palavras* (1997) [*The Word Tree* (2013)], and one by Lobo Antunes, *O Esplendor de Portugal* (1997) [The Splendor of Portugal].

In Gersão's *A Casa da Cabeça de Cavalo*, the former, now deceased inhabitants of a house, discuss political events, such as the French invasions, and produce different versions of the same events stemming from distinct focalizations, since they belong to people whose lives had nothing in common. The family – viewed not in its generational linearity, but as a household comprising masters and servants, power relations that may issue from labor contracts or from family

> Their mother tongue was eventually forbidden and replaced by other languages that they could not speak, German, French, and English.
> Her previous life was to be forgotten, as if it was devoid of interest or value.
>
> [Entretanto Júlia saíra de um mundo a cores e entrava noutro onde tudo era a preto e branco, ou, na maior parte dos dias, cinzento. A cidade era escura, o ar, mesmo no Verão, era frio, e todo aquele *habitat* inóspito a agredia.
> A língua que falavam era incompreensível, e ninguém entendia a dela.
> Os contactos com Maria [a irmã] foram reduzidos, para não falarem português as duas.
> A sua língua materna tornou-se proibida, e foi substituída por outras que desconheciam, alemão, francês e inglês.
> A vida anterior devia ser esquecida, como se não tivesse interesse nem valor. (Gersão 2021, 91; emphasis in the original)]

This imposed erasure, or better, this dilution into a wider identity, which Julia Mann experiences as destructive and Freud himself analyzes, we find also expressed in Gonçalo M. Tavares' novels, namely through the choice of strange, foreign names for his characters, confounds a sense of national belonging. Further examples are the characters in *The Middle Bone* – Kahnnak, Maria Lurbai, and Vassliss Rânia – or those in *Uma Menina está perdida no século à espera do Pai* (2014) [*A Girl Is Lost in Her Century, Looking for Her Father* (2024)] – Marius and Hanna.

In Gersão's novel, this purposeful confusion of identities favors the characters' connections to Portuguese and European history, which is delineated in the background and focalized through a private, strictly personal point of view. It is the family that conditions their perception of what is real, and European history is understood and commented upon from Freud's, Mann's, or Julia's viewpoint. Freud comments on the war and Nazism and the way it unsettled his family life. In Tavares' *A Girl Is Lost in Her Century, Looking for Her Father*, one finds numerous references to Jews and their persecution by the Nazis. The relation of these events has a deep impact on the characters' experience, playing an oblique, subterranean role that influences their present actions:

> Books and History, so many photos scattered all over the house.
> In a conference, Grube had maintained that History was like a living element, changing position, accelerating, decreasing its pace, an element with constant weight – a mass which drags itself or accelerates from one point to another – but with a variable center of gravity.
> On one of the walls of the house, the names of different cities, with a date under each of them, were marked with dots with a black marker, as if they were train stations: Moscow (1917), Jerusalem (1948), Berlin (1961).
> For Grube those dots identified the successive centers of gravity of History. Those dates and those cities were the points where all of the world's weight was concentrated. Should somebody

wish to overthrow History, turn it upside down, that was the spot where the blow should be applied, in that precise spot, the center of gravity.

[Livros e História, imensas fotografias espalhadas por toda a casa.
Grube defendera numa conferência que a História era como um elemento vivo, que mudava de posição, acelerava, diminuía de ritmo, um elemento com peso constante – uma massa que de um ponto para outro se arrasta ou acelera – mas com um centro de gravidade variável.
Numa das paredes da casa, como se fossem estações de comboio, assinaladas com pontos a marcador preto, estavam os nomes de várias cidades, e debaixo desses nomes uma data: Moscovo (1917), Jerusalém (1948), Berlim (1961).
Para Grube estes pontos identificavam os sucessivos centros de gravidade da História. Nestas datas e naquelas cidades estava o ponto que concentrava todo o peso do mundo. Se alguém quisesse derrubar, pôr a História de cabeça para baixo, era ali que teria de aplicar o golpe, naquele ponto preciso, no centro de gravidade. (Tavares 2014, 181–182)]

Even if not from a functional or traditional point of view, the characters and the members of the family view European events through a private focalization, as is also the case in other novels with a greater focus on the Portuguese context. For instance, in José Luís Peixoto's *Sunday Lunch*, mentioned above, the main character is presented as an 89-year-old man in a third-person narrative, although he speaks in the first person when recalling episodes from his childhood, youth, and adulthood. This character, Senhor Rui, mentions specific historical political moments that he had witnessed and which, directly or indirectly, had had an impact on his private life: these are mostly discrete events dating back to the Estado Novo (1933–1974) or the April Revolution. His is a private view that reflects the protagonist's experiences at different ages and in different historical moments. These references are always episodic, linked to different experiences, and the character refrains from offering political interpretations or making comments of a partisan nature: "Mário Soares [former leader of Socialist party, Prime Minister and President of the Republic] unabashedly speaks a clumsy sort of goofy Spanish. With his jacket hanging from the back of the chair, his shirt sleeves rolled up and elbows piercing the tablecloth, he leans forward. Felipe Gonzáles seems to understand half of it, having a lot of fun, while he pecks at bread crumbs." ["O Mário Soares lança-se a espanholar sem pudor. Com o casaco pendurado nas costas da cadeira, mangas da camisa arregaçadas e bicos dos cotovelos espetados na toalha da mesa, inclina-se para a frente. O Felipe González parece entender metade, divertido, enquanto depenica flocos de miolo." (Peixoto 2021, 127)] Or, take the following passage:

When the news arrived [i.e. the Revolution of April 25, 1974], we were all at work, a very normal Thursday morning. Machines did not come to a halt; coffee beans were aware of nothing. Word went from mouth to mouth, covered by the noise and the smell of roasting.

Men and women listened to the information with wariness, not wanting to seem scared lest it was a false alarm or a not-so-funny joke.

[Quando chegou a novidade [Revolução do 25 de abril de 1974], estávamos todos a trabalhar, manhã normalíssima de quinta-feira. As máquinas não chegaram a suspender-se, os grãos de café não tiveram conhecimento de nada. A palavra foi passando de boca em boca, por baixo do barulho e do aroma da torra. Homens e mulheres apreendiam a informação com desconfiança, não queriam logo aventar uma reação espavorida ainda assim não fosse alarme adulterado, ou brincadeira sem graça. (Peixoto 2021, 60)]

Similarly, the Spanish Civil War persecutions affect the child protagonist, because in the border town where he lives, he comes into contact with police-inflicted torture, albeit indirectly and unknowingly. The description of screams coming from the police station suggests the violent repression, although this is not fully articulated. The first-person account of the child's perception does not explain the facts; these are merely presented, tasking the readers with interpreting them:

Spaniards were screaming inside the police station. I did never tell my uncle about the horror of those screams, coming from deep down inside the throat and tearing up all the nerves along the way. There were many terrible things I was unaware of. I discovered some of them there, inside those screams, a fear I was unable to bear. In a similar state of panic, despite his age and his wisdom, my brother pulled me away by the arm and we ran from the screams, went up the alley, came inside the bedroom and, even after they were over, we continued to hear those screams in the silence.

[Eram espanhóis aos gritos no posto da polícia. Não chego a descrever ao meu tio o horror desses gritos, nasciam do fundo da garganta e rasgavam todos os nervos à sua passagem. [...] Havia muitas coisas terríveis que eu não conhecia. Descobri algumas ali, no interior daqueles gritos, um medo que eu não era capaz de aguentar. Com o mesmo pânico, apesar da idade e da sabedoria, o meu irmão puxou-me pelo braço e fugimos dos gritos, subimos a travessa, entrámos no quarto e, mesmo depois de terminarem, no silêncio, continuávamos a escutar aqueles gritos. (Peixoto 2021, 231)]

The privately limited nature of the focalization generates a simultaneously neutral and unique tone, since this is the point of view of Senhor Rui (as an adult or as a child), who is never directly or emotionally involved when he describes facts or *faits-divers* in which he participated and which he views only according to his own, inevitably limited experience.

In Lídia Jorge's novel *Estuário* (2018) [Estuary], one of the characters worked in a refugee camp in Ethiopia, where he suffered a mutilating hand injury in an accident. This experience determines the way he acts. Family decadence, the urgency of writing a book (a sublimation of family and historical events), and the existence of refugee camps are at the center of this novel, which points to the inevitable interference between the reality of the camps and the family, or rather, helps focalize the Ethiopian space through a private view that also aims to be critical and activist. For the character, writing this book would be tantamount to achieving redemption: "after all, he was in a hurry to write, with his mutilated hand, a book titled *2030*, which would begin with what he knew and loved best, and what he most wanted to save." ["afinal, tinha pressa em escrever, com a sua mão decepada, um livro intitulado *2030*, que iria começar pelo que melhor conhecia e mais amava, e mais queria que se salvasse." (Jorge 2018, 283; emphasis in the original)]

3 The Present that Can only be Explained by Means of the Past

Let us now focus on the second group of novels, which deal with a present that can only be explained by means of the past. I will start by looking at *The Memorables* (2014), by Lídia Jorge, where a young Portuguese journalist, the daughter of an old member of the resistance against fascism, and now working in the United States, is invited to write a documentary on the Carnation Revolution. The aim is to demonstrate its unique nature when compared to other revolutions in different times and places.

The young woman, Ana Maria, comes to Portugal and embarks on a kind of initiatory journey through both her own and the country's past. Although her memories are fuzzy, she seeks to learn about the revolution (she was a child then) through a photo that she finds in her father's house, by interviewing the people shown in the photo, and by trying to understand their different perspectives and experiences during and after the revolution. This photo seems to bring together important figures of the 25 April Revolution, disenchanted characters who continue to live in a fictive world from which they are unable to escape. One of the most flagrant examples is precisely that of Ana Maria's father, a well-known journalist who cannot adapt to the new times, refuses to go back to work and accepts retirement, but who still leaves home at the same time every day only to stay inside his car and wait for time to pass. When Ana Maria finds out about this strange habit, she begins to understand what the past hides, and focalizes it through the different stories/families of the characters in the photograph. As mentioned above, the photo becomes the starting point for her quest, since "objects have a soul which writes itself" ["os objetos possuem uma alma que a si mesma se escreve" (Jorge 2019, 54)]. This 'soul' triggers various memories, which do not always correspond to reality, but which revolve around the momentous 25 April, an event which Ana Maria's supervisor, an American journalist, considers to have been unique.

As we read the novel, we become aware of the protagonist's alienation vis-à-vis the historical event about which she is supposed to write a documentary and the disjointed versions, near lies or various false accounts that are being told and that refer to private, individual perspectives. History thus emerges in fragments, almost mythical, transfigured into a dimension that may have little in common with reality. One of the characters in the photo, who is endowed with an astonishing charisma, is the one called *El Campeador*, identifiable as Otelo Saraiva de Carvalho, or "*the Portuguese red oak*" (Jorge 2019, 27; emphasis in the original), as the American journalist describes him. This character seems to live in a dreamlike world, imagining to embody the hero-protagonist of a movie that does not exist, in a kind of Cervantine hallucination.

The revolution, then, is also presented as a construction, not just a verifiable event. In her documentary project, the young woman comes across a series of disjointed versions; slippery, deceptive universes are the signs of a collapse. Comparing Otelo and Ana Maria's father, we find similar paths and a common inability to accept dystopic reality. By focusing on individual memories and their reading(s) of History, a history which mercilessly interferes with people's lives, the novel seems to underscore precisely that sense of dystopia: "[t]hat was exactly it, the stark reality, Praia Grande, as a scenic setting for so many movies in the past, would not be a setting for any movie whatsoever called *The Sea Hero*. Neither fiction nor history, it just would not" ["Era assim mesmo, realidade nua e crua, a Praia Grande, espaço cénico que o fora para tantos filmes, não seria cenário para nenhum filme chamado *O Herói do Mar*. Nem ficção, nem história, não seria" (Jorge 2019, 228)].

The title of the film is not chosen randomly: any Portuguese person with an average education immediately associates it with the Portuguese national anthem. This is a tragic, inconsequential heroism, like Ana Maria's quest, her documentary, unable to "decipher what really happened" ["decifra[r] o que verdadeiramente se passou" (Jorge 2019, 342)]. The accumulation of private points of view conditions the various presents of the characters, irremediably influenced by the unreachable past.

4 Personal Focalization of Specific Historical Facts

Let us now look at the personal and familial vision of a concrete phenomenon: the return home of thousands of Portuguese citizens after the African colonies were granted independence. They are the returnees (*retornados*), as they were then called. Dulce Maria Cardoso's novel *O Retorno* [*The Return* (2016)] is a very thorough illustration of those events.

The book, published in 2011, is an exemplary account by an adolescent whose family was forced to leave Angola soon after the country's independence. The title, *The Return*, is in itself quite evocative. Indeed, the name *retornados* is usually applied to people coming from the former Portuguese African colonies either after or immediately before their respective independence, placing the focus on those who came back, or returned, to Portugal, even if they had never lived there in the first place. The noun *retorno* [return], however, emphasizes the process rather than the people. By accentuating the phenomenon of the return to European Portugal (and it should again be emphasized that for many, who had never left Africa, this 'return' is a trip to the unknown), this lexical choice shifts the focalization to something that paradoxically goes beyond the family and becomes a presentation of experiences at the crossroads of the subjective and the objective.

Adopting the first-person narration of a male adolescent whose oral language register has frequent gaps and often lacks references, the novel places the narrator in a position of discomfort and insecurity. The book starts with the adversative 'but' ["mas"] ("But there are cherries in the Motherland" [Cardoso 2016, 7] ["Mas na metrópole há cerejas" (Cardoso 2021, 7)]), thus announcing itself as a text that operates on the basis of small, seemingly insignificant details which in many instances reveal themselves to be highly symbolic and meaningful.

Centered in an exclusive point of view, this novel, as is typical for first-person narratives, plays with internal focalization, as is typical of first-person narratives, generating incomplete perspectives on episodes that the character cannot have witnessed: "Just as it won't do me any harm not to know what happened to Father in prison, what happened to Mother's demons, to Silvana or to Uncle Zé. There's no harm in not knowing any of those things as long as there are things I do know for sure." (Cardoso 2016, 178–179) ["Como não faz mal eu não saber o que aconteceu ao pai na prisão, aos demónios da mãe, à Silvana ou ao tio Zé. Nada disso tem mal desde que ainda haja coisas de que eu tenha a certeza." (Cardoso 2021, 267)] Internal focalization fosters the emergence of dichotomies opposing the *I* and his/her space, the *here* and the others (whether they be family members or strangers) in their other space, which is usually dysphoric and hostile.

In *The Return*, we find two categories of others, those who belong to the family (father, mother, sister and Uncle Zé) and the strangers, from neighbors in Angola and the other people who live in the hotel, in the Motherland, to the Angolans, who are the others *par excellence*, "[b]y they I mean the blacks" (Cardoso 2016, 8) ["Eles são os pretos" (Cardoso 2021, 8)]. Rui, the adolescent, views what is happening in Angola in 1975 through the perspective of his immediate family. All the events are focalized and received by the boy, who adopts his parents' view as well as that of other Portuguese people. The polarization of 'us/the others' also implies a radicalization of discourse and the awareness that an irremediable rupture will necessarily occur between those two worlds. A member of the lower-middle class, Rui combines his and his family's experience in Angola with the spaces in which his life unfolds: his father and his truck company; his sick mother and her illness ("the illness we never talked about" (Cardoso 2016, 108) ["doença de que nunca falávamos" (Cardoso 2021, 155)]), his sister Milucha; his neighbors back in Angola; the hotel dwellers in Estoril, where returnees stay while waiting to be integrated into life in Portugal.

The departure to Lisbon signals the loss of balance and the breakdown of the family structure, as his father is taken by the Angolans and his whereabouts remain uncertain until nearly the end of the novel. The sense of displacement, seen through the teenage boy's eyes, which reflect his family's perspective even if only obliquely, represents the primacy of private opinion and is necessarily incomplete: "Not even the gunfire can undo the silence of our departure, tomorrow we will no longer be here. Even if we like telling ourselves that we will be back soon, we know we will never be here again. Angola is finished. Our Angola is finished." (Cardoso, 2016, 12) ["Nem os tiros conseguem desfazer o silêncio da nossa partida, amanhã já não estamos aqui. Ainda que gostemos de nos enganar dizendo que voltamos em breve, sabemos que nunca mais estaremos aqui. Angola acabou. A nossa Angola acabou." (Cardoso 2021, 14)]

The break with the *here* (which, at a personal level, may correspond to the *I*, or the *self*), as well as not knowing his father's whereabouts, causes the narrator's instability. At first, the figure of the father provides a secret force of hope, followed by the narrator's passive acceptance of his death, followed by the sudden and completely unexpected resurfacing in the end, and the creation of a new survival strategy (the cement factory). Besides the obvious confusion, the displacement from home in Luanda to the hotel in Estoril also marks an involuntary movement away from the family environment (the family home) to a collective space where identity tends to become blurred and negative tendencies condition the focalization, originating in a discourse that is partial, dysphoric and dystopic.

In the *metropolis* nearly everything is perceived as negative, and the sentence that stands out in a chapter which is made up of this sentence only, ("So this is the Motherland, then" (Cardoso 2016, 47) ["Então a metropole afinal é isto" (Cardoso 2021, 65)]) underlines the disillusionment of experiencing a hostile space. This is complemented by a totally utopian vision of America and a planned meeting with a friend from Angola at the Sears Tower (Chicago), which never comes to happen. The abrupt arrival of Rui's father breaks the utopia and seems to restore the balance that had been ruptured by their traumatic departure from Angola.

In parallel with this de-centering of the teenager's worldview, there is another, even more personal de-centering: his sexual initiation with all the insecurities that it generates. His hesitant steps in this direction, both in Angola and in Portugal, culminate in an ambiguous relationship with Silvana, the doorman's wife, whose pregnancy is revealed at the end of the novel. Such insecurities contribute to what is a very partial view of the political circumstances and corroborate the imperfection of a focalization that is conditioned by a personal experience and hence necessarily interferes with the perception of external events.

The disruption of balance brought about by the April revolution elicits Rui's various comments, situated as he is inside a somewhat claustrophobic space with no possibility of escape, since he is confronted with his mother's illness, maybe epilepsy, his father's absence, and his sister's female adolescent world. Isolated within this broken-down family, with a mother who is psychologically damaged, the narrator chooses to analyze the clues that he gets from an external viewpoint. What such clues reveal to him is a world of insecurity and frustration. His mother's state denies him the much-needed support that his absent father, presumably dead, is far from being able to provide. The boy narrates the events that caused his 'de-centeredness' and describes his space and circumstances unilaterally and in some detail. His mother's desperate actions (such as trying to pawn some personal belongings), his relationship with his schoolmates, and his sexual initiation, are all intimately connected to the socio-political environment and create a private narrative, which may also be read as a national one.

Outside the close family circle, there is also Uncle Zé, the mother's brother who came to Luanda with the Portuguese military and later settled there. This character could conceivably have played an important role as a mediator, but as a gay man, Uncle Zé does not belong to a traditionally privileged space, but he rather occupies a transgressive space, generating in Rui a series of ambiguities and uncertainties. A supporter of the revolutionary movement, Uncle Zé seems to be doing nothing to free his brother-in-law from prison. He also never answers his sister and nephews' insistent letters:

> Uncle Zé who appeared in the hotel bar did not mention my letters but said he'd answered Mother's. It's not true, so many letters could not have got lost. Uncle Zé realized we didn't believe him but he swore over and over again that he had done everything he could to get Father released. Perhaps it's true, Uncle Zé almost cried in anger when he realised that we kept saying yes of course yes of course just to make him shut up. It might be that Uncle Zé had not written to us because he had no good news to give us, and instead of a lack of love or interest on his part there may have in fact been a greater love that didn't allow him to do things differently. It doesn't matter. If he liked us, he should have known how to do what we needed him to do, otherwise any love he claims to have for us is simply a nuisance. That's why, in my mind, Uncle Zé never did anything to get father released and as soon as

> he put us on an aeroplane, he ran off to go and suck Nhé Nhé's cock and never wanted to hear from us again. (Cardoso 2016, 176)
>
> [O tio Zé que apareceu no bar do hotel não falou das minhas cartas mas disse que tinha respondido às da mãe. Não é verdade, não se podem ter perdido tantas cartas. O tio Zé percebeu que não acreditávamos nele mas jurou e voltou a jurar que tinha feito tudo o que podia para libertar o pai. Talvez, seja verdade, o tio Zé quase chorou de raiva quando percebeu que íamos dizendo que sim só para o calar. Pode acontecer que o tio Zé não nos tenha escrito porque não tinha boas notícias para nos dar, e em vez de desamor ou desinteresse pode ter havido um amor maior que não soube fazer as coisas de outra maneira. Não interessa. Se gostava de nós tinha de ter sabido fazer o que nós precisávamos, se não for assim o amor que os outros nos têm só estorva. Por isso, para mim o tio Zé nunca fez esforço nenhum para o pai ser libertado e assim que nos enfiou no avião para virmos para cá foi a correr pôr-se a chupar na pichota da Nhé Nhé e nunca mais quis saber de nós. (Cardoso 2021, 263)].

This uncertain certainty is what conditions Rui's thoughts and makes him long, as we have seen, for a mythical America. The father's unexpected return breaks the different stages of Rui's progression towards adulthood, forcing his regression back into adolescence. His description of his father's entrepreneurship further contributes to recreating the atmosphere among the returnees and the possible activities that they consider taking up.

Outside this more or less restricted family unit, the case of Senhor Manuel stands out. This character represents the scheming Portuguese man who manages to leave in time and safeguard all of his possessions. Mistrustful of Senhor Manuel's motives, Rui's focalization describes a set of opinions that perfectly illustrate the political circumstances of the time, to which we have access through the narrator's translucid, blurred lenses. The political discourse, or the discourse about politics, used by the narrator to describe the hotel dwellers, is necessarily conditioned by his expertise in analyzing the circumstances and the atmosphere of a society in deep crisis: "There were returnees from every corner of the empire, the empire was there, in that waiting room, a tired empire, in need of a house and food, a defeated and humiliated empire, an empire no-one wanted to know about." (Cardoso, 2016, 60) ["Estavam lá retornados de todos os cantos do império, o império estava ali, naquela sala, um império cansado, a precisar de casa e de comida, um império derrotado e humilhado, um império de quem ninguém queria saber." (Cardoso 2021, 86)]

It is interesting to note that the blurred view produced by an imperfect (private and partial) focalization is rendered through the use of a somewhat imprecise language, by linguistic taboos, making it impossible to narrate in a transparent or linear way: "I know the words, I'm sure I know the words, I never say them, I'm afraid of them, I don't even say them in my head, but I am sure I know them."

(Cardoso 2016, 108) ["Sei as palavras, tenho a certeza que sei as palavras, nunca as digo, tenho medo delas, nem em pensamentos as digo mas tenho a certeza que as sei." (Cardoso 2021, 155)]

The difficulty of putting concepts into words, the vanishing of a sense of utopian belief in the future, means to accept the limitation and ignorance that stems from internal focalization, and which becomes quite visible in the end, "Just as it won't do me any harm not to know what happened to Father in prison, what happened to Mother's demons, to Silvana or to Uncle Zé." (Cardoso 2016, 178–179) ["Como não faz mal eu não saber o que aconteceu ao pai na prisão, aos demónios da mãe, à Silvana ou ao tio Zé." (Cardoso 2021, 267)], all this propitiates a discourse signaling a reality that goes beyond individual or family experience to signify the social circumstances, conditioned by political events. In *The Return*, readers can clearly see the complicity between the adolescent narrator's view and external facts, a complicity that is achieved through the skewed perspective of his personal experiences and the specific perspectives of his family.

5 Conclusion

As I have sought to demonstrate, the novels published in the last twenty-two years are not principally concerned with exorcising past memories, family memories, or the visions imposed by the ghosts of former times. Instead, we witness a re-dimensioning of the family structure that views the events of national history in oblique ways that are more discreet or translucent. With the exception of Dulce Maria Cardoso's novel, all the other novels discussed here are distinguished by indirect and internalized, though no less reliable, allusions and atomized references. We may conclude that these novels feature family constellations and broken identities, though they often hide behind removable screens and masks.

Bibliography

Antunes, António Lobo. *Para Aquela que Está sentada no escuro à minha espera*. Lisboa: Publicações Dom Quixote, 2016.

Antunes, António Lobo. *The Land at the End of the World*. Transl. Margaret Jull Costa. London: W. W. Norton & Company, 2012.

Antunes, António Lobo. *The Splendor of Portugal*. London: Dalkey Archive Press, 2011.

Antunes, António Lobo. *Que Cavalos são Aqueles que fazem Sombra no Mar?* Lisboa: Publicações Dom Quixote, 2009.

Antunes, António Lobo. *O Esplendor de Portugal*. Lisboa: Dom Quixote, 1997.

Antunes, António Lobo. *South of Nowhere*. Transl. Elizabeth Lowel. London: Random House, 1983.
Antunes, António Lobo. *Os Cus de Judas*. Lisboa: Dom Quixote, 1986 [1979].
Cardoso, Dulce. *O Retorno*. Lisboa: Tinta-da-China, 2021 [2021].
Cardoso, Dulce. *The Return*. Transl. Ángel Gúrria-Quintana. London: MacLehose Press, 2016.
Correia, Hélia. *Lillias Fraser*. Lisboa: Relógio dÀ'gua, 2001.
Gersão, Teolinda. *O Regresso de Júlia Mann a Paraty*. Porto: Porto Editora, 2021.
Gersão, Teolinda. *The Word Tree*. London: Dedalus UK, 2010.
Gersão, Teolinda. *A Árvore das Palavras*. Lisboa: Dom Quixote, 1997.
Gersão, Teolinda. *A Casa da Cabeça de Cavalo*. Lisboa: Dom Quixote, 1995.
Jorge, Lídia. *The Wind Whistling in the Cranes*. Transl. Margaret Jull Costa. New York: Liveright, 2022.
Jorge, Lídia. *Estuário*. Lisboa: Dom Quixote, 2018.
Jorge, Lídia. *Os Memoráveis*. Lisboa: Dom Quixote, 2019 [2014].
Jorge, Lídia. *O Vento Assobiando nas Gruas*. Lisboa: Dom Quixote, 2002.
Mann, Thomas. *Os Buddenbrook*. Lisboa: Relógio dÀ'gua, 2020 [1901].
Marinho, Maria de Fátima. "Il était une fois un arbre (à propos de *Árvore das Palavras* [Arbre à Paroles], de Teolinda Gersão." *Carnets* 19 (2020). https://journals.openedition.org/carnets/11251 (March 15, 2024).
Marinho, Maria de Fátima. "A Memória da Família." *Revista de Estudos Literários* 9 (2019): 115–130.
Marinho, Maria de Fátima. "In Search of Lost Identity – Essay on the Crisis of Identity in the Contemporary Portuguese Novel." *Language, Literature, Culture and Identity – 200th Anniversary of the University of Belgrade*. Eds. Slobodan Grubačić/Dalibor Soldatić. Belgrade: University of Belgrade, 2009. 87–101.
Marinho, Maria de Fátima. *O Romance Histórico em Portugal*. Porto: Campo das Letras, 1999.
Meretoja, Hanna. *The Ethics of Storytelling – Narrative hermeneutics, History and the Possible*. Oxford: Oxford UP, 2018.
Peixoto, José Luís. *Almoço de Domingo*. Lisboa: Quetzal, 2021.
Sue, Eugène. *Os Mysterios do Povo*. Lisboa: Empreza Editora do Mestre Popular. s. d. [1849–1856].
Tavares, Gonçalo M. *O Osso do Meio*. Lisboa: Relógio dÀ'gua, 2020.
Tavares, Gonçalo M. *Uma Menina Está perdida no século à espera do Pai*. Porto: Porto Editora, 2014.

Serena Cianciotto

Memory, History, and the Fragmentation of Family: José Luís Peixoto's Multi-Generational Novel *Book*

Family stories often work as a template for narrating and reflecting upon history, individual as well as collective identities. In this article, I will explicate these topics with regard to José Luís Peixoto's multi-generational novel *Livro* (2010) [Book], in which characters must pass through the complex and painful process of questioning the national and familial past from 1948 until 2010, revealing a transnational and transgenerational dimension of memory and history that shapes their inner world. On the one side, such a process highlights the fragmented subjectivities of the younger generation, on the other side, oblique family relations emerge and manifest themselves – often through the use of innovative narrative techniques and fantastical elements – thus leading to a breaking of the circle of violence. My subsequent analysis considers the novel not only in the context of Portuguese history, but also in a broader transnational perspective on the representation of historical imaginaries.

Born in 1974, José Luís Peixoto is one of the most published contemporary authors in Portugal and is known for several novels regarding family topics, especially the question of paternity and of generational continuity, like *Morreste-me* (2000) [You died on me], *Cemitério de Pianos* (2006) [The Piano Cemetery], or *Em teu Ventre* (2015) [In Your Belly]. Most of Peixoto's novels can be described, at least partially, as autofictions, since they mirror the autobiographical experience of the author; furthermore, they focus on family constellations, with the aim to offer insights into the state of the individual, of familial and social networks, in both national and transnational contexts. This allows the author to investigate how personal and collective identities have been shaped throughout the twentieth century, and through the long Portuguese turn of the century until today,[1] especially as concerns the transition from a rural to a modern world.

1 As Carlos Reis suggests, Portuguese literature at the turn of the century is marked by two chronological limits, the first one corresponding to the Carnation Revolution – April 25, 1974 – and the second one coinciding with the actual beginning of the new century in 2000 (see Reis 2005, 287).

Serena Cianciotto, University of Siena; Leipzig University

https://doi.org/10.1515/9783111208664-006

1 Generations and History

Livro narrates the story of a four-generation family, covering fundamental junctures of Portuguese and European history between the twentieth and the twenty-first century. The time of the story is divided into two parts: the first one starts in 1948 with the mother of the 6-year-old Idílio giving her son a book ("livro" in Portuguese) before she leaves him with her friend Josué, while she abandons Portugal; it ends in Paris on April 27, 1974 – just a couple of days after the Carnation Revolution – with the birth of the mother's nephew, himself named Livro. The second part, much shorter than the first one, and mainly concerned with Livro's life, continues until July 9, 2010. At the end, it becomes clear that Livro has been reading (and paradoxically also writing) the very same book that Idílio had initially received in the first part, and that during the process Livro recognizes his story and his identity as fragmentary and incomplete.

Idílio's mother decides to leave her country, since she doesn't see any chance to survive in the social context of her native village. Namely, she is considered a prostitute for having relations with several men, including the priest. However, the woman accepts this label, only to hide a more terrible truth: since her childhood she has been suffering sexual violence by her father, an alcoholic known as Aquele da Sorna,[2] and thus Idílio is not only the grandson, but also the son of this man. The woman has a deep spiritual legacy with the foreman Josué, who practically adopts Idílio after her departure and turns into a sort of father, or elder brother, for the boy. Above all, he transmits to him his knowledge about his own, beloved profession, therefore Idílio himself becomes a skilled bricklayer.

Another central figure is Adelaide, a girl born into a large family of poor people. For this reason, she is raised by an aunt known as *a velha Lubélia* [the old Lubélia], who became a severe and self-righteous woman after having been expelled by her parents for getting pregnant as a teenager and before marriage. After having lost both her lover and her baby, she has lived a sexually repressed and lonely life, which has led her to torture young Adelaide with excessive rigor, in turn. For example, when, in the early 1960s, Idílio and Adelaide announce to her their plan to marry, both being aged twenty-three, she forces her niece to move illegally to France. The girl brings along the book that Idílio gave her as a promise of love.

As soon as he discovers Adeleida's forced removal, Idílio also leaves in the direction of France together with his friend Cosme, who wants to escape poverty, dictatorship, and military service in the African colonies. After a dangerous and

2 *Sorna* means indolence, laziness in Portuguese.

exhaustive journey, the two friends arrive in France and they slowly build themselves a new life there, Cosme working as a nurse, Idílio as a construction worker, later as an entrepreneur. Yet, despite all their efforts, they do not manage to contact either Adelaide in France or Josué in Portugal, because the old Lubélia works at the only post office of their native village and intercepts their letters. Therefore, the characters remain isolated for many years until the death of Lubélia, when Josué eventually discovers that his 'son' has not forgotten him, while Adelaide receives the old message from her first boyfriend. By that time, however, she has already lost all hope regarding Idílio's love and has become engaged with another Portuguese immigrant, so she doesn't answer Idílio and marries Costantino. Cosme will meet Adelaide by chance only years later, after 1968. He not only becomes the link between her and Idílio, but also a fundamental point of reference, a sort of uncle, for the child they will have, Livro.

2 Protagonist, Reader, Book

Adelaide gets to know Costantino in the mid-1960s during a visit in the public library, browsing through the book received by Idílio years before, and she discovers circles around some words drawn by Costantino while she was not looking; the chosen words form questions and sentences through which they start to communicate with each other. Costantino is a fervent communist, an intellectual interested in the social and political protests of the 1960s and 1970s in Europe, yet he turns out to become a jealous and cold husband. When Adelaide returns to Portugal in 1973 for some days, she briefly meets Idílio, who has never gotten married and is also back for holidays. They have sexual intercourse and Adelaide gets pregnant but, once back in Paris, she makes Costantino think that he is the father of the baby named Livro. Curiously, the baby is born on April 27, 1974, just a couple of days after the Carnation Revolution which signifies the end of the Portuguese dictatorship[3] and marks a decisive limit for the country, closing one epoch and opening another one, at once democratic and postcolonial. The novel *Livro* itself is marked by this limit, because the first part, with its omniscient narration, ends exactly at this point. While this first part, then, deals especially with the history of Portuguese emigration to France from 1960 until 1974, alluding in the process to historical issues like dictatorship, war, censorship, and poor living conditions, the second part, by contrast, amounts to a sort of postmodern game of perspectives, because here

3 The Portuguese regime by António de Oliveira Salazar began officially in 1933 and is known as *Estado Novo*.

Livro is at the same time the auto-diegetic narrator – being both the narrator and the protagonist of the plot – as well as the fictional reader and the material book itself. Livro's statements describe this peculiar conjunction:

> Hold my name. This book that you are reading and that I am writing, where we are, is exactly the same that my mother put in my hands, as in the first sentence. That book was also this one. The beginning is also now, thank you for having brought me until the last page and for continuing with me until the last word.[4]
>
> [Seguras o meu nome. Este livro que estás a ler e que eu estou a escrever, onde estamos, é exactamente o mesmo que a minha mãe me pousou nas mãos, como na primeira frase. Também esse livro era este. O início também é agora [...] agradeço-te por me teres trazido à última página e por seguires comigo até à última palavra. (Peixoto 2010, 262–263)]

These concluding sentences of the novel make clear that many elements circulate not only among past, present, and future, but also between the fictional and the real world, and even among different spaces within the narrated story. In fact, there are at least three *mises en abyme* in the text:[5] the first one consists in the fact that the book that Idílio received in the past is also the book of the future that Livro accepts as a present and reads. The second *mise en abyme* concerns the book that both Livro as fictional reader and the reader of *Livro* hold in their hands and the book that Livro is writing; evidence for this metafictional overlap is provided by the circles around some words in the text through which Adelaide and Costantino are communicating in the library – in the fictional plot – and that are graphically reproduced on each copy of the novel *Livro* – in the world of the novel's readers. The third *mise en abyme* can be deduced from Livro's concluding words: "Hold my name," and "Thank you for having brought me until the last page," thus suggesting that there is an overlap between the character Livro and the very object of the book.

3 Reality, Imagination, Postmemory

In addition to these games of mirroring among real and fictional spaces, there is a clear intersection between the narrator Livro and the real author José Luís Peixoto, which is typical for the autofictional genre: they are both born in the crucial year 1974 and they both experience a transnational family history, that is, a history of

4 Unless otherwise specified, translations are provided by the author of the article.

5 About the use of *mise en abyme* of the second and of the third type in the text, see also Amorim 2017, 447–448.

emigration. Similar to his fictional characters' relatives, José Luís Peixoto's parents emigrated to France and came back to Portugal slightly before the birth of the writer in 1974 (Alberani 2013, 342). Consequently, both the real author and the narrator of the second part of the story are heirs of a complex transnational and traumatic history of emigration and return, which they experience indirectly through oral testimonies, and which they need to 'complete' through historical knowledge, but also through imagination during the writing process. The confrontation with the collective past of their own families amounts to what Marianne Hirsch (2012) has called *affiliative postmemory*, namely a kind of transgenerational memory about traumas that is transmitted to younger family members not only in verbal, but also and mostly in non-verbal forms, like taboos, gestures, or habits. As Astrid Erll explains, this kind of mediated memory was often not considered to be part of that "qualitative, experienced time" (2014, 388) that holds a generation together, but in fact, she argues, second-hand experiences do contribute to one's own personal and familial inheritance and identity, and even to social heritage and cultural memory (2014, 396).[6] Such issues, concerning the correspondence between personal and collective identity, as well as the vacillation between the real and the imaginary, are always present in the work, as both the real writer Peixoto and the fictional writer Livro interrogate themselves about the acquisition and the communication of their own traumatic familial and national histories. As Elisa Alberani has suggested, literature may become a conduit for the establishment of collective memory:

> And here is the problematic subtext emerging in *Book*, the question of transmitting experiences that are not our own, that is: how is it possible to convey the experiences of others? A memory that reflects upon what has been inherited from the past and upon our relationship with it and on how to establish a collective memory. Literature, then, becomes a way to preserve memory, bearer of an archival function, container of something that otherwise would be lost. (2013, 343)

At the same time, it is clear that Livro is a member of the generation of postmemory, having introjected in his identity the traumatic and violent history of twentieth-century Portugal: dictatorship, underdevelopment, violence perpetrated by the secret police, colonial wars, emigration, and poor life conditions suffered abroad. This younger generation's life is marked by inner fragmentation, disillusionment, and solitude – as if they had experienced all of this directly. Moreover, in Peixoto's novel, even the readers are implicitly put in a comparable position

6 Erll partially corrects Hirsch in her definition for *affiliative postmemory*. While Hirsch describes postmemory as vertically structured through family generations, Erll (2014, 400) conceives affiliation as horizontal, intragenerational, and dynamic, with media playing a fundamental role in moving memories across time, space, and social groups.

when they are encouraged to ask themselves similar questions about their own relationship with family and conception of personal identity. This is particularly evident in the cloze test that opens the second part of the narrative and in which readers are asked to imaginatively fill in the required missing words – for example, the mother's name – to create their own story alongside Livro's.

Historical and personal traumas introjected by the generation of postmemory explain why the character Livro grows up with a sense of inner fragmentation, in some way becoming a stranger to himself: he does not study nor work, is incapable of creating real bonds with the women he dates, and has a conflictual relationship with Costantino, whom he significantly never calls father, while in fact both do not know the truth about the love affair of Idílio and Adelaide. The only fundamental legacy that Livro inherits from Costantino is his love for books. Literary works shape Livro's inner world, but when he moves to his parents' native village, he is finally able to discriminate and recuse that part of Costantino's legacy he cannot accept: many books remain abandoned on the floor and are finally burned by Livro because they remind him of Costantino's hate, dissatisfaction, severity, and scarce regard for him and Adelaide: "They were books with worn covers anthologizing Costantino's emotional and intellectual incoherence in volumes, tomes of poison and heartburn. Like an encyclopedia: Aberration to Despair; Despotism to Incapable; Disturbance to Prejudice; Bossy to Angry." ["Eram livros de capas gastas, que antologiavam a incoerência emocional e intelectual do Constantino em volumes, tomos de veneno e azia. Como uma enciclopédia: Aberração a Desespero; Despotismo a Incapaz; Incómodo a Preconceito; Prepotente a Zangado." (Peixoto 2010, 215)]

These imaginary titles reflect the behavior of the Portuguese intellectual disappointed with the experience of living in France and with the failed revolution (Soares 2022, 114). During his conscious life, he has been completely absorbed in his readings about history and politics, while acting disdainful and aggressive towards Adelaide, who is entirely devoted to the private sphere and has not shown much interest in the tumultuous atmosphere associated with either the France of 1968 or the Portugal of 1974. Costantino's strong involvement in a world that situates him at a violent distance – "distância violenta" (Peixoto 2010, 220) – from his wife eventually adulterates his mood and his identity to the point that, in his eighties, he identifies himself with the young Lenin (Peixoto 2010, 220–222). As a mentally ill person, Costantino continues, as it were, to live in his own historical imagination in which he has always been living as an unsatisfied immigrant, husband, and father. As far as his relationship to Livro is concerned, Costantino expresses violent judgements against him, as Livro himself reports:

I've never concluded my master's degree, but I kept going out in the morning and coming back in the evening. Costantino didn't ask anything but, years later, it wasn't very likely that he had any doubts. Since the beginning, he had known that I had only enrolled in the master's course because, after my studies, I couldn't imagine myself looking for a job. I was scared.
You're lacking a direction.
The most humiliating thing was that he knew what he was saying.

[Nunca acabei o mestrado, mas continuei a sair de manhã e a chegar à noite. O Constantino não fez perguntas mas, ao fim de anos, era pouco provável que tivesse dúvidas. Desde o início que sabia que eu só me tinha inscrito no mestrado porque, depois do curso, não me imaginava a procurar emprego. Tinha medo.
Falta-te uma direcção.
O mais humilhante era que ele sabia o que estava a dizer. (Peixoto 2010, 248)]

In addition, Livro, having returned to Portugal in 2008 as a reaction to having accidentally run over an old woman without assuming his responsibility, experiences a crisis of guilt, as well as a deep fracture concerning identity and culture, as he is divided between two realities: he has spent his entire life in France, except for summer holidays; even if Portuguese culture has been transmitted to him by Adelaide and Cosme, he has never considered moving to Portugal until he sees it as a chance to run away from himself. This fragmentation is extended to the question of his affective relation to a father figure, since Livro is divided between Costantino and Idílio. The first one is an estranged father, representing France and its political, economic, and social traditions, which, Livro acknowledges, have shaped his intellectual horizon. The second one is a father representing Portugal and its long and painful way towards democratization and self-realization. The late revelation, at 36 years of age, to be a descendant of this man and this country shocks him (Peixoto 2010, 261).

As a matter of fact, Livro, ever since he was seventeen, had the suspicion that Idílio was his biological father since he was seventeen, as a consequence of Cosme's report about the love affair and Idílio's meeting with Adelaide in 1973 (Peixoto 2010, 236–237). But it is only two years after the arrival in Portugal, in May 2010, that Adelaide and Idílio finally meet again, decide to stay together and reveal to Livro their relationship. Adelaide's speech implicitly confirms Livro's suspicion, yet, faced with this revelation he feels confused and overwhelmed, clearly suffering from the weight of the historical and familial past that he has not lived through personally. This leads to an affirmation of his own persona, although there is no coherent self, but rather – as is rather typical for contemporary literature – fragmentary pieces of identity that are assembled in a provisional configuration (Donnarumma 2014, 129–134). Moreover, this fragmentation reflects the dissolution of the social network of contemporary subjectivities,[7] because Livro escapes self-analysis and responsibility while fleeing into the world of literature and music; paradoxically, this does not happen in a situation of real social isolation, but it is rather the individual who feels increasingly distant from the social network he lives in.[8] In fact, the familial disorientation and national displacement experienced by Livro cannot result in any sense of belonging, or allegiance to the father or country. The issue of nonlinear paternity does not only concern the last family member but all four generations of the family: Idílio has no father or several father figures because he grows up without ever knowing that his biological father is in fact his grandfather Aquele da Sorna. On the contrary, he learns from a popular rumor that probably the priest is the man who gave him life, or maybe a shepherd. Nevertheless, he finds protection and care in Josué, who never adopts the authoritative role of a father, but significantly imparts to him the most important thing in his life, his own profession.

4 Circular Movement, Metalepsis, Memory

Despite all family fractures, the plot is dominated by a sort of circular, and thus infinite, movement driven by the transmission of the book as an almost biological heredity among family members: the volume is left by the mother to Idílio and given as a present by him to Adelaide. Despite the distance, silence, and the difficulties of life, they remain linked by true love through several decades and Adelaide not only delivers the book to their son, but she also gives him his absurd name with the aim to underline the family legacy, the bond between herself, Idílio, and Livro. For the same reason of perpetuating the generational circle, Livro himself declares that he will give his future daughter – in case he should have one – the name of Adelaide's mother, whom he has never met. Even if this does not seem very plausible at the end of the book, when the 36-year-old Livro lives far from interpersonal relations and responsibilities, he does indeed perpetuate the transmission of the story and the book in his role as a fictional author, reader, and narrator.

7 Gianluigi Simonetti observes that such posture is typical for contemporary characters, as exemplified by the novel *Il piccolo isolazionista*: "Symmetrically, what the book narrates is a progressive process of isolation, an abolition of human relations that is paradoxically achieved in the midst of the flow of communication – music, messages, television broadcasts that fill the protagonist's life and constitute their experience." (2018, 76)

8 Simonetti refers especially to Italian contemporary literature, but his observations equally apply, at least in part, to other works of international literature.

The metalepsis of the book also alludes to the possible continuity between the fictional and the real world, a view suggested by a couple of fantastical episodes occurring during Idílio's and Cosme's journey through Spain and France: in one case, Idílio discovers that the woman leading the group of clandestine emigrants is a sort of witch or werewolf, who killed a man who had disappeared from the group (Peixoto 2010, 106–107). Later, Idílio and Cosme find the dead body of the man they were travelling with inside a piece of luggage that has always remained in the compartment with them (Peixoto 2010, 134–136). A possible interpretation for the insertion of such fantastical elements is that they give form to the abstract, but terrible fears connected with the long and dangerous journey of illegal Portuguese migrants: extreme tiredness, hunger, thirst, and coldness, together with the high chance of failure and death. All of this might distort the perceptions and emotions of the travelers to the point that they are not able to distinguish the limits of reality. Following an observation made by Simonetti (2018, 129–132) about contemporary literature, we might say that the extraordinary, as an expression of *romance*, offers a chance for the return of the repressed in the contemporary novel, in the form of a flight from reality. Such non-realist narrative techniques build bridges between the fictional and the non-fictional, between the imaginary and the real, between the inner self and the outside world, showing how everything – just like the book of *Livro* – is constantly moving through spaces and times, as Carlos Nogueira observes:

> But this book also interrogates the reader through the creative view of the postmodern, that is no longer satisfied with the presentation of a linear and foreseeable history; while it dialogues ironically with the historical, literary, and cultural past, it is interested in innovating through metafictional reflection. For the narrator of this *Livro*, who at the end speaks to a fictional reader, everything is on trial and in motion: society, thought, and literature itself. (Nogueira 2012, 157)

In fact, the circular movement of the transmission of the book subverts any sense of linearity both with regard to the plot and the (hi)story of the characters. This circular movement is marked by the violent events of personal and public history, resulting in a sense of fear and instability on the part of the individual, the generation, and the family. In this sense, Livro's lack of consciousness, representative for the generation of postmemory, may be a reaction to the repercussions of the violent history of the twentieth century:

> Besides personal memories, here intentionally universalized, the novel *Livro* constitutes an archive of the last decades of political, economic, and social history in Portugal, from the 40s until the present, with a focus on political persecution, corruption, latent violence, the

promiscuous relations between political power and the Church, impoverishment, the strong social stratification, the conservative and patriarchal morality, and, obviously, clandestine emigration, namely emigration to France.

[Além das memórias pessoais, aqui intencionalmente universalizadas, o romance *Livro* constitui um arquivo das últimas décadas da História política, económica e social de Portugal, desde a década de 40 à actualidade com destaque para a perseguição política, a corrupção, a violência latente, as relações promíscuas entre o poder político e a Igreja, o empobrecimento, a forte estratificação social, a moral conservadora e patriarcalista, e claro, a emigração clandestina, concretamente a emigração para França. (Soares 2022, 112)]

If personal memories are allegorically universalized in the work, examples of violence during the twentieth century obviously constitute second-hand experiences for Livro, because they occurred before his birth and in another country. Therefore, they are not focused on directly, but rather alluded to in the characters' various vicissitudes. Nevertheless, these events are determining in shaping Livro's identity, as if they were part of his genetics (see also Alberani 2013, 341). In this sense, the character of Livro serves as an allegory for the whole generation of postmemory born in the 1970s, the first one to live in a democratic and postcolonial country, but still experiencing the transnational and transgenerational dimensions of history and trauma.

In Peixoto's novel, historical violence refers in the first place to Portuguese dictatorship and to the social dichotomy it has caused: on the one side, there are the privileged authorities governing the village and the country as a whole, especially the Church – in the figure of the priest – and the rich old aristocracy – represented by Dona Milú and her villa. On the other side, most of the population is obliged to live in poor conditions, with the youngest, most dynamic, and productive part of the society either leaving the country for France or risking their lives in an absurd colonial war in Africa. Violent acts are perpetrated by the secret police – known as PIDE – that defends the privileges of the Church, the dictatorial state, and the aristocracy. In the novel, this occurs when Idílio's and Cosme's friend Galopim is arrested by a policeman under the false accusation of having insulted the dictator Salazar. In fact, Galopim has a love affair with the wife of that policeman and can avoid the false charge only because the alcoholic Aquele da Sorna repeatedly claims that it was he who made the declarations against Salazar, although it is not clear whether he consciously offered this as an act of expiation (Peixoto 2010, 127–129).

Furthermore, the novel addresses the disillusion of the million and a half Portuguese emigrants between 1960 and 1974 when they finally achieve their destination and discover that their dreamland is made by hard work, and very poor life conditions. As we have seen, the experience of illegal travel to France and the hard times there are extremely traumatic: the extraordinary happenings during Idílio's and Cosme's journey might be seen as metonyms for the misadventures of all clandestine migrants from dictatorship and poverty, possibly not only from Portugal but also in a more universal dimension. Even if they succeed in building themselves a new life in France starting from the lowest social level, Adelaide, Idílio, and Cosme feel the need to come back to their native land; once there, they are faced with a country where nothing has developed as rapidly as in France but, at the same time, everything has been changing: time has passed, people have died or lost their youth – like the old Josué – and the village has changed rapidly, also thanks to the richness brought by old emigrants coming back; Adelaide, for example, buys the former big house of Dona Milú and has it restored. While this contributes to the material development of the place, it also exacerbates a feeling of disorientation of the characters. They often feel like strangers in the 'homes' they are trying to improve:

> Since we had arrived in France almost two years earlier, it had been mainly the two of us. My mother was short of topics to exchange with the other women of the village. It would have been difficult or impossible to explain to them the happenings of Paris and my mother didn't have much interest in the illness of rabbits, for the mildew of grapevines, or for complaints about arthritis and arthrosis. I felt repugnance for sitting in the pub watching TV and ordering beers, I abominated football and *jogo da sueca* [a card game].
>
> [Desde que chegáramos da França, quase dois anos antes, que éramos sobretudo nós os dois. A minha mãe tinha falta de assunto para trocar com as outras mulheres da vila. Seria difícil ou impossível explicar-lhes os enredos de Paris e a minha mãe interessava-se pouco pelo mal dos coelhos, pelo míldio das parreiras ou por queixas de artrites e artroses. Eu sentia repugnância por me sentar na taberna a olhar para televisão e a mandar vir imperiais, abominava futebol e desprezava jogo da sueca. (Peixoto 2010, 228–229)]

After all the violence suffered as a consequence of historical junctures and political power, after all the solitude experienced, the contrast between the urban reality of Paris and the rural world of the Portuguese village still prevents human relations and proximity among characters. Nonetheless, the novel offers a concluding perspective that can be described, at least in part, as hopeful, because family shows persistence and resistance, despite having been fragmented and dispersed by the effects of public history on several generations in various times and spaces. Love is celebrated in the late union of Adelaide and Idílio; and the affective, rather than biological brotherhood among Idílio, Cosme, and Galopim is affirmed; likewise, paternity is recognized neither in the biological nor in the material heritage, but rather in the emotional bond between Josué and Idílio, in Aquele da Sorna's self-sacrifice, and in Cosme's support to Livro while trying to reveal to him progressively the truth about his father.

As we have seen, family links in this novel are frequently interlaced with issues of a transnational and transgenerational historical imaginary, of memory, and postmemory. In *Livro*, remembering is presented as a possible remedy against the experience of violence, isolation, and death, as Vânia Rego has pointed out:

> A fundamental topic in Peixoto's work, memory appears as an answer to tragedy to the extent that it is a subjective time that escapes the laws of chronology and allows the characters to exist in another way, to perpetuate themselves in the others, thanks to remembrances, gestures, words, professions, which are transmitted. It is in fact the value of transmission that enables to rescue characters through those who eternalize them over time. (2016, 42)

Furthermore, the handover of the book among family members in a circular movement, beginning and ending with the book itself, signifies the chance to perpetuate memory despite all the instabilities and fears endured by the family and especially by Livro: as a character, he is a link in the generational chain; as a fictional author, he can re-write the personal and collective past; finally, in his existence as the material book, he embodies the infinite movement of memory transmission: "The landscape, world of objects, will become real only when we abandon these words. Until then, we'll have our heads submerged in this time without clocks, without calendar days, without seasons, without age, without August, this bound time." ["A paisagem, mundo de objetos, apenas ganhará realidade quando deixarmos estas palavras. Até lá, temos a cabeça submersa neste tempo sem relógios, sem dias de calendário, sem estações, sem idade, sem agosto, este tempo encadernado." (Peixoto 2010, 262)] By reflecting on this process of intergenerational and transnational memory through its own (meta)narrative form, *Livro* demonstrates the permutation and persistence of family links in spite of personal and collective experiences of violent fragmentation.

Bibliography

Alberani, Elisa. "José Luís Peixoto, *Libro.*" *Altre Modernità/Outras Modernidades/Autre Modernités/Other Modernities* 10.11 (2013): 340–343.

Amorim, Sílvia. "Livros e Vidas: Atravessando Fronteiras em *Livro*, de José Luís Peixoto, e *Biografia Involuntária dos Amantes*, de João Tordo." *Letrônica* 10.1 (2017): 443–458.

Donnarumma, Raffaele. *Ipermodernità: dove va la narrativa contemporanea*. Bologna: il Mulino, 2014.

Erll, Astrid. "Generation in Literary History: Three Constellations of Generationality, Genealogy, and Memory." *New Literary History* 45.3 (2014): 385–409.

Hirsch, Marianne. *The Generation of Postmemory: Writing and Visual Culture After the Holocaust.* Columbia UP, 2012.

Nogueira, Carlos. "José Luís Peixoto, *Livro.*" *Alea* 14.1 (2012): 155–157.

Peixoto, José Luís. *Morreste-me*. Lisboa: Queztal Editores, 2021 [2000].

Peixoto, José Luís. *Em teu Ventre*. Lisboa: Queztal Editores, 2015.
Peixoto, José Luís. *Livro*. Lisboa: Queztal Editores, 2010.
Peixoto, José Luís. *Cemitério de Pianos*. Lisboa: Queztal Editores, 2006.
Rego, Vânia. "L'écriture de soi au service de la construction du mythe de l'écrivain: le cas de José Luís Peixoto." *Lublin Studies in Modern Languages and Literature* 40.2 (2016): 37–56.
Reis, Carlos. *História Crítica da Literatura Portuguesa*. Vol. 9. Lisboa: Verbo, 2005.
Simonetti, Gianluigi. *La letteratura circostante*. Bologna: il Mulino, 2018.
Soares, Luísa Afonso. "O Romance *Livro* de José Luís Peixoto: uma Narrativa de Pós-Memória." *Memoria y Narración. Revista de estudios sobre el pasado conflictivo de sociedades y culturas contemporáneas* 3 (2022): 107–116.

2 Transgenerational/Transtemporal Relations

Tamara Hundorova

Transgenerational Trauma and Maternal Criticism in a Decolonial Perspective

Contemporary trauma studies emphasize that the concept of trauma refers not to the event that caused it, but to its spatial and temporal transmission and how it reverberates across generations. The transgenerational transmission of trauma has been part of the field of research since the 1960s and was inspired by Holocaust studies, which focuses on the physical, mental, and social lives of the second and third generation descendants of traumatized victims. The inclusion of the transgenerational aspect in postcolonial discourse means the expansion of psychological, social, and biological factors in contemporary postcolonial criticism.

The relationship between parents and children is of particular importance in a period of transition, which inevitably leads to a crisis of the usual way of life, psychological instability, and the emergence of new subcultural identities. This is especially true of the crisis of totalitarian consciousness. According to Hannah Arendt, when totalitarianism disappears, the experience of it turns into much more disturbing consequences in the future. It destroys personal worlds, tears people away from their existence, stimulates emotional instability, and disrupts communication links between past and present, self and other, parents and children. Colonialism operates in this way, and its consequences reverberate in subsequent generations, leading to a reassessment of parental experience, impeding adaptation to others, and causing various identity shifts. Following Karl Mannheim, in order to belong to a certain generation, a person must have experienced and participated in the events that define that generation "with a common location in the historical dimension of the social process" (1972, 290). Skeptical, destructive, analytical thinking is most likely to be found among the representatives of generations that have experienced radical changes in the sphere of power. For Mannheim, "the continuous emergence of new human beings certainly results in some loss of accumulated cultural possessions; but, on the other hand, it alone makes a fresh selection possible when it becomes necessary; it facilitates reevaluation of our inventory and teaches us both to forget that which is no longer useful and to covet that which has yet to be won" (1972, 294).

Transgenerational trauma opens new perspectives for cultural and anthropological research, as well as memory studies, postcolonial studies, and gender studies.

Tamara Hundorova, Princeton University/National Academy of Sciences of Ukraine

https://doi.org/10.1515/9783111208664-007

This aspect is especially important in periods of transition, when generations find themselves at the center of historical and socio-cultural change. Intergenerational relations reflect the development of cultural consciousness, fill in gaps in individual and collective memory, and reconfigure symbolic relations in the family.

1 The Symbolic Power of the Mother

The conflict between parents and children in colonial history is particularly painful and acute, as Frantz Fanon has noted. The family of the colonized father and the colonized mother, the relationship between siblings, children and parents, and the identity of adolescent sons in the postcolonial world create an extremely diverse and internally antagonistic image. Frantz Fanon discusses the changing roles, in particular the weakening of the role of the father, which is a deeply traumatic experience for children confined to the family circle if "the colonized father at the time of the fight for liberation gave his children the impression of being undecided, of avoiding the taking of sides, and even adopting an evasive and irresponsible attitude" (1965, 100). Fanon emphasized the traumatic nature of colonialism, especially the psychosomatic disorders it causes. He viewed bodily, mental, and psychosomatic illnesses as symptoms that indicate how a person reacts and adapts to constant pressure and inevitable change. In his later works, Freud also raised the issue of the transgenerational pathway of trauma transmission and the memory trace of the murder of the primal father. He argued that the primary trauma, which is imprinted in human psychology, largely determines the behavior of subsequent generations.

However, symbolic identification with the mother and breaking with her plays an equally important role in the processes of socio-cultural representation. The image of the mother becomes one of the key ones in the development of cultural images and imagination, emphasizing the symbolic power of the mother in representing collective values, reflecting the fear of death, and embodying ideal fantasies and entities, in particular those identified with mater patria. Moreover, these processes are crucial in different periods of human life.

According to Yulia Kristeva, the loss of a mother is a necessary step in the process of individual autonomy. "Matricide is our vital necessity," she asserts, "the sine-qua-non-condition of our individuation, provided that it takes place under optimal circumstances and can be eroticized" (2002, 197). Contemporary feminist and postcolonial criticism pay special attention to the role of the maternal complex in family conflicts between generations, particularly in the relationship between mother and daughter. This refers to the concept of matraphobia, which Adrienne Rich defines as "a womanly splitting of the self, in the desire to become purged once and for all of our mother's bondage, to be individual and free. The mother stands for the victim in ourselves, the unfree woman, the martyr" (1986, 236).

I use the concept of maternal criticism in the context of a socio-cultural discourse that is constructed around the idealization of the mother and motherhood in culture and politics. The latter involves the substitution of the real biological experience of motherhood with social and cultural constructs, as well as the subordination of motherhood to ideological goals. In general, normative motherhood is "maintained by many ideological assumptions that cause mothering to be oppressive to women" (O'Reilly 2016, 64) and assumes that "all women want to be mothers (essentialization), that maternal ability and motherlove are innate to all mothers (naturalization), and that all mothers find joy and purpose in motherhood (idealization)" (O'Reilly 2016, 65).

2 Motherhood as a Cultural Construction

The essentialist interpretation and use of motherhood is mainly associated with the silencing and tabooing of the real biological experience of motherhood. The over-idealization of motherhood in past social and cultural discourses, especially patriarchal ones, has contributed to the growth of criticism of motherhood as a public disposal of values associated with motherhood. Motherhood is largely used to create a mental association of the nation with a loving, sacrificial and highly spiritual mother whose purpose in life is to serve national goals. Traditionally, a native land, country, or nation is associated with a woman, or rather a mother, particularly in vulnerable or colonized countries. It is worth noting that the concept of motherhood is an invention of the modern era and is often how "the construction of this version of motherhood was conditioned by strong nationalism" (Shin 2002, 162).

The very concept of the nation, based on the idea of a *gendered* nation, emerges in a male-dominated culture, and its gendered connotations lead to the desexualization of the idealized image of the mother. However, as Yulia Kristeva shows, physical representation is also an integral part of the sacralization of the mother. In particular, both the colonizer and the colonized associate the concept of the nation with the desirable female body. The symbolic identification of a nation with the mother, who becomes a colonized subaltern, leads to maternal phobia as an integral part of anti-colonial consciousness. As a result, the image of the mother is deprived of its sacred character and devalued to associations with the sinful feminine. This is particularly true of the literature of nineteenth-century Ukraine, which had the character of a colonized province under the rule of the

Russian Empire. The Ukrainian national poet Taras Shevchenko, speaking about the fate of Ukraine under the rule of the Russian Empire, associated it with an unmarried mother and a girl raped by Russian soldiers. In his poetry, the colonized Ukrainian world is symbolically built on the "fundamental division of Ukraine into a feminine, settled and peaceful half opposed by a masculine, nomadic, and warlike one" (Grabowicz 1982, 59).

Shevchenko endowed the feminized image of Ukraine with an anti-colonial meaning. He widely used images associated with archetypal symbols of the mother. A terrifying manifestation of femininity and motherhood in Shevchenko's works is the maternal archetype of the *pokrytka* (a young woman who gave birth to a child out of wedlock). *Pokrytka* is on the verge of good and evil, righteous and sinful. She is an innocent lawbreaker, a victim of her own passion, traditional patriarchal morality, and a misunderstanding by society (the *evil* people, lords, and soldiers). As a mother, she suffers and loves her child, but she goes mad with despair, and therefore can commit a crime against the child. Incest and infanticide in the poet's lyrics are the personification of sinful transgression and vulnerability to evil in the colonial world, and symbolize the inability of the enslaved nation and society to protect their values, which are embodied in virginity, family, and happy motherhood. In the 1930s, Yevhen Malaniuk, reflecting on the colonial history of Ukraine, including the enslavement of neighbouring Turkey, Poland, and Russia, identifies Ukraine as a woman and a mother and called her a naughty "whore of khans and tsars" who was "powerless, | weak, drunk, and dumb," and who "gave her barren flesh, her miserable body | to everyone willingly" ["Безсила, | Безвладна, п'яна і німа | Неплодну плоть, убоге тіло | Давала кожному сама" (Malaniuk 1954, 78)].

In the 1990s, after the collapse of the USSR and in the wake of postcolonial reassessment of Ukrainian history, Oleksandr Irvanets uses maternal criticism to parody the idealized iconic image of Ukraine as the Mother depicted in Volodymyr Sosiura's poem *Liubit' Ukrainu* [Любіть Україну; Love Ukraine], which was written in 1944 and reflected the national-patriotic pathos of the post-war years. Sosiura's poem was banned in the Soviet era and became a symbolic poem for the Ukrainian nationalist movement in the 1990s. In Irvanets's interpretation, nationalist rhetoric is transformed into the rhetoric of globalization and acquires a postcolonial multicultural meaning. He desacralizes the image of Ukraine as a mother, calling to love not only Ukraine, but Oklahoma, Indiana, Northern and Southern Dakota, Alabama, Iowa, California, Florida, Nevada, the District of Columbia, Georgia, Montana, Louisiana, Arizona, Alaska, Nebraska, and Virginia. As Myroslav Shkandrij stresses, "[t]he list of states, all of which have feminine endings in Ukrainian, suggest a list of female lovers. The poem hints at the need to share one's affection generously, even to the point of promiscuity" (2010, 68).

3 Postcolonial Trauma of Maternity

Contemporary anti-maternal criticism relies on trauma studies and addresses the psychoanalytic and anthropological aspects of memory and post-memory that reflect traumatic events and violence. Cathy Caruth, in particular, argues that "the language of trauma and the silence about the deafening return of suffering" requires "a new way of reading and listening" (1996, 9). Narrativization of trauma becomes a means of analyzing the generational gap, and transgenerational trauma connects such seemingly disconnected and unrelated issues as the anti-colonial experience, the traumatic consequences of the Second World War, the post-Soviet trauma of Eastern European countries, the trauma of the Holocaust and the Holodomor, and post-Chernobyl trauma.

In the introduction to a special issue of *Studies in the Novel* (2006) devoted to postcolonial trauma novels, the scholars discuss both the integration of trauma studies into postcolonial studies and the fact that trauma studies itself "is almost entirely concerned with the traumatic experience of white Western people" (Craps and Buelens 2008, 2). The analysis of the contexts of trauma in other cultures, including those associated with the so-called Orient, becomes relevant for the development of trauma theory in general, and can also be applied to postcolonial criticism in the post-Soviet space.

The postcolonial novel of trauma is based on the analysis of traumas such as slavery, forced migration, racism, genocide, family destruction, generation gaps, mental and physical violence, etc. Usually, these novels are a testament to the disaster experienced, the narrative conveying a situation of extreme tension. Quite often, such works are immersed in mystical practices, as rational interpretation cannot convey the experience of what has happened. The traumatic narrative, mostly non-linear and fragmentary, is manifested through the images of monstrous characters (the monstrous femininity), the body (wounds or mutilation), and broken language or silence. The traumatic narrative aims to relieve tension through catharsis and help restore the broken connection between ancestors, generations, families, nations, and races.

However, the genre of the trauma novel has also manifested itself in the post-totalitarian literature of Eastern Europe. Maria Matios's novel *Solodka Darusia. Drama na try zhyttia* [*Солодка Даруся. Драма на три життя* (2004); *Sweet Darusya. A Tale of Two Villages* (2019)] is an attempt to write a postcolonial novel of trauma in Ukrainian literature. The story tells of the national liberation struggle in western Ukraine against the Soviet regime before and after the Second World War. The family trauma that is passed down from generation to generation is manifested through the fate of a mute girl, Darusya, who becomes an innocent victim of a broken mother-daughter relationship. She finds herself on the margins of a patriarchal society as a stranger, and her muteness indicates her isolation from people. She has *her language* and only in the cemetery by her father's grave can she speak like she is normal. The central image in the text is Darusya's mother, who turns into a monstrous, mysterious character. The mother embodies a threatening and erotically attractive female character and appears as a young and sinful woman with long, luxurious hair: "Matronka had such a thick and long braid she could wind it around her head three times" (Matios 2019, 98) ["Матронка мала таку грубезну й довгу косу, що нею тричі обвивала голову" (Matios 2005, 88)]. She seemed a stranger to the villagers, she dared to disobey tradition, looked like a child, and ignored the patriarchal village tradition to appear with her head covered.

Having just given birth to a daughter, she is taken into the hands of an NKVD officer who brutally abuses her. Matronka feels guilty and is mocked by villagers, her shame is doubled when her daughter later tells the officer who also seduces a child with the promise of a sweet lollipop about her father's connection to the rebels. Unwittingly, 10-year-old Darusya becomes a traitor, and her mother curses her child for her unintentional betrayal, saying that she "would have been better off poisoning such an unclean force in my womb or giving birth to a mute" (Matios 2019, 186) ["Краще би була струїла в утробі таку нечисть чи родила німою" (Matios 2005, 159)]. The daughter's behavior compounds the mother's sin and she commits suicide. The horror experienced by little Darusya, who becomes a witness to this death and sees her mother hanging, is deepened by the sight of her blackened face and the braid wrapped around her neck. All of this has a traumatic effect on Darusya: "Bareheaded, upbraided Darusya with both of her tiny hands held on to her mother's bare and barefoot legs, so that at first two fully-grown men – Mykhailo and Dmytro, the husband of the neighbor Maria – weren't able to drag away the child" (Matios 2019, 196) ["Простоволоса, розплетена Даруся ручками трималася їй за голі і босі ноги, так що спершу дитину не могли відтягнути два чоловіки – Михайло і чоловік Марії-сусідки – Дмитро" (Matios 2005, 167)]. By committing suicide, the mother passes on her trauma to her daughter. The mother's death represents the trauma of Sovietization, which is passed on from mother to daughter. Darusya loses her voice, has unbearable headaches, and is frequently called stupid.

Darusya's loss of voice is reminiscent of Friday's muteness in the novel *Foe* (1986) by John Maxwell Coetzee, who reinterprets the famous story of Robinson Crusoe, undermining the myth of empire and all the colonial policies promoted in Defoe's canonical text. Friday cannot speak because his tongue was cut out, probably in early childhood. Thus, he is not a full-fledged interlocutor either for Robinson, with whom he lived for a long time on a desert island, or for Mrs. Crusoe, who brings him to a strange and cold London. Friday's silence is the personification of the subaltern.

Unable to tell his story, he remains an *other* who is endlessly colonized. He is racially, physically, and verbally marked by his skin color, his wounds, and his lack of a language that no one hears or understands.

The image of a monstrous mother who kills her child is often found in novels about postcolonial trauma, which depict a *monstrous* femininity that inspires fear through its extraordinary sexual and reproductive power. Usually, this characterization is given to a mother who is in conditions of humiliation and violence-slavery, colonial or totalitarian. This is a woman who is unable to properly fulfill her maternal functions to protect her children, who are either taken away from her or forced to abandon them. These motifs are echoed in postcolonial novels about the lives of black slave mothers. Ngũgĩ wa Thiong'o in *Petals of Blood* (1977) describes the fate of a Kenyan black woman named Wanya. Raped and scorned by the patriarchal laws of the village, she flees to the city to become a prostitute – her only way to find shelter – and kills her newborn child.

In Toni Morrison's *The Beloved* (1987), the story of the horrific times of black slavery eventually turns into a story of life in the terrifying house number 124, where real people and ghosts live, feared by the neighbors. The house is haunted by the ghost of a dead daughter whom her mother killed to free her from slavery. Deprived of her mother's love and affection in life, the daughter demands it back in death as a ghost. She comes and slowly expels the living people from the house. Her mother killed her as a little girl in front of her pursuers to prevent her from becoming a slave. At the same time, the murderous mother is also a victim. Slavery deprives her of the happiness of motherhood: her sons have abandoned her, she has killed one daughter, and she is unable to love the other.

4 Post-Soviet Maternal Resentment

Maternal criticism in Ukraine has also become an important element of post-Soviet literature. In Oksana Zabuzhko's *Pol'ovi doslidzhennia z ukrainskoho seksu* [*Польові дослідження з українського сексу* (1996); *Fieldwork in Ukrainian Sex* (2011)], a maternal critique resembles the postcolonial prose of Toni Morrison, Salman Rushdie, Jamaica Kincaid, and Arundhati Roy. The author uses gender conflict to recreate colonial national history. This is connected to both the oppression of the Russian Empire and the Soviet period. The novel unfolds as a monologue of a deeply traumatized woman, a stream of her thoughts and a psychotherapeutic discourse about the traumatic relationship between a man and a woman, which reflects the entire colonial history of Ukraine, that gave rise to the phenomenon of a humiliated man and a strong woman. The female body becomes a metaphor for the country, "like a strange, alien 'other' that she must try to revive over and over despite the history and trauma that encroach on her and try to consume her" (Berbenuik 2012). Zabuzhko portrays the love drama as a deep colonial trauma that affected an entire nation and destroyed the intimate space of the family. A colonized man, humiliated, subjugated, and weakened by the empire, who no longer feels like a winner, directs his aggression not at the colonizers, but at his countrywoman or wife, treating her as an object of his power. Colonial history has given rise to a gender crisis and the so-called male *hermeticism* (closed-mindedness) – self-sufficient, self-absorbed, and aimed at humiliating the other. On the contrary, colonized women take on masculine responsibilities and become their male counterparts. This is how Zabuzhko's protagonist speaks to a foreign audience: "What can I tell you, Donna-dearest. That we were raised by men fucked from all ends every which way" (Zabuzhko 2011, 158) ["Що я можу тобі на це відповісти, Донцю? Що нас ростили мужики, обйобані як-тільки-можна з усіх кінців" (Zabuzhko 1996, 140)]. They humiliated after being humiliated themselves; they did the same thing that the other, alien men had done to them. However, "we accepted them and loved them as they were, because not to accept them was to go over to the others, the other side? And that our only choice, therefore, was and still remains between victim and executioner: between nonexistence and existence that kills you." (Zabuzhko 2011, 158) ["ми приймали й любили їх такими, як вони є, бо не прийняти їх – означало б стати по стороні тих, чужих? Що єдиний наш вибір, отже, був і лишається – межи жертвою і катом: між небуттям і чуттям-яке-вбиває?" (Zabuzhko 1996, 140)] Similarly, in his book *Black Skin, White Masks* (1967), Frantz Fanon explores how racism effectively demasculinized and disempowered the black man. It created a double standard and forced him to imitate white hegemonic masculinity: "without my knowledge I am attempting to revenge myself on a European woman for everything that her ancestors have inflicted on mine throughout the centuries" (1986, 70).

The generation gap, which signifies totalitarian trauma, is one of the main themes of Zabuzhko's novel. The heroine's parents are real victims of totalitarianism. The father, a prisoner of Stalin's camps, returns home infected with fear and lives his entire life in anticipation of a new arrest. The mother, having survived the 1933 famine in Ukraine, becomes frigid and lives in constant fear of starvation. The daughter survives by Ukrainizing her boyfriends and combining the images of an intellectual, a witch, and a prostitute, which help her compensate for her lifelong infantilization, nurtured by a totalitarian society. Here, the trauma of colonial history is expressed through the monstrosity of the daughter and her critique of motherhood, as the mother is not only a victim of the totalitarian regime, but also bears the guilt for her daughter's unborn children. Zabuzhko traces the connection between slavery and totalitarian experience, concluding that "slavery is the state of being infected by fear. And fear kills love. And without love – children, poems, painting – all is pregnant with death" (Zabuzhko 2011, 156) ["Рабство є інфікованість страхом. А страх убиває любов. А без любові – і діти, і вірші, й картини – все робиться вагітне смертю" (Zabuzhko 1996, 138)].

Totalitarian drama penetrates the family. It separates the father and mother, takes the children away from their parents, and deprives the daughter of the opportunity to create a full-fledged family and give birth to happy children. "Slaves should not give birth to children!" (Zabuzhko 2011, 76) ["раби не повинні родити дітей!" (Zabuzhko 1996, 87)], this phrase in Zabuzhko's novel is a diagnosis of totalitarian trauma. The period of national revival is an apocalyptic period when motherhood is threatened, when the processes of growing up regress, and entire families become extinct.

Zabuzhko's portrayal of the daughter's relationship to her mother is characterized by mother phobia and critique. The mother is excluded from her daughter's life, becoming a shadowy victim of traumatic national history, a "sacrificial lamb," a "child who survived the famine." Hence "Mother was quite beside the point in all this, Mother was, in fact, frigid" (Zabuzhko 2011, 148) ["бо мами за тим усім не проглядалося, мама взагалі була фригідна" (Zabuzhko 1996, 131)]. In this way, Zabuzhko undermines the nationalist narrative based on the idealization of the image of the mother as nation. The daughter lives in a patriarchal world where her father controls her maturation and her boyfriend is "more than a brother, he was homeland and home" (Zabuzhko 2011, 154) ["більше, ніж брат, бо вітчизна і дім" (Zabuzhko 1996, 136)]. The post-totalitarian crisis of motherhood signals that it is the mother who is to blame for the totalitarian past.

We find a similar conflict in Evgenia Kononenko's novel *Nostal'hiia* [*Ностальгия* (2005); Nostalgia]. The novel tells the story of a mystery that goes back to the collapse of the Soviet Union in the late 1980s. In Shulika's family, a man killed his wife and then committed suicide, and no one could understand why. Oleksa, their son, a child of the postwar years, believes that the tragedy in his family was rooted in his parents' generation. Thirty years later, he asks Larysa, an art historian and the daughter of his father's front-line comrade, to help him uncover this mystery. It turns out that the truth of the murder is that Oleksa's mother, trying to get back the man she loved and waiting for him to return from the war, wrote a letter of denunciation against the girl he was bringing back from the war. This girl is sometimes called Raichka, sometimes Ramina; she is either Moldovan or Romanian, a victim of war who was abused by both German and Soviet soldiers. The girl turns out to be a kind of magic key to an old secret. As the hidden lies slowly unravel, the shadow of the mother's sin from the past penetrates into the present and hangs over the children. In Kononenko's interpretation, maternal sin is not limited to the Shulika family, but rather serves as an allusion to the whole of Soviet history. It binds the parents, typical *homo sovieticus*, to the same fate, separating them from their children and traumatizing them.

It is no coincidence that the brutal incident occurred at the beginning of perestroika, when the KGB archives were opened and many people were able to familiarize themselves with their case files, including denunciations written by those who lived in the neighborhood. It is likely that Oleksa's father, upon learning of his wife's denunciation, killed her and himself, erasing his life from history. But this trauma is haunting the children. By discovering the shadow of the past, children separate themselves from the history of their parents and gain independence. "We have only these parents, they gave birth to us, there will be no others. The only thing you can change is to become the kind of parent you dreamed of as a child"[1] ["В нас тільки ці батьки, які нас народили, й інших не буде. Єдине, що ти можеш – це стати комусь таким батьком, про якого мріяв у дитинстві" (Kononenko 2005, 183)]. This is a statement that children make to themselves. It seems that the removal of the mother as a symbolic code of the Soviet era heals the totalitarian trauma and gives children the opportunity to be free and build their own lives.

5 A Loser "without the Mother"

The Ukrainian post-Soviet novel reflects dissatisfaction not only with the power of the authoritative father, who is associated with the colonial past, but also points to disillusionment with the maternal world of the family and homeland, in which the individual is expected to feel safe. This condition reflects a situation in which politically, economically, environmentally, and culturally post-Soviet Ukraine does not correspond to the individual's expectations.

For the generation that came to literature in the 2000s, a fatherless teenager became the central character. Serhiy Zhadan diagnosed in his novel *Voroshylovhrad* [*Ворошиловград* (2010); *Voroshilovgrad* (2016)] that the loser was born in the last Soviet generation. As one of the representatives of this generation confesses, "we all wanted to become pilots. Most of us became losers" (Zhadan 2010) ["всі ми хотіли стати пілотами. Більшість із нас стали лузерами" (Zhadan 2012, 29)]. Feeling like a loser becomes a consciously chosen outsider and non-conformist position, a way of gaining personal freedom from both society and family. The loser confronts various social and consumerist roles in post-Soviet society. In some sense, it represents a teenager consciousness, without a gender, social and professional definition, a fluid

1 Translations from the Ukrainian are my own.

self-identity that is formed by repulsion by authoritarian and global patterns of behavior. Losers are blamed for lack of activity and antisociality, escaping to a situation of virtual reality, which gives a sense of integrity and security.

These inconsistencies are supposed to be harmonized and reconciled by a "good-enough mother" (Winnicott 1971, 7). According to Winnicott, it is the mother who provides the child with the fulfillment of all needs, including fantasy and illusory ones. "There is no possibility whatever for an infant to proceed from the pleasure principle to the reality principle or towards and beyond primary identification [...], unless there is a good-enough mother" (1971, 7). When the child grows up, the mother-role must gradually withdraw – she can no longer be the source of satisfaction for the individual's needs. This process of psychological detachment from the breast is quite painful for a person because "the mother's adaptation to the infant's needs, when good enough, gives the infant the illusion that there is an external reality that corresponds to the infant's own capacity to create. In other words, there is an overlap between what the mother supplies and what the child might conceive of" (Winnicott 1971, 8).

In the world of a loser, instead, there is no 'good-enough mother' either. One of the reasons for this is economic migration processes and changes in the sociocultural roles of mother and woman in post-Soviet society. Therefore, the psychology of the loser is fueled by aggression towards the maternal world, which turned out to be different than it (ideally) should have been. In the 1990s, the younger generation witnessed the collapse of the ideals of parents born and raised under socialism. The loser becomes an archetypal character of the millennial generation. He is presented in Sashko Ushkalov's novel *БЖД. Crazynovel*[2] (2008) [BZhD. Crazynovel]. The Ukrainian language abbreviation in the novel's title, BZhD, stands for life security, which was the name of a subject that was introduced in Ukrainian schools and universities in the 1990s to help the younger generation socialize quickly and easily. The epigraph to the novel refers to Ivan Vyrypaev's words "It's strange, very strange, where would I have been if I hadn't been there?" ["Дивно, дуже дивно, де б я був, якби мене не було?" (Ushkalov 2008, 3)].

The main situation depicted is associated with disillusionment with the post-totalitarian era and distrust of the family, and especially the mother's protective role. It is quite noteworthy that the characters in Ushkalov's novel do not have their own names, only nicknames, which signals not only the absence of a paternal identification passed down by tradition, but also the loss of one's own name, which denotes a transient subjectivity and lost individuality of a person. The maternal image also loses its ideal character. As the protagonist of the novel, nicknamed Baz,

2 БЖД is the Ukrainian abbreviation of Life Safety, in Ukrainian it is Безпека ЖиттєДіяльності.

notes, he started swearing at six years old, when his mother brought him to a dental practitioner with a strong toothache and, "operating with phrases like 'turn it to the left,' 'fucking tooth,' 'be fucking careful,' got it?" ["оперуючи фразами 'туди його наліво', 'сраний зуб', 'обережно, твою мать', затямив?" (Ushakov 2008, 209)], explained to the intern that he was a bad child. The intern "took out his sadistic forceps" and pulled out a tooth, not the diseased one, but a normal, neighboring one. This episode of initiation can be considered a key one for understanding the childhood trauma, as it serves as a sign of castration. It disconnects a boy from illusory world, as well as breaking him of a 'good-enough mother.' His mother eventually left to work abroad, as Baz says, and he stayed at home with his father, whose image exists more as a background than a reality in Baz's perception. Thus, having been mistakenly emasculated at the age of six (as a pulled tooth can be associated with emasculation), Baz becomes an eternal immature adolescent with a deeply resentful soul. He doesn't want to transform into an adult and hates the social connection because as Baz admits, he was unnerved by the fact that in life it seems that someone is always watching you, like a half-darkened disk of the sun, which resembles "a squinty red eye, sleepy and squinty, watching me" ["зачухане й заспане примружене червоне око, що спостерігає за мною" (Ushkalov 2008, 27)].

It feeds the teenager's subconsciousness and produces an aversion to everything female. The image of his mother is erased, as on the talisman given to him by his grandfather. The last presented Baz with a talisman – an old German medallion with the image of a monastery – "of a mother… I don't know exactly whose, but some kind of mother" ["матері … не знаю точно якої, але якоїсь там матері" (Ushkalov 2008, 74)]. Over time, the medallion wore down, and the monastery simply disappeared from its surface. "I often tried to see at least its outlines, but only my eye blinked at me from the medallion" ["Я дуже часто намагався роздивитися бодай його обриси, але з медальйона на мене кліпало тільки моє око" (Ushkalov 2008, 74)], Baz admits. The mirror stage of identification with the mother thus turns into the hero's own narcissistic self-reflection. He is unable to break through to reality beyond the maternal image (and the insult caused by his mother), to build a coherent and protective world of reality.

From the point of view of society, he is a loser, an outsider, as his psycho-sociotype was defined when he was still in school. The formula of existence that Baz consciously derives is an antisocial counterargument to the world of parents, teachers, and educators. Their society is built on the opposition of enemies and friends and the struggle against an imagined enemy. This world is controlled and divided into winners and losers. And a teenager does not want to live in such a world, he prefers to be in a space of freedom, where there is neither responsibility nor struggle, where there is no need to defend and conquer centimeters and cubic meters of the so-called homeland and one does not have to think about an imaginary enemy. In general, Baz's anti-social escapist mood is identified with infantilism.

In Ushkalov's novel, the resentment towards the mother is transferred to the maternal body of the homeland, which can no longer protect the post-totalitarian individual. Ultimately the *motherland* turns into the figure in an advertisement for officer's beer. Against the backdrop of trenches, war, and soldiers, the Italian beer commercial proclaims "the homeland is thinking of you," which is a computer-generated effect, "as if someone is firing a machine gun on the TV screen and displaying the inscription 'OFFICER'S BEER – THE MOTHERLAND THINKS OF YOU!!!'" ["наче по екрану телевізора хтось стріляє з кулемета й виводить напис 'ОФІЦЕРСЬКЕ ПИВО – БАТЬКІВЩИНА ДУМАЄ ПРО ТЕБЕ!!!'" (Ushkalov 2008, 21)]. This phrase ("The motherland thinks of you!!!") becomes magical and is repeated in different variations and in different situations in the novel. Its counterpoint is profane words such as "mazafaka" and "yor maser fakin kuk" ["мазафака, йор мазер факін кук" (Ushkalov 2008, 64)]. Women, mothers, grandmothers – all of them pass before Baz as if "border guards of some state, not an ordinary state that is on all geographical maps, but some kind of internal state, whose paths and passages they carefully guarded against smuggling, illegal immigrants, and other misfortunes" ["прикордонники якоїсь держави, не звичайної держави, що є на всіх географічних картах, а якоїсь своєї – внутрішньої, чиї стежини й проходи вони ретельно охороняли від контрабанди, нелегалів та інших напастей" (Ushkalov 2008, 54).

These guardians of the "internal state" turn out to be not only weak, but also traumatized: in the perception of a teenager orphaned by his mother who left to work, they become defective representatives of the female gender in general. Resentment towards the mother is manifested in violence against the female body. In Baz's perception, most women embody sexual degradation: "old mops," a watchman, an "old whore" with sagging breast bags, a night moth whore, a "very nice nipple," and other "mantelpieces" converge here. The impression of school is associated with the word "bitches" – it covers the impression not only of a slow-moving teacher but also girl classmates – "bitches who are studious." The dry-as-a-chip barmaid, the drunken hospital nurse, the fat woman on the bus – they all deserve the teenager's contempt. Thus, Baz's world is without his mother – as he confesses, "fifteen years ago I saw her. And now she is somewhere in Portugal... they say" ["Років п'ятнадцять тому я її бачив. А тепер вона десь у Португалії... кажуть" (Ushkalov 2008, 150)]. The last episode of the novel, when Baz is sitting on the seashore and the sun "was BIG and at the same time very far away, so FAR away that if it had deigned to look at me, it would have seen nothing but an empty seashore" ["було ВЕЛИКЕ й водночас дуже далеке, таке ДАЛЕКЕ, що якби воно зволило глянути на мене, то не побачило б нічого, окрім порожнього морського берега" (Ushkalov 2008, 239)], is the apotheosis of escape from society and its parental "eye." But at the same time, the ending can also be seen as a regression to the maternal body traditionally correlated with the water element.

Ushkalov's novel, published in 2007, reflects the disillusionment that follows the Orange Revolution, which becomes fertile ground for the emergence of an outsider loser consciousness. Transgenerational trauma, global migration, fatherlessness, and resentment towards the mother acquire symbolic socio-cultural significance in post-Soviet Ukrainian literature. In some sense it symbolizes the initiation into the new global world because, as Maria Margaroni points out, extreme "clinging to the mother's body can be a form of suicide, since the subject is unable to construct itself as a 'living system'" (2003, 95). Thus, matricide takes on a new meaning in the period of transition and serves as a means of escaping from colonial or totalitarian experiences and becoming free from real and imagined trauma.

Bibliography

Berbenuik, Brianna. "We Are All From The Camps: A Review of Oksana Zabuzhko's Fieldwork in Ukrainian Sex." *Numéro Cinq Magazine* 3.2 (2012). https://numerocinqmagazine.com/2012/02/22/we-are-all-from-the-camps-a-review-of-oksana-zabuzhkos-fieldwork-in-ukrainian-sex-brianna-berbenuik/ (November 7, 2023).

Caruth, Cathy. *Unclaimed Experience: Trauma, Narrative, and History*. Baltimore: John Hopkins UP, 1996.

Craps, Stef, and Gert Buelens. "Introduction: Postcolonial Trauma Studies." *Studies in the Novel* 40.1–2 (2008): 1–12.

Fanon, Frantz. *Black Skin, White Masks*. Trans. Charles Lam Markmann. London: Pluto Press, 1986.

Fanon, Frantz. *A Dying Colonialism. With an Introduction by Adolfo Gilly*. New York: Grove Press, 1965.

Grabowicz, George G. *The Poet as Mythmaker. The Study of Symbolic Meaning in Taras Sevcenko*. Cambridge: Harvard UP, 1982.

Kononenko, Yevheniia. "Nostal'hiia." *Bez muzhyka*. Lviv: Kalvariia, 2005.

Kristeva, Yulia. "The Black Sun." *The Portable Kristeva*. Ed. Kelli Oliver. New York: Columbia UP, 2002. 180–203.

Malaniuk, Yevhen. *Poezii v odnomu tomi*. New York: Vydavnytstvo NTSh i UVAN, 1954.

Mannheim, Karl. "The Problem of Generations." *Karl Mannheim. Essays*. Ed. Paul Kecskemet. London: Routledge, 1972. 276–322.

Margaroni, Maria. "Selling of the Mother/Land: Restaging the Crisis of the Postcolonial Subject." *Camera Obscura* 18.2.53 (2003): 93–123.

Matios, Maria. *Sweet Darusya. A Tale of Two Villages*. Trans. Michael M. Naydan, and Olha Tytarenko. New York: Spuyten Duyvil, 2019.

Matios, Maria. *Solodka Darusia. Drama na try zhyttia*. Lviv: Piramida, 2005.

O'Reilly, Andrea. "We Need to Talk about Patriarchal Motherhood. Essentialization, Naturalization, and Idealization in Lionel Shriver's *We Need to Talk about Kevin*." *The Journal of the motherhood initiative* 7.1 (2016): 64–81.

Rich, Adrienne. *Of Woman Born: Motherhood as Experience and Institution*. New York: Norton, 1986.
Shin, Jiweon. "Social Construction of Idealized Images of Women in Colonial Korea: the 'New Woman' versus 'Motherhood.'" *Women and the Colonial Gaze*. Eds. Tamara L. Hunt/Micheline R. Lessard. New York: New York UP, 2002. 162–173.
Shkandrij, Myroslav. "The Shifting Object of Desire: The Poetry of Oleksandr Irvanets." *Canadian-American Slavic Studies* 44 (2010): 67–81.
Ushkalov, Sashko. *BZhD. Crazynovel*. Kyiv: Fakt, 2008.
Winnicott, D.W. *Playing and Reality*. London/New York: Routledge, 1971.
Zabuzhko, Oksana. *Fieldwork in Ukrainian Sex*. Trans. Halyna Hryn. Las Vegas: Amazon Crossing, 2011.
Zabuzhko, Oksana. *Pol'ovi doslidzhennia z ukrainskoho seksu*. Kyiv: Zgoda, 1996.
Zhadan, Serhiy. *Voroshilovgrad*. Trans. Reilly Costigan-Humes, and Isaac Wheeler. Dallas: Deep Vellum Publishing, 2016.
Zhadan, Serhiy. *Voroshylovhrad*. Charkiv: Folio, 2012.

Michael Karrer

Entangled Temporalities and Symptomatic Revisions of the Family Archive in Gastón Solnicki's *Papirosen*

1 Introduction

At the beginning of the twenty-first century, literary scholar Josefina Ludmer (2002) has observed a growing number of narratives by Argentine writers dealing with the subject of family memory, transgenerational experience and questions of filiation and belonging.[1] Ludmer speaks of a "family-form"[2] (2002, 20) or "cultural formation of filiation" (2002, 26) that emerges as a crucial pattern in the artistic and political engagement with the country's recent past. This boom of the family narrative can be traced to the concrete specific historical context of post-dictatorship and neoliberalism, in which family affiliation played a central role in addressing human rights violations and in voicing demands of justice, and where it functioned as "a temporal mechanism of transition from dictatorship to democracy" (2002, 26).[3] In the literary works discussed by Ludmer,[4] however, multiple cultural formations and temporalities overlap, coexist and condition each other, with the family providing a narrative parenthesis for linking different pasts and

1 This paper is based on a chapter that is part of my doctoral dissertation on the political uses of the family archive in Argentine and Brazilian documentary film. The central notion of *entangled temporalities* goes back to the doctoral program *Entangled Temporalities of the Global South* at the University of Tübingen of which I was a part and from which I benefited substantially.

2 If not stated otherwise, all English translations are mine.

3 From 1976 to 1983, Argentina was ruled by a military regime responsible for the disappearance and death of thousands of political opponents and leftist militants. During the final years of the dictatorship, family members of victims began to take to the streets demanding clarification about the whereabouts of the "disappeared" [*desaparecidos*]. Subsequently, the "grandmothers" [*abuelas*], "mothers" [*madres*] and "sons and daughters" [*hijos*] of victims became symbolic figures of protest against the military dictatorship and central actors in the investigation of the crimes committed by the regime.

4 Among other literary works published in Argentina in 2000, Ludmer refers explicitly to *El teatro de la memoria* (2000) [The Theater of Memory], by Pablo De Santis, *Un secreto para Julia* (2000) [A Secret for Julia], by Patricia Sagastizábal, *El mandato* (2000) [The Mandate], by José Pablo Feinmann and *Lesca, el fascista irreductible* (2000) [Lesca. The Irreducible Fascist], by Jorge Asís.

Michael Karrer, Martin Luther University Halle-Wittenberg

https://doi.org/10.1515/9783111208664-008

presents: "Family in fiction is a specific embodiment of temporality: a way of articulating succession, of filling a gap in time and marking historical continuity. It serves to subjectivize memory, history, the future, the different pasts, it serves to narrate in continuity, in sequence and concatenation." (2002, 26)

As Ludmer notes, the family in its "biological, affective, legal, economic and political forms" (2002, 26) is also ubiquitous in cultural domains other than (fictional) literature. This article addresses the distinct but related field of non-fictional film, offering a close reading of the feature-length documentary *Papirosen* (2011), by Argentine filmmaker Gastón Solnicki, to illuminate how the family, as a specific embodiment of temporalities, offers an alternative approach to history that (re-) constructs the course of time not in terms of a succession of extraordinary events but rather as a process of complex relationships and entangled temporalities. This focus on a single documentary film that straddles Eastern Europe and Latin America is meant to provide a complementary and medium-specific perspective to the study of family narratives in Ibero-American and Slavic literatures of the twenty-first century. For that purpose, I will draw on the notion of "microhistorical documentary," which does justice to the specific nature of the audiovisual in relation both to the family as the focal point of the narrative and to its multiple intersections with history, making "personal memory the foundation of the historiographical enterprise, [and] establishing a specific link between lived memory and public history." (Cuevas 2022, 36)

Particularly in the context of genocidal violence and atrocities committed by state actors, testimonies of survivors and family members of victims are an indispensable source for a historiography that accounts for the point of view of those affected by these events. Here, visual documents from the personal archive – family albums, snapshots, and home movies – play a pivotal role in reconstructing lived history and thus illustrating the (ongoing) impact of historical events on people's everyday life (see Hirsch 1997). Films such as those by Hungarian filmmaker Peter Forgács, which use home movies made in Europe from the 1930s and 1940s to reconstruct the history of Nazism primarily from the perspective of its victims, are paradigmatic for such a microhistorical perspective in documentary film (Cuevas 2022; Nichols and Renov 2011). Moreover, there is still an increasing number of films that deal with historical events and their effects on family structures and everyday relations from a personal and autobiographical perspective (Russell 1999; Rascaroli 2009; Lebow 2012; Piedras 2014). The microhistorical approach of these films, usually centering on one particular family, implies a significant shift in the way history is conceived and thought of, pushing the focus away from History with a capital letter towards a *history from below*[5] as experienced by multiple social actors.

In Argentine documentary film, this microhistorical perspective emerges around the same time Josefina Ludmer writes on the appearance of the family as a pervasive figure in literary fiction. In the years following the turn of the century, filmmakers such as Albertina Carri, María Inés Roqué, Nicolás Prividera, Andrés Di Tella, David Blaustein and Natalia Bruschtein, explore the country's recent history, especially that of dictatorship, displacement and migration, from a highly situated, personal and subjective perspective. By placing the family in the center of their films, the boundaries between memory and history, personal and political, individual and collective tend to be blurred. As Pablo Piedras points out in relation to Argentine "first-person documentary film, these works continue to draw on public and shared history in search of answers to understand personal or family histories and, conversely, maintain the explicit intention that explorations of the private world produce effects on, or serve to explain, events in the public sphere." (2014, 167) In the various documentary films from Argentina dealing with military dictatorship and/or historical fascism, the use of photographs and family films constitutes, despite the diversity of their aesthetic and political approaches, a common point. In these films, home movies and photographs from the family album usually provide a link between two or more generations and thus function as vehicles of memory, imagination, and identification.[6] The recourse to these fragments is often related to an affective demand that generally characterizes postmemory documentaries, and that turns the family archive into a central device to connect materially and emotionally with the stories told or untold by previous generations.

Solnicki's *Papirosen* joins this tradition of the microhistorical documentary, which places the family archive at the center of its examination of historical experience and the intergenerational transmission of traumatic events. However, what distinguishes Solnicki's documentary from other films that revisit twentieth-century political history through the use of domestic material, is its being anchored in and

5 The concept of microhistory can be traced to a variety of sources, but was largely shaped by the work of Italian historians Giovanni Levi and Carlo Ginzburg. For an historical overview, see Cuevas 2022, 21–27.

6 Particularly in the films by children of disappeared and murdered militants, in which the filmmakers keep only vague memories of their progenitors, these images are the only visual legacy carrying an experience inaccessible to the exercises of memory. Thus, images from the family album allow a symbolic encounter, made *de facto* impossible by the State terror, between the two generations. In the case of disappearances, which consist precisely in the elimination of a person's physical presence, the use of the family archive becomes a vindicating gesture that returns an image to someone whose presence was annulled by the political regime.

engagement with the familiar present, from which it brings the past to the surface of the visible. *Papirosen* tells the story of the filmmaker's Jewish grandparents, Pola and Janek, who fled Nazi terror during the German occupation of Poland to settle in Buenos Aires; the story of his father, Victor, who was born in Poland and grew up in Czechoslovakia, and would later amass a considerable fortune as a businessman in Argentina; and finally, the story of the third and fourth generation, represented by the filmmaker's sister, Yanina, a trader of fancy clothing who faces emotional difficulties after separating from her partner, and her son Mateo, on whom the family projects its anxieties, making him the center of attention and concern. Based on the filmmaker's family archive (home movies and video tapes) and other domestic scenes shot directly for the film, *Papirosen* draws on (minor) events of family life – birthdays, travels, religious celebrations, etc. – present in the archival images and reads them against the backdrop of the historical trauma of the Holocaust. In doing so, Solnicki's film not only mediates between family memory and social history, but also reveals the disruptive potential of memory with its long latencies and heterogeneous temporalities that manifest themselves in seemingly insignificant details and fissures of the audiovisual archive.

2 Familial Co(i)mplications: The Present as Symptom

Papirosen starts with a black screen and a mechanical, rumbling sound that seems to be produced by a metallic friction. Only when the image of a snowy landscape appears can this sound be associated with the movement of a chairlift, mixed with environmental noise such as the crunching of the snow under the skis and the wind blowing on the white hill. These sounds, superimposed and slightly modified, constitute the central theme that reappears throughout Solnicki's film at moments that deal explicitly with the remote events in Poland during the Second World War. This connection becomes evident when a voiceover narrates in a thick accent the tragic experience of a young woman during the late 1930s:

> I was in Grodno, the city where I was born. And suddenly, in 1939, the war broke out. At first, they made a ghetto. I went to the cemetery. I was in hiding there for more than a month. At night I would go out with my sister and we dig in the garbage dumps to eat. After half a year the Germans gathered people to take to concentration camps like Treblinka, Auschwitz and several others that I don't remember well, because at that time I was sixteen years old.

[Yo estuve en Grodno, la ciudad donde nací. Y de repente, en 1939, estalló la guerra. Al principio hicieron un gueto. Yo me fui al cementerio. Allá estuve escondida más de un mes. En la noche salía con mi hermana y vamos sacar en los basurales para comer. Después de medio año los alemanes juntaron gente para llevar al campo concentración como Treblinka, Auschwitz y varios más que no me acuerdo bien, porque yo en aquella época tenía dieciséis años. (00:01:04–00:02:21)]

After a cut to black, the image of the snowy landscape is followed by several scenes from rather typical Super 8 home movies. The first image shows the figure of a man (the filmmaker's grandfather, as we learn later) in front of an Israeli airline plane, followed by another equally shaky, scratch-marked image showing a woman, the grandmother, in an arid landscape. After a brief interlude, the voice continues: "We arrived by boat in Argentina" ["Llegamos en barco a Argentina" (00:02:37)]. In the subsequent images we see the two of them on the shore of a pond – recognizable as part of Parque Tres de Febrero in Buenos Aires – followed by images that include other people, probably family members, in the living room of a house, interacting, eating and dancing. As we see the dark, underexposed or backlit images, in which the silhouettes of people are barely distinguishable, the voiceover narrates the losses caused by the Nazi terror: "A lot of people are missing from the family too. My aunts are gone, my cousins. My brother was killed. My husband lost the whole family." ["De la familia también falta mucha gente ya. Mis tías no están, mis primos. Mi hermano me mataron. Mi marido a toda la familia perdió." (00:02:46–00:03:09)] At the moment when a small group of young people appears on the balcony of a modern building, the voice directly addresses the filmmaker: "Your dad was born in Poland, just after the war ended. This also had a great impact. On dad, on the family, and those who were close to your dad." ["Tu papá nació en Polonia, apenas terminó la guerra. Esto también influyó mucho. Sobre papá, sobre la familia, y los que eran cerca a tu papá." (00:03:22–00:03:39)] The scene shows three young people, among them Victor, the filmmaker's father, playing and acting in front of the camera.

In this first part, which offers a sort of prologue to the film, the different elements on which the cinematographic discourse is built are already present: The family's past is evoked from archival material, home movies from the 1950s and 1960s, shot by the filmmaker's grandfather several years after the family arrived in Argentina. These silent images are accompanied by the voice of Solnicki's grandmother, who recounts her experiences of persecution and displacement. Pola's accented voice functions as a thread that organizes the familial memory and offers an interpretation of past events in the light of the present. By mixing archival footage with Pola's testimony, the film establishes meaningful connections between disparate moments, thus creating a disparity between what the images show and what is said on the soundtrack. According to the general observation of Efrén Cuevas, "that strategy of contrast between the happy image and the oral testimony that revisits them

Ill. 1: © Gastón Solnicki. The filmmaker's grandfather in a Super 8 shot.

will be one of the constants that reappear in a good number of films that recycle domestic footage" and "that foregrounds [its] ambivalent character" (2010, 125). In *Papirosen*, the contrast between image and sound is accentuated by the metallic sound of the chairlift added to the soundtrack. The repetition of that theme makes evident its allegorical function (otherwise, *Papirosen* dispenses with synthetic sounds and background music) as a painful reminder of the deportation trains that took part of Solnicki's family to the extermination camps.

Papirosen thus works on different temporal levels that overlap and intertwine with each other. The sound recorded during a skiing vacation in which the filmmaker accompanies his father and grandson is mixed with archival footage of other, more distant vacations, while Pola's voice evokes a past that still precedes these images. One immediately notices the temporal differences among heterogeneous images, between the *then* of the old home movies and the *now* of the more contemporary footage. This *archival effect* is the result of what Jaimie Baron (2014; ch. 1) calls a "temporal disparity" between distinct and distinguishable elements within the same film. According to the film scholar, this effect essentially depends on our ability to recognize certain images as coming from different historical contexts. In *Papirosen*, on the one hand, the grainy and scratchy images of the analog film and the distortions and streaks in the video tapes are evidence of the ravages of time. On the other hand, the changed appearance of the filmed subjects (especially the filmmaker's father who appears throughout the film as a teenager, an adult, and a man well into middle age) gives us an idea of the long period of time covered by the film. Nothing speaks better of the passing of time than the material decay of the footage and the physical change of the people portrayed. Even converted and transferred to the digital medium of Solnicki's film, the archival images are sharply distinguishable from the neat images produced by the digital camera.

However, what makes the *then* of the family archive distinct from the *now* of the filmmaker's contemporary recordings, is not only due to this disparity in temporal terms, but also, and most importantly, to "a disparity based on our perception of a previous intention ascribed to and (seemingly) inscribed within the archival document." (Baron 2014, Ch. 1) This intentional disparity is evident in *Papirosen*, where the 8mm footage and VHS recordings perfectly match what can be expected within the confines of the typical home movie.[7] While this footage is limited to the special moments of family life such as birthdays, weddings, and vacations, Solnicki's own recordings deliberately violate the rules of *good taste* implicit to the home movie genre. Following a different pattern, the filmmaker's camera approaches the family in close-ups and medium shots, showing his father barely in panties and his mother in a nightgown combing her hair, or his sister changing her daughter's diapers and grooming herself in the bathroom next to her husband. At times, the camera follows the protagonists into the most intimate spaces, filming them in situations in which they seem very vulnerable. If the "observational stance" (Nichols 1991, 38) of the film takes on intrusive and even abusive features at times, placing the viewer in the position of a voyeur, this seeming impertinence appears justified by the almost anthropological assumption that a deeper meaning is revealed in the close observations of everyday situations, especially those involving serious tensions and conflicts.

Conflicts between family members run like a thread through *Papirosen*. On a family trip to Miami, the argument between Yanina, the filmmaker's sister, and Sebastian, his brother-in-law, escalates and later ends in divorce. Likewise, the trip to Eastern Europe, by means of which Solnicki's father, Victor, tries to obtain his Polish nationality, is marked by numerous quarrels, showing a particularly nervous and easily irritable father. Solnicki's camera follows these conflicts down to the smallest detail. Their meticulous depiction does not mean a deviation from the plot, as one might think, but rather constitutes its core. For, as the film's

7 Roger Odin (2008, 256) defines the home movie as a film or video "made by one member for other members of the same family, filming events, things, people, and places linked to the family." Although Odin's "semio-pragmatic" approach does not assume genre rules, the French film theorist notes certain regularities: "Nothing resembles a home movie as much as another one. [...] The same ritual ceremonies (marriage, birth, family meals, gift-giving), the same daily scenes (a baby in his mother's arms, a baby having a bath), the same vacation sequences (playtime on the beach, walks in the forest) appear across most home movies." (2008, 261) In this respect, see also the fundamental studies of Richard Chalfen (1987), Patricia Rodden Zimmermann (1995), and James M. Moran (2002).

sophisticated montage suggests, it is the seemingly superficial conflicts between family members that reveal a much deeper conflict – the trauma of the Holocaust and its transmission through different generations – that seriously affects the family into the present. Commenting on their trip to Poland, Pola interprets Victor's mental state in precisely that way: "Victor, when he travels, gets very nervous. Because he suffered a lot in his life. He didn't have papers until he was seven years old. We lied and said he was born in Argentina. Dad couldn't say anything because we were illegal immigrants." ["Victor cuando viaja se pone muy nervioso. Porque él pasó mucho en su vida. Papeles no tuvo hasta los siete años. Nosotros mentíamos y decíamos que nació en Argentina. Papá no podía decir nada porque éramos inmigrantes ilegales." (00:09:13–00:09:42)] As we watch the images of a seemingly happy family in home movies from the 1950s and 1960s, the commentary suggests that the trauma of persecution and forced displacement is expressed symptomatically in the contemporary conflicts recorded by Solnicki's camera, forming a temporal "knot of an arborescence of associations or conflicting meanings" (Didi-Huberman 2005, 19) that brings various temporal connections to the surface of the visible.

By showing the escalation of conflicts between family members, *Papirosen* brings to light the dysfunctionality and vulnerability of family ties or "Familienbande" (00:06:06), as the title of one of the film's chapters reads. As an observer, Solnicki does not explicitly position himself on the family conflicts. However, he cannot completely stay out of it either. The filmmaker's involvement in the profilmic world, that is, in the events registered by the camera, brings with it a number of complications arising from his dual nature as a social actor and observer, as a relative and filmmaker. Michael Renov speaks of a "co(i)mplication" (2004, 218) to describe both the "complexity and interpenetration of subject/object identities" in films that engage "in the documentation of family members, or, less literally, of people with whom the maker has maintained long-standing everyday relations and has thus achieved a level of casual intimacy." In *Papirosen*, the biographical implication allows the filmmaker to delve into family relations, working through unresolved conflicts and illuminating latent ruptures. In doing so, he assumes the role of an analyst whose interpretations of family life might have a "reparative meaning" (Cerdá 2013, 69) for its members. At the same time, Solnicki, a *Grenzgänger* [go-between] on the border between inside and outside, between his passive role as observer and his active role as son, brother, and uncle, takes on the task of a chronicler. The story he tells is at once particular and general, personal and social, individual and collective: the story of a Jewish-Argentine family at the beginning of the twenty-first century and the specific story of the Solnicki family; the story about the afterlife [*Nachleben*] of the Holocaust and about individual survival; the story of the Ashkenazi diaspora and the forced migration of Pola and Janek; the story of a painfully shared trauma and its particular generational transfer to future generations.

3 Temporal Entanglement: Trauma, Repetition, and Repair

Despite Solnicki's effort to organize the diverse and scattered material within a story, the images and sounds integrated into the film maintain a certain autonomy in relation to the larger narrative. The audiovisual fragments of private origins that are taken up and are re-semanticized do not merge into an organic whole but constitute a material and temporal heterogeneity. In the complex temporal modulation of *Papirosen*, where the family archive functions as a kind of echo chamber, a detail, a particular situation, a gesture, or a musical theme evokes spontaneous associations that short-circuit several moments of family history. Among the many examples of this temporal entanglement, two stand out in particular for their evocative power: In the first sequence, we see the filmmaker's sister, Yanina, dancing in the living room to the opening bars of the song *Forever Young* by the German band Alphaville. Then, through an abrupt cut, the scene changes to a home video from the 1980s showing the young siblings in the back seat of a car, with the sister moving her hands in the same way as in the previous shot (00:16:30–00:17:21). In another sequence, we see a scene of a family video in which the director's father and sister are shown at the door of a bathroom being occupied by young Gastón, cutting to another scene in which we see Gastón's nephew, Mateo, brushing his teeth (00:24:35–00:25:38). This montage technique allows new and unexpected combinations to emerge from the raw material, cutting across the various temporal levels of the family archive.

Not by chance, this procedure reminds us of Marcel Proust's literary technique in *À la recherche du temps perdu*. According to Siegfried Kraauer (1969, 182–183), an important but almost forgotten theorist of microhistory, Proust and other modern writers such as Joyce and Woolf, "seek, and find, reality in atom-like happenings, each being thought of as a center of tremendous energies." In Proust's *Recherche* the "seemingly insignificant minutiae of daily existence" (Kracauer 1969, 161) are magnified under the microscopic gaze and thereby gain significance in the biography of the writer's alter ego. "Each such 'close-up'" – as Kracauer metaphorically refers to the Proustian scenes – "consists of a texture of reflections, analogies, reminiscences, etc., which indiscriminately refer to all the worlds he, not only Marcel, has been passing and altogether serve to disclose the essential meanings of the incident from which they radiate and toward which they converge." (1969, 161) Since these close-ups, ephemeral and insignificant only at first glance, are part of a larger texture from which they can neither be isolated nor reduced to, their meaning necessarily transcends the momentary. Yet this assemblage does not follow a causal or hierarchical scheme, but rather contains multiple contingencies. In *Papirosen*, as in Proust's *Recherche*, neither determinacy nor linear succession is crucial to the construction of meaningful associations. On the contrary, both works reject linearity as the default temporal structure in narrative, building on a series of connections (figurative, auditory, or otherwise sensorial) that mutually illuminate past and present events.

Ill. 2, 3: © Gastón Solnicki. Proustian montage. The filmmaker's sister now and then.

This technique of Proustian montage, which links temporally disparate moments in complex ways, operates not only through similarity, but also through contrast. Thus, a scene that witnesses a heated argument between Alan, the "middle brother" ["hermano del medio" (00:17:24)] – as one of the intertitles calls him – and his parents is followed by a video showing the young man dancing with his mother at his sister's *quinceañera* birthday celebration. The montage contrasts the present conflict with the apparent harmony of old home movies. Affectionate glances and slow steps to the ternary rhythm of Johann Strauss's waltz *An der schönen blauen Donau* counter the dissonance caused by Alan in the previous shot, when he announced his disengagement from the family. Followed by the intertitles "The Miserables" ["Los Miserables" (00:19:53)], the juxtaposition of the two scenes has a distinctly ironic and playful tone. Yet, at the same time, the montage arguably functions as a "filmic repair" (Lebow 2008, 85) of family relationships already severely damaged by multiple conflicts. The filmmaker's desire to restore a harmony that, judging from the home video, might have existed in the past, and to reconcile the quarreling relatives, at least in the virtual setting of the film, can be related to what kabbalists call "*Tikkun Ha'Olam,*" or "repair of the world." As Alisa Lebow explains in relation to "Jewish first-person films" (another generic label that might be useful in regard to Solnicki's film), *tikkun* "can also mean emendation or improvement, concepts applicable to the way these films seek to rewrite family narratives to correct or improve the errors, omissions, or grave injustices of the past." (2008, 86) The desire to repair one's family relationships is inextricably linked to a desire for self-repair: "When seen in this light, with family as an extension of the self, and its interrelationships constitutive of self-identity, the films may also be seen as constituting a *tikkun*, or repair, of the self." (Lebow 2008, 86)

As a kind of "supplementary autobiographical practice," *Papirosen* functions both, we might say with Renov, as a portrait of the "familial other" and as a "vehicle of self-examination" that constructs a "self-knowledge through recourse to the familial other." (2004, 218) However, unlike the vast majority of first-person films that highlight the subject of an authorial *I* (Lebow 2012), the visual presence of the filmmaker in *Papirosen* is rather discreet (Cerdá 2013). The filmmaker's self appears only in a few occasions and is temporally diffracted: as a *character* in front of the camera in the home videos, as an operator behind the camera in the more contemporary footage, and as the one who organizes (together with Andrea Kleinman, the editor of *Papirosen*) the audiovisual material. Certainly, within the diegesis there is little to indicate the identity between these different instances, and it is only by extratextual reference to a real subject (the filmmaker) that we can assume an integrity of a self that manifests itself in multiple ways. Each of the instances bears a different temporal mark. Visually, the filmmaker is almost absent, with the exception of the 1980s home videos that are included in the film. In these images, the young Solnicki does not occupy a privileged place, but appears casually next to his siblings and parents. The film presents in a non-chronological way the director's successive selves (as a child and as an adult), alongside the aging of other family members (the nephew Mateo, whom Solnicki films during his first ten years, embodies in an exemplary way this constant change through aging).

The image of the young Solnicki positions the filmmaker not only as a "perpetual child [...] in relation to the family" (Lebow 2008, 57), but also in relation to the film, which is constructed from the perspective of the youngest member of its generation. At the same time, the thirty years that separate the filmmaker from the child we see in the home videos, imply a difference, as the two belong to different times and states of being. But the *I* of the filmmaker as it is visible in the archival images is also another because it is shaped by a gaze alien to him (the self as seen by another). As Barthes explains regarding photography, "[i]n front of the lens, I am at the same time: the one I think I am, the one I want others to think I am, the one the photographer thinks I am, and the one he makes use of to exhibit his art." (1981, 13) By re-appropriating his own image made by another, the filmmaker rebels against the authorial structure underlying the family archive, where the father traditionally acts as cameraman, effecting "a child's triumphalism [...] in recutting home movie footage or revisioning dominant family narratives." (Lebow 2008, XXIX)

In one of the few moments in which the filmmaker appears in contemporary footage, that is, as an adult, we see him through a mirror that multiplies his presence in the image (00:42:45). The scene is central to the film for several reasons: On the one hand, it represents the moment that most directly addresses the trauma of the Holocaust and its severe effect on both survivors and their offspring, thus forming the narrative core of *Papirosen*. The scene shows the bathroom in the grandparents' house, where Victor explains why he never enters this room since it is the place where his father Janek committed suicide. On the other hand, the scene functions as a *mise en abyme*: The multiplied and refracted mirror image alludes to a dissociation of the filmmaker's identity whose successive selves are presented discontinuously throughout the film. At the same time, the repetition of the filmmaker's image within the diegetic world draws attention to the cinematic device as such, as he steps in front of the camera and thus detaches himself from the filmic apparatus.

The scene is also the only one in which son and father are seen in one frame. This visual co-presence of the two is representative of the structure of the entire film, which is largely based on this interaction, otherwise mostly invisible throughout the film, between the filmmaker and his father.

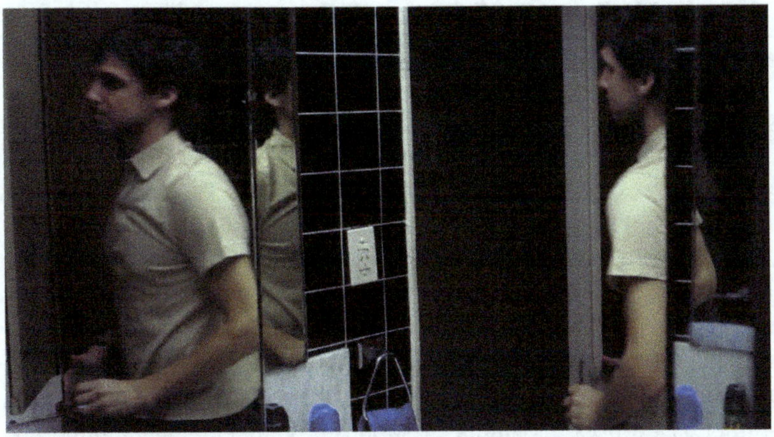

Ill. 4: © Gastón Solnicki. Mise en abyme. The fragmented self of the filmmaker.

"He thought it through" ["La pensó bien"], Victor explains to the filmmaker as we see both in a narrow frontal shot, "because in this thing he put the belt" ["porque en este coso puso el cinturón"]. Pointing to the place where the Solnicki's grandfather put an end to his life, Victor goes on to explain: "He stayed here and took the sleeping pill. He leaned against the wall and fell asleep" ["Se quedó acá y se tomó la pastilla para dormir. Se apoyó en la pared y se quedó dormido" (00:41:26–00:41:44)]. During the shot, Victor illustrates what he just said with gesticulations, bringing his hand to his mouth, leaning against the wall with his arm and slowly lowering his head as he repeats twice "he fell asleep" ["se quedó dormido"]. Interrupted by an image showing the brother Alan (an image that lacks any obvious relation to the sequence in which it is inserted), the scene is repeated in a condensed form in a counter-shot focused on Victor who repeats: "He took the pill and leaned... the weight itself..." ["Tomó la pastilla y se apoyó... el peso mismo..."]. The painful memory of the grandfather's suicide, whose ghostly presence runs throughout the film, finds its concretization in Victor's physical reenactment. According to Nichols, reenacted scenes in documentary film "contribute to a vivification of that for which they stand. [...] Vivification is neither evidence nor explanation. It is, though, a form of interpretation, an inflection that resurrects the past to reanimate it with the force of a desire." (2008, 88) In the same way, Victor's reenactment of the suicide does not evidence an event "as it really happened," but visually and physically expresses a loss, bringing an absence into the realm of the perceptible. In this interpretative and reiterative act "past and present coexist in the impossible space of the fantasmatic" (Nichols 2008, 88). This coexistence is the very space of memory whose labyrinthic paths the film traverses.

4 Final Remarks: A Past to Come

Combining oral testimony, archival images and long-time observations of family life, *Papirosen* mediates between the experience of Holocaust survivors (Pola and Janek), the generation whose lives are directly affected by the trauma of forced displacement (Victor), and the "generation of postmemory" connected to these events through intergenerational transmission and family narratives (the filmmaker and his siblings as well as the following generation) (see Hirsch 2012). In *Papirosen*, the filmmaker's family functions as "a specific embodiment of temporalities" (Ludmer 2002, 26) that links different temporal and experiential layers with the traumatic experience of the Holocaust at its core. Solnicki's microhistorical approach conceives the past not as a series of isolated and self-enclosed events, but rather as a process of complex relationships and entangled temporalities. The film's memory work is necessarily incomplete, an open-ended process that passes through the different generations of the family. It is thus only consequential that the filmmaker's nephew becomes the center of interest as the film progresses. Significantly, the film ends with Mateo's birth (possibly one of the reasons that induced Solnicki to start filming). It is to him and his grandfather that the film is dedicated. In one of the last scenes we see Victor and Mateo on a chairlift going up the white hill that we already know from the beginning of the film. "My father used to sing to me like this" ["Mi viejo me cantaba así" (01:05:46)], Victor says, as he sings the liturgical song *My Father, My King* [*abinu malkenu*]. The film ends with Mateo asking his grandfather about Janek's death:

> And did he die of old age?
> No. He died when he was young because he was very sad. Because of the war.
> Just because he was sad?
> Yes, there are people who die because they are very sad and he used to sing me this song.
>
> [¿Y se murió de viejo?
> No, se murió de joven porque estaba muy triste. Por la guerra.
> ¿Sólo porque estaba triste?
> Sí, hay gente que se mueren porque están muy tristes y él me cantaba esta canción. (01:05:50–01:06:05)]

In this way, *Papirosen* stages tradition and trauma as a past to come, a legacy to be adopted and dealt with by future generations.

Bibliography

Bachelard, Gaston. *The Poetics of Reverie: Childhood, Language, and the Cosmos*. Toronto: Beacon Press, 1971.

Baron, Jaimie. *The Archive Effect: Found Footage and the Audiovisual Experience of History*. New York: Routledge, 2014.

Barthes, Roland. *Camera Lucida: Reflections on Photography*. New York: Farrar, Straus and Giroux, 1981.

Cerdá, Marcelo. "Más allá de la primera persona. Figuras liminares del yo en el último cine argentino." *Kilómetro 111. Ensayos sobre cine* 11 (June 2013): 59–74.

Chalfen, Richard. *Snapshot Versions of Life*. Bowling Green: Bowling Green State University Popular Press, 1987.

Cuevas, Efrén. *Filming History from Below: Microhistorical Documentaries*. New York: Columbia UP, 2022.

Didi-Huberman, Georges. *Confronting Images: Questioning the Ends of a Certain History of Art*. University Park, PA: Pennsylvania State UP, 2005.

Hirsch, Marianne. *The Generation of Postmemory: Writing and Visual Culture After the Holocaust*. New York: Columbia UP, 2012.

Hirsch, Marianne. *Family Frames: Photography, Narrative, and Postmemory*. Cambridge, MA: Harvard UP, 1997.

Kracauer, Siegfried. *History: The Last Things Before The Last*. Completed after the Death of the Author by Paul Oskar Kristeller. New York: Oxford UP, 1969.

Lebow, Alisa. *The Cinema of Me: The Self and Subjectivity in First Person Documentary*. New York: Columbia UP, 2012.

Ludmer, Josefina. "Temporalidades del presente." *Margens/Márgenes: Revista de Cultura* 2 (2002): 14–27.

Moran, James M. *There's No Place Like Home Video*. Minneapolis, London: University of Minnesota Press, 2002.

Nichols, Bill. "Documentary Reenactment and the Fantasmatic Subject." *Critical Inquiry* 35.1 (2008): 72–89.

Nichols, Bill. *Representing Reality: Issues and Concepts in Documentary*. Bloomington: Indiana UP, 1991.

Nichols, Bill, and Michael Renov. Eds. *Cinema's Alchemist: The Films of Péter Forgács*. Minneapolis, London: University of Minnesota Press, 2011.

Odin, Roger. "Reflections on the Family Home Movie as Document: A Semio-Pragmatic Approach." *Mining the Home Movie: Excavations in Histories and Memories*. Eds. Karen L. Ishizuka/Patricia Rodden Zimmermann. Berkeley/Los Angeles/London: University of California Press, 2008. 255–271.

Papirosen. Dir. Gastón Solnicki. Filmy Wiktora, 2011.

Piedras, Pablo. *El cine documental en primera persona*. Buenos Aires: Paidós, 2014.

Rascaroli, Laura. *The Personal Camera: Subjective Cinema and the Essay Film*. London: Wallflower Press, 2009.

Renov, Michael. *The Subject of Documentary*. Minneapolis/London: University of Minnesota Press, 2004.

Russell, Catherine. *Experimental Ethnography: The Work of Film in the Age of Video*. Durham: Duke UP.

Zimmermann, Patricia Rodden. *Reel Families: A Social History of Amateur Film*. Bloomington: Indiana UP, 1995.

Matteo Colombi

Old New Families and (Good) Old Magic Realism between Brazil and Czechia: Markéta Pilátová's *With Bata in the Jungle*

1 A Czech Family Goes to Brazil

There are many ways, I think, to determine the topic of a research. One can for instance start from an abstract issue like a certain theoretical problem and choose accordingly which concrete material shall be analyzed to elaborate on that problem – yet one can also decide to begin with some specific material and let this suggest by itself which theories and abstract questions are relevant to be dealt with. This article is without doubt the result of the latter: I knew immediately, when I got the call for paper from the conference *Family Constellations*, that I have interesting literary material to examine: the novel *S Baťou v džungli* (2017) [With Baťa in the Jungle] by the Czech author Markéta Pilátová (*1973). The book tells the story of the (big) family of the famous Czech shoe entrepreneur Jan Antonín Baťa, whose brother, at the end of the nineteenth century, founded the well-known and successful world corporation known abroad as Bata: Jan Antonín emigrated with his family from the Protectorate of Bohemia and Moravia, the Nazi occupied region of Czechoslovakia, during World War II to Brazil, where his descendants live to this day. The novel depicts this migration experience, linking it by means of many flashbacks and memories to the time before 1939, as a process stretching across different generations and affecting each of them and every family member differently. Pilátová herself is, furthermore, an important voice within the landscape of Czech/South American cultural relationships, since she had been commuting for many years between Czechia, Brazil, and Argentina working both as a teacher of the Czech language and as a journalist and literary author (not only *S Baťou v džungli* but several other literary works by Pilátová are set in South America). Her novel came very quickly to my mind for the following reasons: firstly, it is a story connecting the Central-Eastern European and South American history of the twentieth century to the present, strongly thematizing violence as one of the fundamental features of both histories (the novel deals with the deeds of the Nazi and the Communist regime against the Baťas and, although much less intensively, with the Baťas' attitude towards the military

Matteo Colombi, Leipzig University

https://doi.org/10.1515/9783111208664-009

regime in Brazil, and the conflict between them as Brazilian landowners and the Sem Terra movement today);[1] secondly, it is a transgenerational novel opening the closed representational scheme of the nuclear family and its direct descent (grandparents, parents, children) to other family figures (an aunt, family friends or acquaintances and even a speaking shoe factory...); thirdly, it is a text with a transnational family topic, dealing with the transcultural experience made by the Baťas moving from Czechoslovakia to Brazil.

I chose Pilátová's book for another reason, too, since it partly relies on the aesthetics of South American *realismo mágico*. I have already hinted at this tie by mentioning, among the characters of the novel, a speaking factory – yet there are even more elements of *realismo mágico* in it, since one member of the family, Jan Antonín Baťa himself, is allowed to observe the others *post mortem* as a spirit (although he does not seem to be able to read their minds), and even to speak to one of his relatives, his niece Dolores, in dreams and in a kind of vision at the end of the novel. This reference to *realismo mágico* is from my point of view of considerable interest for our topic: for families are indeed at the core of classical texts of *realismo mágico,* such as *Cien años de soledad* (1967) [*One Hundred Years of Solitude*] by Gabriel García Márquez or *La casa de los espíritus* (1982) [*The House of the Spirits*] by Isabel Allende. Both these magic-realist novels focus moreover on a transgenerational idea of the family and thereby address the relationship between history and violence in South America: indeed, the magic-realist approach to the family already highlights in the second half of the twentieth century a good part of what distinguishes literary family narratives in the twenty-first century. One can nonetheless – relating again to the call for paper of the conference – point out a difference between the features of *realismo mágico* in the twentieth century and Pilátová's appropriation of elements from this tradition: García Márquez and Allende do mostly adopt, as a matter of fact, a national perspective in dealing with their family constellations (at least in the mentioned novels and without considering certain characters) whereas *S Baťou v džungli* tells about a whole family faced with the experience of transnationalization.

The connection I shall reflect upon in the following pages analyzing Pilátová's novel is, to sum up and conclude this introduction, her usage of *realismo mágico* in a transnational context dealing with the subject of history and violence. I will be asking, why and how this connection works on the representation of the family in the novel and whether the way Pilátová makes use of magic-realist elements in the

1 The Brazilian Landless Workers' Movement (Movimento dos Trabalhadores Rurais Sem Terra, MST) is a social movement fighting for the access of poor people to land ownership in Brazil. It is very much discussed because it considers and practices land occupation as a legitimate strategy of political struggle.

text can also be considered as an implicit poetological statement on the tradition of *realismo mágico* and its legacy for the twentieth century – in other words, this might suggest something about the way (some) literature of the twenty-first century may look at (some) literature from the previous century with respect to the narrative handling of the family topic. I will elaborate on these two questions through the following steps: firstly, I will define more in detail the concept of *realismo mágico* for the purpose of my analysis; secondly, I will analyze Pilátová's novel by focusing on the elements of the family, of the relationship history/violence, of the transnational, and of *realismo mágico*; the third and last step in the article will be some interpretational conclusions on the approach to the family topic in *S Baťou v džungli* as a novel written after 2000.

2 *Realismo Mágico* and its Place in Cultural History

Realismo mágico refers to the specific literary phenomenon taking shape in Latin American literature from ca. 1950 onwards, through literary works such as *Pedro Páramo* (1955) by Juan Rulfo and the already mentioned novels by García Márquez and Allende. These works do also combine the natural and the supernatural, reality and fantasy, yet in contrast to older works their aesthetic strategies are based on a very specific form of programmatic blurring of the real on the one hand and of the fantastic imagination on the other hand. For the intertwining of reality and fantasy in *realismo mágico* is not only seen as a mixture of two spheres with equivalent ontological values, but also as a superimposition of reality and imagination that is *not* considered as gnoseologically problematic as, let's say, in Tzvetan Todorov's characterization of the *étrange* and the *fantastique* (1970). Todorov's *étrange* is in fact an aesthetics that solves the tension between reality and fantasy in favor of the former (it explains fantasy rationally), whereas for him the *fantastique* is a representational form playing with the clash between reality and fantasy, whose relation is considered as essentially ambivalent and inexplicable – and exactly because of that as gnoseologically problematic, whereas the unexplained intertwining between reality and fantasy in *realismo mágico* is depicted as a simple matter of fact, as a non-problematic, 'normal,' given precondition of the represented possible world (to put it in the categories of Lubomír Doležel's theory; Doležel 1998). The characterization of *realismo mágico* as the aesthetics of both the ontological equation of reality and fantasy and the gnoseological suspension of the necessity to grasp the exact nature of their relationship, seems to be very consensual in contemporary scholarship. Thus, in an influential essay collection edited by Parkinson

Zamora and Faris, it is stated that the magic-realist supernatural "*is* an ordinary matter, an everyday occurrence – admitted, accepted and integrated into the rationality and materiality of literary realism" (Parkinson Zamora and Faris 1995, 3; italics in the original). The magic-realist ontological consistency of both natural and supernatural reminds us, thus, of Todorov's category of the *merveilleux* characterizing mythology and fairy tales, that is, an aesthetics presupposing that the fantastic, in the sense of something that cannot be rationally explained, is a constituent part of reality – yet it is important to stress that *realismo mágico* is to be distinguished from the aesthetics of older ages in which the supernatural was generally considered as an effective or even the most essential part of the world, that is, as something that is 'more real' than the ordinary real (to paraphrase Mircea Eliade's anthropological history of beliefs; see Eliade 1957). Myths and fairy tales were, therefore, not told or written to bewilder their audience or readership and to question their visions of the world – for they were, on the contrary, expressions of exactly those visions. *Realismo mágico* is, instead, a modern aesthetics coming after the Scientific Revolution and its break with the ancient continuity between the natural/real and the supernatural/fantastic: its literature is written with the awareness of the gap between the magic-realist aesthetics and the foundations of modern thinking. This also explains why one cannot say about *realismo mágico* that it considers the supernatural/fantastic as something real exactly in the same sense as Todorov's *merveilleux* or Eliade's more real than the real – *realismo mágico* simply states the ontological equivalence and continuous blurring between the natural/real and the supernatural/fantastic, but it does not explain the very nature of this equivalence and blurring in detail, very consciously leaving the readers asking about it in their reader responses (one could also say, in other words, that the magic-realist aesthetics very much counts on the fact that readers will, from a gnoseological point of view, waver between acceptance and suspicion of the unclear epistemological presuppositions of *realismo mágico* itself).

The very reason why *realismo mágico* reuses essential elements of a premodern aesthetics in the middle of the twentieth century and allows them to clash against the postulates of the modern visions of the world is at the very core of the critical and scholarly reception of this artistic phenomenon: Parkinson Zamora's and Faris's collection considers the ontological equation of supernatural and natural, reality and fantasy as an "ontological disruption serv[ing] the purpose of political and cultural disruption: magic is often given as a cultural corrective" (Parkinson Zamora and Faris 1995, 3). The authors stress that this corrective is very much related to "non-Western cultural systems that privilege mystery over empiricism, empathy over technology, tradition over innovation," and is insofar "subversive" of the hegemonic *Weltanschauung* imposed by the West to the world (see Parkinson Zamora and Faris 1995, 6). This post-colonially inspired perspective seems to be well established in the broader scholarly reception of *realismo mágico* as it is confirmed, for example, by a renowned collective survey on the history of the novel such as Franco Moretti's *The Novel* (2006). The chapter on the magic-realist novel is entrusted to Ato Quayson (who quotes among others from Parkinson Zamora and Faris) and strongly highlights the transformative potentiality of *realismo mágico*: its aesthetics delivers in his opinion "means by which humanity may renew itself: not by subsuming the fruits of the nonrational under the impress of rationality, but to celebrate and open itself to the fecundity of the unexpected" (Quayson 2006, 754). Quayson also makes the point that the magic-realist ontological blurring of the natural/real and the supernatural/fantastic is not shaped as problematically as in other aesthetics (and literature in general) from the nineteenth and twentieth century (he mentions Kafka as an example). On the contrary, this blurring in *realismo mágico* has to be considered as "an invitation for us to look beyond any settled norms of epistemological ontological forms, rather than as means of instituting a desire for normality, however this may be defined" (Quayson 2006, 730–731).

Quayson links magic-realist aesthetics to the aesthetics of postmodernity because of its refusal of any defined and defining norms and its pervasive disruptive desire, and he thus echoes another chapter of *The Novel*, in which Michael Denning analyses the history of the novel by engaged leftist writers in the twentieth century and notices that *realismo mágico*, albeit being mostly written by leftist authors, is commonly considered "as an antithesis of an earlier social realism" for it represents "a larger shift in the aesthetic from the powerful censoring of desire to an unleashing of desire and utopia, foreshadowing the liberation ideologies of the New Left" (2006, 723–724). Denning does not really work with the concept of postmodernity in his text yet I considered it as implied in the background of his argumentation since the New Left and postmodernity are very much tied to each other in the history of the 1960s, and topics such as the unleashing of desire and liberation ideologies are at the very core of postmodern culture. One could object that Denning also speaks of utopia – and postmodernity is generally seen as the cultural epoch developing suspicion towards every universal master narrative, including utopias, avoiding them as forms of global indoctrination which suppress diversity and preferring to focus on specific forms of emancipation (of women, of black people, etc.). Yet it is also true that such specific forms of emancipation, "the liberation ideologies" in Denning's quote, can be considered as local utopias, utopias concerning some groups – and it is well known that an important aspect of the debate on postmodernity deals with the question whether a fluid interaction of local utopias can lead also, through the "unleashing of desire," to real emancipation within mankind (I refer for the concept of and discussion about postmodernity to Ceserani 1997 and Zima 1997). Denning does not address this question, yet he would perhaps reject this idea because he stresses that *realismo mágico* opens up to desire but its novels mostly show how social struggle can never really overcome oppressive power in history (Denning 2006, 724–725). Therefore, Denning seems implicitly to evaluate the transformative potential of *realismo mágico* differently than Quayson – and in fact the two position themselves on different sides of the general debate on postmodernity, one optimistically considering this epoch as the beginning of new emancipation projects, and the other more pessimistically judging it as the skeptical diagnosis of the impossibility of ultimate emancipation (neither Quayson's nor Denning's position are simply manichaean: it is a question of tendencies).

I will return in the last chapter of this article to the several possibilities to interpret the ontological blurring of reality and imagination in *realismo mágico* as a constitutive part of postmodern sensibility. I just want, for now, to highlight its influence and popularity in the world literature from the second half of the twentieth century until today – a circumstance that cannot be forgotten when examining *S Baťou v džungli*, a very recent novel that relies on magic-realist features to focus on Czech-South American topics. The evident replication (with variations) of many of the features of García Márquez's *Cien años de soledad* by Allende in her *La casa de los espíritus* is already evidence of a certain institutionalization and popularization of the magic-realist aesthetics from the 1980s onwards which goes along – according to some interpretations – with its simplification. The literature of the last decades, that is, also the literary works of the twenty-first century, is nonetheless rich of authors from all over the world relating their poetics *in toto* or *in parte* to *realismo mágico* or being related to it by their readers, whereas the recent approaches to 'good' old magic-realist aesthetics can also be non-conventional and creative. Many of the authors nowadays working with *realismo mágico* – one of the most discussed being for example Salman Rushdie – write in post-colonial contexts supporting therefore the above-mentioned post-colonial interpretation of magic-realist aesthetics – yet European authors without clear post-colonial origins, as for instance Pilátová in Czechia, relate to such aesthetics, too; they therefore possibly show that the post-colonial gaze and its specific criticism of European modern history and *Weltanschauung* has become or is becoming part of the cultural background of European literature in general.

The dynamics of the reception and implementation of realist-magic elements in European literature cannot be analyzed here, yet it is important to stress that they have to be determined according to their specific cultural contexts: *Realismo mágico* was not only known among Czech authors and readers before the fall of the communist regime, it was also presented in Czech communist society as a Latin American alternative way for Socialist Realism to criticize Capitalism (see Denning, above) – and it was mostly for its being leftist that it was less subjected to censorship than other forms of foreign literature (see Zourek 2018 on the relationships between Latin

American authors and Czechoslovakia although his research focus is on the time around 1950, that is just the beginning of *realismo mágico*, and not necessarily on magic-realist authors). Some Czech authors experimented with the magic-realist aesthetics already in the 1980s although they only began to publish after 1989, eventually trying to link *realismo mágico* to the tradition of the Prague fantastic literature *à la Der Golem* by Gustav Meyrink around 1900, or to aesthetics more related to the above-mentioned Kafka's one (see Gӧrӧzdi and Passia 2016). The transnational life of Pilátová shows moreover that the artists' movement between cultures can support the migration of artistic ideas, *realismo mágico* being no exception (think of Alejo Carpentier living in Paris in the interwar period and importing/adapting from France into Latin American the idea of *merveilleux quotidien/real-maravilloso*, or of Allende going to Venezuela and later on to the US, after Pinochet's putsch in Chile).

3 Between Discontinuities and Continuities: The Representation of the Family in *S Bat'ou v džungli*

I have already roughly summed up the content of *S Baťou v džungli* at the beginning of the article, saying that the characters in the novel are several members of the Baťa family and some friends (plus the speaking factory). I mention here just the most important of them, beside the family chief Jan Antonín his daughters Edita and Ludmila, his granddaughter Dolores (Ludmila's daughter), his son-in-law Ljubodrag (a Serbian, Ludmila's husband and Dolores' father) and others such as the worker and drunkard Laďa Pinga. It is noticeable that Jan Antonín had a wife and three other children (two daughters and a son) who are more or less cursorily mentioned in the story but do not play an active role in it. The novel is nevertheless strongly polyphonic since every chapter is told from the perspective of a different character in the first person (some characters as Jan Antonín, Ludmila, Dolores and Ljubodrag speaking alternatively in many, some others in just few, or only one chapter). The story begins with Jan Antonín telling how he is dying in a hospital bed in Brazil, although he wants to go back "far away from the hospital in São Paolo, far away over the ocean" ["daleko od nemocnice v Sao Paulu, daleko přes oceán"] to retell his story:

> I want to look at the story very orderly. Perhaps tear it to small pieces. And then put them together patiently in order to know if it is possible to reassemble the parts so that they can hold together. Get all the threads straight, enjoying that I now know which villain pulled

them, examine everything under the magnifying glass of time. And understand why you did not want to listen to me so long. Why you wanted to tell everything by yourself.[2]

[Chci se podívat na ten příběh pěkně popořádku. Možná ho i rozcupovat na malě kousky. A pak je trpělivě dávat dohromady, abych viděl, jestli je možné znova dílky sestavit tak, aby držely pohromadě. Ujasnit si všechny nitky, pokochat se tím, že už teď vím, který všivák za ně tahal, všechno si prohlédnout pod zvětšovacím sklem času. A pochopit, proč jste mě tak dlouho nechtěli poslouchat. Proč jste všechno chtěli vyprávět sami. (Pilátová 2017, 14)]

The story Jan Antonín wants to look at anew is the one of his life as the younger half-brother of a very successful shoe entrepreneur of the pre- and interwar period who had built up a huge international business with its center in the city of Zlín (located in south-western Czechia in the region of Moravia) – a modern worker city designed according to the visions of the European liberal tradition and its belief in a certain idea of progress. Jan Antonín worked in the US after World War I and helped his brother to expand his business outside Czechoslovakia, becoming, after his brother's accidental death at the beginning of the 1930s, leader of the Baťa enterprise and keeping on expanding the company from Zlín into the world. Jan Antonín's life story however got more and more complicated facing the challenges of big History, since he had first to stand the Nazi menace and later on the German invasion of the Czech part of Czechoslovakia. The fear to see himself too strictly controlled by the Third Reich let Jan Antonín escape Czechoslovakia with his family and go to Brazil via the US – just to realize very soon after the war, that coming back would not ever be possible since he was *persona non grata* for the communist rulers of his country. They accused him of having been a collaborator of the Nazis and condemned him *in absentia* to prison and ordered the expropriation of his goods within the borders of the Czechoslovak state, including the shoe factories. This misfortune was on top of that worsened by an inheritance dispute with his nephew, his half-brother's son, who migrated to Canada and claimed in several trials the major part of the company goods outside Czechoslovakia for himself. Jan Antonín tried to defend himself from his exile, but he ended up keeping for himself only the part of the Baťa enterprise located in Brazil – a business declining after his death, partly because his own son, who inherited his position as company director, was seemingly not very apt for the job. The story ends with Jan Antonín's relatives, who mostly worked for the company, reinventing themselves as *fanzendeiros* or else, and with some of them – especially the two daughters Edita and Ludmila, and Ludmila's daughter Dolores – trying to rehabilitate the memory of Jan Antonín in Czechia after 1989: a difficult project that terminates in 2007 with the revocation of the

2 All translations in the article are mine (if not otherwise indicated).

sentence of guilt from the communist time but without restitution of the family properties.[3]

Jan Antonín's and his family's story is partly retold in *S Baťou v džungli* by Jan Antonín himself in the chapters in which he speaks – reexamined, as the above quotation shows, for a hypothetic Czech audience to discharge Jan Antonín from the accusation of collaborationism with the Nazis and to criticize the long time, the many efforts and the only partial results that his rehabilitation process cost his family. Yet all the other characters in the novel retell the story as well, or at least pieces of it, introducing points of view partly different from Jan Antonín's. The narrative structure of *S Baťou v džungli* is thus based on a repetition/variation scheme, which is quite complex, since the plot of the novel relies on systematic interruptions of the chronological story of the family: all the narrating characters mix up their actual present and their memories, whereas their actual present corresponds with their time in Brazil, with temporal shifts from the 1940s to today, in a way which is roughly chronological but continually crossed by the characters' discontinuous memories. These memories refer in associative, not chronological order to different periods in the past of the family life (in Czechia as well as in Brazil) and are supported by references to and quotations from different sources of familial memory like Ludmila's diaries, various letters by different characters, or Jan Antonín's own poems. Finally, Jan Antonín Baťa speaks as a dead spirit relating both to his past life, and to the past, present and future in the life of the other characters.

Pilátová explains the genesis of the novel's complex narrative structure in her afterword of the book, calling her work procedure "nedělní metoda" ["Sunday method"]: she recalls how she got interested in the figure of Jan Antonín thanks to her acquaintance and then friendship with his granddaughter Dolores, and how she had decided to write his story on the basis of what she had heard from Dolores and what she had read in some of Jan Antonín's letters and other family material that had been made available to her. Pilátová adds, though, that it was only "after some years" ["až po letech"] that Jan Antonín "began to speak" ["začal [...] mluvit"] to her: "Yet it would not have been Jan Antonín, if he had not wanted to tell his story personally and in his way. And so I let him. After all, he was not given the chance to speak for a good 50 years" ["To by ale nebyl Jan Antonín, aby nechtěl vyprávět svůj příběh osobně a po svém. A tak jsem ho nechala. Koneckonců celých padesát let se ke slovu moc nedostal"] (Pilátová 2017, 259). Pilátová

3 I cannot deal with a historiographical examination of Jan Antonín Baťa's life, the several trials he had and the rehabilitation here. See the conference proceedings *Jan Antonín Baťa – život a dílo, pokračovatel práce Tomáše Bati* 2007.

claims that her intent in writing the novel was, as it were, to give the floor to Jan Antonín, yet she also stresses that it is not only him speaking in the book: The writing method is called *nedělní metoda* because the very fact that Jan Antonín begins to speak to Pilátová in her imagination lets her retake the discussions with Dolores about her grandfather, meeting her regularly for two years on this subject, mostly on Sundays. The story is thereafter also written from Dolores' perspective – but also from the perspective of Jan Antonín's daughters Edita and especially Ludmila, whose diaries Pilátová had got to read from Dolores (who was afraid to read them herself, according to Pilátová): "I tried to smuggle into the arid historical facts his [Jan Antonín's] idea and his image as it was in the mind of especially his daughters Ludmila and Edita and his granddaughter Dolores" ["Snažila jsem se do suchých historických faktů propašovat jeho názory a jeho obraz, který měly v hlavě především dcery Ludmila a Edita a vnučka Dolores" (Pilátová 2017, 259)]. Finally, Pilátová also acknowledges that there is also something of her own authorial perspective in the story – although she stresses again that she has intended her own role being primarily the one of a writer's pen channeling Jan Antonín's voice and the voice of his granddaughter Dolores, the author's direct interlocutor: "Dolores and I simply wanted that Jan Antonín Baťa gets speaking. It is his and our version of the story. Based on facts and on such deceptive, non-objective things as the human memory." ["Já i Dolores jsme prostě chtěly, aby se Jan Antonín Baťa dostal ke slovu. [...] Je to jeho a naše verze příběhu. Založená na skutečnosti a na tak ošidné, neobjektivní věci, jakou je lidská paměť." (Pilátová 2017, 260)]

The kaleidoscopic structure of *S Baťou v džungli* and the variety of points of view displayed in it makes it difficult for the readers to say if the novel really accomplishes the wish expressed by Jan Antonín in the first chapter, namely of "reassembl[ing] the parts [of the story] so that they can hold together" (both for him as a character and for the book's readership itself). The novel seems more based on the idea to put different pieces of the story near each other and let them react to one another in a not-predefined way, which can very much vary according to the reader – a strategy that recalls the idea of a paradigmatic, non-syntagmatic narration of family events (see remarks on the historical imaginary in the introduction to this volume).[4] Regarding Jan Antonín's spirit, it finds only a partial satisfaction

4 I have tested with some advanced students of Czech Studies at Leipzig University the complexity of multiperspectivism in *S Baťou v džungli* within the activities of a Czech reading circle in 2020. We made the experiment to read the novel so that each of us chose or got assigned a character in the story and could read only the chapters in which his:her character was speaking – and therefore had to rely for the other chapters on the way the others retold them during our meetings (Jan Antonín was the only common character for all to read). We very soon realized in our

in the examination of his story in the penultimate chapter of the book: he is able to invisibly attend the tribunal session in Czechia proclaiming his innocence, but he does not feel only relief. The juridical reconstruction of his own story is in fact not enough – according to Jan Antonín – to change the memory of people:

> And that's all, perhaps. The people and history have further in mind Jan Antonín, the fascist. It is vain. Too complicated. People and history are complicated. So what's now. I should perhaps be happy. Yet I got accustomed after all these years to the feeling that the world is unjust and that you cannot reasonably talk to confusion. For the moment, I just feel exhausted and abandoned.
>
> [A to je asi tak všechno. Lidi i dějiny mají dál v hlavě Jana Antonína Baťu, fašistu, [...]. Je to marné. Příliš složité. Lidé i dějiny jsou složití. Tož co už včil. Měl bych se asi radovat. Po těch letech jsem si ale zvykl na pocit, že svět je nespravedlivý a se zmatkem se nedá rozumně domluvit. Zatím se cítím jenom vyčerpaný a opuštěný. (Pilátová 2017, 250)]

Jan Antonín's spirit is afraid to leave the world because he is aware of the fact that even the official memories about him could change again, that "in a couple of years another tribunal proclaims something different" ["za pár let nevyhlásí nějaký jiný soud něco úplně jiného" (Pilátová 2017, 250)]. He leaves eventually, in the last chapter, after having made an apparition in front of his granddaughter Dolores who is waiting for a storm on the edge of the Brazilian jungle – yet the final scene of Jan Antonín's definitive departure sounds like a confirmation of the idea that both one's own story and big History have something chaotic in their essence and cannot entirely make sense to human beings (and their spirits departing from life) in a way capable to satisfy them: "'So, girl, I'm going. It's up to you now,' grandfather says. What, he won't say. A lightning goes down the sky. As unaccountable, wild, cruel and beautiful as the half-tamed jungle all around." ["'Tož, děvčico, já du, včil je to na tobě,' říká děda. Co, to už neřekne. [...] Nebem sjede blesk. Stejně nevypočitatelný, divoký, krutý a krásný jako napůl zkrocená džungle všude kolem." (Pilátová 2017, 257)]

The analysis shows that *S Baťou v džungli* displays to its very end a complex family narrative that cannot be reduced to order and linearity – yet it would be a mistake to think that the novel stresses only discontinuities and gaps in the story of the Baťa family. I think on the opposite that an aim of the book is to show that this story is also marked – for better or worse – by a strong element of continuity: that is, the one represented by the charismatic and willful presence, *ante* and

discussions that the different characters were quite often speaking of the same things but saw them in different ways. I wish to thank my students and Markéta Pilátová, who attended our last meeting, for the insights they gave me on the novel.

post mortem, of the family head Jan Antonín, a beloved patriarch for whom every other member of the family is ready to restrain parts of her or his wishes in order to adapt to Jan Antonín's purposes. All of this may be related to the topics of history and violence, to the transnational aspects of the novel and last but not least to the elements of *realismo mágico* – the last one being in my opinion the very tool through which Pilátová introduces in her representation of the Baťa family a framing counterbalance to the diverse and quite fragmentary foundations of her narration, as they have been posed by the talks and archive work of the *nedělní metoda*.

I have already highlighted how Jan Antonín appears in *S Baťou v džungli* tormented by the violence he had to suffer on history's behalf when he decided to escape to Brazil during World War II and had to accept his exile as a permanent condition after his condemnation and expropriation by the Communists. Yet Jan Antonín's worry does not lead him – not in the beginning at least – to depression, for he is in fact depicted as very reactive to his situation, and he tries to defend himself to the point, as we have seen, that he is not willing to give up even after his death. Jan Antonín is anyway not the only character in the story remembering historic episodes of violence, for this is in fact realized on different levels: more or less all characters (also the ones not belonging to the family) do consider the Baťas (and themselves, if they are not family members) as victims of history's violence – of World War II and the Cold War – although they partly differ from each other in their attitude to remembering and repressing memories. Dolores is the only character who seems as reactive to violence and its memory as her grandfather (concerning the challenges he experienced during World War II and afterwards as well as the ones of her own later life in Brazil), while Edita and Ludmila, in the chapters narrated by them in the first person, oscillate between remembrance and repression of memories; Ljubodrag, Dolores' Serbian father who has spent World War II in Serbia and has been persecuted, does not want, for his part, to think of this period of his life at all. The more guarded approaches to the past Edita, Ludmila and Ljubodrag have in comparison to Jan Antonín, are explicitly expressed by their thoughts in which they admit that they consider Jan Antonín a little obsessive. They remark and even regret that he is too strongly tied to his Czechness to try to forget what has happened to him – especially the fact that the Communists defamed him and forced him to stay in Brazil: he therefore cannot entirely adapt to his new life and his new country, although he likes it, speaks Portuguese well and has good connections to politics. Ljubodrag cannot even understand Jan Antonín's attachment to the happy memories of his life, that is, the one connected to his activities as a visionary entrepreneur from the 1920s and 1930s who did not just want to be a businessman, but pretended to be a great reformer of modern work culture, basing it on an utopian idea of good capitalism as a moral force of progress. Such memories are from Ljubodrag's point of view a little arrogant and naïve at the same time.[5] Indeed, Edita's, Ludmila's and Ljubodrag's points of view confirm the multiperspectivity at the base of *S Baťou v džungli*, yet it is important to highlight that the differences among these characters and Jan Antonín do not lead to any interpersonal conflict: all these (and all other) characters try – despite their own wishes – to be always very supportive of Jan Antonín and his desire to continue his activity as a visionary entrepreneur in Brazil as well as to be rehabilitated in his native country. Edita and especially Ludmila accept to work for the family enterprise, although the former would have probably wanted to study and the latter to become a pianist; Ljubodrag is one of Jan Antonín's closest assistants in the company although he prefers to be a *fazendeiro* (and seems to be relieved when he can devote himself to that). Jan Antonín seems to take his family's support for granted during his life without truly realizing that his relatives do not necessarily see things as he does and make important personal sacrifices to adapt to his feelings and ideas. It is only after death that Jan Antonín's spirit understands this at least in part and acknowledges some of the efforts made by his family as well as some of their silent criticism of his attachment to and ideas of the past: "Yet no one has the chance to see himself from the distance until he dies. After that, everything is clearer. Mistakes are like red blazing exclamation marks and you cannot put them out" ["Nikdo ale nemá šanci vidět sám sebe z odstupu, dokud neumře. Pak je všechno jasnější. Chyby jsou jak červené plápolající vykřičníky a vy je nemůžete uhasit" (Pilátová 2017, 217)].

The second topic to be analyzed here, the question of transnationality, is implicit in the consideration that Jan Antonín cannot – according to some of his relatives – but see Brazil through the eyes of his Czech past, without really adapting to his new situation. Indeed, *S Baťou v džungli* represents the relationship of the different characters to their transnational experience in the same way as it puts on stage their relationship to history and violence: their attitudes are fashioned as diverse and potentially conflicting, but their divergences do not result in any explicit tension, since everyone is trying to support Jan Antonín. Edita and Ludmila struggle as much as their father between their Czech past, in which they were still teenagers, and their Brazilian present, yet they open themselves to Brazilianizing more thoroughly – and they do this not only because they are a generation younger than their father and can adapt more easily to the new situation, but also because

5 It is also true, on the other hand, that multiperspectivism gives to Pilátová the possibility to counter-relativize Edita's, Ludmila's and Ljubodrag's thoughts about Jan Antonín, who reveals in his own thoughts that he feels, at least partly, a strong affinity with Brazil, its nature and the sense of wilderness and possibility the country communicates (it is, as a matter of fact, an affinity at least partly based on a colonial gaze).

their father encourages their assimilation to the new culture since he needs their assistance in his new Brazilian business. The young Czech Edita, an intellectual *in spe*, and the young Czech Ludmila, a musician *in spe*, therefore have to disappear in favor of Edita, the Brazilian mother, and Ludmila, the Brazilian shoe designer and *fazendeira*, because their personalities do not really match with their father's expectations for their new Brazilian life. Dolores struggles, in turn, between her Brazilian identity and the Czech past of her family from the opposite direction: she is a Brazilian-born person who as a child idealizes Czechia and Czech culture as something very special and realizes as an adult firstly that coping with this heritage has been problematic and painful for the older generations of her family; secondly (after her first journey to Czechoslovakia in the 1980s), that the reality of Czech life is more ordinary than she thought; and thirdly, that her Czech identity and language are actually regional and not national, being *qua* family history very much connected with the Moravian city of Zlín and its surrounding. The analysis shows, thus, that the main characters in *S Baťou v džungli* think intensively about their own transnational problems, yet we see also that everyone decides to solve them alone and to hide every trouble in front of the relatives. Each family member is, in fact, acting as if fully identifying with Jan Antonín's narrative about the Baťas, that is, the narrative of the clever family of a clever Czech entrepreneur that has been forced with him to exile but is determined like him to continue the family business – and that is ready to accept as much assimilation to Brazilian culture as it is required for fulfilling the family's managerial project. It is only after Jan Antonín's death that the other family members begin to feel, at least partly and not always consciously, more independent in their transnational identities (Edita comes back to her Czechness, Dolores de-idealizes it).

It is an interesting aspect of *S Baťou v džungli* that its representation of the Baťa family (with its multiperspectivism sustained by the combination of oral memories, written sources and fictional invention) is used to give some internal dynamism to the picture of a family that seems, on the contrary, to be afraid of potential conflicts and mainly interested in a durable harmony based on compromises. Pilátová's display of such compromises shows, moreover, that the Baťas are, at the end of the day, a traditional family, i. e. an old patriarchal clan in which everyone and particularly women accept to support Jan Antonín solving his or her own internal struggles in favor of the patriarch's needs.

Realismo mágico – to come to the last aspect of the novel I wanted to highlight – plays a tricky role in the novel since, on the one hand, it corrects Jan Antonín's patriarchal attitude, without, on the other hand, endangering the consent-seeking attitude on which the Baťa's family life is based: in fact, Jan Antonín's magic-realist existence after death does not work in the novel as an element of disruption (*à la* Parkinson Zamora and Faris, or Quayson), but rather as a cathartic element of re-composition that allows the family to go further on the path of harmonization. The play with *realismo mágico* namely gives Jan Antonín the possibility to assist as a spirit in the future life of his relatives, to revise at least partly his self-centered behavior, and, in a sense, to silently apologize to the members of his family for how he egocentrically bound them to his needs. Jan Antonín's approach towards the other characters is, albeit *post mortem*, an acknowledgment of their adjustments to his position during and after his life.

One can wonder, given the special genesis of the novel by means of the *nedělní metoda*, whether Pilátová's decision to tinge Jan Antonín's spirit with a touch of regret can be read as an answer to her friend Dolores' conscious and unconscious wish to frame her family history in a meaningful way, finally expressing underground tensions which have marked her family for decades but at the same time solving them thanks to the remorse of Jan Antonín, as expressed, through the means of magical realism, after his death. This supposition may indeed be plausible – but it has to be noticed that *S Baťou v džungli* does not make out of his main character a fully repented patriarch on the way to completely revise his role in the story of his family. Jan Antonín may think to have sometimes been mistaken in his conviction to be a progressive and attentive man moved by the right visions – especially in relation to the women of his family to whom he granted education and working experience, thinking of this as very modern and emancipatory, even though his concessions were still expressions of a patriarchal way of thinking. Yet there still is a certain satisfaction in the way Jan Antonín recalls the limits of his own visions:

> I loved and honored the women around me, I sometimes even listened to them, but as if I did actually not see them. They lived with me, but I was living in my own world, much more important and adventurous. In the world of hunters and big predators. Of players and history movers. There I belonged. And Mrs. Baťa and my daughters were allowed to accompany me there. They might provide me peace at home. Comfort me, hear me. And it was perfect, if they on top of that also played the piano.
>
> [Ženské kolem sebe jsem miloval a ctil, někdy je dokonce i poslechnul, ale jako bych je vlastně neviděl. Žily se mnou, ale já žil ve svém mnohem důležitějším a dobrodružnějším světě. Světě lovců a velkých predátorů. Hráčů a hybatelů dějin. Tam jsem patřil. A paní Baťová a dcery mě tam směly doprovázet. Směly mi poskytnout klid domova. Utěšit mě, vyslechnout mě. A když mi k tomu ještě hrály na klavír, bylo to dokonalé. (Pilátová 2017, 217)][6]

6 I can just briefly mention here that I have talked to some readers of the books who were not satisfied with the perspective from which Jan Antonín Baťa is presented in the novel exactly because they expected more elements of criticism from the author's side in the text. These interpreters argue that the choice to retell Jan Antonín's story from within the point of view of different family

4 Constrained Agencies: Family Issues in the Literature of the Twenty-First Century

I would like to conclude this article with some considerations that take the *dénouement* of *S Baťou v džungli* as their starting point. The ending of the novel has indeed something positive about it since Jan Antonín's spirit eventually makes peace with his past after the official rehabilitation of his memory in Czechia and accepts to go beyond this world, in a way also releasing his family. My impression is, though, – as I have already suggested in my textual analysis – that the conclusion of the story is not univocally optimistic if one considers that catharsis is possible for Jan Antonín only *post mortem*, whereas the lives of his daughters Edita and Ludmila, albeit not tormented by the violence of history as much as the one of their father, are nevertheless marked by the compromises and renunciations they make to help him. Dolores is the only character in Pilátová's novel for whom catharsis comes when she is still alive (although already an old woman) – yet the catharsis of the story is, as I have shown above, also ambivalent, since it means both for Jan Antonín and Dolores the acceptance that one cannot really change history to one's well-being but has to learn how to cope with it, knowing that it is "unaccountable, wild, cruel and beautiful as the half tamed jungle all around". On the whole, one does not have the impression that the agency of the characters in *S Baťou v džungli* has many possibilities to assert itself in relation to what they

members and friends does not prevent – notwithstanding the differences between single characters – a certain social bias of the narrative perspective: for all members of the Baťa family speak, all considered, for a certain upper class milieu and its *Weltanschauung* based on the connection between Liberalism and patriarchy (whereas the family friends are either upper class themselves or admirers). This criticism overlooks in my opinion some relativization of the upper-class mentality carried out in the novel by certain characters (for example Ljubodrag), and the fact that important female characters such as Ludmila and especially Dolores do distance themselves, at least partly, from Jan Antonín's patriarchal thinking, after his death. Yet it is understandable that the critical readers I spoke with very much insist on the fact that the story recalls the violence of Brazilian history in the second half of the twentieth century until today only very sporadically and only from Dolores' perspective – which reveals itself to be the one of a Brazilian *fazendeira* critical of, but not hostile to the right wing military dictatorship of the years 1964–1985, and who is openly in conflict with the movement of the *sem terra* that she describes as vandals wanting to destroy her property (Pilátová 2017, 143–144; 248). I nonetheless wonder if this critical position is aware of the fact that introducing another point of view on these issues would mean breaking off with the *nedělní metoda*, part of which also implies that *S Baťou v džungli* is also a product of the friendship between the author and Dolores – and this circumstance does not make it very easy to write from points of view completely alien to Dolores, even if Pilátová had wanted to do it.

undergo: the violence of history (past or present) and the structure of family constellations in the novel are evidence of the limits of self-assertion.

The relativization of agency that characterizes *S Baťou v džungli* is for me all the more interesting because it seems to question the above-discussed interpretation of *realismo mágico* as an aesthetics deeply believing in the transformative potential of humans and culture: the story seems, in other words, to resonate more with Denning's view, as when he remarks that magic-realist literature often puts the failure of emancipation struggles on stage – than with Quayson's view, when he suggests that *realismo mágico* opens up to the fecundity of the unexpected. Pilátová's novel reveals itself insofar as an interesting starting point to reflect, out of a literary work, upon the divergent interpretations of realist-magic aesthetics as they have been codified in the scholarly reception: in my opinion, Denning is in fact partly right when he states that *realismo mágico* is not only optimistic in its perspectives, since it is true that even a vital text of *realismo mágico* such as García Márquez's *Cien años de soledad* depicts nothing but the path from a village's and a family's exuberant life to death and destruction (to mention again Moretti and his interpretation of *Cien años de soledad* in Moretti 1994, 219–235). Yet I do also think that Quayson is right when he highlights, on the contrary, the disruptive potential of *realismo mágico* – for even if García Marquez' novel may not lead to final emancipation of the world it is describing, as Denning stresses, it is nevertheless an example of the transformative potential that magic-realist literature grants to its characters: figures such as the big patriarch José Arcadio Buendía as well as other characters show that humans in García Márquez' work may not change things forever but they can nonetheless shape the world for a certain time with their magical-realist wishes and powers. At first glance, Pilátová seems to be, in this respect, quite close to García Márquez – for her patriarch Jan Antonín has somehow the strength of a José Arcadio. Yet Pilátová has in my opinion an approach to *realismo mágico* which is at the end more similar to Denning than to Quayson: the protagonists of García Márquez' novel can in fact impact their surroundings much stronger than every member and friend of the Baťa family – and even Jan Antonín, the only character of *S Baťou v džungli* who possesses the magic-realist power to exist further in this world after death, does not succeed in augmenting his influence on things, but he learns on the contrary to (partly) relativize himself and the importance of his strength. His internal development as a spirit makes him, thus, actually more similar to the other characters of the novel, who from the very beginning try to cope with Jan Antonín's idiosyncratic vitalism through their readiness to make compromises to overcome the past and accept their new life as migrants. Pilátová appears, therefore, to be not only more cautious about the disruptive potential of *realismo mágico* than Quayson or García Márquez, but also seems to relativize the one-sided positivity of such disruptive vitalism, showing how much people less uncompromising than a Jan Antonín/José Arcadio have to renounce in order to adapt to the will of such charismatic characters (and yet it is also possible to argue that Pilátová is in a certain sense more optimistic than García Márquez since it is exactly the sobering approach to *realismo mágico* of *S Baťou v džungli* that allows a relative catharsis for Jan Antonín in the end – who, as a spirit, has the possibility to critically reflect upon his life and to cope with his mistakes, reaching a sense of relief that is missing in the conclusion of *Cien años de soledad*).

One can ask whether Pilátová's (critical?) relativization of the strong human agency implied by many classic magic-realist texts is somehow related to the fact that she is an author of the twenty-first century writing some decades after García Márquez and inclined to innovate the aesthetics of authors like him (notwithstanding the fact that there are foundational texts of *realismo mágico* fashioning much less strong agencies than García Márquez, as for example the already mentioned Rulfo). *S Baťou v džungli* has indeed characteristics that are not to be found in the classics of *realismo mágico*: for Pilátová shows herself very interested not only in the power of the fantastic imagination intermingling with realism, but also in the material traces left by previous times – like the letters, diaries, poems etc. she found in the family archives of the Baťas and in the oral memory of Dolores, which she puts together in the reconstruction work of the *nedělní metoda*. Pilátová even strengthens, integrating archive sources to magic-realist elements in her text, the gnoseological play with the readers' consciousness at the basis of *realismo mágico* of which I spoke in the second part of the article: for the readers of *S Baťou v džungli* have to decide how much credit and which meaning they should give to Jan Antonín's afterthoughts *post mortem* and to his path towards relief, that is, to fantastic occurrences that are in *S Baťou v džungli* magically-realistically stated as perfectly normal in their equivalence to reality – yet which do not completely match with the sources Pilátová is basing her story on. Readers have thus to decide what they think of Pilátová's integration of an archive-based story through the reality/fantasy ontological equivalence of *realismo mágico* and its gnoseological indifference to the accountability of such an equivalence – and it is not certain that everyone will interpret this mixture as I did above, namely as a kind gift to a friend, Dolores, to whom the author offers a (minor) narrative catharsis imagining her last intimate meeting with the departing soul of the finally half-pacified Jan Antonín. *S Baťou v džungli* is a complex piece of literature for it makes, I think, a conscious use of the gnoseological irritation of the readers caused by the magic-realist features of the story: they may identify with the small catharsis at the end of the book, they can even really wish for it to come true, for Dolores' and Jan Antonín' sake – yet they can also decide not to forget that such a catharsis is only possible as long as the equation of reality and fantasy postulated by *realismo mágico* is maintained. Some readers could, however, find the whole construct one-sidedly in favor of Baťa, and historically not critical enough (see footnote 7).

One can have different ideas about the way *S Baťou v džungli* combines archival research and magic-realist elements, yet I would like to emphasize again that it shows undeniably a greater explicit interest in working with historical sources than the *realismo mágico* of the twentieth century (in which the work with such sources is, if there is one, rather implicit). Some interpreters stress that many authors of contemporary literature share with Pilátová a similar interest in the reconstruction of the past through sources, and they consider this fact as an overcoming of postmodern sensibility whose aesthetics is, according to them, more related to a playful invention of the past than to its reconstruction – yet they also stress that this new form of realism does not forget the lessons of postmodernity since the reconstruction of the past is always presented in this literature as the reconstruction of what might have been and it is eventually diversified through multiple perspectives and possibilities, as is indeed also the case for Pilátová (Donnarumma 2014, see for an application of this perspective on South American literature Welge 2021).

I cannot elaborate here on the question whether the interest in the reconstruction of history that one can detect in the literature of the twenty-first century can be considered as already post-postmodern. I think that it depends on how postmodernity is defined – and I define it, as I have already argued in the second part of this article, as Ceserani, Zima and other scholars do, as the epoch in which culture gets gradually attuned to work without the fundamental horizon of universal master narratives one can trust in (whereby, according to the interpreters, this may be seen both as a chance and as something inevitable but not necessarily positive). Nowadays culture is still getting used to a world without reliable universal *récits*, and we are therefore, from my point of view, still in the era of postmodernity – but this is not the point I really want to argue in my conclusions. I would rather like to limit myself to the suggestion that the case of *S Baťou v džungli* illustrates that the interest showed by recent literature in reconstructing the past does not exclude that literature can intermingle this reconstructive work based on actual traces (like the ones Pilátová collects thanks to her *nedělní metoda*) with postmodern aesthetics like the magic-realist one. One could conversely claim that also in the second half of the twentieth century postmodern literature was not always just playfully fictionalizing history but sometimes also at least partly dealing with its reconstruction on the basis of traces of the past. It is surely an interesting realization, though, that, given the coexistence of both approaches before and after 2000, there has actually been a shift in emphasis from the fiction to the 'faction.'

I would like to devote my last remark to another shift in (not only) literary culture which can be observed in Pilátová's novel, too: I am alluding to the very fact that the death of universal master narratives stated by postmodernity is nowadays less considered as a chance for radical change and emancipation than it was in the last decades of the twentieth century – when the optimistic voices were probably stronger than the skeptical ones. One seems today to be more resigned: people know that there are no master narratives to believe in, but they also think that they cannot live in eternal fluidity because one lacks the energy either to truly sustain such an unstable state of being or to oppose the stabilizing instances always present in the human condition. It is therefore not by chance that *S Baťou v džungli* tells a story that highlights the constraints forced upon its characters' agency – a story of compromises which make the life of a family practicable although not entirely satisfying (even after death, although Jan Antonín reaches some relief at the end).

It is perhaps significant, regarding the relativization of human agency in *S Baťou v džungli*, that this novel deals with an 'old' family – in the sense that the Baťas have a quite traditional patriarchal structure. I am highlighting this circumstance because one could have the reasonable expectation that at least part of the contemporary literature dealing with non-patriarchal families – like the feminist or queer ones and the so-called families of election – may be more charged with an optimistic commitment than Pilátová's novel. This belief in the emancipatory potential tied to new and alternative family narratives can be seen as an example of those local/group utopias which I have discussed in the second part of the article as a typical phenomenon for postmodernity.[7] Such narratives are particularly apt to have a utopian charge because the public discourse about feminist, queer and several sorts of 'chosen' family constellations is *de facto* a new cultural horizon of our present and of our projections on the future (although one could, as always, find older practices and discourses that can be considered as predecessors of the feminist/queer/chosen families). Time will tell if these narratives, too, as other local/group narratives developed by postmodernity, will in the future undergo a process of self-relativization similar to the one experienced *post mortem* by Jan Antonín Baťa in relation to his own family model and its significance for society in *S Baťou v džungli*: Jan Antonín must in fact realize that his still patriarchal idea of the family and his vision of society are not as progressive as he thinks, and that they do not lead to a perfect utopia, but rather restrain the role of women (among others) even if they intend to enhance it – yet he always considers his intentions good, although he admits some inadequacies of his family model, regarding them, on the other hand, as an inevitable part of the constitutive fallacy of mortal beings ("yet no one has the chance to see himself from the distance until he dies"). It is thus also possible that one day the new family narratives of today like the feminist/queer/chosen ones – which are presently sometimes depicted as utopian by their supporters and that are often condemned as

7 See the contribution by Pablo Valdivia in this volume on the criticism of the patriarchal model of family, including the patriarchal schemes implicit in many magic-realist texts.

dystopian by their opponents – will be considered just as well-intended, partly positive and partly fallacious models. Time will also tell whether and which new family constellations will eventually succeed the by then de-utopianized non-patriarchal families in carrying on the utopian impulse of human culture, which seems to be no less constitutive for human beings than their fallibility.

(The author would like to thank Owain Griffith, Hannah Kusak and Hannah Morris for the linguistic revision of the article. Very long sentences and other stylistic oddities are according to his taste, not the revisors'.)

Bibliography

Allende, Isabel. *La casa de los espíritus*. Barcelona: Plaza & Janeś, 1982.

Ceserani, Remo. *Raccontare il postmoderno*. Torino: Bollati Boringhieri, 1997.

Denning, Michael. "The Novelists' International." *The Novel*. Vol. 1: *History, Geography, and Culture*. Ed. Franco Moretti. Princeton: Princeton UP, 2006. 703–725.

Doležel, Lubomír. *Heterocosmica: fiction and possible worlds*. Baltimore: John Hopkins, 1998.

Donnarumma, Raffaele. *Ipermodernità. Dove va la narrativa contemporanea*. Bologna: Il Mulino, 2014.

Eliade, Mircea. *Das Heilige und das Profane*. Reinbek bei Hamburg: Rowohlt, 1957.

García Márquez, Gabriel. *Cien años de soledad*. Buenos Aires: Sudamericana, 1967.

Görözdi, Judit, and Radoslav Passia. Eds. "Magic Realism in Central European Literatures." *World Literature Studies* 2.8 (2016).

Jan Antonín Baťa – život a dílo, pokračovatel práce Tomáše Bati. Mezinárodní conference. Sborník. Zlín 2.–3. května 2007. Zlín: Statutární město Zlín, 2007.

Meyrink, Gustav. *Der Golem*. Leipzig/München: Kurt Wolff, 1915.

Moretti, Franco. Ed. *The Novel*. 2 vols. Princeton: Princeton UP, 2006.

Moretti, Franco. *Opere mondo. Saggio sulla forma epica dal* Faust *a* Cent'anni di solitudine. Torino: Einaudi, 1994.

Parkinson Zamora, Lois, and Wendy B. Faris. Eds. *Magical Realism. Theory, History, Community*. Durham: Duke, 1995.

Pilátová, Markéta. *S Baťou v džungli*. Praha: Torst, 2017.

Quayson, Ato. "Fecundities of the Unexpected. Magical Realism, Narrative, and History." *The Novel*. Vol. 1. *History, Geography, and Culture*. Ed. Franco Moretti. Princeton: Princeton UP, 2006. 726–756.

Rulfo, Juan. *Pedro Páramo*. Ciudad de México: Fondo de Cultura Económica, 1955.

Todorov, Tzvetan. *Introduction à la littérature fantastique*. Paris: Seuil, 1970.

Welge, Jobst. "Historical Reference and (Auto)Fiction in the Recent Latin American Novel." *Fictionality, Factuality, and Reflexivity Across Discourses and Media*. Ed. Erika Fülöp. Berlin: De Gruyter, 2021. 138–151.

Zima, Peter V. *Moderne/Postmoderne*. Tübingen: Francke, 1997.

Zourek, Michal. *Československo očima latinsko-amerických intelektuálů 1947–1959*. Praha: Runa, 2018.

Jobst Welge

Autofiction, Transnationality, and Family Constellations in the Work of Eduardo Halfon

All of my books are intimately related, like brothers who live far away.
Eduardo Halfon, "In Conversation: Eduardo Halfon" (2018a)

1 Literary Form, (Non-)Belonging, and *El boxeador polaco* (2008)

When Eduardo Halfon (*1971, Guatemala) entered the Spanish-speaking and international literary scene in the early years of the twenty-first century, he was part of a somewhat broader 'memorialist' trend among younger Jewish-Latin American writers (often members of the second post-Holocaust generation) who used literature to delve into their individual family stories and ask questions about their Jewish identity.[1] Typically, these authors use hybrid literary forms that confound the boundary between reality and imagination, such as autofiction (Moszczyńska 2022, 136; 190). The term autofiction is generally understood as being based on the intersection of two distinct pacts of reading, the one of life-writing and the other one of fiction, where the name/person of the author and the 'fictional' character coincide (Marchese 2021, 183).

Halfon's work is concerned with the author's Jewish identity, as it is refracted in a series of various family constellations that link together not only different members of the family but also the distinct literary articulations in Halfon's short stories and (short) novels. The brevity of the literary form (the novels rarely exceed about 120 pages) undoubtedly favor the impression that the individual texts correspond with each other like the pieces of a puzzle: a puzzle of texts and of family relations. Far from the idea of the traditional family novel, or even the autofictional

1 For a useful, brief survey of autobiographical forms and/or (transgenerational) family narratives in Jewish-Latin American literature, including, for instance, *Las genealogías* (1981) [*The Family Tree* (1991)] by the Mexican writer Margo Glantz, or *O que os cegos estão sonhando?* (2012) [*What are the Blind Men Dreaming?* (2016)] by the Brazilian Noemi Jaffe, see Lockhart 2022, 338; for a reference to Halfon, see 343.

Jobst Welge, Leipzig University

https://doi.org/10.1515/9783111208664-010

family saga of Jewish diaspora (such as Andrés Neuman's *Una vez Argentina* (2003) [Once Upon Argentina]), Halfon's fictions tend to focus on single episodes and specific relations between the autofictional narrator and individual members of his widely and internationally disseminated family. For instance, and broadly speaking, the novel *Duelo* (2017) [*Mourning* (2018)] is primarily concerned with the relationship to his brother; the novel *Monasterio* (2014) [*Monastery* (2014)] takes its cue from the relationship to his sister and maternal grandfather; the novel *Canción* (2021) [*Canción* (2022)] focuses on his paternal grandfather; a recent collection of essays (*Un hijo cualquiera* [2022] [An ordinary son]) is, as the title suggests, partly concerned with paternity, the relation to his own son.

As autofictional works, Halfon's novels and stories exemplify the idea of postmemory, a concept introduced by Marianne Hirsch (1997), in that they deal with the transmission of traumatic memories to the second and third generation. Moreover, as some critics have suggested, given the multicultural family inheritance of Halfon's family and his own nomadic existence, these works are concerned with the formation of a cosmopolitan identity (Campisi 2018; Kobyłecka-Piwońska 2018, 366). The possible references to various sub-orientations of contemporary literature (autofiction, literature about Jewish identity, Latin American literature) underscore the kaleidoscopic quality of Halfon's literary project, which thus situates itself squarely in the 'global,' transnational orientation of contemporary literature (Kobyłecka-Piwońska 2018, 368; Welge 2022).

What distinguishes Halfon's literary project from these broader tendencies of contemporary ('Latin American') literature, then, is not the fact that the self's relationship to family and history brings to the fore questions of origin, belonging, or cultural identity, nor the structural device of the self on a quest for the familial past, but rather the insistently serial character of this endeavor, whereby individual texts approach the relation to specific (constellations of) family members, while intersecting with parallel narratives in other texts. The cumulative effect of this approach is certainly to reinforce the importance of 'family,' yet at the same time the very notion of 'family' gets thereby fragmented and multiplied.

Eduardo Halfon's parents were born in Guatemala, yet, ten years old, he moved with his family to the United States – before moving back to Guatemala for eight years as a professor of literature. He now lives in Nebraska and frequently visits Guatemala and Europe. While English thus has become his second language, Halfon writes exclusively in Spanish and therefore apparently has to be situated primarily in an Ibero-American literary field. But things are not that easy, for language does not in itself guarantee a solid sense of belonging, and in fact the author's (and his family's) cultural and national affiliations encompass the Jewish, the Arab, the Polish, and the Guatemalan. In fact, the recurrent theme of displacement, the living 'between worlds' in Halfon's fictions is echoed by the "mobile cognitive cartography" of the literary form itself (Ortiz Wallner 2014, 34). Accordingly, Nicolás Campisi has grouped Halfon's literary persona (especially in *Monasterio*) with a series of other contemporary 'Latin American' writers whose works feature "globetrotting protagonists" who embody "a state of precarious homelessness" and the "temporality of transit" (2018, 114; 115).[2]

Campisi is referring here to a concept developed by Mariano Siskind, who has argued that the Heideggerian notion of dwelling has become entirely anachronistic in contemporary culture. Although Siskind is careful to insist that forced migration and displacement are experiences that should not be universalized, he writes that, "dwelling is impossible for everyone everywhere, no matter the bodily or world-historical scale of the experience of dislocation," as a consequence of "the structural undoing of the world and its symbolic horizons" (2018, 114). This trait he identifies as characteristic for "many of the most interesting contemporary narratives whose aesthetic contributions consist in a programmatic drive to dislocate the possibility of their own Latin American, national, or generally identitarian reterritorializations" (2018, 215). Not surprisingly, among the list of authors embodying this aesthetic of non-belonging he also lists Halfon (2018, 216).

While Halfon's narrator-protagonist is certainly dislocated, the serial exploration of affective bonds with family members or multiple identities holds out the possibility, if not of "dwelling," of establishing temporary or singular points of contact, or retrievals of origins and cultural belonging, across borders and nations. While this typically involves interpersonal contacts, memories, travels, or archival research, there is also often a margin of mystery, of the unexplained. This ambivalence can be illustrated with the short story "The Polish Boxer," included in the homonymous collection *The Polish Boxer* (2012) [*El boxeador polaco* (2008)], Halfon's breakthrough publication, translated into many languages. Here the young self of the autofictional narrator 'Eduardo'[3] has been intrigued by the five digits impressed on his maternal, Polish grandfather's arm. If the grandfather has long surrounded this traumatic fact with silence and the 'fiction' – or "joke" (Halfon 2012, 78) ["broma" (Halfon 2019, 87)] – that the numbers are a memory aid for his phone number, young Eduardo himself has long indulged in a 'game' to imagine all kinds of fantastic stories how the grandfather would have received the tattoo by the Germans during their occupation of Poland:

2 Campisi mentions writers such as João Gilberto Noll, Julián Fuks, Sergio Chejfec, César Aira, Valeria Luiselli.

3 In the course of this essay, I will consistently refer to Halfon's autofictional narrator as 'Eduardo,' although he appears not always under this name in the works themselves.

> I [...] suddenly realized that in my childhood game, in each of my boyish fantasies, I had imagined him already old, already a grandfather. As if he'd been born a grandfather, or as if he'd aged once and for all at the very moment of receiving that number, which I was now examining so meticulously. (Halfon 2012, 80)

> [[Y] de pronto caí en la cuenta de que en aquel juego de niño, en cada una de aquellas fantasías de niño, me lo había imaginado ya viejo, ya abuelo. Como si hubiese nacido un abuelo o como si hubiese envejecido para siempre en el momento mismo que recibió aquel número que yo ahora examinaba con tanta meticulosidad. (Halfon 2019, 89)]

The young Eduardo is thus unable to imagine the past experience of the grandfather, even if the notion of the instantly aged figure suggests an inkling of the unimaginable. The grandfather's deliberate silence about the past and his assertion that his tattoo represents his telephone number, is the traumatic kernel that haunts the consciousness of the next generation: "For Halfon, the image of the tattoo embodies the affective link between him and his grandfather's unknown past, and its persistence in his memory demonstrates Halfon's tenacious desire to uncover secrets buried within his grandfather and now himself" (Gartenberg 2021, 131). Although the grandfather eventually gets around to tell his grandson that he got the number in the concentration camp of Sachsenhausen, there remains an area of not-knowing. The grandfather tells him that his life was saved thanks to a council by a Jewish boxer from Łódź, who told him which exact words to use in front of the authorities. Yet these words remain shrouded in mystery, and, based on this information, the narrator has to imagine everything else: "I tried to imagine the face of the Polish boxer, imagine his fists, imagine the possible white pockmark the bullet had made after going through his neck, imagine his words in Polish that managed to save my grandfather's life" (Halfon 2012, 91) ["Intenté imaginarme el rostro del boxeador polaco, imaginarme sus puños, imaginarme el posible chisguetazo blanco que había hecho la bala después de atravesar su nuca, imaginarme sus palabras en polaco que lograron salvarle la vida a mi abuelo" (Halfon 2019, 100–101)]. This oscillation between given information and the imaginary projection of how things might have been, can be seen as a meta-literary reflection on the nature of autofiction.[4]

The short story "The Polish Boxer" is the symbolic center of the volume, and even as some sort of allusion to the grandfather occurs in every single one of the nine stories of the collection, making it a sort of leitmotiv, these stories otherwise

---

4 A symptomatic response to the 'unreliability' of the genre of autofiction is an article by a Polish journalist, who retraces some of the details of Halfon's visit in Łódź, as mentioned in the short story "Oh Ghetto my Love" (included in Halfon 2018b, 37–68), only to be startled that some of the details appear to be invented; Adamczewska 2023. For this reference I am indebted to Anna Artwińska, as well as for other critical response to this essay.

center on different aspects of Eduardo's identity or affiliations (from indigenous people to gypsies). In this sense the volume as a whole can be said to be programmatic for the poetics of Halfon's subsequent works (Laorden 2016, 592; van Hecke 2020, 23). In a short preface to the new edition of the book (ten years after the publication of the original version), the author refers to the narrator as "that other Eduardo Halfon, who at that time was barely born and who still accompanies me today" ["ese otro Eduardo Halfon, que en aquel entonces apenas nacía y que hoy aún me acompaña" (Halfon 2019, 11)].[5] The sentence encapsulates at once the autofictional nature of the work (the difference/identity between narrator and author) and the serial nature of the literary project.

This maternal grandfather, then, who escaped from Auschwitz and later settled in Guatemala, occupies the symbolic center of Halfon's work. For instance, the passage from "The Polish Boxer" reoccurs almost verbatim in the later novel *Monasterio* (2014): "I washed my hands, thinking about my grandfather, about Auschwitz, about the five green numbers tattooed on his forearm that throughout my entire childhood I'd believed were there, as he himself had told me, so that he wouldn't forget his phone number" (Halfon 2014b, 109) ["Luego me lavé las manos pensando en mi abuelo, en Auschwitz, en los cinco dígitos verdes tatuados en su antebrazo que durante toda mi niñez creí que estaban allí para que, como él mismo me decía, no olvidara su número de teléfono." (Halfon 2014a, 62)]. The repetition of scenes, phrases, and figures across several literary works creates an effect of dissolved boundaries, as if they all were parts, or facets of a narrative continuum.[6] In the remaining part of this essay, I will look more closely at two novels (*Monasterio, Canción*), in order to discuss how specific familial constellations are foregrounded (through emplotment and imagery) to both interrogate the narrator's identity and to suggest relations of proximity or comparison between different times and locations.

2 *Monasterio* (2014): Sister, Maternal Grandfather

Monasterio (2014) is a novel divided into four chapters. It begins with the voyage of the autofictional narrator, together with his brother, to Jerusalem, on the occasion of his younger sister's wedding to an orthodox Jew from Brooklyn, his parents having also travelled to Israel from Guatemala some days before. The novel's dedication,

5 Unless otherwise noted, all translations are my own.

6 As Kobyłecka-Piwońska has observed (2022, 307), this intertextual repetition of scenes and names also reinforces the impression of autobiographical and historical veracity.

"For my sister, for my brother" (Halfon 2014b, 5) ["Para mi hermana, para mi hermano" (Halfon 2014a, 7)] is enough to ensure the autofictional contract with the reader, alongside an allusion to the writer's former training as an "engineer" (Halfon 2014b, 22) ["ingeniero" (Halfon 2014a, 25)]. In the initial scene of the novel, having arrived at Ben Gurion airport in Tel Aviv, the narrator describes his sister as being estranged from her family, changing her name legally into the Hebrew version, while the narrator and the rest of the secularized family have in turn become alienated by what they see as her excessive religious devotion:

> She'd been living in a women's yeshiva in Jerusalem, studying the Torah and other rabbinical texts, for nearly two years. At first we all thought it was just a touch of Zion fever or Hebrew fever, or some juvenile obsession with finding a deeper manifestation of our grandparents' religion, and that it would eventually pass. But soon her discourse began to evolve. In letters, in phone calls, her words were no longer her own. (Halfon 2014b, 12)
>
> [Llevaba ella casi dos años viviendo y estudiando la Torá y otros textos rabínicos en una yeshivá de mujeres en Jerusalén. Al principio todos pensamos que era nada más una leve fiebre sionista o hebraica, un arrebato juvenil por encontrar manifestaciones más profundas de la religión de nuestros abuelos, y que ya se le pasaría. Pero pronto empezó a cambiar su discurso. En cartas, en llamadas, sus palabras ya no eran suyas. (Halfon 2014a, 14)]

In contrast to his sister's reconnecting to her Jewish origins in Israel, the narrator makes fun of, or denies his own Jewish heritage. Moreover, the initial encounter with Israel does not respond to any expectations of 'home': Eduardo finds himself in places that, starting with the no-place of the airport, fly in the face of clear categories of belonging. Thus, having settled in the hotel in Jerusalem, he remarks: "I was a bit disappointed to note that nothing in there looked like Israel. It could have been any restaurant, in any hotel. It had the same decorations and furniture and maybe even the same background music as any other cheap hotel." (Halfon 2014b, 21–22) ["Me decepcionó un poco notar que nada allí dentro parecía Israel. Era un restaurante cualquiera, de un hotel cualquiera, con la misma decoración y mobiliario y hasta la misma música de fondo que cualquier otro hotel barato." (Halfon 2014a, 24)] At the airport, he has accidentally met an old acquaintance, Tamara, now working as a Lufthansa stewardess. The second chapter begins with his memory of how he had initially met Tamara (he recognized her as Israeli by her accent) in a "Scottish" bar in Antigua Guatemala: "It wasn't actually a Scottish bar, but an ordinary bar in Antigua, Guatemala, that served only beer and was called (or at least known as) the Scottish bar." (Halfon 2014b, 104) ["No era aquél un bar escocés, sino un bar cualquiera en Antigua Guatemala que sólo servía cerveza y que se llamaba (o le decían) el bar escocés." (Halfon 2014a, 57)] Even with this random detail, the question of national belonging and identity is brought to the fore.

To the question of a taxi driver whether he is Jewish, Eduardo answers "sometimes" (Halfon 2014b, 23) ["a veces" (Halfon 2014a, 26)], and to Tamara he quips that he is "no longer" Jewish, that he has "retired" (Halfon 2014b, 105) ["Ya no soy judío, [...] me jubilé." (Halfon 2014a, 58)]. To the further question by the cab driver, whether he is Arab, he replies in the negative. Yet, confronted with the cab driver's exclamation that all Arabs are bad and have to be killed (uttered in "deficient English" [Halfon 2014b, 24] ("pobre inglés" [Halfon 2014a, 26]), yet rendered in Spanish in the novel), 'Halfon' cannot but think about his family history that, through its various cultural crossings and intermingling, defies the logic of us-versus-them: "I was going to tell him that my grandfather had been an Arab Jew from Beirut, and my grandmother an Arab Jew from Alexandria, and my other grandmother an Arab Jew from Aleppo, and so that made me a little Arab too – three parts Arab, in fact, one part Polish –" (Halfon 2014b, 24) ["Iba a decirle que mi abuelo había sido un árabe judío de Beirut, y mi abuela una árabe judía de Alejandría, y mi otra abuela una árabe judía de Alepo, y que eso entonces me hacía a mi también un poco árabe – tres partes árabe, de hecho, una parte polaco –" (Halfon 2014a, 26)]. Following this scene, Eduardo further muses on the family genealogy: his maternal grandmother is the daughter of Syrians who have escaped to South America, and due to an itinerary life, had children who were born in Panama, Cuba, and Guatemala; his paternal grandfather and his seven brothers and sisters fled Beirut, and settled each in another place of the world – the grandfather first living in Paris but then settling in Guatemala as well (Halfon 2014a, 28–29; Halfon 2014b, 26–27).

In Antigua Guatemala Eduardo had also met a friend of Tamara, Yael, whose last name, Tenenbaum, happens to be also the last name of Eduardo's mother's side of the family. This coincidence leads him to imagine "an entire novel about two Polish siblings who believed their family had been exterminated and then, after not seeing each other for sixty years, were suddenly reunited thanks to two of their grandchildren, one a Guatemalan writer and one an Israeli hippie" (Halfon 2014b, 106[7]) ["una novela entera sobre dos hermanos polacos que creían a toda su familia exterminada, pero que de pronto se encontraban, tras sesenta años sin verse, gracias a dos de sus nietos, un escritor guatemalteco y una hippie israelí" (Halfon 2014a, 59)]. Apart from the exploration of 'real' family connections, Halfon engages sometimes in such imaginary or comic-sounding asides, as if to offset the severity and topicality associated with literary representations of the Holocaust and its traumatic afterlife.

7 Curiously, this quote from the English version (from the chapter "White Smoke," rather late in the novel) corresponds to the second chapter of the original version. Cf. also note 8.

In any event, the sojourn in Israel sets in motion the narrator's coming to terms with his own family's genealogy and, by extension, his relation to his Jewish identity. For instance, while in the vicinity of the wailing wall, he refers to it as "that *final vestige* of the Temple of the Jews, of my ancestors." (Halfon 2014b, 29; emphasis mine) ["ese *último vestigio* del templo de los judíos, de mis antepasados" (Halfon 2014a, 31; emphasis mine)]. Amidst all the turbulence around the wall, he says that except for being reminded of a song by *The Cure*, he does not "feel" (Halfon 2014b, 30) ["sentir" (Halfon 2014a, 33)] anything but the stone. Yet in the memorial-associative logic of the narrative, this brings him to remember his past contact with another wall in another city, where he similarly didn't feel anything – namely his touching "the *last remnants* of what had once been the wall of the Warsaw ghetto." (Halfon 2014b, 30; emphasis mine) ["el *último vestigio* de lo que fue el muro del gueto de Varsovia." (Halfon 2014a, 33; emphasis mine)]

The bodily contact with these material remnants apparently remains insignificant for Eduardo. Yet precisely the associative connection between the two experiences, underscored by the construction "the last vestige," goes to show that they are part of a skeptical, unresolved, often reluctant process to come to terms with the "vestiges" of a sort of Jewish identity. And precisely because this 'identity' is anything but given for Eduardo, who shows himself comically irreverent of the orthodox creeds and practices paraded by his brother-in-law, he repeatedly remembers and dwells on scenes of family life, scenes of the past, such as his "mechanical" learning of the six words of a Hebrew prayer as a young boy, which gradually lost all meaning to him (Halfon 2014b, 35–36; Halfon 2014a, 38–39). Instead of grounding identity in a fixed or circumscribed location, Eduardo/Halfon are more interested in finding linkages between different experiences. In fact, the entire novel is composed of short fragments, which often refer to Eduardo's travels – typically introduced by the formula, "[on] a different trip, to a different city" (Halfon 2014b, 30) ["[e]n otro viaje, a otra ciudad" (Halfon 2014a, 33)] – and which in a constant back and forth transport the reader to different moments from the past (his own youth in Guatemala, his previous visits to Poland, his grandfather's early life in Łódź and Auschwitz).

In Israel, he feels most alienated when the brother-in-law gives him and his brother a tour of the ultra-orthodox neighborhood of Kiryat Mattersdorf, and when he sees there the multiple, layered mantles, *talit*, worn by the rabbi. This in turn brings him back to scenes of his childhood, when he himself wore a *talit* in the Sephardic synagogue of Guatemala (Halfon 2014b, 42–43; Halfon 2014a, 46). His bewildered observation of the orthodox religious practices leads him to such an enraged disgust that he says to his brother he won't assist the wedding, to which his brother retorts that he is more intolerant than the orthodox Jews: "you're as Jewish as all of them. [...] That's your heritage. [...] It's in your blood."

(Halfon 2014b, 45) ["usted es tan judío como ellos. [...] Ésa es su herencia. [...] Lo lleva en su sangre." (Halfon 2014a, 48)] This might sound like a possible moral of the novel, yet the narrator remains skeptical, the idea of inherited blood reminds him of the speeches of Hitler (Halfon 2014b, 45; Halfon 2014a, 49).

The grandfather's option to be silent about his history and/or identity is compared to the tattooed number of Primo Levi, in whose case the number, alongside his name, was inscribed on his tomb stone in Turin, both being "intrinsic parts of his identity" ["partes intrínsecas de su identidad" (Halfon 2014a, 81)].[8] However, toward the end of the novel, in the fourth chapter, Eduardo recalls the moment (that is, temporally prior to his visit in Jerusalem) in which his dying grandfather has, after *his* long resistance, finally allowed him to visit the places in Poland where he had lived: "It was a mandate. An order. A dictate. An itinerary. A travel guide. A few coordinates on the mysterious and uneven map of our family." (Halfon 2014b, 145) ["Era un mandato. Una orden. Un dictamen. Un itinerario. Una guía de viaje. Unas coordenadas en el oculto y accidentado mapa familiar." (Halfon 2014a, 108)]

Earlier in the novel, and hence in reversed order, the narrator had already recalled memories from this visit to Poland. During his stay at Warsaw, on his way to visit Auschwitz, he remembered that his grandfather "had been trained by a boxer, in 1942." (Halfon 2014b, 143) ["había sido entrenado por un boxeador, en el 42." (Halfon 2014a, 106)] This is an obvious allusion to the earlier work *El boxeador polaco*, and indeed, through his own visit to Poland (in 2011, and as represented in *Duelo*),[9] Eduardo wants to get in touch with the experience of his grandfather. In one scene he enters a simple milk bar, a popular restaurant that appears to him like "vestiges of another time" (Halfon 2014b, 110) ["[v]estigios de otra época" (Halfon 2014a, 63)]. Faced with the problem of linguistic communication, he is assisted by a young friendly couple, and thus receives something good to eat. However, the whole atmosphere, his feeling alienated as a foreigner among the older Polish people, the standing in line for soup, the tattoos on the arms of the young couple – all of these are signs of an uncanny haunting, through which this otherwise trivial scene appears to be overdetermined. As Ewa Kobyłecka-Piwońska observes, these elements "contribute to infect the scene with

8 My translation. Curiously, two chapters in the English translation ("Surviving Sundays," "Prologue at Saint-Nazare," [Halfon 2014b, 114–127]) diverge entirely from the 'third chapter' in the Spanish original (version Halfon 2014a, 70–78). I have not found any editorial or authorial comment on this substantial divergence. In any case, it is further evidence of the serial, combinatory nature of Halfon's poetics, even with regard to an authorized translation.

9 In *Duelo*, 'Halfon' travels to the Gedenkstätte Sachsenhausen, to find out that his grandfather worked as a forced laborer for an aircraft factory (Halfon 2017, 44; Halfon 2018b, 98).

flashes of a past more remote than communism, namely that of the Jewish experience during the Second World War. [...] In Warsaw, 'Halfon' seems to confirm, at every step, the memory of the grandfather, to cultivate his alienation within Polish society, anticipating the signs of anti-Semitism" (2022, 375). Supported by the fact that some of the older Poles remind Eduardo somewhat of the figure of his grandfather, the scene is informed by his inclination to perceive the foreign place as a "vestige from the past," as a way to identify, however obliquely, with the past experiences of his grandfather. As the nephew of a Holocaust survivor, Eduardo is affected by a transgenerational transmission of trauma, or by what has been called "secondary trauma" (Logie and Navarrete 2020).[10] During his visit to Poland, he sees the elderly Polish people, imagines them, when they were young, to play domino with his grandfather, and he strives to not see them as "traitors" – precisely the reason why the grandfather for a long time did not want his nephew to visit his country of origin, and whose language he has deliberately renounced ever since. The same resistance of the grandfather occurs almost verbatim also in *Duelo*: "You must not go to Poland, he said. The Polish, he used to say, betrayed us." (Halfon 2018b, 44) ["No hay que ir a Polonia, decía. Los polacos, decía, nos traicionaron." (Halfon 2017, 47)]

At another point, Eduardo refers to the history of his grandfather as "a history that in a way was also mine. In the end, our history is our only patrimony." (Halfon 2014b, 145) ["una historia que, de algún modo, también era la mía. Al final, nuestra historia es nuestro único patrimonio." (Halfon 2014a, 108–109)] Refusing the admonitions of others to demonstrate his Jewish identity, Eduardo recognizes history – familial history – as the form in which he experiences a sense of commonality. Again, this occurs *after* his prior taking distance from both family and Judaism. In an earlier scene, he recalls the death of his grandfather, which was assisted by a (rather unsympathetic) old rabbi, who, as Eduardo narrates this scene, reminds him of another rabbi, a young and sympathetic one. The narrator recalls the moment of his life when he met him on the street: "I had just left my father's house, my father's religion, my father's glassed-in world." ["Recién me había marchado de la casa de mi padre, de la religión de mi padre, del mundo acristalado de mi padre." (Halfon 2014a, 72)] The sympathetic rabbi comments the confused sentiments of the young Eduardo with a reference to the story of Abraham, invoking the words of *Genesis* 12:1: "Go from your land, and from your family, and from your father's house..." ["Vete de tu tierra, y de tu familia, y de la casa de tu padre" (Halfon 2014a, 73)]. The verbal echo ("the house of

10 Such a form of transgenerational relation is also explored in the novel *Diary of a Fall* (*Diário da queda* [2011]) by the Brazilian writer Michel Laub. See Moszczyńska 2022, 300–318; Welge 2016.

my/your father") is a subtle and ambivalent one. The distancing from his family – and from the religion represented by the older rabbi – is paradoxically countered and confirmed by the biblical quote (the source of tradition), which is turn implicitly 'cited' by the narrator himself.

In this vein, through verbal echoes and the repetition of images the novel lays out a network of echoes and analogies. One of these occurring images, as we have already seen, is the wall in Jerusalem, which is first invoked with regard to the orthodox neighborhood, a secluded ghetto-like space within a country, Israel, which is itself "physically confined, decidedly self-contained, cloistered somewhere between yellow security gates and huge invisible walls." (Halfon 2014b, 41) ["físicamente aislado, decididamente encerrado en sí mismo, enclaustrado entre talanqueras amarillas y grandes muros invisibles." (Halfon 2014a, 44)] Furthermore, at different moments throughout the novel, mention is made of the "wall" (Halfon 2014b, 30) ["muro" (Halfon 2014a, 33)]; and of the "wall of racial segregation" (Halfon 2014b, 136) ["el muro de la segregación racial" (Halfon 2014a, 99)], separating the Palestinians from Israel. All walls, the narrator proposes, are futile attempts to separate us from the other (Halfon 2014b, 137; Halfon 2014a, 100). The recurring image of the wall, as associated with the past and present in Israel and in Poland, clearly serves as a linkage that stresses the permeability of spatial and temporal boundaries within the novel (Kobyłecka-Piwońska 2022, 377). In this capacity, it also might be seen as an example for the poetics of multi-directionality (Rothberg 2009) in Halfon, encouraging comparisons and parallels across time and space.[11]

In the final scene of the novel, Eduardo finds himself together with a sensual, bikini-clad Tamara at the Dead Sea – and there is a long conversation (grotesquely interspersed with Eduardo's erotic arousal) – in which Eduardo replies to Tamara's accusation that he would deny his roots and Jewish heritage (Halfon 2014b, 149; Halfon 2014a, 112), by recounting various examples that demonstrate the necessity of Jews to disavow their own identity during moments of antisemitic danger or historical periods of persecution. Thus, he adduces the example of the Polish-American writer Jerzy Kosinski (1933–1991), whose family pretended they were Catholic, and who, disguised as a girl and with his real name suppressed, survived in a "monastery" (Halfon 2014b, 153) ["monasterio" (Halfon 2014a, 117)] on the outskirts of Warsaw (Halfon 2014b, 153–155; Halfon 2014a, 117–119). During Eduardo's visit in Warsaw, due to his misplaced suitcase at the airport, he had acquired a feminine "pink raincoat" ["femenino gabán color rosa" (Halfon 2014a, 33)] that in various scenes of his movement through the city simultaneously 'conceals'

11 On the wall as a sign of ethnic segregation in the Israeli-Palestine constellation, with implications also for other urban conflicts, see the pertinent remarks in Settis 2017, 73–75.

him and draws the attention to him. This comical apparel, then, is another oblique allusion to the theme of confessing/suppressing one's identity. The scene exemplifies Halfon's often provocative approach of suggesting (not necessarily unproblematic) analogies and *Monasterio*'s ambivalent stance toward the question of cultural belonging.

3 *Canción* (2021): The Paternal Grandfather

Halfon's most recent novel (*Canción*, 2021) moves the focus to the figure of the paternal grandfather, specifically the story of his kidnapping in the midst of the Guatemalan civil war, during the year 1967. While this event of the past reaches back before the birth of the author, it is one of the reasons why the family left Guatemala in 1981 for New York. As for the chronological order (which gets in any case confounded in Halfon's narrative project and approach) this book might be considered the 'first' with respect to the other books published by the author. In a sense, and with all the necessary qualifications, it might also be called Halfon's most 'Latin American' novel. In an interview, Halfon comments on the reasons why it has taken him some time to address in fiction the historical contexts of violence during his upbringing in Guatemala as well as on the necessity of his investigative approach: "The family suffered, especially my grandmother, my father, who had to negotiate. In my childhood it was a taboo subject, it was not talked about much, it was not commented on. So much so that when I started to investigate, I found out many details that my family did not know." ["La familia lo sufrió, sobre todo mi abuela, mi padre, que tuvieron que negociar. En mi infancia era un tema tabú, no se hablaba mucho, no se comentaba. Tanto es así que cuando yo empiezo a investigar me entero de muchos detalles que mi familia no conocía" (Rodríguez Ballester 2021)].

The fact that this grandfather's name is equally Eduardo Halfon, gives occasion to the narrator to find his own identity within the structure of the family. When his grandfather dies, the narrator receives from him a box with personal belongings (a paper seal, business cards, letterhead paper), all with his personal name imprinted or engraved. The identity of the name constitutes a short circuit between the material objects of memory and the identity of self and writing: "My grandfather had left me these things because I was the only person who could still use them, because I was the only other Eduardo Halfon. My inheritance, literally, textually, was my name." (Halfon 2022, 119) ["Mi abuelo, pensé, me había dejado esas cosas porque yo era el único que aún podía usarlas, porque yo era el único otro Eduardo Halfon. Mi herencia, literalmente, textualmente, era mi nombre." (Halfon 2021, 84)]

However, as is customary for Halfon, this identity is anything but clearly defined and is caught up in a network of cosmopolitan orientations and imaginative possibilities. Thus, similar to *Monasterio*, also *Canción* begins with a scene of the autofictional narrator arriving at an airport – this time in Tokyo, where he participates in a congress by Lebanese writers. Programmatically, the first sentence of the novel reads: "I arrived at Tokyo disguised as an Arab." (Halfon 2022, 11) ["Llegué a Tokio disfrazado de árabe" (Halfon 2021, 9)]. Eduardo's association with Lebanon via his grandfather, who was born in Beirut, gives rise to a partly comical self-conscious reflection on his status as a Hispanophone author not to be easily contained within the framework of a single national literature:

> I had never been asked to be a Lebanese writer. A Jewish writer, yes. A Guatemalan writer, obviously. A Latin American writer, of course. A Central American writer, less and less. A U.S. writer, more and more. A Spanish writer, when traveling on that passport was desirable. A Polish writer, on one occasion, at a Barcelona bookstore that insisted – insists – on shelving my books in the Polish literature section. A French writer, since I lived for a time in Paris and some people assume I'm still there. (Halfon 2022, 13–14)

> [(…) nunca antes me habían solicitado ser un escritor libanés. Escritor judío, sí. Escritor guatemalteco, claro. Escritor latinoamericano, por supuesto. Escritor centroamericano, cada vez menos. Escritor estadounidense, cada vez más. Escritor español, cuando ha sido preferible viajar con ese pasaporte. Escritor polaco, en una ocasión, en una librería de Barcelona que insistía – insiste – en ubicar mis libros en la estantería de literatura polaca. Escritor francés, desde que viví un tiempo en París y algunos aún suponen que sigo allá. (Halfon 2021, 11)]

Even the national affiliation (and self-identification) of the grandfather with Lebanon turns out to be doubtful, for Eduardo tells us that in the process of the archival research he did on the grandfather's first-born son Salomon (whose fate is in turn centrally explored in the novel *Duelo* [2017]) he found out that the grandfather is in fact of Syrian descent – but that the migration officer in New York changed this to 'Lebanese.' (Apart from the fact that the state of Lebanon was only established in 1920, three years after his grandfather left Beirut [Halfon 2022, 15; Halfon 2021, 13]). Eduardo therefore confronts his public (and his readers) with a paradoxical interrogation of the notion of national belonging: "And so I am the grandson of a Lebanese man who was not Lebanese, I told the audience at the University of Tokyo" (Halfon 2022, 16) ["Y es que yo soy el nieto de un libanés que no era libanés, le dije al público de japoneses en la universidad de Tokio" (Halfon 2021, 14)].

This tendency to interrogate and confound the supposed identity between names, identities, and nationhood is also visible in the very title of the novel: 'Canción' (meaning 'song' in Spanish) is the nickname of the guerrillero from the FAR (Fuerzas Armadas Rebeldes) who kidnapped the grandfather, his name resulting from a linguistic play with his day-work in a "carnicería" (Halfon 2021, 31) ["butcher shop" (Halfon 2022, 59)]. By choosing to have the novel not named after his grandfather, but after the person who kidnapped him, the author implicitly stresses the decisive significance of this event for the history of the family, but he also signals that he means to address the history of violence that has marked Guatemala for 36 years. In fact, a brief account of the origin of the revolutionary and guerilla movement, as a reaction to the servile stance of the government toward the US, seeks to create an understanding for the causes that led to this movement (Halfon 2022, 68–69; Halfon 2021, 39–40). The reason for his grandfather's kidnapping, Eduardo muses, had probably less to do with the 'official' reason, namely that he allegedly treated his employees badly, but rather with the fact that the guerilla needed to extort money to finance its activities (Halfon 2022, 116; Halfon 2021, 81). However, Eduardo tells us also about the circumstances that had led to his grandfather's arrangement and compromises with the political situation in Guatemala, so that we may also understand *his* situation.

In the memories of the narrator, the grand house of the grandfather is evoked through a long list of the smells and aromas of the kitchen, where dishes from the Sephardic and the Guatemalan cuisine coexist: "There they fried falafel and *kibbe.* They baked bagels, pita bread, *sambouseks* filled with cheese [...]. They made *mujadarra,* [...] a Sephardic stew [...], called *hamin.*" (Halfon 2022, 18–19; emphasis mine) ["Allí freían falafel y kibbes. Horneaban bagels, pan pita, sambuseks de queso, [...]. Hacían mujadarra, [...] un guiso sefardí [...], llamado jamín." (Halfon 2021, 16)] Thus, even these very sensuous memories are testimony to a 'multicultural' familial heritage that defies unitary identifications.[12] While researching in the Bibliothèque Nationale in Paris, he finds further evidence for his grandfather's multiple migrations: After having fled Beirut in 1917 during the period of the Great Hunger, after

12 As Logie and Willem point out in their study of recent postmemory fictions concerned with the dictatorial past in the Cono Sur, such memories attached to a family house may be tinged by nostalgia. Recent narratives centered in the "return to the house"-genre are frequently distinguished by "an intimate and familiar atmosphere, which privileges the domestic sphere and is expressed in a rescue of the most everyday details of the past, such as the evocation of children's games, homemade food rituals or school experiences" (2015, 4). While Halfon's fictions share some of these traits, the history of the Jewish diaspora is responsible for the fact that the association between house and family is much more punctual and does not work as an organizing trope for the text.

various international way-stations he eventually settled in Paris, where he established a small textile business together with a French Jew named Gabai, in order to trade and send these wares to "his eight brothers, all spread out in several countries in the Americas." (Halfon 2022, 79) ["sus hermanos repartidos por varios países de América" (Halfon 2021, 48)]

Eventually, in 1931, when the grandfather travels to Guatemala to help one of these brothers, he falls in love with a woman (Eduardo's grandmother) and comes to settle there. Eduardo discusses these aspects of his family history with a friendly librarian of the Parisian library, who, when hearing about the grandfather's successful attempt to obtain a safe conduct for Gabai, to get him out of the country, apparently has also his own personal memories about this period: "I immediately understood or thought I understood that he was speaking from experience, that he'd personally lived through or suffered through something similar during German occupation." (Halfon 2022, 81) ["yo de inmediato comprendí o creí comprender que hablaba por experiencia propia, que algo había vivido o sufrido él mismo en los años de la ocupación alemana." (Halfon 2021, 50)] While the memories of the librarian are not further specified and thus remain on the level of speculation, the 'multi-directional' poetics of memory in Halfon's work feature – as here – scenes of archival or documentary research, which then give rise to 'imaginary' reconstructions of possible pasts and empathic identification with the lives of 'others' (including the figure of 'Canción').

In *Canción*, the superimposition of different time periods and the implicit, or explicit relationality between different geographical and/or national spaces is not only a 'natural' aspect of the migratory and transnational experience of the characters, but it is also connected to the notion of a multi-directional memory, according to which the history of German/European totalitarianism is ironically juxtaposed to the experience of dictatorship in Guatemala. For when the grandfather eventually manages to get his former business companion to Guatemala, this is made possible by the signature of general Jorge Ubico (1878–1946), dictator since 1931, nicknamed the 'Napoleon of Central America,' and dubbed by Halfon as the (self-confessed) "Hitler of Guatemala" (Halfon 2022, 82) ["El Hitler de Guatemala" (Halfon 2021, 51)].

According to the Argentine theorist Leonor Arfuch hybrid literary genres working with autobiographical or autofictional elements in the face of a traumatic past establish a link between memory, history, and identity, and they constitute an "intersubjective circuit" (2009, 36) that opens up the private experience toward broader and collective dimensions. Such a tendency, that is, not only of transgenerational transmission, but also of a horizontal dimension of intersubjective relationality ultimately also involves the readers, namely by way of a "narrative mode that emphasizes the incessant need to open historical narratives to the concrete, material conditions of situated, embodied readers" (Kaakinen 2017, 20).

In fact, the final pages of the novel circle back to the opening scene: Eduardo is now addressing the public of 'Lebanese' writers in Tokyo. After having given his talk, he meets there a woman named Aiko, a student of the university, and he learns that her family comes from the city of Hiroshima – to where Eduardo plans to travel in the next days. The conversation about Hiroshima soon reveals that Aiko's grandfather has survived the bomb (Halfon 2022, 138; Halfon 2021, 101). During the scene of Eduardo's lecture he reads a scene about the life of his grandfather (originally, he planned "four excerpts from four different books recounting aspects of my grandfather's life" [Halfon 2022, 138] ["cuatro fragmentos de cuatro libros distintos que narran aspectos de la vida de mi abuelo" (Halfon 2021, 102)]), dwelling on the internal conflict between the military and the guerilla fighters. The readers are thus doubly interpellated as a stand-in for the Japanese audience of Eduardo's lecture and as 'readers' of the novel(s) by Halfon.

Now, these culminating scenes of the lecture about the grandfather (as an answer to the question of the writer's Lebanese heritage) are paratactically intercut with Aiko's narrative about *her* grandfather.[13] Her narrative begins with one of those matter-of-fact, brief sentences that are typical for Halfon: "My grandfather's kimono remained on his skin." (Halfon 2022, 142) ["En la piel de mi abuelo quedó su kimono." (Halfon 2021, 106)] We eventually learn that the pattern of the kimono has been "imprinted onto his skin" (Halfon 2022, 144) ["estampado sobre la piel" (Halfon 2021, 107)] because of the heat wave of the atomic bomb. Significantly, Aiko narrates this from her limited perspective of a child, when, at first, she could not understand why her grandfather had this pattern on his skin. Finally, she understands:

> But that night I understood my grandfather. I understood the reason for his silence. I understood that the bomb had forever marked his skin not with just any old article of clothing, not with a shirt or jacket, but with one of the traditional kimonos he had inherited from his father and his grandfather, and which no longer even existed. The bomb had incinerated it, Aiko said. Or rather, the bomb had embedded it in his skin. (Halfon 2022, 145)

> [Pero aquella noche entendí a mi abuelo. Entendí el porqué de su silencio. Entendí que la bomba había marcado para siempre su piel no con cualquier prenda de vestir, no con una

13 Grouping the concept of parataxis with analogy and juxtaposition, Kaakinen proposes that it allows for the analysis of "undetermined linkages" in narrative: "The concept of parataxis enables talking about different modes of unspecified relation on various levels of the text while highlighting the undetermined nature of linkage that is common to all these instances of narrative linking" (2017, 18).

camisa o un saco, sino con uno de los kimonos tradicionales que había heredado de su padre, y su abuelo, y que ya ni siquiera existía. La bomba lo había incinerado, dijo Aiko. O más bien la bomba se lo había metido en la piel. (Halfon 2021, 108)]

This is a remarkable passage, since the violent inscription in the skin is paradoxically also the sign of a transgenerational, material and bodily memory. The transgenerational chain extends not only into the past, but also into the future: for the Japanese word 'hibakusha' ('bombed person'), sometimes used in a scornful sense, is applied not only to the survivors, but it extends also to "us, too, their children and grandchildren, for fear of the possible effects of radiation." (Halfon 2022, 145) ["sino también a nosotros, a sus hijos y nietos, debido al miedo a los posibles efectos de la radiación." (Halfon 2021, 108)] Readers of Halfon – namely of "The Polish Boxer" – will notice that the memories of young Aiko (her ignorance as a child, the long "silence" of the grandfather) recall the scene of young Eduardo wondering over the mysterious digits imprinted on the arm of his other, maternal grandfather. In *Canción*, the narrator Eduardo makes this linkage (almost) explicit to Aiko: "I was going to tell her that I very much understood the silence of a grandfather survivor, that I very much understood the marks they then wear on their skin for the rest of their lives." (Halfon 2022, 145–146) ["Iba a decirle que entendía bien el silencio de un abuelo sobreviviente, que entendía bien las marcas que ellos luego llevan en la piel durante el resto de su vida." (Halfon 2021, 109)]

This final approximation (including gestures of physical approximation) between Eduardo and Aiko (echoing in turn the final scene with Tamara in *Monasterio*) creates a constellation of echoes and analogies between the figures of the three grandfathers. The 'paratactic' possibilities of comparison include the notion of bodily memory (violence born in the skin) and the notion of (textual) inscription (as in the material heritage of the paternal grandfather). The intersubjective and multidirectional movement of memory suggests how such transmissions within the history of the family point also to larger constellations of comparison, through which different memories of historical catastrophes are not equated, yet juxtaposed and shared. Thus, in *Canción*, Eduardo agrees to Aiko's proposal that she may show him a primary school in Hiroshima (Halfon 2022, 152; Halfon 2021, 114). The affective bonding between Eduardo and Aiko ultimately occurs in the shadow of transgenerational, embodied memories of Hiroshima and the Holocaust.[14] While the approximation of familial pasts is enacted by the novel's

14 The juxtaposition between these two signature historical catastrophes of the twentieth century is far from unprecedented. In literature, one of the most significant precedents is perhaps Elsa Morante's novel *La Storia* (1974) [*History: A Novel* (1977)]. On "Auschwitz and Hiroshima" in

characters, the reader is asked to ponder the repercussions and transmissions of (different) historical catastrophes of the twentieth century.

4 Conclusion

> We all need a grandfather, so I insist on writing to you. If you're not around, let me make you up.
>
> [Todos necesitamos un abuelo, así que insisto en escribirte. Si no estás, déjame que te invente.] Andrés Neuman, *Una vez Argentina* (2003, 118)

By considering here mainly two novels of Halfon (*Monasterio, Canción*) we have seen that the author uses his relation to individual family members (sister, grandfathers) to explore the question of his (highly ambivalent) Jewish identity and of (trans)national belonging or affiliations. While in recent times many writers of Jewish and/or Latin American descent have employed autofictional/memorial or hybrid literary forms to establish connections between personal family memories (or memories of individual family members) and collective histories in order to confront traumata of historical or state violence,[15] Halfon's literary project is distinctive for its serial, iterative and fragmentary approach to these matters. Thus, the memory of his maternal grandfather, a survivor of the Holocaust, is distributed and repeated over various texts, as if in a traumatic compulsion to repeat and to 'work through.' At the same time, the question of uncertain belonging, of multiple trajectories and identities (Jewish, Arab, Polish, Guatemalan), associated especially with the paternal grandfather, leads in turn to ever new constellations of affective identifications with other pasts, identities, or histories of violence. The central importance of the two grandfathers for these companion works is grounded in the fact that the temporal distance provides a transgenerational link to the events of the Shoah and diaspora, even as it opens up a space of not-knowing that must be filled by investigation and imagination. At once deeply rooted in autobiographical

Morante, see Mariani 2022, 112–116. Similar to Rothberg or Kaakinen, also Mariani defends comparison between different historical traumata: "Connecting traumatic events does not necessarily degenerate into neutralizing the exceptionality of the atrocity or creating a zero-sum game between the victims. The cultural elaboration of trauma can be conceived of as an accumulative, not competitive process" (2022, 117). On the transatlantic memory debate, see also Lim 2021, 113–119.

15 Among the many possible examples, let me just mention Nona Fernández' recent *Voyager: Constellations of Memory* (2023) [*Voyager* (2019)], in which she blends memories of her mother and of the dictatorial past of Chile.

experience and continuously open to other experiences and locations, Halfon's texts encourage multidirectional modes of reading and may be seen as exemplary for the multiple orientations, dislocations, and different temporalities that may be said to be typical for the contemporary 'Latin American' novel (Welge 2022).

Bibliography

Adamczewska, Izabella. "'Wyblakła gwiazda porno' w bałuckim getcie. Jak mnie nabrał pisarz Eduardo Halfon." *Gazeta Wyborcza*, April 11, 2023. https://lodz.wyborcza.pl/lodz/7,35136,29651416,wyblakla-gwiazda-porno-w-baluckim-getcie-jak-mnie-nabral.html (January 1, 2024).

Arfuch, Leonor. *Memory and Autobiography. Explorations at the Limits*. Transl. Christina MacSweeney. Cambridge: Polity, 2020.

Campisi, Nicolás. "The Dislocation of Cosmopolitan Identities in Eduardo Halfon's *Monasterio*." *INTI. Revista de literatura hispánica* 87/88 (2018): 113–124.

Fernández, Nona. *Voyager: Constellations of Memory* [2019]. Transl. Natasha Wimmer. Oxford: Daunt Books, 2022.

Gartenberg, Charlotte. "Inheriting Ghosts in Latin American Jewish Literature: Forging Stories and Selves Out of Deathly Pasts in Sergio Chejfec and Eduardo Halfon." *Shofar: An Interdisciplinary Journal of Jewish Studies* 39.1 (2021): 120–140.

Halfon, Eduardo. *Canción*. Transl. Lisa Dillman, Daniel Hahn. New York: Bellevue Literary Press, 2022.

Halfon, Eduardo. *Canción*. Barcelona: Libros del Asteroide, 2021.

Halfon, Eduardo. *El boxeador polaco*. Barcelona: Libros del Asteroide, 2019.

Halfon, Eduardo. "In Conversation: Eduardo Halfon." *Asymptote*, June 18, 2018a. https://www.asymptotejournal.com/blog/2018/06/18/in-conversation-eduardo-halfon/ (January 1, 2024).

Halfon, Eduardo. *Mourning*. Transl. Lisa Dillmann, Daniel Hahn. New York: Bellevue Literary Press, 2018b.

Halfon, Eduardo. *Duelo*. Barcelona: Libros del Asteroide, 2017.

Halfon, Eduardo. *Monasterio*. Barcelona: Libros del Asteroide, 2014a.

Halfon, Eduardo. *Monastery*. Transl. Lisa Dillmann, Daniel Hahn. New York: Bellevue Literary Press 2014b.

Halfon, Eduardo. *The Polish Boxer*. Transl. Ollie Brock et al. New York: Bellevue Literary Press, 2012.

Hirsch, Marianne. *Family Frames: Photography, Narrative, and Postmemory*. Cambridge, MA: Harvard UP, 1997.

Kaakinen, Kaisa. *Comparative Literature and the Historical Imaginary. Reading Conrad, Weiss, Sebald*. Cham: Palgrave Macmillan, 2017.

Kobyłecka-Piwońska, Ewa. "Perturbar el orden de sentido: los viajes polacos de Eduardo Halfon." *Studia Neophilologica* 94.3 (2022): 365–390.

Laorden Albendea, María Teresa. "Lidiar con el pasado familiar. Posmemoria y trauma en *El Boxeador Polaco* de Eduardo Halfon." *Tuércele el cuello al cisne. Las expresiones de la violencia en la literatura hispánica contemporánea (siglos XX y XXI)*. Eds. Cristóbal José Álvarez López/Juan Manuel Carmona Tierno/Ana Davis González/Sara González Ángel/María del Rosario Martínez Navarro/Marta Rodríguez-Manzano. Sevilla: Renacimiento, 2016. 589–600.

Lim, Jie-Hyun. “Triple Victimhood: On the Mnemonic Confluence of the Holocaust, Stalinist Crime, and Colonial Genocide.” *Journal of Genocide Research* 23.1 (2021): 105–126.
Lockhart, Darrel B. “The Jewish-Latin American Novel.” *The Oxford Handbook of the Latin American Novel*. Eds. Juan E. De Castro/Ignacio López-Calvo. Oxford: Oxford UP, 2023. 329–347.
Logie, Ilse, and María Teresa Navarrete. “Trauma transgeneracional y trauma secundario: padres, hijos, nietos.” *Trauma y memoria cultural. Hispanoamérica y España*. Eds. Roland Spiller/Kirsten Mahlke/Janett Reinstädler. Berlin/Boston: De Gruyter, 2020. 39–60.
Logie, Ilse, and Bieke Willem. “Narrativas de la postmemoria en Argentina y Chile: La Casa revisitada.” *Alter/nativas. Revista de estudios culturales latinoamericanos* 5 (2015): 1–25.
Marchese, Lorenzo. “L’autofiction.” *Fiction e non fiction. Storia, teorie e forme*. Ed. Riccardo Castellana. Roma: Carocci editore, 2021. 183–205.
Mariani, Maria Anna. *Italian Literature in the Nuclear Age. A Poetics of the Bystander*. Oxford: Oxford UP, 2022.
Moszczyńska, Joanna. *A memória da Destruição na escrita judaico-brasileira depois de 1985. Por uma literatura pós-Holocausto emergente no Brasil*. Berlin/New York: Peter Lang, 2022.
Neuman, Andrés. *Una vez Argentina*. Barcelona: Penguin Random House, 2018 [2003].
Ortiz Wallner, Alexandra. “Una escritura más allá de las fronteras. La narrativa f(r)iccional de Eduardo Halfon.” *Hispanorama* 144 (2014): 34–38.
Rodríguez Ballester, Alejandra. “La guerilla secuestró a su abuelo y su familia debió exiliarse: la nueva novela de Eduardo Halfon.” Interview with Eduardo Halfon. *Clarín*, May 19, 2021. https://www.clarin.com/cultura/guerrilla-guatemalteca-secuestro-abuelo-familia-debio-exiliarse-nueva-novela-eduardo-halfon_0_fNmFI2XhU.html (January 1, 2024).
Rothberg, Michael. *Multidirectional Memory. Remembering the Holocaust in the Age of Decolonization*. Stanford: Stanford UP, 2009.
Settis, Salvatore. *Architettura e democrazia. Paesaggio, città, diritti civili*. Torino: Einaudi, 2017.
Siskind, Mariano. “Towards a Cosmopolitanism of Loss: an essay about the end of the world.” *World Literature, Cosmopolitanism, Globality. Beyond, Against, Post, Otherwise*. Eds. Gesine Müller/Mariano Siskind. Berlin/Boston: De Gruyter, 2019. 205–235.
Van Hecke, An. “Memoria, ficción y multilingüismo en ‘El boxeador polaco,’ un cuento de Eduardo Halfon.” *Connotas. Revista de crítica y teoría literarias* 21 (2020): 9–31.
Welge, Jobst. “Locations, orientations and multiple temporalities in the contemporary, ‘global’ Latin American novel.” *Claiming Space. Locations and Orientations in World Literature*. Eds. Bo Ekelund/Adnan Mahmutovic/Helena Wulff. New York: Bloomsbury Academic, 2022. 193–215.
Welge, Jobst. “Transgenerationelle Erinnerung in der argentinischen und brasilianischen Gegenwartsliteratur (Sergio Chejfec, Michel Laub).” *Artefrakte: Holocaust und Zweiter Weltkrieg in experimentellen Darstellungsformen in Literatur und Kunst*. Ed. Esther Kilchmann. Köln: Böhlau, 2016. 269–282.

Anja Tippner

Legacies of Repression and the Siege: Ol’ga Lavrent’eva’s Graphic Novel *Survilo* as a Family History of Trauma

Soviet history was marked by a multitude of extreme and catastrophic events beginning with the death and destruction of the Civil War, the hunger of the 1920s and 1930s, the Great Terror, mass deportations, the Second World War and Chernobyl. Some of these events have been commemorated extensively in official culture, while others were suppressed and hardly ever remembered and discussed openly. The homogenization of violence under a common – mostly Russian-Soviet – denominator glosses over the specifics of local and ethnic experiences. The fate of ethnic minorities in the Soviet Union was a contested and rarely addressed topic in Soviet times that suppressed differences and erased ethnically motivated violence, repression, and discrimination. Since the beginning of the 2000s, authors make use of their family histories to deal with the difficult and traumatic aspects of Russian twentieth century history, often focusing on the specific experiences of ethnic groups such as Russian Germans, Tatars, Jews,[1] or Ukrainians. Investigating private pain and researching the lacunae of family memory, these authors tap into a wider trend of autofiction and documentary writing. Private family history becomes public and political. All the while, history is still contested and complicated territory, even more so due to its instrumentalization to devastating effect in current politics. Authors such as Guzel Iakhina, Mariia Stepanova, Sergei Lebedev, Elena Chizhova, and Liudmila Ulitskaia[2] make use of the family novel to address family histories marked by ethnically motivated violence and repression.

While a shared collective remembrance of the Great Terror was almost impossible, due to its “self-inflicted nature,” which complicated the “strife for justice” as

1 On Jewish family histories as counter-histories see Tippner 2019, 203–223.

2 Transnational German family novels written by authors with trans-ethnic Soviet backgrounds, e.g. Nino Haratischwili (*Das achte Leben (Für Brilka)* [2014] [*The Eighth Life (for Brilka)* (2019)]), Eleonora Hummel (*Die Fische von Berlin* [2005] [The Fish of Berlin]) or Katerina Poladjan (*Hier sind Löwen* [2019] [Here are lions]) can be read as examples of this trend. They also turn the reader’s attention to the difficult fate of transnational families and ethnic minorities in the USSR. Anna Rakhmanko and Mikkel Sommer’s *Din bedstefar Vasja* (2021) [Vasja, your granddad] translates the transnational family story into the medium of graphic novel addressing Western audiences.

Anja Tippner, Hamburg University

https://doi.org/10.1515/9783111208664-011

well as the need to learn about the catastrophe (Etkind 2013, 8–9), World War II remembrance was ubiquitous, with the siege figuring prominently. Post-war Soviet generations were confronted with a ritualized and formalized memory culture of World War II that oftentimes shaped private memories and their narrativization. Leningrad, the 'hero city,' took pride of place in a host of texts, films, monuments, and pictures that stressed heroism but kept mute about the scale of death and the incomparable suffering in the city. Just as the horrendous aspects of the siege were not acknowledged, the suffering caused by the Great Terror was impossible to even be mentioned in public. In official remembrance "private pain went underground," as Catherine Merridale wrote (2000, 46). Painful memories were told only in the inner circle of family and friends, if at all, and siege texts trying to voice suffering were censored and subdued. Generations of Soviet citizens only "whispered" (Figes 2008) about the past. The family history and related narrative genres such as memoir and biography are shaped by this historical framework and often marginalize the memory of siege atrocities as well as those of the Great Terror.

1 *Survilo* as Transnational Family Novel and Graphic Recreation

Ol'ga Lavrent'eva's graphic novel *Survilo* [*Сурвило* (2019)][3] is an especially salient example of multi-temporal and multi-directional literature resulting from a Soviet family constellation marked by totalitarianism and transnationality. Lavrent'eva's book was published with Bumkniga, a publishing house focusing on graphic literature and comics that publishes foreign and domestic authors.[4] Its backlist contains titles by international graphic artists like Marjane Satrapi or Edmond Baudoin as well as famous Russian artists like Viktoria Lomasko, who is known for her project "We draw the trial," a work documenting political trials in Russia. As a graphic artist, Lavrent'eva has been associated with graphic documenting, graphic journalism and graphic autofiction due to her first work *Shuv* [*Шув* (2016)] and has become a prominent representative of the "non-fiction turn" or fact-based comic literature (Alaniz 2022a, 185–213; Alaniz 2022b). As one reviewer remarked, Lavrent'eva's book is the first graphic novel about the Leningrad siege and the Great Terror in

3 At the publication date there is no English translation of Lavrent'eva's book. In the following all translations from Russian are mine.

4 While the backlist of the publishing house also contains children's literature, the lieu of publishing does not indicate that Lavrent'eva's book was created as children's or young adult literature, as Sylwia Kamińska-Maciąg purports (2023).

Russia (Pavlovskii 2019). This may be due to the conflicted attitudes towards graphic literature in the USSR (Alaniz 2010) and its relatively late revival since the collapse of the Soviet Union. While "pictorial narrative proliferated in many different media: poster art, applied art, installations, children's books, Gulag memoirs, painting, even propaganda," graphic literature never flourished in the USSR (Kuhlmann and Alaniz 2020, 11). All things considered, Lavrent'eva's book is even more astonishing since it tackles traumatic topics with the repertoire of graphic literature in an environment that was, and to a certain degree still is, hostile towards it.

Like strictly textual reworkings of family history, her novel is saturated with material from the family archive and her personal memories of her grandmother. In addition, it creates a specific visual poetics for the transmission and (re)presentation of this material. In her "biographical novel" ["биографический роман" (Lavrent'eva 2019, impressum] the author tells the story of her maternal grandmother Valentina Survilo using an impressive, almost expressionist black and white grammar to convey her family history as viewed by her grandmother, a survivor of both the Great Terror of the late 1930s (in this case directed at the Polish community in Leningrad) and the siege. In interviews Lavrent'eva has expanded on her search for a graphic style suitable for representing the devastating stories and the process of remembering them, deciding in the end on a textured style of "lots of pencil strokes, fills, [and] wet painting" ["множество штрихов, заливки, рисования по мокрому" (Bederov 2019)]. For the author the "unevenness" ["неравномерность"] of the panels conveys the "unevenness" of the memories (Bederov 2019).

By introducing herself as a character in the narrative, Lavrent'eva uses a strategy developed by the graphic artist Joe Sacco and described by Nina Mickwitz as being "able to reflect, by way of verbal commentary, and by visual and compositional cues" (2016, 67) on her position within the family frame and her grandmother's narrative. She constructs the post-catastrophic mindset of her traumatized grandmother and contextualizes Valentina's experience as a central aspect of the family history. Scenes of communication or shared activity of grandmother and granddaughter are interspersed with the largely chronologically told biography of Valentina. The narrator is thus shown in her intimate dealings with her grandmother as well as in the process of gathering the information that turns her into a secondary witness, thereby "signaling that [she] is the filter through which" (Mickwitz 2016, 69) Valentina's experiences are visualized and mediated.

Ol'ga's great-grandfather, Vincenty Survilo, was born in 1884 and moved to Petersburg before her birth, looking for work and freedom. Survilo is at once a

Ill. 1: © Ol'ga Lavrent'eva. Lavrent'eva 2019, 14.

toponym denoting a small rural settlement called 'Survily' in the borderlands between Belarus, Lithuania, and Poland, and a common family name in the local Polish community. Although the place that was then Poland and is now Belarus, was incorporated into the Soviet Union in the times after the father's emigration to Leningrad and the family members thus were Soviet citizens, they were perceived as foreign and hence suspect. The unusual family name continues to indicate the transnational nature of the family history and becomes a central marker of exclusion and discrimination in the text.

The 1920s, when Valentina and her sisters were little, were good times for the family and her father, an ardent party activist. They live in a tight-knit community of factory workers and Polish emigrés, believing in the values of the new Soviet Union. However, in the wake of the assassination of the popular Leningrad party leader and Stalin rival Sergei Kirov in 1934, her father is arrested and executed unbeknownst to the family. This event turns Valentina's life upside down. Because they are family members of an 'enemy of the people,' Valentina, her sister, and her mother are deported to Bashkortostan near the Ural Mountains. While Valentina and her sister manage to return to Leningrad in 1940 to take up their studies, their mother dies in exile from hunger and illness. Because of her association with a repressed, politically unreliable relative, Valentina and her sister have trouble finding work and live in precarious circumstances even before the siege. Their personal situation during the siege is aggravated by the fact that they have no relatives or friends willing to help and support the daughters of an enemy of the people. The extreme hunger, terror of air raids, and the death of her sister haunt Valentina for the rest of her life. The siege experience forms the core of the novel and becomes its dark center. Having lived through the repression and the siege, the heavily traumatized Valentina exists in a state of constant fear – fear of the authorities, fear of losing her next of kin, fear of darkness and having not enough food. Even though her husband is supportive and is not put off by her family history, she struggles and suffers from anxiety. It is only during the Thaw and the Perestroika that some of the psychological weight of the Great Terror is lifted, first when she receives confirmation of her father's death and posthumous rehabilitation in 1958, and then when she can access his secret police files during the Perestroika. Nevertheless, fear has become part of her personality and cannot be erased neither by love, nor by knowledge.

Lavrent'eva stresses the fact that her grandmother had neither knowledge about her father's fate, nor a rational explanation for the persecution of her family. She perceives the repression as chaotic, inexplainable, and confusing. The double victimization during the Great Terror and the siege defines her life. The transnational family history, namely the fact that her family migrated from Poland, adds another layer of concern to her family history. At the center of Lavrent'eva's family history is the enormous pain that her grandmother has suffered and the almost unspeakable trauma that is predominantly transmitted via a million gestures and little quirks of Lavrent'eva's deeply beloved grandmother. Her book falls into the category of post-memorial literature as described by Marianne Hirsch (2008). It is noteworthy here that Hirsch developed her concept writing about Art Spiegelman's *Maus*, the architext of all graphic family histories. The Russian author follows an aesthetic framework mapped out by Spiegelman in *Maus*. Since *Maus* first was published in 1986, "visual witnessing" (Chute 2016, 39–69) has gained momentum, especially when it comes to representing disaster and trauma. As Chute demonstrates, in a visual world graphic witnessing has become a privileged genre. If a second-hand testimony is to convey meaning, it must be transmitted by an involved and engaged mediator. Lavrent'eva translates these trends in graphic and postmemorial literature into the Russian context and its different waves of violence.

The Soviet Union produced a singular environment for family histories that still holds post-Soviet texts in its thrall. In other literary and historical contexts, communities that have been oppressed had the possibility to tell their story and work out the effects of persecution on families, with some temporal distance. People told and listened to stories, books were written, films made while contemporary witnesses were still able to convey their truth. In the Soviet Union, however, family members of the repressed did not dare to speak about their experiences for the fear of incriminating themselves. The recreation of Russian family histories was and is further complicated by the fact that the distinction between perpetrators and victims is not always clear-cut in the Soviet context. One of the defining aspects of Soviet family politics was the immense pressure on family structure in the times of societal transformation and terror since "there could be only one primary allegiance and it was to the state, not the untrustworthy family" (Ginsborg 2014, 417).

Thus, focusing on family matters and family history could be observed as already disloyal, individualistic, and bourgeois. Starting with the Russian Revolution, collective violence and persecution fragmented families and often destroyed the natural generational order. The (il)logic of persecution confronted family members with difficult choices of either associating themselves with party lines and personal safety or staying loyal towards loved ones and risking persecution themselves (Tippner 2024).[5] For Valentina this is not only a historical truth but a personal experience. When the family of her husband learns whom, he has married, they abuse him as an "idiot" ["дурак" (Lavrent'eva 2019, 226)] for getting involved with "the daughter of an enemy of the people" ["дочь врага народа" (Lavrent'eva 2019, 226)], even though they have known Valentina and her family for their whole life. This rejection by people close to her only heightens Valentina's sense of isolation and abjection.

It seems to be almost a genre convention now, to convey historical experience of the generation of grandparents via grandchildren. This is a constellation that can be found in the family histories written by Ulitskaia, Lebedev, or Stepanova. Contemporary family novels often favor the perspective of grandchildren over that of parents because relations between grandparents and grandchildren are less fraught. Also, the temporal distance between grandparents and grandchildren moves questions of legacy and memory to the forefront.[6] While Lavrent'eva and other younger authors such as Lebedev are removed by one generation from the experience generation even authors who belong to different generational cohorts, e.g. Liudmila Ulitskaia, uses the perspective of the grandchild as narratorial device. In many ways, the grandchildren are the stand-in for the contemporary reader and his or her desire to learn more about the Soviet past. Or to use the words of Sabrina Wagner, you need not be a grandchild to write from the perspective of grandchildren (Wagner

5 This article focusses on transnational family histories that elaborate on the way the Soviet experience and family histories are reimagined within the frame of contemporary German literature. Nevertheless, Germanophone and the Russophone texts tap into the general trend of autofictional literary projects.

6 A similar trend can be observed in in German 'Enkelliteratur'. This literature focusses on grandparents who are heroes and/or victims and less on the conflicted relationship to (perpetrator) parents, as did for example the so-called 'Väterliteratur' [father literature]. As Artwińska and Mrozik have noted the concept of generation emphasizes both the genealogical order in the family as well as the collectivity of a generationally shared experience (2021). The generational order is different if we look at literary generations and actual Soviet generations. Thus, Soviet, and German generations are not compatible either, the most prominent representative of the generation of grandchildren, Tanja Dückers, was born in 1968.

2014, 53).[7] In conclusion, instead of using birth dates as a foundation for the generational order, we should look at the family constellation that is inscribed in the text and regard the grandparent-grandchildren dichotomy as a literary device which constitutes a subtype of the family novel.

As 'post'-texts, Lavrent'eva as well as other authors stress the positionality of witnessing by emphasizing repetitions and after-effects, expressing thus, a certain "multi-temporality," to quote Mieke Bal (2018, 234), albeit one that is limited to the Russian historical frame. Lavrent'eva's text does not address the siege as an isolated event in Russian history but rather as one of several interrelated instances of totalitarian biopolitics, as do authors like Chizhova or Stepanova who also make the siege part of their family history. In addition, Lavrent'eva's text is retrospective as well as prospective, trying to describe the after-effects of the siege but also the obligations and bonds it created with future generations (Miller and Tougaw 2002, 7). But while the novel stays thematically within the confines of Russian history, it relies on transnational theories of fiction, trauma transmission, and memorial culture as well as the conventions of "disaster drawn", by making the act of "textualization" graphically manifest (Chute 2016, 33). This emphasis on textualization corresponds to the emphasis on the receptiveness of the generation of grandchildren towards the historical experiences of their grandparents.[8]

Lavrent'eva frames the recreation of her grandmother's life with two episodes that put herself in the picture as secondary witness and researcher. In the first, she remembers walking in the countryside outside St. Petersburg in 1997. Her grandmother panics when she loses sight of her grandchildren, since this evokes the primal fear of the disappearing father (Lavrent'eva 2019, 11–13). This episode gives the reader a first impression of the lingering effects of trauma on her life and that of her descendants. The second episode takes place in 2017, when Ol'ga goes on a search for the birthplace of her great-great-grandparents, the mythical Survily, and listens to her grandmother's life story. Episodes like these complement the biographical narration of Valentina which moves from the 1920s to the 2000s. They also verbally and visually symbolize "the family [as] the individual's personal

7 This sounds more poignant in German: "Der Autor muss offenbar gar kein 'Enkel' sein, um 'Enkelliteratur' zu verfassen." (Wagner 2014, 53)

8 In this aspect, it most closely resembles Rakhmanko and Sommer's comics *Vasja, your granddad* (*Din bedstefar Vasja* [2021a]) which was published in Danish and German (*Vasja, Dein Opa* [2021b]) almost simultaneously. Rakhmanko and Sommer have collaborated on the comic with Rakhmanko as author and Sommer as visual artist. The book tells the story of Anna Rakhmanko's grandfather and his family who were deported from Podolia on the eve of World War II solely on the bases of their ethnic German background. Here, too the story is the result of a dialogue between the witness generation and the generation of their grandchildren who were both born in late Soviet times.

connection to history, [as a] vehicle for the transmission of tradition and heritage" (Mason 1981, 18). In her book Lavrent'eva makes effective use of the graphic novel as a medium to reconfigure the family history, represent trauma, and rearrange memory. The medium of the graphic novel lends itself especially well to representing multi-temporality. Lavrent'eva depicts how her grandmother plunges back into past traumas and is engulfed by her memories, seeing a bomb crater that transports her back to the war or waiting for a loved one which triggers memories of her father. Drawings of her young and beautiful grandmother after the war are accompanied by the caption: "My whole life, I lived in fear. It was always close by. The fear was locked inside, and fear surrounded me – I was used to it. Fear, and also … a feeling of guilt, without knowing what it was I felt to be guilty of" ["Я всю жизнь прожила страхом. Он всегда шёл радом. Страх был внутри меня и вокруг – я к нему привыкли. Страх, а еще чувство вины непонятно за что"] (Lavrent'eva 2019, 241)]. The overwhelming and all-pervading trauma is visualized by a split reflection

Ill. 2: © Ol'ga Lavrent'eva. Lavrent'eva 2019, 241.

of Valentina's shadow in a dark Leningrad canal that almost dissolves into black and white abstraction.

Lavrent'eva thus points the reader towards the after-effects of trauma, introducing a Russian version of survivor guilt, a phenomenon often found in those surviving the Holocaust (Juni 2016). In addition to her grandmother's narrative, the graphic novel adds another temporal layer by providing the reader with Lavrent'eva's own feelings and attitudes towards the depicted events. In its capacity as a hand-drawn narrative the novel offers its "own kind of thicket of time," adding the "manifestation of marks," as every graphic novel does (Chute 2016, 21). Time lapses into the present or the near past, where the author is being shown as interviewing her grandmother, add another layer to the text. Nearly all episodes situated in the present time feature acts of witnessing. Furthermore, she avoids exhausted elements of the family novel, especially the supplementation of missing information via archival and textual research, which has become a common narrative strategy. Given the author's decision to present the story almost exclusively from the point of view of her grandmother, mostly presenting Valentina as the verbal subject of narration, the one who sees and tells, and sometimes even literally adopting her perspective, the novel deprives itself of the possibility of supplementing Valentina's often limited perspective. So, even if the text creates a layered temporality and convincingly represents the workings of memory through shading and fading, the step towards an assessment of the historical events from the point of view of the post-catastrophic and post-memorial narrator is not taken.[9]

Lavrent'eva's family history is complicated further because her family is associated with foreignness. Despite the official ideology of the all-encompassing *sovetskii narod* [Soviet People] and the highlighting of socialist universalism, the Soviet Union acknowledged ethnic particularism and national identities. With a high degree of ambivalence, the Soviet Union "celebrat[ed] separateness along with communalism" (Slezkine 1994, 415), all the while conceiving of national and ethnic identities as remnants of a bourgeois if not counter-revolutionary past. While "Russia was multinational country, Leningrad [...] a cosmopolitan city, [...] its national minorities were the people most at risk" during the Great Terror (Snyder 2010, 97).

Although the family ties to Poland become increasingly lose after the father came to Leningrad to build a career (the family members do not speak Polish among themselves and Vicenty russifies his name – Vikentii instead of Vincenty,

9 Even in retrospect Valentina never transcends her own biography or hints at collective experiences. The story told by her, and her granddaughter has thus its limits, as Sylwia Kamińska-Maciąg remarks (2023). This is a criticism shared by Aleksei Pavlovskii (2019).

adding a patronymic [Lavrent'eva 2019, 27]), being associated with a country that is perceived as hostile, becomes a burden. In his study *Bloodlands*, Timothy Snyder highlights the fate of Poles in the Great Terror: "Biographies became death sentences, as attachment to Polish culture or Roman Catholicism became evidence of participation in international espionage" (2010, 96).[10] Being Polish already makes the family suspect via national affiliation and, as ardent Kirov supporters, the family is doubly stigmatized. Though the political activism is restricted to her father, Valentina and her sister being too young to engage in party politics, the whole family is affected by the father's arrest. Only when accessing his file, Valentina learns that her father was arrested together with ten other workers, "also Poles, also from the Kanonerskii plant" ["тоже поляки, тоже рабочие Канонерская завода" (Lavrent'eva 2019, 285)]. In hindsight, the "Polish ethnic character of the operation" is apparent, while at the time it was less obvious. Still, the fact remains, that in her contemporary recreation of the Great Terror the concept of ethnic persecution is not further explored. Here, as elsewhere in the novel, the father's fate is individualized and neither put into perspective with other victims of the Great Terror, nor with the violence directed against Poles in this period. Valentina's sense of alienation is never linked to her ethnic family constellation but to political repression and the haunting effect of the siege.

Valentina, who herself has never been to Survily and does not know where it is located exactly, thus cannot transfer any sense of Polishness or Polish customs, sayings, or culture to her children and grandchildren. Later in her life, her granddaughter remembers asking her, "where is Survily? Somewhere in Poland? Does it still exist?" ["Где они, эти Сурвилы? Где-то в Польше? И существуют ли до сих пор?" (Lavrent'eva 2019, 291)] – which makes the persecution more absurd and Survily more phantasmagoric. The village retains this imaginary quality even though the narrator finally travels there with her brother. The pictures she takes for her grandmother dissolve in a page-filling panel of black pencil strokes on white (Lavrent'eva 2019, 305). For the following generations, especially her granddaughter, the transnational family constellation is almost entirely meaningless, apart from the fact that it caused her great-grandfather's arrest.

10 Timothy Snyder contests that among the victims of the Great Terror were more than 300.000 Poles and Ukrainians (2010, 411) and gives the number of 6.597 Soviet citizens who were shot in the Leningrad region in the Polish operation (2010, 97).

2 Writing Family History of Pain

Although the root cause of trauma is the arrest of Valentina's father, his unknown fate, and the resulting destruction of the core family, as well as the ensuing stigmatization and trauma, the siege takes up more than hundred pages and constitutes the narrative/visual center. While the repression is a family affair, the siege is a collective experience. In fact, the event of the siege functions as a point of reference for the Great Terror, since it comes with a shared memory (albeit a distorted one), a fully developed literary template and iconic images. Commemoration means here positioning a narrative about the Great Terror alongside siege literature. Lavrent'eva's graphic novel aims to give voice to the forgotten victims of the Soviet regime that have rarely found representation in either verbal or visual literature. These people "lived in a constant state of fear because their relatives had been repressed" (Figes 2007, xxx). They needed to find a balance between the love for their father (in Valentina's case) and the need to conform. But as Valentina's story shows, the lost relatives are never forgotten. This also meant that the transmission of family history was complicated, memories were lost, pictures burned, and storytelling only became possible during the perestroika years, too late for many victims.

Within Russian memory politics today, there is almost no room for the commemoration of the Great Terror and repression, and thus remembering repressed family members has become increasingly complicated and undesirable, as is evident in the closure of Memorial in 2021. The remembrance of repression is further complicated by a scarcity of publicly available images of the victims or the plight of families of enemies of the people. Thus, while images of the siege abound in public memory, the repression cannot be conjured up as easily and is almost devoid of visual icons and topoi. The visual-verbal narrative in *Survilo* also calls our attention to this fact. Where we have the frozen bodies on the streets, the children's sleighs, and the broken-down street cars serving as visual metaphors for the siege, the Great Terror is a black hole without iconic images. Manifest documentation is only to be found in files. While the graphic novel re-mediates iconic images of the siege such as corpses transported on sleighs or streetcars frozen to a standstill in the visual depiction of the siege, the Great Terror has left very few visual traces. Consequently, the siege is represented in a great number of frames, referencing iconic images on page after page, evoking the well-known visual documentation of the event. On the contrary, the persecution of Valentina's father during the Great Terror is not visualized in a similar way, since the great mass of unknown victims to which Vikentii Survilo belongs, has left almost no traces. There are no widely circulating iconic images that could stand in for the lack of personal images of the repression, either. When Valentina finally gets access to her father's file in the former NKVD, then KGB archives, she is devastated by the fact that the file is minimal, the pages mainly devoid of meaning: "... [W]hat did I find in the file? There was nothing." [... И что там было в материалах дела? Там было ничего." (Lavrent'eva 2019, 283)] The whole material consists of some pages, and she realizes that there was not really a case against him, that "the case was made out of nothing." ["Дело составлено из ничего." (Lavrent'eva 2019, 285)] Her hope to find a last picture of him is also thwarted. "There were no photographs. Only text." ["Фотографий в деле не было. Только текст." (Lavrent'eva 2019, 288)] As Valentina says, despite having read up on repression and the Great Terror, she still did and does not understand its driving forces and mechanisms. Lavrent'eva finds a visual equivalent for this confusion, for the meaninglessness of the files, and the hole that was left by the arrest and execution of her father in her grandmother's life, by covering the pages with excerpts from the files, Valentina's

Ill. 3: © Ol'ga Lavrent'eva. Lavrent'eva 2019, 288.

commentaries and, on the last page, with an array of outlines of police photographs, resembling empty shells.

The memory of Vikentii Survilo looms large over his child's life. On the next page an image of her father taken from the family album dissolves into a large cloud hanging menacingly over an empty landscape, symbolizing Valentina's lifelong longing and search for answers as well as her trauma. Still, in comparison with the extended visualization of the siege, the visual representation of the repression remains marginal. The narrator does not find a graphic language to fill this void. While Aleksei Pavlovskii regards this as a shortcoming, a lack of visual inventiveness, and calls for fictionalization (Pavlovskii 2019), it is also possible to read this as an acknowledgment of the void. In Lavrent'eva's work, the void is not only a visual signifier of lack of documentation, it also often results in a lack of framing or a surplus of framing, as is the case with the above-mentioned silhouettes, drawing our "attention both to the creation of evidence and to what is outside the frame" (Chute 2016, 20). The apparent impossibility to visually represent what has left no visual traces, points us towards the fact that we need public images to construct private stories, that we must "feel public memories" (Landshut 2004, 19) to conceptualize our own stories. This holds true for family histories as well, as Lavrent'eva demonstrates. Family histories too, cannot escape the dilemma of visual representation or witnessing when confronted with a lack of documents. They either veer towards bracketing documentation in favor of fictionalization, or towards an acknowledgment of this absence. Commemoration serves as means to highlight this discrepancy, to underscore the blank spaces in Russian memorial culture. It also underscores that both events have affected Valentina in equal measure. These extreme experiences have a cumulative effect, as Lavrent'eva's graphic novel contests. With every dead family member, the mission of witnessing and surviving becomes more important. Or as Valentina tells her grandchild: "I often repeat to myself: I live for all of them." ["Я часто себе повторяю: Я живу за всех." (Lavrent'eva 2019, 167)] Passages like this one, but also Ol'ga's metatextual commentaries, support the claim that this is not solely Valentina's story but a family history, a "joint family effort" (Paperno 2009, 33),[11] that is, a text that breaks the silence of the past and turns whispers into shouts, but also a text that shows the lasting effects of the totalitarian experience on the family as whole, grandchildren included. In addition, it is also a text aiming for more than describing individual suffering, namely trying to give voice to a multigenerational

11 Irina Paperno (2009) shows that many memoirs written during the memoir boom of the 1980s and 1990s were written and reworked by several family members. The collaborations often acknowledge the lasting effects of trauma but also supply information that was not accessible during Soviet times.

family experience that is representative for all those whose relatives were oppressed or suffered through the siege.

The way in which the work narrates and visually represents hunger is especially indicative of temporal transcendence and focalizes the importance of biopolitics. While hunger forms the core of the siege narrative, Valentina is quick to point out that her hungry and lean years started even before the Germans bombed the food storages in Leningrad. She speaks about going hungry after her father's arrest and relegation to Bashkir exile, and during her time in Leningrad before the war. Noting that she was prepared for the great hunger of the siege, she remarks: "I had been starving for a long time, even before the war. This is what saved me. I understand now that I survived the siege because I was prepared, I had hardened myself." ["А я задолго до войны столько наголодалась. Это меня спасло. Сейчас я понимаю, что выжила в блокаду, потому что была подготовлена." (Lavrent'eva 2019, 103)] Thus, she uses the well-known and terrible hunger in Leningrad to highlight the ubiquity of hunger in Soviet history and she references the plight of the deportees during the terrible times of 1937/1938.

The insight into the Soviet politics of hunger as means of biopolitics, punishment, and oppression as witnessed by millions during collectivization, the Ukrainian famines of the 1930s, and in the Gulag, is equally present in other narrative representations of the siege, for example by Elena Chizhova. She, too, acknowledges that "the siege memory of her generation is the slow and long process of rethinking [the siege] that gradually leads to the conclusion that Hitler and Stalin are to blame for the tragedy of the Leningrad siege in equal measure" ["Das Blockadegedächtnis meiner Generation ist ein langsamer und langer Prozess des Umdenkens, der allmählich zu dem Schluss führt, dass Hitler und Stalin Schuld an der Tragödie der Leningrader Blockade tragen" (Chizhova 2019)], thus commemorating different totalitarian events. Additionally, Aleksei Pavlovskii regards the fact that Lavrent'eva creates a visual metaphor for the Leningrad catastrophe as "double blockade – Hitler's siege and Stalin's disciplinary restrictions" (Pavlovskii 2019), a concept developed by siege survivors Lidia Ginzburg and Ol'ga Freidenberg, as her greatest achievement. Thus, there is no irony in the fact that Valentina finds refuge in the sick ward of a prison.[12] Commemoration here means the realization that these epochal events share a similar biopolitical approach towards Soviet

12 In other aspects Lavrent'eva does not share the critical attitude authors like Chizhova and researchers like Tat'iana Voronina have developed towards the official siege narrative. In many ways her novel stays within its confines, stressing solidarity and the overwhelming wish to defy the German invaders. Pavlovskii (2019) is critical of this aspect of her novel (2019) which he considers to be not on the height of contemporary siege discourses. One could argue that this is because Lavrent'eva's goal is to write family history, not siege history.

citizens.[13] Lavrent'eva's family novel commemorates the siege and the Great Terror within the family (and national) frame, but she points her readers, especially the non-Russian ones, towards ways in which those experiences may be integrated into a European culture of remembrance.

Lavrent'eva's drawings preserve the shocking and haunting quality of her grandmother's experiences, when she depicts her surrounded by an empty landscape littered with bomb craters, symbolizing her constant fear of being absorbed by traumatic memories and erased like her dead family members (2019, 10–11). For example, Lavrent'eva uses panels without words to depict the traumatic effect of bombings (2019, 122–123) or the freezing cold (2019, 178–179). Valentina does not call the arrest and ensuing murder of her father by its name, she rather speaks of "neschast'e" ["несчастье" (Lavrent'eva 2019, 15)], which means the 'catastrophe' or 'disaster' that came upon her family. Her life is broken in half, the happy life before the disaster of 1937 and the siege and the time after. 'Disaster' is another word for 'meaningless suffering' which presents itself as the fundamental problem of postsocialist memory, as Alexander Etkind has noted (2013, 186). The postcatastrophic character of *Survilo* (see Artwińska and Tippner 2021) is underscored by its aesthetics, which do not differentiate between then and now, pointing the reader towards the fact that Valentina still inhabits the black-and-white chronotope created during the 1930s and the siege. As noted above, the mnemonic landscape of the novel is dominated by the siege narrative and thus by the war narrative. The remembrance and celebration of heroic sacrifice during World War II undoubtedly is the focal point of official but also familiar narratives, while invocations of the repression under Stalin have become increasingly rare in the last two decades. Even though, as this article contends, memories of persecution are less vivid and prominent, forming a backdrop rather than being foregrounded in the text. Despite its critical engagement with Russian public memory of the Putin era, *Survilo* falls in line with public calls for heroic family memory while also placing family memory of persecution along its side, a popular strategy in Russian contemporary collective memory in general, as Haskins has pointed out (Haskins 2023). Taking this critical view, it could be argued that Lavrent'eva's novel is representative of a less subversive tendency in contemporary Russian memory culture that writes victims of the state into the general narrative of sacrifice, as means of "exonerating" (Haskins 2023, 367) them without criticizing wider memory culture.[14]

---

13 This is a thought that can already be found in the writings of Lidia Ginzburg or Ol'ga Freidenberg who compare both regimes.

14 Haskins is interested in the ways in which official and private memories interact and official discourse seep into private memories, becoming habituated and privatized. She argues that including

3 Conclusion

Lavrent'eva's graphic investigation into her grandmother's life is a narrative of heightened individuality. Despite its roots in visual witnessing, it is not intended to educate the reader beyond the individual case presented here. The framing as family history stresses the private, rather than the public side of family life. Furthermore, it goes to show that a lack of documents and iconic images complicates the narration of private suffering. This is achieved not through research and critique but through the act of storytelling. What links Lavrent'eva's graphic family novel to other family

Ill. 4: © Ol'ga Lavrent'eva. Lavrent'eva 2019, 308.

---

victims of repression in the narrative of sacrifice which dominates Russian memorial culture, is an inherently non-critical approach, as she demonstrates regarding other examples.

histories and research in the family archive is its conviction that the present can liberate us from the past and purge the ghosts of the past. Lavrent'eva concludes her family history with the image of light streaming through a window that almost fills the last panel in the book. Readers are invited to perceive this last image as both the end of the oppressive hold the past had on the family, but also as a larger metaphor for the logic of enlightenment that pervades these texts of search and research.

Bibliography

Alaniz, José. *Resurrection: Comics in Post-Soviet Russia*. Columbus, OH: Ohio State UP, 2022a.

Alaniz, José. "Survilo and Historical Trauma in Contemporary Russian Comics." *International Journal of Comic Art* 22.1 (2022b): 5–32.

Alaniz, José. *Komiks: Comic Art in Russia*. Jackson, MISS: UP of Mississippi, 2010.

Artwińska, Anna, and Anja Tippner. "Postcatastrophic Aesthetics." *The Afterlife of the Shoah in Central Eastern European Cultures: Concepts, Problems, and the Aesthetics of Postcatastrophic Narration*. Eds. Anna Artwińska/Anja Tippner. London: Routledge, 2021. 3–22.

Artwińska, Anna, and Agnieszka Mrozik. "Generation and Gendered Memory of Communism in Central and Eastern Europe: Methodological Perspectives and Political Challenges." *Gender, Generations, and Communism in Central Eastern Europe and Beyond*. Eds. Anna Artwińska/ Agnieszka Mrozik. London: Routledge, 2002. 9–22.

Bal, Mieke. "In the Absence of Post-." *Narratology & Ideology: Negotiating Context, Form, and Theory in Postcolonial Narratives*. Eds. Divya Dwivedi/Henrik Skov Nielsen/Richard Walsh. Columbus, OH: Ohio State Press, 2018. 231–250.

Bederov, Viacheslav. "Repressii i blokada – surovym iazykom komiksa." *Godliteratury*, March 25, 2019. https://godliteratury.ru/articles/2019/03/25/repressii-i-blokada-surovym-yazykom (December 31, 2023)

Chizhova, Elena. "Das doppelt verriegelte Gedächtnis." *Neue Zürcher Zeitung*, May 6, 2019. https://www.nzz.ch/meinung/tabuisierte-blockade-leningrads-das-gedaechtnis-meiner-familie-doppelt-verriegelt-war-von-innen-und-von-aussen-ld.1466171 (December 31, 2023).

Chute, Hillary. *Disaster Drawn: Visual Witness, Comics, and Documentary Form*. Cambridge, MA: Belknap, 2016.

Etkind, Alexander. *Warped Mourning. Stories of the Undead in the Land of the Unburied*. Stanford, CA: Stanford UP, 2013.

Figes, Orlando. *The Whisperers. Private Life in Stalin's Russia*. London: Penguin Books, 2008.

Ginsborg, Paul. *Family Politics: Domestic Life, Devastation and Survival, 1900–1950*. New Haven, CT: Yale UP, 2014.

Haskins, Ekaterina. "Remembering the war, forgetting Stalin's repressions: appeals to family memory in contemporary Russia." *Handbook on the Politics of Memory*. Ed. Maria Mälksoo. Cheltenham: Edward Elgar Publishing, 2023. 362–376.

Hirsch, Marianne. "The Generation of Postmemory." *Poetics Today* 29.1 (2008): 103–128.

Juni, Samuel. "Survivor guilt: A critical review from the lens of the Holocaust." *International Review of Victimology* 22.3 (2016): 321–337.

Kamińska-Maciąg, Sylwia. “Postmemory of Stalinist Repressions and the Siege of Leningrad in Olga Lavrentieva's Graphic Novel *Survilo* (2019).” *Children's Literature in Education*. https://doi.org/10.1007/s10583-023-09553-9. 2023 (December 31, 2023).
Kuhlman, Martha, and José Alaniz. “General Introduction: Comics of the ‘New’ Europe.” *Comics of the New Europe. Reflections and Intersections*. Eds. Martha Kuhlman/José Alaniz. Leuven: Leuven UP, 2020. 7–25.
Landsberg, Alison. *Prosthetic Memory. The Transformation of American Remembrance in the Age of Mass Culture*. New York, NY: Columbia UP, 2004.
Lavrent'eva, Ol'ga. *Shuv. Goticheskii detektiv v vos'mi glavach*. Saint-Petersburg: Bumkniga, 2019.
Lavrent'eva, Ol'ga. *Survilo*. Saint-Petersburg: Bumkniga, 2019.
Mason, Kenneth Clifton. *The Family Chronicle and Modern America*. PhD University of Nebraska, Lincoln, 1981.
Merridale, Catherine. “The Collective Mind: Trauma and Shell-Shock in Twentieth Century Russia.” *Journal of Contemporary History* 35.1 (2000): 39–55.
Mickwitz, Nina. *Documentary Comics: Graphic Truth-telling in a Skeptical Age*. Houndmills, Basingstoke: Palgrave Macmillan, 2016.
Miller, Nancy K., and Jason Tougaw. “Introduction: Extremities.” *Extremities: Trauma, Testimony, and Community*. Eds. Nancy K. Miller/Jason Tougaw. Urbana: University of Illinois Press, 2002. 1–25.
Paperno, Irina. *Stories of the Soviet Experience. Memoirs, Diaries, Dreams*. Ithaca, NY: Cornell UP, 2019.
Pavlovskii, Aleksei. “Pervyi graficheskii roman o docheri ‘vraga narodov.’ Pokolenie postpomiati i chernyi iashchik nevyrazimogo.” Colta, March 27, 2019. https://www.colta.ru/articles/art/20863-pervyy-graficheskiy-roman-o-docheri-vraga-naroda (December 31, 2023).
Slezkine, Yuri. “The USSR as a Communal Apartment, or How a Socialist State Promoted Ethnic Particularism.” *Slavic Review* 53.2 (1994): 414–452. https://doi.org/10.2307/2501300 (December 31, 2023).
Snyder, Timothy. *Bloodlands: Europe Between Hitler and Stalin*. New York, NY: Basic Books, 2010.
Sommer, Mikkel, and Anna Rakhmanko. *Din bedstefar Vasja*. Copenhagen: Cobolt, 2021a.
Sommer, Mikkel, and Anna Rakhmanko. *Vasja, Dein Opa*. Kassel: Rotopol, 2021b.
Tippner, Anja. “The Transnational Family Novel as Memory Form: Mnemonic Migration in Marina Frenk, and Sasha Marianna Salzmann.” *Transcultural Transmission, Translation and Circulation of Memory Across and Into Contemporary Europe*. Eds. Eneken Laanes/Jessica Ortner/Tea Sindbæk-Andersen. Berlin: De Gruyter, forthcoming.
Tippner, Anja. “Familiengeschichte als Gegengeschichte – Jüdische Identitäten in der zeitgenössischen russischen Literatur bei Elena Čižova, Marija Stepanova und Ljudmila Ulickaja.” *Osteuropa* 69.9–11 (2019): 203–223.
Wagner, Sabrina. “Distanziert, nüchtern, unbefangen? Zur Konstruktion und Zuschreibung ‘generationentypischer’ Emotionen im Diskurs um eine Erinnerungsliteratur der ‘Enkel.’” *Familiengefühle: Generationengeschichte und NS-Erinnerung in den Medien*. Ed. Jan Süselbeck. Berlin: Verbrecher, 2014. 45–67.

3 Imagined Bonds, New Formations

Pablo Valdivia Orozco

On the (Im-)Possibilities of Family Narratives in Times of Violence. Writing Family Novels after García Márquez: Roberto Bolaño, Héctor Abad Faciolince, and Pilar Quintana

> Are we mistaken to suspect that history – at least in this instance – repeats itself yet again?
> Hortense Spillers, "Mama's Baby, Papa's Maybe: An American Grammar Book" (1987, 78)

1 Family Narratives: On Mythical and Historical Violence

It is safe to say that family narratives are in a very fundamental sense narratives of violence. Greek mythology might be the most striking example. The most terrible things happen in families and because of passions related to family relations. Family narratives, read as narratives on violence, make it plausible to think of violence as a fundamental and even foundational aspect in the most intimate part of human existence. Not surprisingly, Freudian psychoanalysis referred precisely to Greek mythology and its family narratives in order to formulate its theory of the subject. The archaic violence made explicit in the myth of Oedipus is something the self needs to cope with to become a socially functional subject. This and other myths allowed Freud to describe the violent and unconscious desires the self has to work through and repress.

Narratives play here a central role – not only as mythical narratives about primordial violence in our inner reality, but also as reflecting on narrativity as such. Psychoanalysis can be understood as a work on and with (family) narratives (see Schafer 1980). The *work* realized in the analytical praxis can be summarized as the intent to find a language and narrative for the subject's emotional biography. Its capacity to narrate will allow him or her to suffer less and overcome the (neurotic) urge to fulfill the *fate* that the (individual family) myth has *predicted* for the subject. To narrate one's own (family) story is part of the strengthening of the self. Finally, the consolidation of the conscious I can be understood as an

Pablo Valdivia Orozco, European University Viadrina Frankfurt [Oder]

https://doi.org/10.1515/9783111208664-012

ongoing narrative process, of including and excluding elements, of stabilizing and sense-making. From this perspective, family narratives are the most essential narratives in human existence, the systematic place where the individual and the collective history coincide – a coincidence that – given a mature self – is also the condition for a more active and freer life of the subject.

This therapeutical setting tends to offer strong evidence for an assumption that has huge metahistorical implications: Narratives are tools of civilization to overcome primordial violence and to transform it into a cultural and socially acceptable and even productive force. The fact that archaic desires are made accessible and functional through a narrative is an act of symbolization that already liberates the subject from the urgency to respond immediately to its first drives and desires. Narrating a myth is – as Hans Blumenberg (2006, 8) insisted – already a first expression of enlightened reason. The act of narrating something creates a (sovereign) distance, namely from mythical violence and the *absolutism of reality*. Only *homo narrans* is able to overcome the beastly nature of man and become an agent of his own story.

However, this *enlightening, empowering* and *emancipating* conception of narratives – generally valid in an analytical setting and beyond – is nonetheless only one side of the coin. Freudian psychoanalysis also insisted on the fact that culture and society require us to renounce certain pleasures. The transformation of the primordial violence does not translate exclusively as civilizational refinement, but is also a loss, not only a conciliation, but also a deepening of the inner conflicts. The Freud of the death drive and the later Freud of *Civilization and its Discontents* [*Das Unbehagen in der Kultur* (1929)] was well aware of the fact that if a narrative is too teleological, best exemplified in the mature subject's capacity of sublimation, this might not necessarily be the best model for society. This has several reasons: First of all, humans do not renounce that easily a once experienced pleasure, and 'culture' is not necessarily a synonym of refinement but can also be the path to an even more devastating and destructive violence than any primordial violence. The very same corpus of the ancient Greek (family) myths can be also read as an allegory of the fact that violence is not just a prehistorical and mythical force, but something that remains active in history, and is repressed when we read these narratives merely as myths or as figurations of something already overcome and only present in the aesthetic experiences of pity and fear.

From this perspective, family narratives that treat violence in one or the other way can be read as a reminder that violence is not something primordial relegated to the past, but an omnipresent and persistent phenomenon in human society. It is therefore not absurd to assume that also narratives can be part of this persistent violence. The optimistic and civilizational narrative about narratives now seems itself a narrative that is haunted by the repression of the violence produced by the narratives themselves. The violence of narratives consists not only in their force of determining, but also of repression. In psychoanalytical terms, the most decisive aspect of narrative violence is not its manifest violent content, but its complicity in the process of repression, be it by allegorizing or normalizing violence. Narratives can be powerful means to affirm the process of repression. This is also the reason why psychoanalysis focuses especially on inconsistencies, little breaks, seemingly secondary aspects, etc. This focus on the process of repression is of particular interest in this case because it is here where the formal processes of psychic life inevitably acquire their social and cultural specificity. While repression as such is necessary for every subject, the concrete means and contents of repression are always specific and regulated by social and cultural norms and needs.

In the following pages, and with reference to Latin American literary family narratives, I want to address this latter dimension of narratives and specifically of family narratives – not only because of their unique status as being at turns mythical and historical, social and individual, but because these family narratives are especially apt to illustrate the violence exercised by narratives and the search for other narrative logics. Concretely, the narrative violence of family narratives is effective both on a structural and on a pragmatic level. Family narratives evidence more than other narratives that the sequential logic of narratives is also a determinant logic. Sequence (especially if framed as expression of a determining origin or progress or development) presupposes a clear path where every element is conditioned by its prior element. In the case of family narratives, this sequential logic often translates into a clear sense of genealogy. Only then family narratives can be narratives of constitution and of a constitutive power, that is: a narrative powerful enough to have a specific meaning, a plot, and a distinctive symbolic power.

On a pragmatic level, family narratives manifest more than other narratives the constraint to tell, the obligation to be able to narrate one's story in a certain (that is: genealogical) way. The 'well-built' family narrative illustrates how *homo narrans* does not simply narrate in order to constitute its humanity but is also able to use narratives in order to establish a difference within humanity itself. Subjects in a fully realized sense are those individuals who know how to narrate, construct, and present their story in a way that makes them distinct, that renders a past readable and a present meaningful. A subject is considered less liable or worthy when he or she is not able or willing to tell his/her genealogy. The fact that family narratives in Greek mythology and tragedy tell the story of aristocratic families proves that having a genealogy is not the same as having ancestors. Social distinction – so important for bourgeois society – surely echoes this ultimately political difference between those who have a story and those who are outside of history.

Narratives can be a medium to perpetuate violence, and to be more precise: the (biopolitical) violence of becoming distinct that is associated with the potentially lethal exclusion of those who are not able or willing to become distinct and therefore exposed to social death, not having a body, but being just flesh, deprived of any form of 'respectable' kinship (see Spillers 1987, 67–75). This violence is invisible and repressed as long as we focus only on its constitutive effects in the dominant sector of society, negating the fact that this violence is not only a founding one, but a constitutive part of modern society and its structure.

This more suspicious view on the possibility of overcoming violence through (mainly patriarchal) narratives is inspired by critical approaches that question the colonial-bourgeois promise of overcoming mythical violence thanks to history and its supposedly enlightened and civilized subjects. The (hidden) persistence of violence is the other side of the civilizational narrative that generally is only admitted as a collateral, not a necessary damage. The excessive and at the same time repressed presence of violence specifies the narrative violence mainly as a segregating force that separates the space of the civilized and the space of the beast in order to repress the nexus between civilization, destruction, and extinction. This – and not the supposed overcoming of violence – is the reason why histories need to be told again and again. The uncanny question raised here is: what if history – at least a certain kind of modern history – is not the overcoming, but the perpetuation of a supposedly constitutive and mythical violence precisely by the continuous reproduction of this divide between the space of civilization and a space that is just material? What if, as Walter Benjamin said, the real catastrophe is the continuity, or as Rebecca Comay said: "The continuum – continuation as such – *is* the catastrophe." (1994, 262; emphasis in the original) If family narratives are narratives of a (catastrophic) continuum, they might be a natural place where we can study paradigmatically how and why this continuum is reproduced. Maybe Tolstoy also had in mind this close relationship between the continuum and the catastrophe, when, in the opening of *Anna Karenina*, he insists that only unhappy families are distinctive. Distinction is a high value in modern society and for modern subjectivity and to associate it with unhappiness might be a reminder of the violence that distinction implies.

Family narratives are a privileged form to allegorically reflect the constitution of society and to interrogate its very logic. The question is, then, whether meaning or distinction are only given by (lethal, destructive) exclusion or if we can think of a meaningful narrative that is not reigned by the (patriarchal) ideal of distinct subjectivity. The question is whether *meaning* or *distinction* are only given by (lethal, destructive) exclusion or if we can think of a meaningful narrative that is not reigned by the (patriarchal) ideal of distinct subjectivity. Do relations between family members liberate the potential of relationality as a source of meaning and sociality or do they function in an antagonistic way? Family narratives, I submit, can be a privileged genre for questioning the teleological and *civilizational* narrative of modern society by insisting more on the principle of relation than on excluding difference, by questioning the concept of a distinct present and the linear character of hegemonic narratives (Kaakinen 2017, 15–19), and by reminding us that the problem of violence is not a question of a primitive past, but an always urgent and actual question of distribution.

2 Latin American Family Narratives: The Colombian Paradigm

The persistence of violence is a commonplace if one thinks of Colombian history. The more recent history of this South American country even knows a period that is called *La violencia* [the violence] that began with the riots after the assassination of the liberal leader Jorge Eliécer Gaitán in 1948, known as the *bogotazo*. Official historiography tried to interpret it as an archaic backlash that the consolidation of the modern nation state would eventually overcome. A more attentive look contradicts this narrative: *La violencia* was in fact just a further manifestation of a permanent state of violence, a permanent civil war passed on from generation to generation.

The Colombian case, far from being an idiosyncratic abnormality, can be understood as a particularly explicit case where the formation of the nation state cannot be told as the story of initial formative violence. National history is better described as an ongoing violence. The narrative of national cohesion is an ideal that requires permanent exclusion, domination, and extinction.

One structural reason for this persistent violence is – in the Colombian case at least – the fact that this country was and still is profoundly fragmented and diverse, and thus opposes the idea of national unity as uniformity. This fact is clearly reflected in its foundational fictions (Sommer 1991) from the nineteenth century, as in the novel *María* (1867) by Jorge Isaacs where Bogotá and the idyllic *valle* [valley] are presented as two opposed worlds, representing the modern and rational state and the emotional landscape of the interior as two irreconcilable spaces. This fragmentation is even more pronounced in the most famous Colombian novel until now: García Márquez's *Cien años de soledad* [*One Hundred Years of Solitude*], published in 1967.

This novel is much more than just a Colombian novel. It is a novel that narrates the fate of the Buendía family, which became the archetypal family narrative in modern Latin American literature. The Colombian case becomes a paradigmatic one. In a heterodox reading of this novel, I want to propose that this archetypical status is also connected to the way in which violence is treated in it. From the peripheric and yet heavily entangled position of the Colombian Caribbean this novel illustrates how a genealogical national narrative is, especially in the context of a colonial society, necessarily a violent one. This novel opposes official national narratives, partly because the politics of the distant and isolated capital Bogotá and the national conflicts translate in the provincial Macondo into a civil war whose reason no one seems to understand. At the end, the difference between the two parties is only visible in the color of the ceilings that are changed according to the ruling party. Moreover, the novel opposes official narratives because it questions the genealogical paradigm of national narratives. Against this background it is more than just a curious fact that the founding couple of Macondo, Ursula and José Arcadia, found Macondo in order to hide the fact that they, being cousins, are an incestuous couple.[1] Only by negating this fact it seems possible to establish the idea of a proper genealogy that will be permanently challenged by the following generations. This first *sin* haunts the whole family. The founding couple is obsessed with the urge to hide its initial transgression that endangers the family's capacity to be an integral part of the nation. José Arcadio dreams of modern science as a means of liberation; and Ursula intervenes every time an incestuous relationship appears on the horizon.

Since the desire of incest is not overcome, it seems at first glance that this novel refers to this desire as an archaic mythical desire. But this leitmotiv is treated in a remarkable manner. First, there is no *real incest* in the strict sense of the word (the relationship between cousins is not considered incestuous), but there are several nearly incestuous relationships. The taboo is not a mythical prohibition that it is banned from the discourse of everyday life. It operates more on a symbolic level, representing the (hegemonical) desire to constitute *a proper family*. Furthermore, the ongoing variations of a near-incest do not only express a fixation but can also be read as a creative way to deal with an apparently absolute and unequivocal law. By continuously challenging its limits, the incest taboo no longer signifies the opaque and itself mythical passage from a primitive to a historical and civilized state. As is well known, the incest taboo, founding myth of Freudian psychoanalysis, has found an important echo in Lévi-Strauss' structural

1 Note that in Isaacs' novel the two protagonists and lovers are also cousins. This has been already commented by Efraín Kristal (2000, 400).

anthropology (1962), and has a metahistorical dimension that can be read in different ways. In the established interpretation of the incest taboo, this taboo exemplifies the fact that a society cannot exist if it is not able to establish an absolute basis for its laws. The incest taboo is the paradigmatic instance of a constitutive law as prohibition, making prohibition the kernel of the law. No other taboo affirms that clearly the close relationship between the repression of desire and the process of civilization. Having said this, it is interesting to note that while constitutional law is based on the incest taboo, national cohesion necessitates the exclusion of the other, that is: in its operative logic it realizes an incestuous desire of a homogeneous national population.[2]

But there is also another way to read this law – an interpretation that requires a more literal reading of the taboo. The incest taboo reminds us that a society cannot survive solely based on exclusion, in total isolation. Every society needs its other, a foreign element. The other is constitutive not only as filling the potentially void position of the one who is not part of the family, the antagonistic other against whom a collective identity is formulated. The other is also a vital element in a very concrete sense, as exemplified by the novel in a suggestive way. In *One Hundred Years of Solitude*, the weakened incest taboo undermines the politics of exclusion and inclusion that are associated with the law of modern society and the proper family. The Buendía family, clearly a patriarchal family, is also quite an impressive patchwork family, an example for a family-like "support-structure" (Spillers 1987, 75) that undermines the patriarchal order. Sexist and phallocentric as this novel may be, it is also progressive in the sense that family is not conceived as an essential and biological relationship, but rather in the sense of who is or becomes part of the continuously growing house with a lot and very diverse 'others.'

The leitmotiv of the horror of incest can be read as an allegory for the persistent violence that is bound to the national narrative and its quest for a properly teleological history (a distinct identity in the name of national modernization). However, the continuous silencing of the initial quasi-incest also affects the transgenerational family narrative: the history unfolding from one generation to the next is precisely represented as a story of solitude because this first repression forces the family to narrate its evolution/involution with an absolute beginning that already implies a loss. In the context of the colonial history of Latin America, the premise of an absolute beginning of history, cited ironically at the beginning

2 The explicit recognition of Colombia as a multiethnic state, beyond any phantasies of ethnic fusion, is a very recent phenomenon and was surely not conceivable when the novel was written.

of the novel (see García Márquez 2008, 9), comprises the repression of the destruction of all pre-Columbian culture. If, however, incest is desired by every new generation, if the transgression of the foundational law is continuously desired, this desire is not to be read as an archaic desire, but rather as an allegory for the quest of a history that has been neglected by official history and that cannot be totally repressed. This iconic Colombian novel can be read as the desperate attempt to detach family narratives from the model represented by the foundational fictions of the modern state. *Cien años de soledad* invites us to think of a family narrative not in terms of a foundational difference and identity, urgently desired by the nation state, but as a constellation of multiple positions that do not obey a *telos*, that is: the official rules of (social or national) foundation. The novel undermines this traditional structural pattern closely related to the hegemonic narrative of progress and civilization, by presenting a story of seemingly eternal repetition, as becomes clear already by the repeated variation of the names of the family members. *Cien años de soledad*, a book full of doublings, is a narrative that resists the narratives of progress, but also the image of the mythical that is reproduced by the allegedly enlightened mind.

It is important to insist on the fact that since there is no real (repeated) incest, there is no real repetition, but variations of almost incestuous relationships. The innovative and critical potential of the novel lies in its intent to free the circularity from what appears to be mythical thinking from the perspective of the *enlightened* mind. Repetition is not overcome in the name of progress and its absolute (that is: mythical) beginning, but – and this is allegorized by the highly ambivalent leitmotiv of incest – by variation. Unlike perfect repetitions or teleological developments, variations neither depend on purity nor do they operate according to an antagonistic logic in the formation of a well-defined (family) identity. The ultimate horizon of the novel might be also summarized as a politics of narration: the obligation to narrate (one's genealogy) is transformed into the pleasure to narrate, in always new variations, resisting the hegemonic desire/injunction to become a properly *modern* family/society.

The history of the Buendía family ends at the very moment when variation is no longer possible because the family now lives in isolation and solitude. Macondo, reduced to the house of the Buendía family, is destroyed by an apocalyptic wind that comes after the city has been modernized and fully incorporated into global capitalist production and its promises of progress and development. The dream of the founder of the village, José Arcadio, turned out to be a nightmare. The capitalist circulation of goods and labor did not bring truth and wisdom, but a 'progress' that turned out to be much more lethal than the previous state of 'ignorance.' As García Márquez himself insinuates in his Nobel Prize speech, the question the Buendía family raises is if there can be another model civilization, a civilization where "the races condemned to one hundred years of solitude will have, at last and forever, a second opportunity on earth." (García Márquez 1982)

This interpretation of the narrative of the Buendía family might seem provocative. We are used to refer to this book as a mythical work, and surely it has become one in the reception. Without a doubt, this is a book, as many critics insisted, that establishes a Latin American myth by rewriting several Western myths. Yet it is also a book that narrates a family narrative that opposes the national narrative by presenting another form of history. Of course, there are mythical and archetypical (and highly problematic) female and male figures such as Ursula and the Coronel Aureliano Buendía. The motive of the title – solitude – addresses an existential problem, which has been treated also by Octavio Paz (2015). Magical Realism, as pointed out by Parkinson Zamora and Faris (1995), has a certain affinity with mythical and non-rational narratives. And finally, as Josefina Ludmer's (1972) masterful structuralist analyses proved, the novel's narrative is structured as a myth, with its oppositions and repetitions. While not ignoring these readings and facts, I will nonetheless argue that this family narrative is a narrative in search of another civilizational model that is not simply the Latin American version of Western myths, but another way to constitute society – and this might be a further reason for the specifically Latin American significance of this novel. The Buendía narrative allows a perspective on the violence of modernization which shows itself as such an overwhelming and continuous force that it turns out to be the real mythical and repetitive force of destruction. Not unlike Adorno's and Horkheimer's *Dialectics of Enlightenment* (2022 [1948]), this family narrative exposes the repressed violent side of the supposedly modern and enlightened narrative of the nation. While the modern nation state pretends to create history and presents itself as the entrance into history, it is actually the end of history insofar as it does not offer an option for quitting the circle of violence and exploitation that is intrinsic to its 'progress.'

3 Killing the Father

The fate of García Márquez' famous book is somewhat ironic. The novel became itself – almost immediately after its publication – a mythical narrative that silenced other expressions. What was meant to be a counter-narrative of official memory and history became itself a quasi-official formula, the textbook for a tropicalist identity. The question for the generation writing after García Márquez was: How to narrate after and against this father of magical realism, how to escape the mythical trap of his model?

One of the most remarkable efforts to overcome a stereotypical Magical Realism is realized by the Chilean author Roberto Bolaño. In a short and remarkable passage of his mega-novel *2666* (2004; engl. 2008) Bolaño rewrites the novel of the Colombian in a rather spectacular way.[3] The context of this family narrative is not an isolated and phantasmagoric place like Macondo, but the still ongoing feminicides in Northern Mexico, just behind the U.S. border. These feminicides, as Bolaño (2004b, 335) once said, are the allegory of the inferno of Latin American history as well as of the total frustration of any revolutionary promise of a better future. In this short narrative digression Bolaño narrates the story of a family that also covers six generations and where the repetition of names is brought to its extreme: the names of the women are identical because every new generation is the result of a previous violation. In other words: Bolaño replaces the mythical sexual figure of incest with the more historical sexual figure of a continuous violation, reminding us that family violence is also a gendered violence, thus highlighting an obvious blind spot in the novel of the Colombian winner of the Nobel Prize.

Naturally, the question of how to narrate after García Márquez is especially virulent in the Colombian context. One example of a Colombian post-García-Márquez-family narrative is the novel of Hector Abad Faciolince: *El olvido que seremos* (2006) [*Oblivion. A Memoir* (2010)]. This autobiographical novel narrates the story of the author's family in a rather conventional way. However, it differs profoundly from *One Hundred Years of Solitude.* First of all, we have a personal narrator, an 'I' that narrates, not an omnipresent narratorial voice. Secondly, the motor of this family narrative is a fundamental loss: it's the murder of his father in 1987 that turns Abad Faciolince into a writer. As in Bolaño, the violence is presented not in a proto-mythical setting, but as a very concrete and contemporary event.

But Abad's major intervention against the hegemonic model of the Buendía might be a remarkable short story, inspired by Heinrich von Kleist's *Die Marquise von O ...* (1808) [*The Marquise of O*]. In *La señorita Antioquia* (2008) [Miss Antioquia], the Latin American setting is not evoked to understand a Latin American specificity but is developed in order to tie the persistence of violence to the bourgeois society and its ascension fantasies. Citing Cervantes and Kleist who respectively wrote novellas about a violation that became legalized a posteriori by the fact that the violated woman married the (wealthy) violator, Abad Faciolince's short story reveals how a social ritual is used to cover up violence, reproducing it

3 For a more detailed discussion, see Valdivia (2013).

constantly in order to save the good reputation that is so important for bourgeois society. The supposedly universal female desire to become a mother and the bourgeois imperative to be a mother in legal terms lie at the basis of this recurring story of violence. Let us not forget that it is only during the 1990s that violation in marriage (i.e.: in an 'acceptable' context) is recognized by criminal law in Colombia or Germany.[4]

Seen from this perspective, we could say that Latin American family narratives can be read as an effort to indict the mythification of the continuous and omnipresent violence in Latin American history. It is a plea for another history, freed from the catastrophe of an intrinsically violent modernization. But who should be the actors of this different story, how will it begin?

While the narratives of these three male writers give us an impressive diagnostic of the violence in Latin American history (and beyond), they are quite abstract when it comes to imagining concrete changes, and to be more precise: to write about the body where this violence is rooted. How can we imagine another story, can there be a family narrative without violence and violation? "How can we move from *the plot of violence's undoing* to *the undoing of the plot* (Hartman 2022, 5)?"

4 After the Father: *La perra*

In 2017, the Colombian writer Patricia Quintana published a book titled *La perra* [The Bitch]. It is a provocative title because the most common use of this word in Spanish is not to designate a female dog, but a promiscuous, so-called 'easy woman.' In other words: it is a synonym for bitch, whore or slut. The editors were smart enough to understand this. In the cover we don't see a female dog, but a rotten boat, producing a remarkable sense of ambivalence, between past and present, death and life, sea and land.

I want to finish these reflections by taking a closer look at this example that could be considered as an attempt of 'undoing the plot,' insofar as this narrative reveals once more that family narratives are narratives about women and mothers. Motherhood is the neuralgic point of family narratives in modern society. As Hortense Spillers reminds us in her famous essay *Mama's Baby, Papa's Maybe: An American Grammar Book* (1987) that inspired the following reading, family narratives are powerful "cultural fictions" (66) that structure society and express a

4 Also here, I am referring to a recent and more extensive discussion of Abad Faciolince, see Valdivia (2022).

"grammar" that not only organizes the (patriarchal) structure but also the exclusion and repression.[5] The *perra* in this pejorative and vulgar sense is, obviously, the opposite of the mother in traditional family narratives.

Quintana's novel is about the relationship between a female dog and a woman, Damaris, who suffers profoundly because she cannot become pregnant. The relationship with the dog is determined from the beginning by Damaris' infertility. Damaris calls the very young puppy, very likely to die like most of its siblings, Chirli. This was the name she wanted to give the daughter she never had. Damaris and her husband Rogelio already have several dogs with totally different names: Danger, Mosco and Olivo. The first name was given to the dog by the former owner who wanted a dangerous dog, the second name was given to the dog because a fly came out of his infected body, and the origin of the third name is not explained in the book. We only get the information that Olivo is the offspring of danger. The only female dog and the only dog that receives its name from Damaris is Chirli. Already this fact indicates that this dog is the announcement of a major change: "Damaris told herself things would be different with this dog." (Quintana 2020, 16) ["Damaris se dijo que con la perra todo sería diferente." (Quintana 2017, 13)

The dog's name is also of interest because it evokes in a very dense way the cultural setting and its conflicts. The way it is spelled refers to the transcription of the *bad* pronunciation of the English name "Shirley." Linguistic accents are often an index of class and race. This peculiar transcription reflects the accent of the Pacific coast, the most neglected and poorest region in Colombia where most of the population is Afro-Colombian. Against this background, it is worth mentioning the origin of the name in this case. As the novel indicates, "Chirli" refers to the prototypical Caucasian beauty queen from Bogotá, Shirley Sáenz Starnes, who represented Colombia in the Miss Universe competition in 1978.[6] The fact that Damaris and her cousin Luzmila, both Afro-Colombian women, admire the white and western-style beauty of Shirley Sáenz is a clear hint at the racial hierarchies in Colombia. Damaris is described as a clumsy woman and is far from considering herself a beauty – there seems to be no space for black beauties. Ironically, the name Damaris is also easily referable to a beauty queen. Damaris Dediego Torres was Miss Chocó 1994, that is: an Afro-Colombian beauty queen representing the

5 In her study focusing on the views on and the experiences of Afro-American families, Spillers shows convincingly how motherhood in modern society cannot exist on its own and is always depended on a patriarchal structure. Motherhood is therefore only 'acceptable' if it is integrated in this structure. Otherwise, it is considered a "state of pathology" (1987, 66).

6 The importance of the Miss-competitions for popular national culture in Colombia cannot be overestimated. For instance, also Abad Faciolince writes in the mentioned short story of a beauty queen.

region where the novel is set. Damaris Dediego became a celebrity because she was the wife and is now the widow of the most famous Salsa composer and band leader in Colombia during that period, Jairo Varela, founder of the Salsa band *Grupo Niche*. *Niche* is a synonym for black people and Salsa music began in Cali as an expression of urban Afro-Colombian popular culture. This Afro-Colombian background is fundamental to understand the questions raised about motherhood in this novel. Having Spillers' essay (1987) in mind, it does not seem incidental that these questions are formulated in a novel that narrates the story of an afro-diasporic woman. The history of slavery led to a racially structured sociality in the Americas that also affected family relations. For the afro-diasporic community, Spillers concludes, "'motherhood' is not perceived in the prevailing social climate as a legitimate procedure of cultural inheritance." (1987, 80)

This lack of legitimacy is reflected in the all too obvious fact that this dog is a kind of *Ersatz* – which is true to a certain degree. But the close relationship between the woman and the dog is not only determined by Damaris' frustrated desire to be a mother. Although she cares about the young puppy with a love we are used to identify as motherly love, their bond has also another origin. Both Chirli and Damaris have been abandoned by their mother at a very young age. The name given to the dog is not only a testimony of Damaris' frustrated desire and her (racist) idealization of western beauties, but also a subtle indication of the exclusion from motherhood both beings suffered. Their respective mothers were not allowed or able to be mothers since their right to be mothers was not considered of worth. Against this background, it is no coincidence that Damaris and Chirli are named after beauty queens, who, while being so different, nonetheless have one thing in common: they are not and must not be mothers.[7]

The exclusion from motherhood, more than the *Ersatz*, turns out to be the deeper reason why Damaris is finally able to liberate herself from a subjugating desire, so intertwined with sexual, racial, ecological, and economic violence. Parodying the well-established method of replacing a child with a dog, Damaris' behavior puts into question the way a woman can respond to a supposedly natural desire under conditions of structural violence, poverty, and social exclusion. What begins as an inter-species mother-child-relation turns out to be a family-like solidarity that does not follow the patterns implied by the model of motherhood established by patriarchal society and is directed against this (tragic) model of motherhood.

7 Even today, a woman who competes for Miss Universe is not allowed to be married or a mother.

Pilar Quintana affirmed in an interview given to the Spanish newspaper *El País* in July 2021, that this novel is about the horrors of motherhood, its ambivalences that normally are repressed in official family narratives:

> In *La Perra*, for example, I poured out all my worst fears as a mother: that my son would die and that I would mistreat him. Because in the same way that your son makes you a better person, he also makes you bring out your deepest rage, the most terrible monster, the one I don't want to see because it's the same one my mother had. Because it is frowned upon for a mother to say that she can't stand her child or that sometimes she feels like giving it away or killing it, which in the end are absolutely normal feelings but which, nevertheless, are frowned upon because the role of the mother is sacralized.
>
> [En *La Perra*, por ejemplo, volqué todos mis peores miedos como madre: que se muera mi hijo y maltratarlo. Porque de la misma manera en que tu hijo te hace ser mejor persona, también te hace sacar tus rabias más profundas, el monstruo más terrible, el que yo no quiero ver porque es el mismo que tenía mi mamá. [...] Porque no está bien visto que una madre diga que no soporta a su hijo o que a veces tiene ganas de regalarlo o de matarlo, que al final son sentimientos absolutamente normales pero que, sin embargo, está mal visto nombrar porque el rol de la madre está sacralizado. (Quintana 2021)][8]

The obscurities of motherhood refer obviously and primarily to the fact that the dog is somehow the daughter Damaris never had, so the treatment of the dog by Damaris shows how she would have behaved as a mother: loving and caring at the beginning; possessive, jealous, and cruel at the end. The story of the relationship between Damaris and Chirli changes after the dog begins to leave home. When the dog finally comes back, Damaris first thinks that she came back because she had missed her. But the real reason for her return is – as Damaris' husband tells her – her pregnancy and the instinct to give birth to her puppies in a place she considers her home:

> "That's just because she's pregnant," he said.
> Damaris felt as she'd been punched in the gut: she couldn't breathe. Couldn't even refuse to accept it because it was so obvious. The pup's teats were swollen and her belly round and firm. It was unbelievable he'd even had to tell her. Damaris was engulfed in sadness [...]. Damaris couldn't stand the sight of her. (Quintana 2020, 104–107)
>
> [–Eso es solo porque está preñada –dijo.
> Para Damaris fue como un golpe en el estómago sintió que se quedaba sin aire. No pudo ni siquiera negarse a aceptarlo porque era evidente. La perra tenía las tetas infladas y la barriga redonda y dura. Era increíble que él se lo hubiera tenido que decir.
> A Damaris la cubrió la tristeza [...]. Damaris no soportaba verla. (Quintana 2017, 74–75)]

8 Translation: Jobst Welge.

To face this fact is so terrible for Damaris that she must negate it; her delusion, anger, and pain seem justified since the dog turns out to be a bad mother:

> The dog turned out to be a horrible mother. On the second night she ate one of her puppies and in the days that followed abandoned the remaining three so she could go lie in the sun by the pool or sprawl in the washtub, where it was always cool, or under one of the houses with the other dogs – anything not to be with them. [...] They weren't even a month old when she ran away yet again, and when she didn't come back they had to learn to eat left-overs. By the time the dog returned, several days later, her milk had dried up and she shunned them completely. (Quintana 2020, 109)

> [La perra resultó ser una pésima madre. La segunda noche se comió a uno de los cachorros y los días siguientes dejaba abandonados a los tres que le quedaron para asolearse en el andén de la piscina o echarse en el lavadero, donde siempre estaba fresco, o debajo de alguna de la casa con los otros perros, en cualquier lado con tal de no estar cerca de ellos. [...] No habían cumplido un mes cuando la perra volvió a escaparse y como no regresaba les tocó aprender a comer sobras. A su vuelta, varios días después, se le había secado la leche y se desentendió por completo de ellos. (Quintana 2017, 77)]

The obscurity of motherhood, then, at first glance points to the scandal of *bad mothers*, mothers who are not able or willing to fulfill their duty as mothers. *La perra* would be a healing narrative, allowing the author and reader to overcome the dark sides by talking about them, in a kind of aesthetic exorcism. Yet there is another dimension of this obscurity that is visible only if we do not read exclusively the curing force of narrative, but also its excluding violence on a social level and this means: if we take into consideration the specific context of this narrative. The novel is constructed in a way that reveals another dimension of the genitive 'obscurity of motherhood.' Maternity is not only an individual question but also a historical and social one. The novel essentially tells a story of *bad mothers*: (female) children abandoned by their mothers for several, but always violent reasons, mothers who will eventually also leave their future children, forced to give them away. The mother of Chirli was killed and Damaris' mother had to leave early for economic reasons. Both are marked by the absence of the mother. And this absence constitutes the first and most painful memory of Damaris:

> [B]ut the image stored in Damaris' memory was one of her mother walking out to the sea until she disappeared from sight. It was one of her first memories and always made Damaris felt lonely, and cry. (Quintana 2020, 140)

> [[L]o que Damaris guardaba en su memoria era a su mamá alejándose a pie mar adentro hasta que se perdió de vista. Era uno de sus recuerdos más viejos y siempre la hacía sentirse sola y llorar. (Quintana 2018, 98)]

Chirli and Damaris did not 'learn' to be good mothers because 'the conditions' did not allow their mothers to be good mothers. The questions raised here about the 'obscurity of motherhood' are not individual but structural: How is it possible to be a mother in a context of a persistent structural violence? For those who live in a society where violence is not the exception but the rule the paradox of motherhood becomes even more evident: this supposedly strongest and natural of all ties between to members of a species is also the most vulnerable. Motherhood is the place where social, economic, and ecological violence becomes most visible and *effective*. The loss of the mother is a traumatic loss with long-lasting effects. And we should be more precise: the loss here is not contingent, but expression of a social structure.

In a remarkable effort of memory and recollection of her deleted African past, the Afro-American feminist Saidiya Hartman writes about this trauma and the specific nature of this loss in the case of the afro-diasporic community. Hartman describes the loss entailed by this violence with a very precise language, making use of the motive of the orphan that is also very established in Latin America literature and especially in literature written by female authors (see Dröscher 2005): "To lose your mother was to be denied your kin, country, and identity. To lose your mother was to forget your past. [...] I was an orphan." (Hartmann 2007, 85)

The 'obscurity of motherhood' should invite us to ask for the origins of this obscurity. What Quintana's novel also does is to raise the challenging question if and how a family-like love between different species is possible beyond the notion of a motherhood that has been shaped by a patriarchal capitalist society. The relationship between Damaris and Chirli can be read as a relationship against motherhood. Only by refusing motherhood, Damaris is able to love. This extreme exclusion and negation of motherhood is necessary to break with the endless circle of violence that is associated with motherhood in a patriarchal society. Negation is the only opposition available to those who are not in power and who are outside history. The only thing that is left to them is their present and the only way to preserve this present of a family-like 'solidarity-structure' – opposing all genealogical family narratives – is to abolish 'traditional' motherhood.[9]

Dogs and the black woman are here paralleled in respect to their exposure to voluntary and arbitrary patriarchal violence and desire. In Quintana's novel there is a remarkable and seemingly minor event that testimonies to this knowledge passed from one generation to another, a painfully embodied knowledge on how to live with violence, violence inflicted on those beings who are not human

9 In a similar way, with respect to Damaris' and Chirli's parents, Saidiya Hartman notes the fixation on the present: "they decided the present was all they could bear." (2007, 15).

or not humans in its fullest sense. As a child, Damaris used to play with Nicolás, a white boy from Bogotá, the son of a rich or upper-middle-class family that bought a holiday house in the area. One day, the boy, despite the warnings by Damaris, goes into the sea and is taken away by the strong tide and drowns. His body is returned by the sea after 34 days. Damaris' uncle Eliécer decides to beat her every day until the boy is found.[10]

What follows is a dense narration that evokes the experience of a "structural, and above all, gratuitous" (Wilderson 2003, 229) violence the body of the black slave experienced in the Americas and that is nonetheless necessary insofar, as this anti-black violence, according to Wilderson, is necessary for human civilization to define the space of humanity.[11]

> Tío Eliécer was helping with the search and, in the afternoons, when he came back with the bad news, he'd sit on a tree trunk by the door to the shack. Damaris knew that this was the sign for her to approach.
>
> She did so without dawdling, as she didn't want him to get any madder than he already was. Then her uncle would grab a hard, flexible switch cut from a guayaba tree and whip her. Tía Gilma had told her not to tense up, that the more she relaxed her thighs, which was where her uncle struck her, the less it would hurt. She tried, but fear and the cracking of the first lash made her clench every muscle tight, and each new blow hurt more than the last. Her thighs looked like the back of Christ. The first day he'd given her one lash, the second two, and so on, adding one for each day Nicolasito didn't turn up. (Quintana 2020, 43–44)
>
> [El tío Eliécer estaba ayudando en la búsqueda, y por las tardes, cuando llegaba con las malas noticias, se sentaba en un tronco que tenían en la entrada de la cabaña. Damaris sabía que esa era la señal para que se acercara.
>
> Lo hacía sin demora, pues no quería que él se enojara más de lo que ya lo estaba. Entonces el tío agarraba una rama de guayabo dura y elástica y la azotaba. La tía Gilma le había dicho que no se tensara, que entre más flojos tuviera los muslos, que era donde el tío

10 It is surely no coincidence that this name makes reference to Jorge Eliécer Gaitán, a left-wing political leader whose assassination in 1948 was the spark that unleashed the insurrection called *el bogotazo* that eventually ended up in the civil war of *La violencia*).

11 See Wilderson (2003, 230–237): "If, by way of the black subject, we consider the underlying grammar of the question 'What does it mean to be free?' that grammar being the question 'What does it mean to suffer?' then we come up against a grammar of suffering not only in excess of any semiotics of exploitation, but a grammar of suffering beyond signification itself, a suffering that cannot be spoken because the gratuitous terror of white supremacy is as much contingent upon the irrationality of white fantasies and shared pleasures as it is upon a logic – the logic of capital. It extends beyond textualisation. [...] Marxism [...] cannot come to grips with America's structuring irrationality: the libidinal economy of white supremacy, and its hyper-discursive violence that kills the black subject so that the concept, civil society, may live. [...] The gratuitous violence begun in slavery."

le pegaba, menos le dolería. Ella lo intentaba, pero el susto y el estallido del primer latigazo hacían que apretara todos los músculos, y cada nuevo latigazo la lastimaba más que el anterior. Sus muslos parecían la espalda de Cristo. El primer día le había dado uno, el segundo dos, y así había ido aumentando por cada día que Nicolasito no aparecía. (Quintana 2017, 32)]

This episode, seemingly not related to the main action, is nonetheless crucial in order to understand the disturbing end of the novel also in its structural and historical dimension. The definitive break in Damaris' and Chirli's relationship is the dog's second pregnancy. Damaris decides to give the dog away to a lady named Ximena (who owned a brother of Chirli and wanted a female dog). Ximena, usually drunk in the evenings, does not care very well for the dog, and so one day the dog comes back to the place she considers her real home. Instead of being touched, Damaris treats the dog as badly as possible to scare her away once again. The very personal and precise mistreatment – "Suddenly Damaris knew what she had to do" (Quintana 2020, 125) ["De pronto Damaris supo lo que tenía que hacer" (Quintana 2017, 89)] – is intended to break definitively their relationship once and for all. Knowing how much the dog hates any contact with water – some drops are enough to scare her away –, Damaris waits for the dog being distracted to throw a bucket full of water on her. The dog is totally perplexed and both seem to know that their special relationship just broke into pieces: "Damaris, who got the feeling that this time she'd broken an irreparable bond between them. Contrary to what she expected, it hurt." (Quintana 2020, 126–127) ["Damaris tuvo la impresión de que ahora sí se había roto entre ambas algo irreparable. Contra lo esperado, le dolió." (Quintana 2017, 89)]

However, the dog comes back once again, pregnant once again. Although their relationship is broken, the instinct of motherhood forces the dog to come back to the place where she grew up, where she survived the loss of her mother, and to expose herself once again to the violence of Damaris who, in anger, decides to kill the dog by strangulation. This extreme reaction is clearly a reaction to the pregnancy of the dog. Damaris feels even some kind of satisfaction in killing the dog: "'Pregnant again,' she said to herself, and tugged even harder." (Quintana 2020, 144) ["–Está preñada otra vez –se dijo y siguió apretando con más ganas" (Quintana 2017, 101)].

I would propose to read this scene of anger, fury, and excessive violence as an extreme form of resistance of those who are fundamentally and systematically deprived of the possibility to realize their humanity. Likewise, Damaris' infertility can also be seen as an allegory for this exclusion. The only option to escape this extreme, dehumanizing exclusion is to refuse reproduction, which is precisely what Damaris does. As Silvia Federici (2004) has pointed out, this imperative of biological reproduction is a blind spot of Marxist theory of labor and the violence of capitalist production. From the position of the black female this critique is articulated even more radically. The resistance of women therefore is not only directed against production, but also against reproduction[12] – an extreme measure known also from enslaved mothers who killed their babies to save them from slavery.

Damaris seems to have a clear intuition that she committed a terrible crime, a crime that implies much more than *just* killing a dog. The end of the novel leaves it open if Damaris commits suicide. The reason for this is not, as one would expect, an unbearable sensation of guilt, but the insight that no one will be able to punish her adequately, she who dared to fight motherhood:

> At first, she considered the possibility of staying put until Ximena got there, considered letting the woman see her killer's hands and expression and notice the smell of urine, considered accepting the blame and the punishment she deserved but then told herself that neither Ximena nor the townsfolk could punish her the way she deserved. So she thought maybe she should head into the jungle, barefoot, in nothing but her spandex shorts and faded sleeveless blouse, and go out past La Despensa, past the fish farm, the navy land, the places she and Rogelio had gone and those that they hadn't, and get lost the way the dog and the boy on Nicolasito's curtains had, out where the jungle was most terrible. (Quintana 2020, 155)

> [En un primer momento contempló la idea de quedarse ahí hasta que Ximena llegara, dejarse ver las manos y la mirada de asesina y que se diera cuenta del olor a orines, aceptar su falta y el castigo que le correspondía, pero se dijo que ni Ximena ni la gente del pueblo podrían castigarla como se merecía. Así que pensó que tal vez debería irse al monte, descalza y apenas en su licra corta y su blusa de tiras desteñida, y caminar más allá de La Despensa, la estación de cultivo de peces, los te-trenos de la Armada, los lugares que había recorrido con Rogelio y los que no habían llegado a conocer, para perderse como la perra y el niño de las cortinas de Nicolasito, allá donde la selva era más terrible. (Quintana 2007, 108)]

The questions provoked by Quintana's compact novel might be the following, echoing the debates inspired by Gayl Jones' novel *Corregidora* (1975): What other forms of resistance against this violence are conceivable other than the total negation of reproduction? How can we free motherly love from a seemingly inevitable process of subordination and repression? The family narrative to come might help us to imagine ways to free reproduction from colonial-capitalist production, free our capacity to love, free our desires from the colonial-capitalist matrix and its narratives in order to "rewrite after all a radically different text for a female empowerment" (Spillers 1987, 80).

---

12 See Wilderson (2003, 230): "The worker demands that productivity be fair and democratic [...], the slave, on the other hand, demands that production stop".

To think of (Latin American) family narratives as narratives on violence and motherhood requires a structural and historical reflection on an all-too-often repressed violence. Ironically, it is the myth of motherly love that is a major reason for the silencing of the historical and structural dimensions of violence that controls reproduction and those involved in it. The major obscurity of motherhood refers to the fact that motherhood turns out to be the central place where the loss and the struggle for recovery of history have their very concrete beginnings. We will not be able to understand the *big* history, History with a capital H, if we do not care about the repressive violence both of motherhood and enacted upon motherhood. Against this background, it should not surprise us that Latin American family narratives, including those that are male-centered and patriarchal, talk almost obsessively (and not always consciously) of violence against women and mothers. This violence is surely one dominant aspect of modern colonial-capitalist society and its deep grammar is readable for those who are excluded from its 'progress' and whose stories of resistance might help to *undo this plot.*

Bibliography

Abad Faciolince, Héctor. "La señorita Antioquia." *El amanecer de un marido*. Bogotá: Alfaguara, 2014. 149–164.

Abad Faciolince, Héctor. *El olvido que seremos*. Bogotá: Editorial Planeta Colombiana, 2006.

Blumenberg, Hans. *Arbeit am Mythos*. Frankfurt a. M.: Suhrkamp, 2006.

Bolaño, Roberto. *2666*. Barcelona: Anagrama, 2004a.

Bolaño, Roberto. "Final: Entrevista de Mónica Maristain." *Entre Paréntesis*. Barcelona: Anagrama 2004b. 329–344.

Comay, Rebecca. "Benjamin's Endgame." *Walter Benjamin's Philosophy. Destruction and Experience*. Eds. Andrew Benjamin/Peter Osborne. London: Routledge, 1993. 251–291.

Dröscher, Barbara. "Orfandad. Configuraciones de una figura en la literatura escrita por mujeres en Centroamérica (1975–2000)." *Revista Iberoamericana* 71.210 (Jan–Mar 2005): 145–164.

García Márquez, Gabriel. *The Solitude of Latin America*, December 8, 1982. https://www.nobelprize.org/prizes/literature/1982/marquez/lecture/ (March 15, 2024).

García Márquez, Gabriel. *Cien años de soledad*, Bogotá: Alfaguara, 2008 [1967].

Federici, Silvia. *Caliban and the Witch. Women, the Body and Primitive Accumulation*. New York: Autonomedia, 2004.

Freud, Sigmund. "Das Unbehagen in der Kultur." *Gesammelte Werke*. Vol. 14. *Werke aus den Jahren 1925–1931*. Eds. Anna Freud et al. Frankfurt a. M.: Fischer, 1999 [1930]. 419–506.

Freud, Sigmund. "Jenseits des Lustprinzips." *Gesammelte Werke*. Vol. 13. *Jenseits des Lustprinzips. Massenpsychologie und Ich-Analyse. Das Ich und das Es*. Eds. Anna Freud et al. Frankfurt a. M.: Fischer, 1940. 3–69.

Hartman, Saidiya: *The Plot of Her Undoing*. Feminist Art Coalition, 2020 [ebook].

Hartman, Saidiya. *Lose your mother*. New York: Farrar, Strauss and Giroux, 2007.

Horkheimer, Max, and Theodor W. Adorno. *Dialektik der Aufklärung: philosophische Fragmente.* Foreword Eva von Redecker. Frankfurt a. M.: Fischer, 2022 [1944].

Kaakinen, Kaisa. *Comparative Literature and the Historical Imaginary. Reading Conrad, Weiss, Sebald.* Cham: Palgrave Macmillan, 2017.

Kristal, Efrain. "The Incest Motif in Narratives of United States and Spanish America." *Internationalität nationaler Literaturen. Beiträge zum ersten Symposion des Göttinger Sonderforschungsbereichs 529.* Ed. Udo Schöning. Göttingen: Wallstein, 2000. 390–403.

Lévi-Strauss, Claude. *Anthropologie structurale.* Paris: Plon, 1962.

Ludmer, Josefina. *Cien años de soledad. Una interpretación.* Buenos Aires: Tiempo Contemporáneo, 1972.

Parkinson Zamora, Lois, and Wendy B. Faris. *Magical Realism: Theory, History, Community.* Duke: Duke UP, 1995.

Paz, Octavio. *El laberinto de la soledad.* Madrid: Cátedra, 2015 [1950].

Quintana, Pilar. "No aceptamos que una madre diga que no soporta a su hijo, a pesar de ser algo normal." *El País*, July 3, 2021. https://elpais.com/mamas-papas/2021-07-03/pilar-quintana-no-aceptamos-que-una-mujer-diga-que-no-soporta-a-su-hijo-a-pesar-de-ser-algo-normal-el-rol-de-madre-esta-sacralizado.html (March 15, 2024).

Quintana, Pilar. *The bitch.* Transl. Lisa Dillman. New York: World editions, 2020.

Quintana, Pilar. *La perra.* Bogotá: Penguin Random House Grupo Editorial Colombia, 2017.

Schafer, Roy. "Narration in the Psychoanalytic Dialogue." *Critical Inquiry* 7.1 (Autumn 1980): 29–53.

Sommer, Doris. *Foundational Fictions.* Berkeley: University of California Press, 1991.

Spillers, Hortense. "Mama's Baby, Papa's Maybe: An American Grammar Book." *Diacritics* 17.2 (Summer 1987): 65–81.

Valdivia Orozco, Pablo. "Eine unversöhnte Marquise von O … : Über eine Allegorie sexueller Gewalt bei Héctor Abad Faciolince und Heinrich von Kleist." *Kleist-Jahrbuch* (2022): 195–213.

Valdivia Orozco, Pablo. *Eine romantheoretische Studie im Ausgang von Gabriel García Márquez, Sandra Cisneros und Roberto Bolaño.* Berlin, New York: De Gruyter, 2011.

Wilderson, Frank B. "Gramsci's Black Marx: Whither the Slave in Civil Society?" *Social Identities* 9.2 (2003): 225–240.

Anna Gaidash

Transgenerational Imagery in Sofia Andrukhovych's Novella Collection *Old People*

1 A New Generation Representing a National Imaginary

A representative of the younger generation of women writers in independent Ukraine, Sofia Andrukhovych (*1982) contributes to the postcolonial national fiction with her texts, creating a collective Ukrainian identity. Studying early independent Ukrainian literature, Mark Andryczyk detects a tendency to deconstruct official histories and national myths already in the texts of the 1980s, which are still applicable to the development of further Ukrainian fiction. The euphoric time of Independence unleashes "upending [of historical accounts and national mythology], playing with them, and dethroning them of their authority" (Andryczyk 2012, 48). The scholar repeatedly emphasizes that at the dawn of its development post-colonial national writing needs stability and structure (Andryczyk 2012, 123; 125; 141), although he sees the basic means of realizing this need in postmodern literary techniques (Andryczyk 2012, 46; 122), including spatial and temporal displacement of (central) characters to places outside Ukraine (Andryczyk 2012, 102). Andryczyk's understanding of Ukrainian postcolonial writing is close to Bhabha's consideration of nation and narration in respect of the "international dimension both within the margins of the nation space and in the boundaries in-between nations and peoples" (1990, 4). Andrukhovych's prose has a certain tonality and is at the same time in tune with the national imagery alongside the other women's voices of Natalya Snyadanko, Irena Karpa, Tania Maliarchuk, and Yaroslava Lytvyn, to name but a few. Developing the paradigm set by their predecessors (Oksana Zabuzhko, Yevhenia Kononenko, and Maria Matios) at the dawn of the country's independence, "engagement with the 'great' national issues, such as those of the traumatic Soviet past and Ukraine's post-Soviet challenges" (Wallo 2019, 5), women authors help diversify their representations of national identity, transgressing the confines of geographical boundaries in the topoi of their fiction and experimenting with the literary tools for their implementation in the prose of the new millennium.

Anna Gaidash, Borys Grinchenko Kyiv Metropolitan University

https://doi.org/10.1515/9783111208664-013

Analyzing the national imaginary through historical and literary lens, Oleksandra Wallo goes deep into Ukrainian idealistic "striving for unity" (2019, 8), which for quite some time has been an issue even after Independence. Her reflections conclude with a position favorable of imaginative literature, which, as opposed to narrative history, can fill in the gaps of documentary sources (2019, 13) following the Aristotelian differentiation between history and fiction: "The real difference is this, that one tells what happened and the other what might happen. For this reason, poetry is something more scientific and serious than history, because poetry tends to give general truths while history gives particular facts" (Aristotle). During the decade before and after the collapse of the USSR Ukrainian fiction is overtly postmodernist. In his analysis of the construction of post-Soviet Ukrainian identity in prose, Andryczyk affirms, that "[n]ever in the history of Ukrainian literature has the Ukrainian intellectual been given so much attention in prose as in the period [between 1990 and 2001]" (2012, 12). Yet in the framework of women's literature of the period the incompatibility or impossibility of relationships between female and male Ukrainian intellectuals prevails, as in the novels by Zabuzhko and Kononenko (Andryczyk 2012, 89–99). Tamara Hundorova considers the postmodernism of Ukrainian women's literature through the prism of feminism focusing on the double female marginality in the traumatic history of nation and the "search for paradise, for virgin land" (2019, 186; 197). Among pioneer women writers Hundorova praises Zabuzhko whose postcolonial fiction is equal to that of US-American and British novelists: in her texts the search for identity and the heroine's road to herself, themes of sisterhood, infantilization, corporeality, eroticism and sexuality, a blend of popular literature with the intellectual essay (2019, 190–195), define the development of Ukrainian women's writing for the following decades. In the examination of the national plots, Wallo champions how in their novels the canonical writers (Zabuzhko, Kononenko, Matios) insert "women into the national story in ways that often contradict or complicate the traditional woman/nation plots" (2019, 23). Even though the following generations of Ukrainian women writers continue [to tackle] the collective national identity [,] they do not "foreground" it (Rewakowicz 2018, 11). Grouping Karpa, Andrukhovych, and Maliarchuk under the umbrella term of post-feminism, Rewakowicz singles out in their texts "progressive ideas of empowerment and choice as substitutes for political activism. Their female characters, by and large liberated and independent, enjoy their sexuality and freedom, and yet, at the same time, dream [of finding the] right man" (Rewakowicz 2018, 120). Younger women writers, among them Sofia Andrukhovych, address other issues in their narratives, apart from national traumatic experiences, which are oftentimes at the core of the modern Ukrainian novel.

2 Transnational Narrative in Andrukhovych's Fiction

This article studies the transnationality of Andrukhovych's short prose texts, focusing on the historical imaginary and temporal aspects of the family stories in the early twenty-first century. At the forefront of a Pleiades of post-Independence Ukrainian women writers, in her texts Andrukhovych reflects on nationwide identity beyond the traditional or established earlier narrative frames of the literary discourse, advancing human mobility processes and decreasing the distance between such ontological binaries as Self and Other, past and present, and outside and inside. Andrukhovych experiments with content and form in her writings and modifies the canon established by Zabuzhko. Andrukhovych's prose is transnational in the broad understanding of the notion, due to its highly transcultural nature. Ukrainian identity is far from fixed, stereotyped, or homogenous in the system of characters in the collection *Stari Ludy* [*Старі люди* (2008); Old People], consisting of two novellas written earlier: *Stari Ludy* [*Старі люди* (2003); Old People] and *Lito Mileny* [*Літо Мілени* (2002); Summer of Milena].[1] The transcultural mode of Andrukhovych's writing is represented by diverse narrative strategies, the shift in character focalization, the dialogical interaction of different generations within one family group, and the variation of topoi. These features reveal the protagonists' ambivalence, exceeding the boundaries of national belonging in each novella. Additionally, in *Lito Mileny* Andrukhovych employs elements of magical realism, a common tool in postcolonial fiction which creates a transcultural imagery with a potentially universal appeal.[2]

The above features in Andrukhovych's early texts, including the fusion of the boundaries of the Self/Other opposition, especially salient in the binary old/young, lay the ground for the transcultural syncretism in modern Ukrainian prose in which the "family saga, centered on the history of the restoration of family and national history relevant to postcolonial writing, represents the positive meanings associated with old age. [The] saga's elderly character acts as a historical memory agent, a symbol of the wholeness of life, an example to follow" (Bashkyrova et al. 2021, 220). The reconsideration of the old family saga is found in Volodymyr Lys's novels *Stolittia Yakova* [*Століття Якова* (2010); Jacob's Millennium], *Solo dlia Solomii* [*Соло для Соломії* (2013); Solo for Solomiya], *Kraina hirkoi nizhnosti* [*Країна гіркої ніжності* (2015); A Land of bitter Tenderness], Marina Hrymych's *Frida* [*Фріда* (2015); Frida], and Luko Dashvar's *PoKrov* [*ПоКров* (2016);

1 All translations from the Ukrainian are my own.

2 See also the contribution by Matteo Colombi in this volume.

PoKrov]. Foregrounding the elderly characters in her collection, Andrukhovych debunks the notion of the boundary as a discriminatory practice of alienating and making older adults invisible in society. Cultural geography and, partially, memories of older adult characters constitute transnationality in Andrukhovych's collection in question.

In terms of literary genre, *Lito Mileny* might be said to be a fusion of the *Bildungs-* and *Reifungsroman* (in Barbara Waxman's terms) in the context of an extended family story. In this novella, the Ukrainian multiethnic palette (Gypsies and Africans act as minor characters), imagined and experienced geographical space (Africa), and migration across the continents, form individual, collective, or national identities that resonate, firstly, with the long-cherished intentions of Soviet-era Ukrainians to break through the Iron Curtain and to end the stifling system of the regime before the country's independence. Secondly, the migration trauma for Ukrainians in post-Independence times, which limited the freedom to travel westward to a significant extent before Euromaidan, is equally tangible in the period of *Lito Mileny*'s creation: the ease with which the novellas' characters travel is a literary way of verbalizing the postcolonial experience, resulting in a prophetic vision of Ukraine today. After all, "[w]e live in an era of transnational migrations, when displacement becomes voluntary or desirable, and rootlessness itself becomes a symbol of globality" (Hundorova 2023, 72). One of the remarkable features in Andrukhovych's collection is the blurring of the conventional dichotomy between the familiar setting (home) and alien territory (new and sometimes quite distant locations for the characters of both novellas). In their journeys, the characters get to know strange people and different places which in the process of crossing the boundaries turn out to be close and understandable for them.

In the vein of globalization, Andrukhovych subverts the identification between a person and a citizen, especially in *Lito Mileny*. The characters strengthen the already established figure of decolonized Ukrainians and also form their cross- or transnational experiences. In connection with emancipatory images of the older adults, the texts signal positive transformations in society, which slowly but surely heals itself from the traumatic colonial past and develops in tune with the democratic values of Western civilization. Freedom of travel is one of the fundamental values granting transcultural mobility that often leads to the formation of a hybrid personality able to share experiences enriching one's individual and national identity.

In her understanding of the family, Andrukhovych, in both texts, is quite open in presenting communities with non-trivial family bonds, not necessarily blood-related, and thus with various family histories constellating transcultural and transgenerational narratives. Focusing alternately on the first and third generations, the family constellation in the eponymous novella *Stari Ludy* facilitates the treatment of the incurable disease of the female protagonist whereas in *Lito Mileny* each family age group interacts actively with the central character. As Maria Rewakowicz underlines, "[b]oth works emphasize the importance of family relations but also reverse the accepted notions of what it is that constitutes family" (2018, 123). Intentionally imaginative stories or memories shared by the characters of *Stari Ludy* widen the contemporaneous horizons of the institution of the family, which for many decades in the history of Soviet Ukraine was labeled a *unit of society*.

Even though Sofia Andrukhovych follows her own literary path with a unique yet already identifiable authorial voice, it is hard to detect the pursuit of a national identity in her novellas so imperative in the canonical Ukrainian women's prose of Independence; evident is rather a focus on the regional collective within the global context, in the form of the self-reflection of the carnivalesque postmodern literature of Bu-Ba-Bu.[3] One of the approaches relevant to tackling the family constellations in Andrukhovych's collection *Stari Ludy* is age studies.

The stigma of late adulthood is subverted by Andrukhovych by means of the historical imaginary, too. For instance, Marta, one of the protagonists in the *Stari Ludy*, narrates various kinds of stories, both invented and real. Addressing them not only to Luka, her young lover, who is the grandson of Marta's stepsister, and one of the narrators, but also potentially to larger audiences, Marta rewrites her family's, the town's, and the nation's histories, thus decolonizing them on these levels. With her made-up stories, the elderly character fills in the gaps which had been left unfilled by the Soviet hegemony. Andrukhovych's multiple endings to the novella, combined with often unexpected shifts of narrators, and especially a number of stories-within-a-story, creates a computer game effect with alternative choices, close to the experience of millennials and subsequent generations. *Stari Ludy* is as heterogeneous in content and structure as in its resonance with Kaisa Kaakinen's reception aesthetics (2017, 9).

As a representative of Eastern European literature, Andrukhovych articulates a new Ukrainian identity beyond the post-Soviet in her transtemporal, transcultural, and transnational imagery. The characters in both novellas transcend the postcolonial transition, acting in a transtemporal dimension. The protagonists undergo transformations of their identities, reconsidering their selves in the postcolonial reality. In their transcendence they become models for the readers to follow.

3 Bu-Ba-Bu is a literary postmodern performance group founded in Lviv in 1985 by the Ukrainian writers Yuriy Andrukhovych, Viktor Neborak and Oleksandr Irvanets. The Bu-Ba-Bu in the name of the group stand for "burlesque, balahan [chaos] and buffonada."

Andrukhovych's prose aims to decolonize the collective Ukrainian identity in the sense outlined by Lydia Hiraide; it "not only seeks to overthrow colonialism, but also to remove and redress its lasting traces and legacies afterwards" (2021, 14). Andrukhovych's therapy is not as sharp and painful as in the prose of the older women writers' generation but is rather imbedded in the less realist subgenre of magical realism, enabling the "rehistoricizing" (Kaakinen 2017, 4) of the traumatic past and present under the guise of the fantasy world, as opposed to the realist novel that "gives readers a coherent 'mental picture' of the nation, grounded in historical time" (Wallo 2019, 9). What is really debatable in the collection *Stari Ludy* is the history of collective time: in both novellas the temporal dimensions are unidentifiable by default, following the laws of fantasy/magical realism genre regulations. Rehistoricizing, applied in reference to Kaakinen's reception aesthetics, seems to be relevant in connection to the authorial intention of Andrukhovych, whose novellas narrate family sagas, making them comprehensible worldwide. The dynamics of family constellations in Andruchovych's imagery is achieved through the continuity and active interaction of their generations.

The Ukrainian woman writer produces an *erregendes Moment* (inciting incident in Gustav Freytag's pyramid of dramatic structure terms) in challenging and simultaneously celebrating late adulthood. Considering old age as a temporal reference point, Andrukhovych fills in the gaps existing in the national literature in the early twenty-first century and indirectly portrays the demographic crisis in Ukraine as an aging country. The continuity indicative of family constellations in *Stari Ludy* tackles time and timelessness as both an affirmation of Ukrainian national identity and Ukraine's belonging to a Western past and present.

3 Narrative Diversity in *Stari Ludy*: Intergenerational Voices

In her 1996 study of monstrosity, Rosemary Thompson observes "a movement from a narrative of the marvelous to a narrative of the deviant" (1996, 3); "what aroused awe now inspires horror" (1996, 3). This diagnosis resonates with the perception of age in the development of Western civilization: de Beauvoir's *La Veilleuse* (1970), D.H. Fischer's *Growing Old in America* (1978) and T.R. Cole's *The Journey of life. A Cultural History of Aging in America* (1992) process social changes in Western civilization, including Ukrainian culture, in relation to late maturity, which ranged from veneration of old people to their neglect. In literary texts of different eras, elderly characters are almost always represented as Others, regardless of whether they are revered or disrespected. In her novellas, Andrukhovych changes the attitude of disdain for late maturity to sincere admiration for old age, which is represented by her older adult characters.

Rosemarie Thompson assumes that the nature of the monstrous represented by freaks is based on the cultural perception of Others (Thompson, 10). In the framework of age studies, this assumption is developed by Margaret Gullette, who argues that "[h]uman beings are aged by culture" (2004, 12). The age scholar calls stories forms of aging "time machines" and points out that insofar age/aging is culturally constructed, it could therefore be critiqued and reconstructed (2004, 12). Common to all social strata, age and aging are represented implicitly in fiction, "from survival, resilience, recovery, and development, all the way up to collective resistance to decline forces" (2004, 17). In her collection of novellas, Andrukhovych represents old age explicitly and undermines the stereotype of the invisibility of older people who are often ignored by younger generations. Filled with hedonistic flavor, the texts of the Ukrainian author create an appealing vision of late adulthood, often devoid of the fear of aging and death.

In this respect, the theoretical staples of feminist study of aging developed by Barbara Waxman are applicable to Andrukhovych's family stories. One of the key positions in Waxman's analysis of women's prose in the context of age studies is the counter-narrative, the destruction of ageist stereotypes rooted in the consciousness of the modern world. Following her feminist agenda, the scholar subverts opposition between youth and late adulthood, advancing "positive associations with [old – A.G.] age" (Waxman 1990, 2). Waxman proposes the genre of the *Reifungsroman*, or the novel of ripening, as a variation on the classic *Bildungsroman*. If the latter is focused mainly on the problems of the younger generation, the former depicts the processes of aging and the later life of middle-aged and elderly characters. The metaphor of the open road, mentioned in the title of Waxman's book, focuses attention on the changes and the development of the protagonists of fictional texts. Those older adult characters, traditionally assigned secondary, stereotypical roles, are placed in the limelight in the new literary discourse of aging. Likewise, in the novellas *Stari Ludy* and *Lito Mileny*, elderly female characters (Marta and Cecilia, respectively) travel with pleasure and joy, not considering going back to the family hearth, although in the finale both characters return home.

The joy and pleasure experienced by her characters serve as a calling card of Andrukhovych's prose. Yuriy Telets singles out the concept of hedonism in postcolonial Ukrainian narrative fiction both in terms of content and as an aesthetical tool. The scholar finds the literary strategy of hedonism specifically popular with the Ukrainian readership as a therapeutic form of decolonization of a traumatic past, which he defines as

> a way of forming an array of artistic texts of the post-totalitarian era, which aim to deconstruct and interpret the moral-ethical and socio-cultural dogmas established by socialist realism, aimed at silencing and tabooing topics important for the spiritual and physical development of the individual, and also to debunk the myths codified by the Soviet authorities regarding the place and role of man in society, according to which the only possible mechanism of satisfaction is service for the benefit of the state. (Telets 2023, 6)

Hedonistic practices employed by modern Ukrainian writers take corporeal and extracorporeal forms. On the one hand, there is a distinctive preoccupation in their texts with the body as a postcolonial marker; on the other hand, "not only the sexual manifestations of the human body, but also other phenomena of emotional and existential experiences" (Telets 2023, 8) help combat the colonial mythology imposed by the Soviet regime, which still echoes in the mentality of the postcolonial era.

The leitmotiv of Andrukhovych's collection is the goal expressed by the elderly protagonist of the story *Stari Ludy*, Marta, who enjoys every moment of her life: "I wanted life to be pleasant for me at the age of ninety-odd years" ["Я хотіла, щоб для мене життя в дев'яносто з гаком років було приємне" (Andrukhovych 2008, 47)]. Marta uses the past indefinite, one of the reasons for which is the terminal illness of the female character. In the fiction of age, late adulthood sometimes overlaps with the condition of illness narrated in (auto)biographical form and known as *pathography* (a medical humanities term coined and defined by Anne Hunsaker Hawkins). Despite epistemological quibbles over the genre concept, Maria Vaccarella further defines pathography as a story of illness written from the experience of survival, comprising four elements – battle, journey, rebirth, and health-consciousness (Vaccarella 2012, 193). In reference to Andrukhovych's hedonistic fiction of aging, two elements of pathography are relevant: the journey and health-consciousness of the older adult Marta whose final 102 days of life take on a carnivalesque character.

The author of the story *Stari Ludy* offers a unique pathography: in addition to her terminal disease, the main character falls ill due to tonsillitis. In contrast, Marta overcomes a lingering infection. Curiously enough, Andrukhovych describes a hedonistically exciting treatment process (Andrukhovych 2008, 44–45). Moreover, the open ending of the novella, in which Marta's destiny remains unknown, serves as a euphemism for death: the four characters and a dog will sit over a yellow lake, "at the bottom of which the reflection of old people, puppies, trees and stars will remain. Time is not mandatory for the lakes" ["відображення старих людей, цуценят, дерев і зірок. Час для озер не обов'язковий" (Andrukhovych 2008, 82)]. The use of the future indefinite creates the continuity of human experience and hope for the existence of life in distant future generations. Setting "old people, puppies, trees and stars" in one synonymous row neutralizes the Otherness of the older adult characters in the story, especially from the perspective of Luka, an artist and a photographer, one of the three homodiegetic narrators of the novella.

The novella's plot unfolds around Luka's amorous relations with his grandmother's stepsister, resulting in their journey around Ukraine and finding home. Two generations younger than Marta, Luka stereotypically refers to other older adult characters (who play a minor role) as gray and pitiful in comparison with Marta, whom he often compares with a girl or a young woman. Presented in the exposition of the novella, the countdown of time left for Marta records only the 102nd, 101st, 97th and 9th days in detail, ending with the infinity of human existence due to several options in the development of the plotline and the timelessness of the final scene. The past, a mandatory component of the present, and the future form a whole, fluid and frozen at the same time.

Stari Ludy begins with the wedding of Luka's grandparents, the sixth in a row. Yet the novella's main character is Marta, the second narrator. Luka meets Marta at his grandparents' wedding and they go on an unplanned trip together. Though the action takes place in autumn and winter, the denouement reveals timeless reality close to transcendence.

The transtemporal dimension is formed in the novella by a carpe diem appeal by the female protagonist, repeated in different variations a number of times: "we live now, not tomorrow" ["живемо зараз, а не завтра" (Andrukhovych 2008, 47; 59; 64–65)]. Andrukhovych reinforces it with Marta's observation: "From an early age, a person has a habit of not reacting to his doom in any way. The further, the more not to react" ["Людина змалку вже має звичку ніяк не реагувати на свою приреченість. Чим далі, тим більше не реагувати" (Andrukhovych 2008, 39)], which, together with the lines of other older adult characters in the novella, form a poignant reflection on late adulthood for modern Ukrainian society, which should be taken into account at all stages of human life, from childhood onwards.

Marta comes forward with the three following forms of coping with late adulthood: first, "live by memories. This method helps alleviate many unpleasant things, often it can act as a substitute for life itself" ["жити спогадами. Цей спосіб допомагає полегшувати чимало неприємних речей, часто він може виступати як замінник самого життя" (Andrukhovych 2008, 46)]. Marta's prescription correlates with the *life review* (coined by Robert Butler), which, when structured, amounts to psychotherapy in gerontology. When applied to analyze the literary representations of older adult characters, the concept of life review brings sense and meaning to the otherwise desperate elderly: it "presupposes a conscious and comprehensive immersion of an elderly person in the past in order to find mental balance (older adults feel better about past mistakes if they perceive them more leniently)" (Gaidash 2019, 38).

Second, the protagonist declares: “Another way to endure old age is not to think about it [...] That’s what my grandfather and grandmother did. As long as I can remember, they worked without looking around, bustled about, helped everyone in a row, not giving themselves the opportunity to even think about anything” [“Інший спосіб витримувати старість – не думати про неї [...] Так робили мої дідо і бабця. Відколи я себе пам’ятаю, вони працювали, не озираючись навколо, метушилися, допомагали всім підряд, не даючи собі можливості навіть подумати про щось” (Andrukhovych 2008, 55)]. Marta’s memories of her own grandparents are an important two-layered component of the aging code in the novella: the older woman establishes the continuity of generations, proving that she is not alone in her late adulthood and that there is a family example that serves her as both a support and a role model. It is distinctive of postcolonial Ukrainian prose to fill in the lacunas in family stories, namely insofar as “the elderly often act as mediators, becoming a painful narrative ‘core’ that seeks to be verbalised and at the same time avoids verbalisation” (Bashkyrova et al. 2021, 218). Furthermore, the social engagement of Marta’s grandparents demonstrates an active strategy of aging, one of the means of harmonious life of an older adult (Palmore 2005, 165).

Finally, the woman character observes that people: “[...] try to drive away the fear of old age and death with constant thoughts about them [...] That’s what my aunt did” [“Страх перед старістю і смертю намагаються відігнати ще й постійними думками про них [...] Так робила моя тітка” (Andrukhovych 2008, 64)]. In her observation, Marta’s age and death are united by fear that her aunt eventually overcomes, as a result of which the relative’s life goes on and she becomes “the kindest person in the whole family” [“найдобрішою людиною з усієї [...] сім’ї” (Andrukhovych 2008, 66)].

The transgenerational modus in the novella is encoded in the sexuality of the aged Marta, “unpredictable and wild” [“непередбачуваної і дикуватої” (Andrukhovych 2008, 21)], a self-confident woman (“Isn’t there anything you want from me?” [“Невже від мене немає чого хотіти?” (Andrukhovych 2008, 22)]) whose intimate experience is directly and elegantly depicted (Andrukhovych 2008, 47; 49–50, 61–62; 64). In this respect, these depictions resonate with the prose of Taras Prokhasko, in particular his collections *Inshi dni Anny* [*Інші дні Анни* (1998); Anna’s Other Days] and *NeprOsti* [*НепрОсті* (2002); The UnSimple]. Andrukhovych intensifies her imagery with the dichotomy older woman/young man, in which there is no aggravation of age differences, or any other differences:

> [T]hey lived together like brother and sister, son and mother, like friends, lovers, like a woman and a man, like a cat and a dog, like two drops of water, like Papua and New

> Guinea, like blood and milk, tea and lemon […] like alpha and omega, old age and youth, right and wrong, like he and she.
>
> [вони жили разом, як брат і сестра, син і матір, як друзі, коханці, як жінка і чоловік, як кіт і пес, як дві краплі води, як Папуа і Нова Гвінея, як кров з молоком, чай з цитриною […] як альфа й омега, старість і молодість, правда і кривда, як він і вона (Andrukhovych 2008, 40)].

Applying a catalogue-like style, the author somewhat glamorizes the relationship between Luka and Marta, as in a May–December romance, through the means of "corporeal hedonism" (Telets 2023, 121).

As opposed to more conventional representations of the relationship between a young woman and an old man, Andrukhovych develops the idea of an inverted relation in the liaison between Marta and Luka. Waxman argues that in *Reifungsromane* the images of "young old" women destroy the stereotype of "unfeeling aliens" (1990, 105), forming instead an attractive picture of late adulthood: older adult female protagonists fall in love with younger characters and are passionately loved in return. In addition, Jeannette King provides an insight into the lack of representations of intimate liaisons of transgenerational couples in Western literature: Relationships between older women and younger men subvert patriarchal power relations between the sexes, in which the male's greater age reinforces his position of dominance. To neutralize such threats, the older woman must be ridiculed, or demonized, and the relationship must prove a failure (2013, 147). Social awareness of age issues in the second half of the twentieth century has a positive effect on the representation of older women in literature. In *Stari Ludy*, Marta

> imposes her will on him [Luka – A.G.] but in such a way that in the end he accepts it as his own and cannot imagine it to be any other way. A more common in real life 'sugar daddy' relationship is turned on its head here to become a 'sugar mammy' tale. Andrukhovych empowers her female characters but, ideally, in this fictional world man and woman, equal and understanding, tend to live harmoniously, loving each other till death does part them. (Rewakowicz 2018, 123)

The protagonist of *Stari Ludy* reinforces the vision of older adult woman liberated from prejudices and ageist stereotypes: "The woman who is willing to make that change must become pregnant with herself, at last. She must bear herself, her third self, her old age, with travail and alone" (Popova).

Luka's comparisons of Marta with a young woman (Andrukhovych 2008, 17; 21) or even a child (Andrukhovych 2008, 32–33), signal a reverse stereotyping that devalues the achievements and features of old age per se: "I looked at pink heels, which cheerfully peeked out from black sandals – women of that age usually have cracked heels, right? Marta had completely childish ones" ["Я дивився на рожеві п'яти, що весело визирали з чорних босоніжок – у жінок такому віці п'яти, як правило, потріскані, правда ж? У Марти вони були зовсім дитячі" (Andrukhovych 2008, 22)]. In the context of age studies, the comparison of older characters with younger generations is considered ageist (Dzyuba 2016, 67). At the same time, Andrukhovych emphasizes graphically Marta's reflections on her age, illness, and the feeling of what is happening to her: her short lines are interwoven with Luka's narration and highlighted in bold letter, forming a mental dialogue with her companion. Marta's lines, along with her memories of her grandparents, explore the topic of death and after-death (Andrukhovych 2008, 56), its aesthetics, the manifestation of which takes on a grotesque form (Andrukhovych 2008, 56–58).

The transgenerational layer of the novella is built on the narrative triangle of Marta, Luka and Fiona, in which Marta's voice consisting of fifteen imbedded stories (on 80 pages of text) prevails. Of different length (from two pages to one paragraph), Marta's stories are united by their enchanting or mysterious nature. The protagonist explains the need to share her stories: "I just imagine everything that can happen in life. I want to continue and expand it at least a little" ["Я просто уявляю собі все, що може статися у житті. Хочу хоч так його трохи продовжити і розширити" (Andrukhovych 2008, 69)]. In the finale to the novella, some components of her made-up stories are combined like a kaleidoscope into a series of variations on the further development of events. Thus, the main storyline of Marta's and Luka's journey, both physical and spiritual, ends trifold: 1) with uncertainty: "It is not known for sure what exactly happened to Luka later" ["Невідомо напевне, що саме сталося з Лукою потім" (Andrukhovych 2008, 70)]; 2) with a conditional state, when the third narrator Fiona models various adventures that could have happened to Luka due to Marta's stories: "Everything could have been different" ["Усе могло бути й інакше" (Andrukhovych 2008, 74)]; "After all, anything could have happened to him. I can't even imagine, where did all the stories she told Luka lead to. What I combined from them are pitiful comic strips compared to what could have been in reality" ["Зрештою, з ним могло трапитися все що завгодно. Я навіть уявити не можу, куди завели Луку всі історії, які *вона* розказала. Те, що скомбінувала з них я, – жалюгідні комікси в порівнянні з тим, що могло бути насправді" (Andrukhovych 2008, 75)]; and finally, as mentioned above (see note 3) with an open finale that transgresses the distinction between old age and death (Andrukhovych 2008, 64).

The novella is partly composed in an epistolary form, and not only Luka, but also Marta thus addresses Fiona, whose identity is revealed at the end of the story. Actually, Fiona herself acts as the narrator at the end of Marta's and Luka's journey. The author's technique of changing the focalization and the multiplicity of scenarios is a compositional component of the aging code in the novella, which is marked by the continuity of generations and intergenerational interaction.

4 The Ukrainian Variety of Magical Realism in *Lito Mileny*

In the Ukrainian fiction of the 1960–1980s there forms a rather new literary phenomenon known as *khymerna prosa* [*химерна проза*], close in its style to magical realism. Yet in its numerous studies of this "chimerical prose," Ukrainian scholarship tends to identify the uniquely Ukrainian nature of this literature that originates from Ukrainian baroque, folklore, and the vernacular. Representatives of this poetics, such as O. Ilchenko [О. Ільченко], V. Drozd [В. Дрозд], V. Zemliak [В. Земляк], V. Shevchuk [В. Шевчук], Ye. Hutsalo [Є. Гуцало], V. Yavorivskyi [В. Яворівський], V. Miniailo [В. Міняйло], P. Zahrebelnyi [П. Загребельний], influenced with their novels mostly the younger generation of writers of independent Ukraine, who continued developing the traditions of non-socialist realism. In the chimerical prose, Nataliia Kobylko singles out the engagement of Ukrainian authors with mythology, oral folk art, mythological and biblical motifs, interwoven with the realistic texture of the books (2017, 8). Yet the scholar is convinced that the writers of chimerical novels normally "did not follow the path of direct borrowing of mythological plots or images, but offered sufficiently subjective, individual-authorial interpretations of mythological material" (Kobylko 2017, 8). The powerful voice of authors of chimerical prose was spurred on not only by the "Khrushchev thaw" and dissident movements, but also by the following factors: "1) the interest of writers in various conditional forms as one of the means of intellectual and philosophical knowledge of human existence; 2) 'defense reaction of literature,' when rethinking the folk 'past' became a salvation from stereotyping, leveling, aggressive 'mass culture'" (Kurylenko 2017, 7).

Thus, the important feature of the genre and its carnivalesque mode is its literary response to the Soviet reality, "as the most acceptable model of opposition to normative socialist realist poetics and deformation of Ukrainian literature" (Voshchenko 2019, 19). This feature differentiates Ukrainian chimerical prose from the Latin American magical realism, represented first and foremost by Gabriel García Márquez, in its employment of a "comic strategy (carnivalization, in particular of tragic events, grotesque, parody, irony, humor, sarcasm, so-called 'fooling'), which creates a humorous (non-serious, playful) pathos of chimerical novels" (Voshchenko 2019, 19). The common denominator of chimerical prose and magical realism is "deformation of spatial lifelikeness, the subjectivity of time"

(Zhuravska 2018, 11). The above-mentioned features of chimerical prose, in combination with features of magical realism, are widely employed by post-Soviet Ukrainian prose writers, such as Yu. Vynnychuk [Ю. Винничук], T. Prokhasko [Т. Прохасько], H. Pahutiak [Г. Пагутяк], Yi. Vesny [Ї. Весни], M. Hrymych [М. Гримич], or, in drama, P. Arie [П. Ар'є].

In contrast to the relatively realistic writing of *Stari Ludy*, the novella *Lito Mileny* is constructed in a fairytale mode. The story of one family, which is represented by several generations, fascinates with undisguised hyperbolic imagery, as in the case of the imprisonment and liberation of the bird woman Wanda, the birth of Cassandra echoing the Christian myth of the God's Son, the improbable death of the old hunter Oba, and the birth and rapid growth of Cecilia's twin sons in Africa.

The novella begins with Milena's birth and ends with her death. At the same time, the plot events are not limited to the life of the main character, but they extend deep into the history of the ancestors and ahead into the life of the descendants, thereby forming the continuity of human existence. The novella's magical realism is encoded in the title, *Lito Mileny,* in which 'summer' (in the Ukrainian language the noun *lito* [*літо*] can denote the number of lived years *lit* [*літ*]) means therefore also the life lived by the protagonist: "Everything was changing, and only where Milena lived was there always eternal summer" ["Усе змінювалося, і тільки там, де жила Мілена, завжди було вічне літо" (Andrukhovych 2008, 143)]. Only after Milena's death does the season change: "Young emerald grass instantly covered the fresh grave, and purple petals slowly fell from the bushes on it, plucked by the first, still timid breath of the autumn wind" ["Молода смарагодова трава миттю вкрила свіжу могилку, а з кущів на неї поволі опадали пурпурові пелюстки, зірвані першим, ще несміливим подихом осіннього вітру" (Andrukhovych 2008, 143)].

Death in the fairytale world of *Lito Mileny* is a magical transformation: "The next day Zemyslava's grandmother was not found. She simply disappeared, as if dissolved somewhere in the air of the garden, among the tree trunks" ["Наступного дня не знайшли бабці Земислави. Вона просто зникла, ніби розчинилася десь у повітрі саду, поміж стовбурами дерев" (Andrukhovych 2008, 132)]. Later, they found a slope "like a huge centipede queen," and "Summer went on" (Andrukhovych 2008, 133). Milena's family is dominated by matriarchy, although Milena's grandfather, father, uncle, and husband and their sons are an organic part of the family.

One of the dynamic plotlines in the novella is formed by an elderly couple in love, Cecilia and Narcissus, who "loved and knew how to dress like a young man" ["любив і вмів одягатися, як дженджуристий молодик" (Andrukhovych 2008, 87)]. They taught Milena's mother, Cassandra ("the gray mother"), "to taste life and enjoy every minute of it" ["відчувати життя на смак і щохвилини отримувати від нього задоволення" (Andrukhovych 2008, 89)]. The hedonism of the characters emphasized in both of Andrukhovych's novellas deconstructs the colonial consciousness in which the subject was not supposed to enjoy life (Aheeva 2003, 47). The loving couple brings up Cassandra together with Zemyslava, forming a happy community of older adults. Like Luka's grandparents in *Stari Ludy*, Cecilia and Narcissus arrange a wedding, which, however, breaks down because the older bride abandons the ceremony.

The love story of another elderly couple, Milena's grandparents, Zemyslava and Leon, who is much older than his beloved, is marked by such a fantastic feature as the birth of their child, Cassandra, many years after Leon's death, which was

> a real miracle. Some mischievous and stupid neighbors began to spread disgusting gossip, but mostly people understood that this talk was just ordinary lies and nonsense, because everyone was well aware of the power of Zemyslava's love and the fact that, apart from Leon, she did not know any man in her life.
>
> [справжнім дивом. Деякі лихі і дурні сусіди почали, було, розпускати огидні плітки, але переважно люди розуміли, що це говоріння – просто звичайна брехня і нісенітниця, адже всі добре знали про силу Земиславиного кохання і про те, що, окрім Леона, вона не знала жодного чоловіка в своєму житті (Andrukhovych 2008, 88)].

Leon is a minor character, one of the founders of the family, who, on the one hand, is the embodiment of the family's core: he is powerful, cheerful, all-powerful, experienced, unique. On the other hand, unlike Zemyslava in her late adulthood, his manifestation of old age is much more prosaic: "his hair turned gray, teeth fell out, eyes watered, hands trembled, insomnia visited every night, doctors almost every day, Leon coughed and croaked, and grew old, old, old" ["волосся сивіло, випадали зуби, очі сльозилися, руки тремтіли, щоночі навідувалося безсоння, майже щодня – лікарі, Леон кашляв і кректав, і старів, старів, старів" (Andrukhovych 2008, 87)]. Before his death, Leon's body became weakened, destroyed by time, crowned with a bald head. In addition, deterioration of another male character and indirect member of Milena's family, Father Lavr, in his ripe old age equally reveals markers of physical decline. Yet the servant of the church could manifest either dementia or spiritual enlightenment: Father Lavr has a "toothless mouth" ["беззубим ротом" (Andrukhovych 2008, 99)], whose "old, decaying look spoke of indescribable quiet bliss" ["старечий, струхлявілий вигляд говорив про невимовне тихе блаженство" (Andrukhovych 2008, 97)].

In contrast to the unaesthetic manifestations of the old age of the male cast of characters in *Lito Mileny*, female images are presented in a rather attractive light. For example, two 80-year-old twin sisters, Matilda and Marcelina, have always "had a trail of ardent fans" ["ніколи не відставав шлейф з палких шанувальників"

(Andrukhovych 2008, 110)]. Organizers of monthly parties, the twins and their fans are a sophisticated company that definitely defies ageist stereotypes about the unkempt and withdrawn representatives of older adults: "These were not conservative, screwed-up virtues, dry and correct, like walnut shells. On the contrary, madness, eccentricity and even genius were usually hidden behind calmness and restraint. There was simply no end to wit" ["Це не були консервативні зашкарублі доброчесності, сухі і правильні, як лушпайки волоських горіхів. Радше навпаки – за спокоєм і стриманістю ховалися зазвичай шаленство, дивакуватість і навіть геніальність. Дотепності ж просто не було кінця і краю" (Andrukhovych 2008, 112)]. After a two-year stay in the company of the elderly twins, young Milena is ready for her own old age, which the main character will spend with dignity and warm memories: thus, having kept a collection of gifts from the twins and their friends, Milena "in the last decade of her life [...] liked to look at these pieces of the past" ["в останнє десятиліття свого життя [...] любила розглядати ці шматочки минулого" (Andrukhovych 2008, 112)].

Transgenerational imagery in *Lito Mileny* is also formed by short fragments with minor characters: for instance, 'Granny In a Knitted Skirt,' a former teacher who did not immediately recollect the correct answer to the child's question concerning Kipling's Mowgli, to which the audience reacted politely, because "who will laugh at an old person, especially if they themselves do not know the correct answer" ["хто ж сміятиметься зі старої людини, особливо, якщо й самі не знають правильної відповіді" (Andrukhovych 2008, 116)]. The author's remark is a powerful comment on the perception of old age in the Ukrainian consciousness. At the same time, the writer reproduces rather creepy images of older adult characters in the novella: for instance, an aged couple looking like fish, "skinny, dry, ragged" ["худих, сухих, обірваних" (Andrukhovych 2008, 118)], who later turn out to be kidnappers of other elderly hostages. Even their further destinies are described with veneration: after meeting the demands of the kidnappers and releasing the hostages, the Fish regularly send Milena postcards and a gift.

5 The Transgenerational Family (as a Backbone) of Andrukhovych's Short Prose

Andrukhovych's family stories narrate transnational stories, transcending the spatial and cultural confines of Ukraine, through journeys, letters, and memories. The heterogeneous perspectives in her novellas resonate with globalization, inscribing her texts organically into modern literature, with regard to the context of reception aesthetics. Andrukhovych offers a hybrid type of knowledge and its transmission, insofar as storytelling and self-discovery avoid the linear forms of the family narrative and approach a fluid and flowing type of writing that reveals the multigenerational interaction in a wider transnational context.

The collection of novellas *Stari Ludy* is a hymn to late adulthood; the Otherness of the world completely shatters persistent ideas about old age that still exist in the public consciousness. The collection is important in introducing into Ukrainian literature aging strategies, even if some of them are utopian, and the perception of old age by other generations. The main message of the work is the visibility and dignity of late adulthood. In the eponymous novella *Stari Ludy*, the transgenerational code is formed by the topos and metaphor of an open road, which performs both the therapeutic function of the psychological recovery of the main character and the didactic function of undermining established stereotypes about the lives and ways of life of representatives of late adulthood. The ageist stereotyping of older adults is contrasted with the philosophy of enjoying life at any age. From the point of view of the pathography genre, and within the framework of medical humanities, Andrukhovych actively uses some of the proposed motifs of the genre, in particular the journey and health-consciousness. In the character of Marta, the following options for adaptation to late adulthood are expressed in the eponymous novella *Stari Ludy*: living both memories and an active life (in the case of Marta, traveling, sharing stories, and planning for the future); thinking of old age not as decline and loss, but as a time of the greatest spiritual development of the individual and enjoying life. Hedonistic practices in late adulthood and productive intergenerational interaction due to the lack of exacerbation of age differences between elderly and young characters form a common background in the collection of novellas. In addition, Andrukhovych undermines ageist stereotypes and sexual taboos surrounding female old age in the images of Marta, Cecilia, and other female older adult characters. At the same time, a gender bias is observed in the reproduction of ripe old age in the novella *Lito Mileny*: the last hours, days, weeks, and years of the female characters (Zemislava, Milena) are somewhat romanticized, while descriptions of old age in male characters (Leon, Father Lavr) are presented in a rather naturalistic manner. The engagement with magical realism in *Lito Mileny* becomes a productive decolonizing strategy, too. The late adulthood of Milena and other characters in the novella is one of the stages of human existence, not overshadowed by the unknown and fear of the afterlife, but full of activity and gratitude for the life lived. Transgenerational imagery in Andrukhovych's novellas help readers transcend the historical imaginary of a given age to envision age free from stereotypes.

Bibliography

Aheeva, Vira. *Zhenskoe prostranstvo. Femynystycheskyi dyskurs ukraynskoho modernyzma*. Moscow: Idea-Press, 2008.

Andrukhovych, Sofia. *Stari Ludy*. Ivano-Frankivsk: Lileya-NV, 2008.

Andryczyk, Mark. *The Intellectual as Hero in 1990s Ukrainian Fiction*. Toronto: University of Toronto Press, 2012.

Aristotle. *Poetics*. https://www.perseus.tufts.edu/hopper/text?doc=Perseus:abo:tlg,0086,034:1451b (November 7, 2023).

Bashkyrova, Olga, Anna Gaidash, and Mykola Lutsiuk. "The Archetype of the Wise Old Man in Modern Ukrainian Prose: A Diachronic Perspective." *Slavia Centralis* 14.1 (2021): 210–223.

Bhabha, Homi K. *Nation and Narration*. New York: Routledge, 1990.

Dziuba, Jelena. "Recepcja starości i wizerunek postaci literackiej osiemnastowiecznego starego człowieka w literaturze rosyjskiej." *Slavica Wratislaviensia* 163 (2016): 59–69.

Gaidash, Anna. *Discourse of aging in the US drama: problem field, semantics*. Dnipro: Aksent PP, 2019.

Gullette, Margaret Morganroth. *Aged by culture*. Chicago: The University of Chicago Press, 2004.

Hiraide, Lydia Ayame. "Postcolonial, Decolonial, Anti-Colonial: Does it Matter?" *New Voices in Postcolonial Studies Magazine* (2021): 10–15. https://newvoicespocostudies.wordpress.com/hiraide (November 7, 2023).

Hundorova, Tamara. "Upward Roots and the Fear of Migration." *State of War*. Chernivtsi: Publisher Svyatoslav Pomerantsev, 2023. 69–73.

Hundorova, Tamara. *The Post-Chornobyl Library: Ukrainian Postmodernism of the 1990s*. Transl. Sergiy Yakovenko. Boston: Academic Studies Press, 2019.

Kaakinen, Kaisa. *Comparative Literature and the Historical Imaginary. Reading Conrad, Weiss, Sebald*. Cham: Palgrave Macmillan, 2017.

King, Jeannette. *Discourses of Ageing in Fiction and Feminism: The Invisible Woman*. New York: Palgrave Macmillan, 2013.

Kobylko, Nataliia. *Mifolohema "doroha" v ukrainskomu literaturnomu dyskursi (na materiali tvoriv khymernoi prozy)*. Berdiansk: Tkachuk O.V., 2017.

Kurylenko, Dana. *Zhanrovo-stylova polifoniia prozy kin. 50–70–kh rr. XX st. (na prykladi romanu O. Ilchenka "Kozatskomu rodu nema perevodu, abo zh Mami i Chuzha Molodytsia", dylohii V. Zemliaka "Lebedyna zhraia" ta "Zeleni mlyny")*. Kyiv: Kyivskyi Natsionalnyi Universytet imeni Tarasa Shevchenka, 2017.

Palmore, Erdman B. *Encyclopedia of Ageism*. Eds. Erdman Palmore/Laurence Branch/Diana Harris. New York: The Haworth Pastoral Press, 2005.

Popova, Maria. "Ursula K. Le Guin on Change, Menopause as Rebirth, and the Civilizational Value of Elders." *The Marquinalian*. https://www.themarginalian.org/2023/09/30/ursula-k-le-guin-menopause (November 7, 2023).

Rewakowicz, Maria. *Ukraine's Quest for Identity: Embracing Cultural Hybridity in Literary Imagination, 1991–2011*. Lanham: Lexington Books, 2018.

Telets, Yuriy. *Hedonizm yak posttotalitarna literaturna stratehiia (na materiali suchasnoi ukrainskoi prozy)*. Kyiv: Borys Grinchenko Kyiv University, 2023.

Thomson, Rosemarie Garland. "Introduction: From Wonder to Error – A Genealogy of Freak Discourse in Modernity." *Freakery: Cultural Spectacles of the Extraordinary Body*. Ed. Rosemarie Garland Thomson. New York/London: New York UP, 1996. 1–19.

Vaccarella, Maria. "Medical Humanities: Renewing Praxis across Disciplines." *Medical Humanities, Status Quaestionis* 3 (2012): 181–202.

Voshchenko, Olena. "Zhanrova dominanta khymernoi prozy." *Synopsis: text, context, media* 25.1 (2019): 16–22.

Wallo, Oleksandra. *Ukrainian Women Writers and the National Imaginary: From the Collapse of the USSR to the Euromaidan*. Toronto: University of Toronto Press, 2019. http://www.jstor.org/stable/10.3138/j.ctvsf1pr3 (November 7, 2023).

Waxman, Barbara Frey. *From the Hearth to the Open Road: A Feminist Study of Aging in Contemporary Literature*. New York: Greenwood Press, 1990.

Zhuravska, Oksana. *Dykhotomiia "realnoho" y "irrealnoho" khronotopu yak katehorialna zhanrova oznaka Ukrainskoho khymernoho romanu 2-yi polovyny XX st*. Kyiv: Kyivskyi Universytet imeni Borysa Grinchenka, 2018.

Adriana Rodríguez-Alfonso

"They are my family": Cross-Border and Alternative Communities in Cuban Cold War Narratives

1 Introduction

The last few decades have been witnessing the emergence of a trend in Cuban fiction that delves into the era of the Cold War, particularly focusing on the collapse of the Soviet Union in 1991. The works that might thus be referred to as 'Cuban Cold War narratives,' frequently explore the theme of 'cultural encounter' and follow the journeys of Cuban students, workers, or intellectuals who ventured into European Communist countries thanks to various collaboration agreements between Cuba and the countries of the Eastern Bloc.

These fictional works are driven by the objective of coming to terms with the dissolution of a world order through the perspectives of Cuban characters, bridging Central and Eastern European history with the destiny of Cuba. In contrast to the locally grounded narratives published during the 1990s,[1] which primarily concentrated on the consequences of the Soviet Union's collapse for the Cuban crisis known as the *Periodo Especial* [Special Period], these narratives strive to portray not only Cuba's historical past but also its interconnectedness with European history. This approach inserts Cuba's catastrophe within a broader, global dimension, and, more intriguingly, uncovers the essential role played by Cuba and Latin America in the complex system of power relations during the era of the Cold War.

According to Jacqueline Loss and José Manuel Prieto, despite the Cuban government's emphasis on the limited impact of Soviet culture on the island, "the influence of the Soviet Union in Cuba is undeniable" (2012, 2). My article will illustrate the significance of two of such narratives, the autofictional novel *Las*

1 Cuban writers, such as Amir Valle, Alberto Garrido, and José Mariano Torralbas, came together in 1984 to establish the literary group known as 'Six of the Eighties' ['Seis del Ochenta']. Meanwhile, Ronaldo Menéndez, Karla Suárez, Verónica Pérez Kónina, Raúl Aguiar, Sergio Cevedo, and Ena Lucía Portela were part of 'The Stable' ['El Establo'], which emerged in 1987. These authors would later come to be known as *Los Novísimos* by local literary critics, a term used to describe a generation of writers dedicated to portraying issues closely connected with the local context during the Special Period, including marginalized social groups and areas in Cuban cities as well as addressing taboo topics that were typically excluded from the political official discourse on the island.

Adriana Rodríguez-Alfonso, University of Tübingen

https://doi.org/10.1515/9783111208664-014

cuatro fugas de Manuel (2002) [Manuel's Four Escapes], by Jesús Díaz, together with the novel *Estoico y frugal* (2019) [Stoic and Frugal], by Pedro Juan Gutiérrez. These fictional works represent a trend that is often overlooked, since the critical focus is typically on trips to Cuba by Western travelers (Hollander 1981). In contrast, these other kind of 'travel literature' draws upon their authors' or characters' experiences in European communist countries in the early 2000s.

While these narratives can be associated with autobiographical and testimonial texts representing the journeys of Latin American intellectuals to the Soviet Bloc, these fictions often adopt a different tone. In contrast to the Latin Americans, for whom Soviet realities elicited admiration or rejection (Rupprecht 2015)[2], and were perceived as entirely different environments, Cuban fictions tend to compare their familiar *communist* Caribbean reality with the European version. These fictions are predominantly written by Cuban authors residing outside the island, and even when they offer critical perspectives on both the Cuban and Soviet socio-political systems, they tend to convey a parallel portrait of the regime behind the Iron Curtain and its 'little sister' in the Caribbean Sea.

The question of what has motivated these narratives about Cuban encounters with Soviet countries has arisen in recent years. For instance, Rafael Rojas (2009) has suggested that Moscow has become a 'symbol' in Cuban literature at the turn of the twentieth century, serving as both a 'souvenir' from the past and an urban cartography to contrast with Havana. In a similar fashion, Damaris Puñales-Alpízar argues that this literary return to the era of cultural Sovietization can be seen in connection with the construction of a collective national imaginary. In this fictional re-creation of a past world, narratives concerned with the Cuban diaspora are inspired by the search for a common identity, a shared experience among Cuban writers born in the 1960s and 1970s, prompted by the "rootlessness" caused by the widespread Cuban emigration across the globe in recent decades (Puñales-Alpízar 2012). Irina Garbatzky (2016), in turn, maintains that these narratives function as critical negotiations of core notions in the official discourse of the Cuban Revolution, such as the Marxist approach to history or Che Guevara's ideal of the 'New Man.' Nevertheless, it is undeniable that these texts can be inscribed within the context of the *ostalgie* of the communist past (Loss and Prieto 2011; Loss 2013), in tune with a vogue in other countries of the Eastern Bloc, as recently pointed out by Anna Artwińska and Agnieszka Mrozik (2021). As they have argued, the questioning of those political-social regimes cohabits with the nostalgic

2 Tobias Ruprecht's book traces through testimonies, memoirs, books and chronicles the travels to the Eastern Bloc of Latin American intellectuals and artists such as Pablo Neruda, Nicolás Guillén, Miguel Ángel Asturias, Jorge Amado, María Rosa Oliver or Gilardo Gilardi.

remembrance of the experiences, practices, and habits that characterized those social organizations.

Cuban authors such as Jesús Díaz, Anna Lidia Vega Serova, Carlos Aguilera, Antonio José Ponte, Emilio García Montiel, Pedro Juan Gutiérrez, Antonio Armenteros, Antonio Álvarez Gil, Reina María Rodríguez, or José Manuel Prieto are among those who have thematized the *cultural clashes* between subjects from the Tropics and the *exotic* and unknown realities they found behind the Iron Curtain. By conducting a close reading of *Las cuatro fugas de Manuel* and *Estoico y frugal*, I will argue that these novels engage critically with discourses of communist and socialist ideologies, dismantling them through a singular use of time and space and the creation of alternative 'families' and cross-border communities. As I will show in the following, this unsettling of ideologies involves a wide range of topics, including categories such as nature, technology, science, power, and propaganda, and thus proving the novels with a specific *chronotope*.

2 "That Endless Road": *Las cuatro fugas de Manuel* and the Formation of a Transnational Network

Jesús Díaz's novel, *Las cuatro fugas de Manuel*, endeavors to explore the last months leading up to the collapse of the Soviet Union and the subsequent chaos at the beginning of 1992, through the experiences of the character Manuel Desdín, a Cuban physics student in Kharkiv, Ukraine. Portrayed as a brilliant young scientist, Manuel's life takes a dramatic turn when he is compelled to return to Cuba, not only due to his unwelcome intellectual arrogance but also because of his support for Mikhail Gorbachev's *Perestroika* and *Glasnost*.

In the pursuit of his dream to become a physicist, Manuel embarks on the four escapes the title alludes to. Through these attempts he endeavors to migrate to Europe, initially trying to reach Switzerland, followed by Finland, Sweden, and eventually Germany. His initial three attempts end in failure, while the novel intricately weaves through the myriad twists and turns in Manuel's life. The broad range of *peripeties* – a term I employ here in its twofold meaning[3] – to which the protagonist is exposed, clearly aligns Díaz's novel with the tradition of the *Bildungsroman*, as it follows the *coming of age* of Manuel. This formation, or *Bildung*,

3 On the one hand, I am employing the term 'peripety' in the Aristotelian sense, signifying a profound and contrasting shift in a character's circumstances. On the other hand, the Spanish term *peripecia* suggests a series of sequential incidents, at times accompanied by a disorienting transformation, which is what in fact happens to the protagonist in Díaz's novel.

as I will argue, is intricately linked to the rapid changes in time and space that the novel encompasses, as well as his successive detachment from the official Cuban state propaganda.

In fact, politics plays a crucial role in the narrative, not only due to the historical backdrop in which the story is set, but also because of Manuel's ideological evolution. He evolves from early communist ideas aligned with the Cuban government's discourse to a critical perspective on the communist system as a whole as well as the global left-wing movement,[4] which has remained oblivious to Cuban autocracy. At the same time, transcending political polarization, the novel also challenges neoliberalist ideas and the rise of nationalisms during the early 1990s. Eventually, the reader discovers that the last friend made by Manuel on his tour is Pablo Díaz, that is, Jesús Díaz's son, adding an autofictional dimension to the story. This discovery not only blurs the boundaries between fiction and reality but also aligns the narrator's viewpoint with the one of the author: Díaz founded the magazine *Encuentro de la Cultura Cubana* [Encounter of Cuban Culture], which was the first to be critical to the Cuban government while striving to build bridges between writers in Cuba and those in exile, thus transcending ideological radicalisms.[5]

The novel's configuration of space and time is closely related to the sense of community it portrays. During his escapes, the main character traverses Eastern and Central Europe, visiting cities such as Kyiv, Moscow, Warsaw, Bern, Basel, Ystad, Dresden, and Berlin. The nature of these journeys is shaped by a sense of secrecy and the clandestine, and each of these places is represented through rather fuzzy and ephemeral images, akin to the brief and reflective facets of a kaleidoscope. Consequently, the perception of space often becomes a matter of time and mobility, as trains move from one station to another, often viewed through the train's windows. That is as close as Manuel gets to these unknown places, since whenever he sojourns in one location, he is forced to stay in the confines of a room in a city or a rural farmhouse. Space perceptions, then, typically

4 This political position is exemplified by Ayinray, the Chilean communist lover of Manuel, who remained oblivious to the realities of Cuban regime. She claimed that "Cuba is our little flame of hope" ["Cuba es nuestra llamita de esperanza" (Díaz 2002, 139)], alluding to the military dictatorship in Chile and the symbolism of hope that the island represents for a socialist future in her country along with other Latin American nations. Similarly, in Switzerland, law enforcement authorities do not recognize Manuel as a political refugee. They insisted on distinguishing the Cuban political system from the Soviet Union regime, pondering the island as an 'example' for the political progressivism (Díaz 2002, 178).

5 *Encuentro de la Cultura Cubana* (1996–2009) was established in Madrid by Jesús Díaz, later succeeded by Manuel Díaz Martínez as its director.

occur in an indirect and indistinct fashion, since he senses and experiences those cities only while in motion, only through window panes.

Trains tend to gain speed as they approach the West, with the concomitant distortion of spatial perception. Even when Manuel is on foot, the constant feeling of being lost contributes to his sense of a frenetic whirlwind: "That endless road to the heart of Europe was also a journey where space and time were compressed until they reached the agonized perfection of the chronometer" ["Aquel interminable camino hacia el corazón de Europa era también un viaje en el que el espacio y el tiempo se comprimían hasta alcanzar la agónica perfección del cronómetro" (Díaz 2002, 61)]. The categories of time and space are described as variable and inextricably linked to each other.

It is noteworthy that the theme of locomotive or other forms of travel serves as a central motif in various narratives within Cuban Cold War literature. Novels such as *Livadia* (1999) [*Nocturnal Butterflies of the Russian Empire* (2001)] by José Manuel Prieto, *Siberiana* (2000) by Jesús Díaz himself, and *Ánima fatua* (2007) [Fatutos Soul] by Anna Lidia Vega Serova, delve into the interplay between journeys and modes of transportation. In *Livadia,* for instance, the protagonist's escape from Istanbul to Odessa takes place on board a cargo ship, while *Siberiana* begins with the distressing, non-stop plane flight of Bárbaro from Havana to Moscow and Siberia.

However, train travel emerges as the most frequent form of transportation, often assuming symbolic significance with regard to the relation between technological advancement and modernity. For instance, *Ánima fatua*'s main character moves across Soviet cities such as Moscow, St. Petersburg and Odessa by regional trains. The novel contrasts the overwhelming bustle of Moscow, a megalopolis, with the prevailing deceleration experienced in St. Petersburg. Train stations epitomize the divergences between the cities: In Moscow, Alia, the protagonist, is described as being "swallowed" (Vega Serova 2007, 86) at the grandiose station of Belorussky, where she is absorbed by the frantic haste, incorporated into the perpetual anthill of passersby, and quickly forgotten. In St. Petersburg, however, she expresses disappointment with the subway (Vega Serova 2007, 160), a sentiment which arises from the city's grayness and the unhurried pace of the commuters and passersby along the Neva River. While St. Petersburg exudes an ancestral splendor, compared to a certain "Russian essence" (Vega Serova 2007, 160–161), technology and modernity are epitomized in Moscow.

In the places where the frenetic pace of cosmopolitan life slows down, such as in the ruined buildings or homeless camps on the outskirts of the city, temporal constraints that dictate the work routines of urban centers vanish. This leads to a suspension of the relentless rhythm, fostering social interaction among individuals from various strata, as those established by Vega Serova's protagonist.

Now, in Díaz' novel, the extensive train journeys also encourage such alternative forms of social interaction, as travelers often spend days in the overcrowded quarters of the train carriages, fostering newfound friendships with fellow passengers. This aspect of the story also suggests a connection between speed and modernity, engaging in a dialogue with the dichotomy between East and West through the mobility of trains. Indeed, Manuel's constant mobility becomes a means of circumventing the strict border controls in Soviet regions, even as they were transitioning into democratic states.[6] As a journey through the *heart of darkness* of Eastern Europe, trains play a key role in facilitating Manuel's four escapes, as chronicled in Díaz's novel. Without a doubt, the sense of derealization that Manuel experiences through these displacements can be interpreted as an echo of the technological disparities between the East and the West – a point that he also makes when comparing trains' speed and comfort in the USSR, Poland, and Germany (Díaz 2002, 61). Nevertheless, the increasing lack of familiarity can also be understood as a symbol of the protagonist's gradual loss of reference points, since in approaching the West, Manuel's familiar world disappears. Therefore, the novel implies that displacement is also tinged with a political connotation, since Manuel did not feel dislocated in Ukraine after leaving Cuba, for both countries are part of the international communist landscape. As he moves closer to liberal democracies, however, Manuel is abandoning his familiar world and entering the unknown.

This loss of reference points finally reaches its peak when the main character meets Jesús Díaz's son, an event coinciding with Manuel's arrival in West Berlin, where Manuel will eventually regain his spatial orientation. The shift in the configuration of space and time might be read as an indicator of the end of Manuel's movement of flight. In this sense, the novel might suggest that Western capitalism is the character's final destination, as this is where the chronotope finally recaptures its regular pace. This reading, however, is called into question as we discover, towards the story's end, that Manuel once again embarks on a journey, this time to Spain. Consequently, the novel ultimately portrays Germany as nothing more than a temporary halt in the character's everlasting odyssey.

In light of this, Manuel's movement across Europe ultimately alludes to a broader theme: the pilgrimage of those who leave their countries of origin and

---

6 This theme also recurs in other Cuban Cold War narratives. In the short story collection titled *Nunca antes habías visto el rojo* (1996) [You Have Never Seen Red Like This Before] by José Manuel Prieto, the narrator recounts how the limited or non-existent control by Russian authorities on trains enabled him to traverse the country without the necessary documentation (Prieto 1996, 5). This motif resurfaces in *Livadia*, where J.M. recounts that simply feigning sleep was sufficient to elude the scrutiny of the train guards (Prieto 1999, 20).

enter the realm of exile. I am deliberately using 'exile' instead of 'migration' here, not only because of the evident political subtext of Manuel's journey, as he is removed, persecuted, and imprisoned more than once, but also because of the political nature of Jesús Díaz's own migration. By 1992, the last year portrayed in the novel, Díaz's book *Las iniciales de la tierra* (1987) [*The Initials of the Earth* (2006)] had already been censored in Cuba. Having been removed from every national institution, Díaz was forced to leave the country. Consequently, the disruption of time and space in *Las cuatro fugas de Manuel* goes beyond representing the transition from communism to capitalism, or from totalitarianism to democracy. It becomes a wider and more complex depiction of the experience of exile and displacement.

The frenetic rhythm imposed by these multiple relocations can also be viewed as an expression of individual self-determination against the strictly regulated lives dictated by the Soviet system. In narratives such as *Las cuatro fugas de Manuel* trains serve as a sort of *mobile interstices* from which one can evade the continuous surveillance imposed by authoritarian control. In contrast to the biopolitical regulation exercised over bodies and their movements, trains provide "other places" (Foucault 1998). *In them* and *through them* transnational "porosity" emerges as an alternative to the "naked life" under totalitarian regimes (Agamben 1998), as well as the choice to establish a social network based on individual affinities rather than conforming to the dictates of collective coexistence imposed by the State. In fact, since under those political systems, the boundary between the private and public spheres tends to blur, Manuel's escapes provide him with the 'blank spaces' in which to foster social ties, free from the interference of the public sphere.

This is likewise associated with the experience of displacement and exile which entails the problem of alienation and isolation as prominent themes permeating the novel, thus creating a narrative that revolves around Manuel's quest for belonging and connection. Here, the novel depicts a support network around Manuel, which serves as a counterweight to the profound impact of his frequent dislocations. In Manuel's narrative, the friends and lovers he encounters during his journey form a complex network of relationships that prove crucial for his survival and personal development.

Invoking here concepts from social network theory,[7] this transnational grid comprises individuals intricately interconnected to one another, with each person leading to the next. These characters hail from diverse nationalities and age

7 Basic notions within Social Network Analysis such as 'nodes' and 'edges' are useful to describe the social circle around Manuel. The network consists of a set of persons (nodes) that revolves around Manuel, connected with him and among them through different types of relations (edges).

groups and, significantly, hold varying ideological positions. From Manuel's lover Ayinray, who is a Chilean militant and admirer of the Cuban Revolution, to his Ukrainian friend Sacha, who aspires to an idealized capitalist future for Ukraine, these characters collectively create a dense network of relationships that ensures Manuel's survival, despite their differing ideological stances. As a consequence, the multiplication of time and space is deeply rooted in this support network, as these individuals provide shelter and community for the disoriented Manuel.

Manuel's relations of friendship, love, and brotherhood form a network of solidarity that transcends state control and political affiliations. Right from the outset, the narrator refers to them as a "family": "Javier, the Peruvian, Sacha, the Ukrainian, and Natalia, the Chilean, are his family; they provide the food, the wine, the songs, and the shoulders to cry on" ["Javier, el peruano, Sacha, el ucraniano, y Natalia, la chilena, son mi familia: ellos proveen la comida, el vino, las canciones, y los hombros en los que llorar" (Díaz 2002, 32)]. In this vein, Manuel also refers to Natalia as his "sister" ["hermana" (Díaz 2002, 37)]. The likening of these relations to blood relations becomes even more pronounced when it comes to father figures, as at least three different characters are referred to as "father" [*padre*] by Manuel throughout his journey: firstly, his academic advisor Derkáchev (Díaz 2002, 46); secondly, the *mafioso* Ibrahim Al Pratter (Díaz 2002, 213), and finally, the novel's author Díaz, who acknowledges that while Manuel gained a "family," he himself gained a "son" ["hijo" (Díaz 2002, 244)].

By portraying this solidarity network as a *family*, the novel suggests a system of *familial relationships* that transcend blood ties. This idealized belief in human collaboration stands in stark contrast to the negative view of official governmental and non-governmental institutions of 'solidarity,' exemplified by political bodies such as the Socialist Committee of Cuban Students in Ukraine, the Swiss and Finnish authorities, and even the Red Cross, all portrayed as intolerant, biased, and corrupt organizations. In this sense, the discourse of solidarity is detached from government administration and instead embodies alternative forms of interaction beyond state control. As for the official discourse of the communist government, Díaz Maceo and Habel (2020, 51) have noted that solidarity frequently was used with respect to the transnational bonds between communist and socialist countries, leaving citizens with limited capacity to engage in independent aid projects outside of state influence (2020, 52).

A rebuttal of this sort of official discourse is especially evident in the novel's conclusion, when Manuel decides to tear his official Cuban passport into pieces, symbolizing not only his rejection of identity-based nationalism but also his refusal to identify with government policies. As a result, the novel proposes an alternative community that challenges the prevailing relationships among Communist Bloc countries. These 'familial' relationships and networks exist outside the purview of state administration, relying on individual agency, situated beyond the realm of power and international foreign politics.

3 Challenging Official Narratives: *Estoico y frugal* and a New Family Paradigm

Estoico y frugal by Pedro Juan Gutiérrez follows the journey of Pedro Juan, a Cuban writer who has recently published a novel that reflected on the extreme poverty – both ethical and economically – during the 1990s in Cuba, known as the *Special Period.* Rooted in a continuous dismantling of boundaries between fiction and reality, the novel not only encourages *autofictional* readings due to the shared name of the author and the main character, but also draws parallels with the real-life controversy surrounding the author's *Trilogía sucia de La Habana* [*Dirty Havana Trilogy* (2002)] in 1998.[8]

Gutiérrez' novel (originally published by the Anagrama publishing house in Barcelona), focuses on the writer's tour across Spain, Italy, Germany, and Switzerland. It provides a somewhat acerbic glimpse into the mechanisms of the publishing industry, portraying it as a business driven by marketing strategies and sensationalism. For instance, the various translations into different languages have roundly ignored the complexities arising from how to adequately render the numerous examples of Cubanisms and local slang (Gutiérrez 2019, 25). In this vein, the novel somewhat idealistically distinguishes between art as a pure and inspirational practice and the publishing business as a purely profitable and opportunistic endeavor. The tension between those idealized values and the sensuous impulses driving the main character's actions permeates the novel: thus, the protagonist's intellectual reflections on politics and literature intertwine with his multiple shifts from one romantic partner to another.

Despite its setting in 1998, the narrator highlights that the underlying causes of national and individual *misfortune* in Cuba began already in 1991. This temporal frame aligns the Cuban crisis of the 1990s with the socio-economic challenges faced by former communist countries after the collapse of the Soviet Union in 1991. As the narrator states: "The entire utopia had collapsed. First, the Berlin Wall fell in November 1989. Then the USSR was shattered on December 25, 1991,

8 The *Trilogía sucia de La Habana* comprises the short stories "Anclado en tierra de nadie" ["Anchored in No Man's Land"], "Nada que hacer" ["Nothing to Do"] and "Sabor a m." ["Flavor of S*."]. Known for its Bukowskian and critical depiction of the Cuban capital, this collection ignited a widespread debate in 1998.

and everything crumbled" ["Toda la utopía se había derrumbado. Primero cayó el Muro de Berlín, en noviembre de 1989. Después la URSS se hizo pedazos el 25 de diciembre de 1991 y todo se vino abajo" (Gutiérrez 2019, 18)]. However, this time frame is actually inaccurate, as the early impact of the Soviet Union's dissolution did not reach Cuba until the end of 1992, with its peak between 1994 and 1995, when the reserves of Soviet resources that had sustained the Cuban economy finally ran out.

By juxtaposing the fates of Communist Europe and Cuba, the novel suggests that the main character's past and present are consequences of this global historical landmark; it constructs a transnational historical narrative that transcends national and local differences. This becomes also evident in the representation of the protagonist's memories of the Cold War era, focusing on his trips to the Soviet Bloc as a tourist or worker rather than his life in Cuba. Through its entwining of the character's life with European communist history, the novel engages what I previously referred to as *Cuban Cold War narratives*. It is no coincidence that Pedro Juan was born in 1950, which means that his life intersects with the post-War period. Accordingly, the narrative emphasizes the global context rather than the local factors that led to the "Special Period" on the island.

With regard to temporality, the novel initially proceeds with a linear narrative stemming from what are supposedly the writer's diary notes from the winter of 1998. However, it soon becomes apparent that multiple temporalities coexist within it, ranging from childhood reminiscences and his role as an outstanding young worker under the Cuban Revolution, to the narrative's present during the 1990s, and retrospective comments and evaluations made from the future, as the novel was written two decades later, in 2018. Instead of being presented as a series of flashbacks and prolepses, these temporalities draw frequent comparisons with the post-Cold War present, as they are brought directly into the main narrative line. Consequently, the novel amounts to a chaotic sequence of various experiences where present reflections coexist with past events from two previous decades, without clearly marked transitions. In this sense, Gutiérrez's novel constructs what might be called a *multi-chronological* perspective, as the narrator conveys his current beliefs alongside his earlier, different thoughts on the Cuban political regime.

This overlapping of temporalities is closely linked to the novel's narrative representation of space. The narrator's journey encompasses over twenty different geographical locations, with Spain alone being a substantial part of it, including cities such as Madrid, Burgos, Vigo, Valencia, and Alicante, to name just a few. This ambitious array of movements across the European map, for a novel with less than 200 pages, entails a rather shallow portrayal of these different places. With some exceptions, places receive only superficial descriptions, relying on conventional features and stereotypes. What is more intriguing is that these movements serve as 'demarcations' within the narrative progression. In other words, the numerous, interconnected episodes are primarily defined by the space in which they occur and by the characters introduced within these locations. The sense of temporal disorientation is amplified by the extended paragraphs, the absence of full stops, section breaks, or division into chapters. Consequently, narrative progression is indicated primarily by *displacement*, with changes in location serving as the primary markers of the story's advancement.

Undoubtedly, this kaleidoscope of intersected temporalities resonates with recent theories about narrative time in contemporary Latin American literature. For instance, the phenomenon of overlapping, asynchronous, or extemporaneous temporalities has been pointed out by Francisca Noguerol (2013) as a characteristic feature of Ibero-American fiction of the first decade of the twenty-first century. Similarly, Graciela Speranza (2017) has identified a privileging of "topological time" over "chronological time." However, the narrator of *Estoico y frugal* suggests that there is a local difference with regard to the temporal coordinates prevalent in contemporary fiction from Europe and Cuba:

> Sometimes it seems to me that Europe repeats itself. At first glance, it gives the impression that everything has been said. In my country, however, we live at the other extreme. Everything is so unpredictable, shifting, and complicated that one lives in confusion. It is disturbing and vertiginous, as if today were the first day of creation, and we were always starting from scratch. We quickly forget and start over.
>
> [A veces me parece que Europa se repite a sí misma. A primera vista da la impresión de que todo está dicho. [...] En mi país, en cambio, vivimos en el otro extremo. Es todo tan imprevisible, cambiante y complicado que uno vive confundido. Es perturbador y vertiginoso. Como si hoy fuera el primer día de la creación y estuviéramos siempre empezando desde cero. Olvidamos rápido y comenzamos de nuevo. (Gutiérrez 2019, 50)]

By implying that Cuban literature echoes the vortex and ever-changing pace of life on the island, Gutiérrez's representation of time aligns with the idea of a specific temporality embodied by Caribbean literature. This has been variously theorized by scholars and writers (Walcott 1957; Benítez Rojo 1997; Welge 2023), who have addressed the circular and juxtaposed temporalities that result from the mixture of languages, ethnicities and races that has shaped Caribbean history.[9]

9 Walcott's essay collection, *What the Twilight Says* (1957), explores Caribbean history through a non-linear framework characterized by repetition and flux. In *The Repeating Island* (1997) by Benítez Rojo, the Caribbean cultural landscape is examined through the lens of chaos theory, portraying it as an island of paradoxes that persist across time. Welge's analysis of *Los pasos perdidos* [*The Lost Steps*] by Cuban writer Alejo Carpentier suggests that "the notion of juxtaposing

Yet also beyond the specific conditions of the Caribbean, the notion of a heterogeneous temporality is a recurring theme in other narratives from the Cold War era, namely concerning those of the countries from the Eastern Bloc. Here, the slowing down of time is often accompanied by a description of space as boundless and infinite. An example for this can be found in José Manuel Prieto's *Enciclopedia de una vida en Rusia* (2003) [*Encyclopedia of a Life in Russia* (2013)], which precisely couples a non-linear dimension of time with a sense of unbounded space. In an entry dedicated to Russian natural reserves titled "Bosque de coníferas" ["Coniferous forest" (Prieto 1998, 27)], Prieto points out that "Russia has the world's largest reserve of timber trees" ["Rusia tiene la mayor reserva mundial de árboles maderables" (Prieto 1998, 27)]. This perception is also echoed in *Siberiana* by Díaz, where the protagonist underscores Russia's status as the "largest reserve in the world, home to the inexhaustible taiga forests" ["la reserva más grande del mundo, los bosques de la inagotable taiga" (Díaz 2000, 87)], going as far as to proclaim that "only a deity of immense power could encompass such a multitude of trees" ["solo el gran Dios sería capaz de abarcar tantos árboles" (Díaz 2000, 87)].

This representation of time and space has the effect of juxtaposing a mythical, almost timeless sense of existence with the temporality characteristic of the modern present. The phenomenon of synchronicity is aptly illustrated in passages that describe the cosmic grandeur of the Ust Ilimsk sawmill in Siberia: "The processing plant under construction," declares the responsible official, "was also the largest in the known universe. The sheer scale of the construction site is so vast that it cannot be explored in a single morning, a day, a month, or even a year. It would require an entire lifetime to fully comprehend the grandeur of the Ust Ilimsk plant" ["La obra en construcción era tan grande que no podrían visitarla en una mañana, ni en un día, ni en un mes, ni en un año. Haría falta toda una vida para ver la gran planta de Ust Ilimsk" (Prieto 2000, 86–87)].

In addition to being associated with the emerging ecological consciousness of the Eastern Bloc during the mid-1980s, which subsequently influenced environmental policies in Cuba,[10] the narratives by Prieto and Díaz draw a stark contrast

different temporal layers may reflect the fact that 'post-colonial' countries in Latin America (or in the Caribbean, for that matter) are not fully synchronized with Western modernity." (2023, 106)

10 The disinterest in the protection of natural ecosystems and the exploitation of resources that characterized the initial decades of the Eastern Bloc underwent a transformation in the mid-1980s. Environmental policies, which emerged during the era of *Perestroika*, began to take a prominent place in the government's agenda (Zaharchenko 1990). This shift toward environmental concerns also extended to the Cuban coastal regions, echoing a discourse that linked capitalist consumption with environmental pollution, while simultaneously suggesting socialism as an economic and social system more conducive to ecological preservation. Following the dissolution of the Socialist bloc the Marxist dichotomy between capitalism and socialism was supplanted by the between developed and underdeveloped nations. This juxtaposition replaces the conventional dichotomy between capitalism and socialism, as a consequence of the disintegration of the Soviet Union. The spatio-temporal imageries are inextricably linked with the notion of the West as an emblem of ecological degradation, and of the East as a paradise for the conservation of nature. This may occasionally even lead to metaphysical overtones, as in another passage from Prieto's *Enciclopedia de una vida en Rusia*, where a character bemoans the "loss of holiness" (1998, 114), depicting Western society as a realm dominated by utilitarianism, egoism, and the absence of transcendentalism.

However, the depiction of the distant West as a domain dominated by individualism and the absence of transcendence does not necessarily imply that the Eastern Bloc is devoid of technological modernity. In fact, *Las cuatro fugas de Manuel* itself begins by asserting that experiments conducted in the extreme temperature laboratories of the University of Kharkov had yielded results unprecedented in the Western world (Díaz 2002, 14).[11] These narratives tend to mythologize technocracy, distinguishing between the chronological as well as chaotic *chronotopes* associated with the West and the circular, static model found in the East.

In many of these texts, the notion of a mythified technology serves as a counterpoint to the secularization and dehumanization attributed to the West. A temporally 'backward' world appears thus as a last refuge for the natural, the human, and the metaphysical – qualities that have been silenced in the Western societies of the twenty-first century –, giving way to a specific form of *nostalgia* identified in recent Eastern Bloc fictions (Boym 1995; 2001; Mrozik and Tippner 2021). However, as exemplified in Gutiérrez, Prieto and Díaz's works, the critical examination of the Cuban regime also concerns philosophical and ideological issues involved in these deviations from the notion of Western progress.

contrast between developed and underdeveloped countries, the former becoming associated with ecological degradation (Díaz-Briquets and Pérez-López 2000).

11 In *Siberiana*, the protagonist grandiloquently proclaims that the TU 104 model, which carried him from Havana to Moscow via the Arctic Circle, was not only the world's largest airplane but had also just completed the longest commercial flight in history (Díaz 2000, 18). Even in *Livadia*, the objects smuggled to the West by the protagonist are considered evidence of cutting-edge technology. In the opening pages of *Siberiana*, the protagonist not only christens the plane transporting him to Russia as "The Beast" (Díaz 2000, 10) but also describes the airborne journey as if it were a contemplative experience, akin to a stroll through the skies (Díaz 2000, 20). In a similar vein, we may recall the imagery employed by Vega Serova in *Ánima fatua* – a title steeped in mysticism – where she vividly describes her protagonist's entry into the Moscow train stations as entering in a monster's mouth.

In this context, the dizzying and non-linear utilization of time and space can be interpreted as a deconstruction of the logical progression of history as presented in communist discourse. This is especially noteworthy with respect to Cuba, where the government has chosen to align itself with 'socialism' rather than 'communism,' portraying its regime as a stage preceding communism. This discourse not only serves the political justification of an eternal 'work-in-progress,' it also embodies a notion of the Hegelian linear progression of history and a constant improvement of human life. In contrast, Gutiérrez's novel as well as the other works mentioned above encourage a temporal disposition which is contrary to the teleological standpoint adopted by the rhetoric of the Cuban state.

In fact, the official propaganda promoted for decades by the Cuban government is also reflected by other features within these narratives. For example, it is a recurrent motif that Gutiérrez's main character frequently *hyperbolizes* the Cuban Revolution's "achievements" (Gutiérrez 2019, 23; 45) regarding public health, education, the eradication of racism and misogyny, and hence reproducing the sound of the usual official government communications. As mentioned before, the question of scientific progress is also challenged within Díaz and Prieto's novels.[12] With regard to environmental pollution, even the opposition between communism and capitalism is dismantled. Thus, in the aforementioned entry on the coniferous forest in Prieto's *Enciclopedia*, we read that, despite the immensity of the forests, in the springtime tons of wood never reach their destination and go to the bottom of the rivers of Siberia, for Russia, it is claimed, is also a "consumerist country" (1998, 87), namely one based on primary materials. The language of the encyclopedic entry mimics the triumphalist tone of official propaganda, even as it points to the overexploitation of natural resources in Russia. Written in a parodic key, the fragment, without denying the clear responsibility of the West in ecological degradation, insinuates that neither the political system nor underdevelopment have exempted the East from damaging the ecosystem.

The critical view on key tenets of the official propaganda is also evident in the sense of *community* conveyed in Gutiérrez's novel. Alongside the change of geographical settings, the main character encounters on his travels a diverse array of individuals, of which many serve as catalysts for various further journeys and encounters. These individuals, although most of them are women, cannot be categorized by age, social status, or nationality. Each of them is connected to a specific time and place in the novel, and the bonds formed between them and the main

12 It is no mere coincidence that these grandiose pronouncements emanate from either governmental authorities or from the protagonists of *Las fugas de Manuel* and *Siberiana*, who initially engage with and echo the official Soviet-Cuban state declarations.

character are ephemeral yet strong. As in Gutierrez's previous work, romantic and sexual encounters often serve as the foundation for these connections, though other types of relationships are also possible. In spite of their differences, the main character explicitly underscores their commonality: a shared inclination toward transgressing social norms, intertwined with a distinct sense of freedom (Gutiérrez 2019, 56).

As we have seen above with regard to *Las cuatro fugas de Manuel*, the sustenance of these alternative social circles, constructed and maintained by both Díaz and Gutiérrez's main characters throughout their travels, plays a crucial role. In contrast to Manuel, Pedro Juan's community lacks not only blood ties but also the notion of a collective bond among its members that endures over time. These connections once again challenge the traditional concept of 'family,' offering instead an ephemeral support group centered around the protagonist. Still, it is worth noting that also he invokes the familial metaphor, stating on multiple occasions that his 'family' comprises "a few lifelong friends and a hundred acquaintances" ["Tengo unos pocos amigos de toda la vida y cientos de conocidos" (Gutiérrez 2019, 123)]. When considering this community's structure from a social network perspective, one might describe it as having a central or *egocentric* node, Pedro Juan, surrounded by several other nodes linked by informal, short-term and undefined relations. It is worth noting that both Díaz and Gutiérrez's novels resist and deconstruct the established concept of 'family,' even as they keep using the same 'traditional' paradigm to describe these alternative bonds: Manuel and Pedro Juan still refer to the individuals with whom they connect as *sisters*, *brothers*, and *fathers*. Even when designing entirely new forms of affective ties, it appears that these authors cannot, or do not want to fully distance themselves from the centrality of the family paradigm.

It seems to me that the concept of a *micro-society* metaphorically associated with blood relationships, as depicted in Gutiérrez's novel, is also rooted in the circumstances in recent Cuban history. Here we might note a significant contrast to contemporary Polish literature, where Anna Artwińska and Agnieszka Mrozik (2021, 14) argue that issues of nationalism, traditional family, and religion have made a resurgence. While European countries have moved beyond their communist past, Cuba continues to cope with it in the present. The attempt to forge connections that stand in opposition not only to the traditional family but also to other related concepts in Cuban official discourse, such as *nation* or the global *communist* 'family,' is evident. Beyond adhering to a political system where individuals are expected to subsume their personal differences in favor of a collective *people*, the idea of 'family' as a synonym for the entire Cuban people [*pueblo*] lies at the core of the regime's narratives. Hence, this unique use of 'family' is also discernible in Fidel Castro's speeches, such as when he emphasized global solidarity among countries:

"I think we should behave as a family, and share what we have: some must share oil, others food, those who are far away, doctors ... and so on" ["Creo que deberíamos comportarnos como una familia, y compartir lo que tenemos: unos petróleo, otros alimentos, los de más allá médicos ... " (2011, 4)].

Moreover, this use of familial terminology also extended to the national public sphere, where Fidel Castro was often referred to as *the head of the Cuban family*. While the familial circle was reconceived as the homogeneous totality of the island's citizens, Castro was promoted as its patriarchal leader, an identification that also carries undertones of male control, messianic leadership, and caudillo roles. Similarly, terms like *motherhood* and *sisterhood* were absorbed into state organizations like the Federation of Cuban Women [Federación de Mujeres Cubanas (FMC)], while *brotherhood* was politically co-opted by neighborhood Committees for the Defense of the Revolution [Comités de Defensa de la Revolución (CDR)]. Against the backdrop, then, Gutiérrez's creation of an alternative community can also be seen as a departure from the official institutionalization of *family* and familial relations. *Estoico y frugal* attempts to portray the possibility of forging *other* social bonds as a means of creating non-normative and unorthodox relationships that stand in contrast to the governmental control.

4 Conclusions

The novels analyzed in this essay are representative for a particular viewpoint of the end of the Cold War period, portraying Cuban history in dialogue with the recent histories of Eastern and Central European countries. This orientation may be related to the field of *New Cold War History* studies, which aim to pursue a restitution of the geopolitical importance of *peripheral* regions (Westad 2012). Furthermore, works of Cuban fiction as those discussed here also draw the attention to the significant impact of more than thirty years of global relations, usually missing from official accounts of the island's history.

These narratives not only chart the temporal and spatial journeys of their protagonists but also delve into issues intricately connected to the realities of the Eastern Bloc. They examine the interplay between power and official discourse, as well as the complex relationships between views of technology, nature, and secularization. These elements are inextricably interwoven with the trajectories of characters such as Manuel and Pedro Juan, who progressively learn to take critical distance from the distortions of state propaganda. In this context, the renunciation of triumphalist rhetoric can be interpreted as a sign of political *maturity* and of the freedom to cultivate their own interpersonal relationships, distinct from conventional modes of socialization. By disrupting the construction of time and space and blurring established reference points, these narratives undertake a critical revision of the crisis and the ultimate demise of a bygone world. This portrayal is offered in dialogue with the perpetual present of their country of origin, where only alternative and independent communities may provide a sense of familial belonging.

Bibliography

Agamben, Giorgio. *Homo sacer. El poder soberano y la nuda vida*. Valencia: Pre-Textos, 1998.

Artwińska, Anna, and Agnieszka Mrozik. *Gender, Generations, and Communism in Central and Eastern Europe and Beyond*. London: Routledge, 2021.

Benítez Rojo, Antonio. *The Repeating Island. The Caribbean and the Postmodern Perspective*. Transl. James E. Maraniss. Durham: Duke UP, 1997.

Boym, Svetlana. *The Future of Nostalgia*. New York: Basic Books, 2001.

Boym, Svetlana. "From the Russian Soul to Post-Communist Nostalgia." *Representations* 49 (1995): 133–166.

Díaz, Jesús. *Las cuatro fugas de Manuel*. Madrid: Espasa, 2002.

Díaz, Jesús. *Siberiana*. Madrid: Espasa, 2000.

Díaz Maceo, Anairis, and Johanna Habel. "The Construction of Solidarity in Public Spaces between Germany and Cuba before and after the German Reunification." *Global Histories: A Student Journal* 6.1 (2020): 48–70.

Foucault, Michel. "Of Other Spaces." *Diacritics* 16.1 (1986): 22–27.

Garbatzky, Irina. "Inscripciones postsoviéticas en la literatura cubana actual. Futuros negativos y desfiguraciones de lo humano en El imperio Oblómov de Carlos A. Aguilera." *Taller de letras* 58 (2016): 111–126.

Gutiérrez, Pedro Juan. *Estoico y frugal*. Barcelona: Anagrama, 2019.

Loss, Jacqueline. *Dreaming in Russian: The Cuban Soviet Imaginary*. Austin: University of Texas Press, 2013.

Loss, Jacqueline, and José Manuel Prieto. *Caviar with Rum: Cuba-USSR and the Post-Soviet Experience*. London: Palgrave, 2011.

Mrozik, Agnieszka, and Anja Tippner. "Remembering Late Socialism in Autobiographical Novels and Autofictions from Central and Eastern Europe: Introduction." *European Journal of Life Writing* 10 (2021): RLS1–RLS14.

Noguerol Jiménez, Francisca. "Barroco frío: simulacro, ciencias duras, realismo histérico y fractalidad en la última narrativa en español." *Imágenes de la tecnología y la globalización en las narrativas hispánicas*. Eds. Jesús Montoya Juárez/Ángel Esteban. Madrid: Iberoamericana Vervuert, 2013. 17–32.

Prieto, José Manuel. *Livadia*. Barcelona: Mondadori, 1999.

Prieto, José Manuel. *Enciclopedia de una vida en Rusia*. Ciudad de México: Consejo Nacional para la Cultura y las Artes, 1998.

Prieto, José Manuel. *Nunca antes había visto el rojo*. La Habana: Letras Cubanas, 1996.

Puñales-Alpízar, Damaris. *Escrito en cirílico: el ideal soviético en la cultura cubana posnoventa*. Santiago de Chile: Cuarto Propio, 2012.

Rojas, Rafael. *El estante vacío: literatura y política en Cuba*. Barcelona: Anagrama, 2009.
Rupprecht, Tobias. *Soviet Internationalism after Stalin: Interaction and Exchange between the USSR and Latin America during the Cold War*. Cambridge: Cambridge UP, 2015.
Speranza, Graciela. *Cronografías: Arte y ficciones de un tiempo sin tiempo*. Barcelona: Anagrama, 2017.
Vega Serova, Anna Lidia. *Ánima fatua*. La Habana: Letras Cubanas, 2007.
Walcott, Derek. *What the Twilight Says: Essays*. New York City: Farrar, Straus and Giroux, 2014.
Welge, Jobst. "Tropical Temporalities: Literary Landscape and Multiple Times in Alejo Carpentier's *Los Pasos Perdidos*." *Literary Landscapes of Time: Multiple Temporalities and Spaces in Latin American and Caribbean Literatures*. Eds. Jobst Welge/Juliane Tauchnitz. Berlin: De Gruyter, 2023. 99–114.
Westad, Odd Arne. *The Global Cold War. Third World Interventions and the Making of Our Times*. Cambridge: Cambridge UP, 2012.
Zaharchenko, Tatiana. "The Environmental Movement and Ecological Law in the Soviet Union: The Process of Transformation." *Ecology* 17.3 (1990): 455–475.

Ángela Calderón

‘The More Blood Ties, the More Family.’ Deconstructing Biological Bonds in Sara Mesa’s *The Family*

1 Talking and Telling about the Family

Sara Mesa’s *La familia* (2022) [The Family] presents family constellations as its subject in two ways: On the one hand, the narrative instance never misses a moment to construct opposing character tandems of two family members through schematic characterizations and explicit oppositional features. On the other hand, it makes questions of positioning, hierarchy, and ranking the constant theme of the numerous character comments, whether these are perceived from a specific viewpoint via the characters or attributed heterodiegetically. All behavior and every interaction are refracted in the light of the respective family constellation – usually the father figure in relation to another – and evaluated primarily on this basis.

The novel is about a family consisting of the parents, Damián and Laura, and their three children – the eldest son, also called Damián, the middle daughter Rosa and the youngest son Aquilino – as well as an adopted daughter, Martina. Martina is in fact Laura’s niece, the daughter of her deceased sister. Finally, Laura’s brother, uncle Óscar, is also part of the narrative. The focus lies largely on the children’s characters, primarily in relation to their father.

Although, structurally speaking, all positions are occupied in this novel – father, mother, daughter, son – there can be no talk of an ‘intact family,’[1] as its genealogy as a family is semantically placed in the context of a massive conflict situation; but *La familia* is not about the family as a structure that may be incomplete in the wake of a disruptive event. The conflict resides in a form of dysfunctionality. It’s a specific form of communicative decomposition within the family that takes place. This raises the question of whether *La familia* can really claim to be a representative family novel if the family is not part of an overall social structure or a place where the political or at least the public sphere is negotiated. Does Laura and Damián’s family therefore have a representative or even allegorical-symbolic dimension? By uncovering a discursive structure, I would like to argue,

1 For the German-language context, Michalski (2015) has examined the ‘radiance’ of the ‘intact family’ and its implications as a model.

Ángela Calderón, Leipzig University

https://doi.org/10.1515/9783111208664-015

Sara Mesa points to an immaterial historical legacy the children of the 1970s and 1980s had to deal with.

The novel is divided into fourteen chapters. Each one is protagonized by a family member. However, the chapter portraying Aquilino ("Aqui in seven fragments" ["Aqui en siete fragmentos" (Mesa 2022, 135)]) is in turn divided into seven chapters with subheadings; all the other chapters form their own narrative unit. Additionally, Aquilino is particularly marked in that he is the only child character to whom only a single chapter is dedicated. Aquilino, who is generally described as an oddball – "he was a very rare child" ["[e]ra un niño muy raro" (Mesa 2022, 14)] – crystallizes the problems of this family. In particular, he stands out within the family structure because he manages to emotionally escape the regiment of his parents: "no one could ever bend him in the slightest" ["nadie jamás pudo doblegarlo lo más mínimo" (Mesa 2022, 136)]. Another contributing factor to his apparent success in a realm denied to his siblings is his proactive engagement with the familial circumstances: "Damián, Rosa, and Martina had learned to lie with ease and were very careful not to make comments that could give them away. On the other hand, Aqui never had any qualms about telling the truth, because where was the problem? Was he to blame?" ["[Damián, Rosa y Martina] [h]abían aprendido a mentir con soltura y se guardaban mucho de hacer comentarios que pudieran delatarlos. Aqui, en cambio, no tuvo nunca reparo en decir la verdad, porque ¿dónde estaba el problema? ¿Acaso tenía él la culpa?" (Mesa 2022, 142–143)] Aquilino is thus marked by the fact that he is the one child that not only speaks openly but also specifically addresses the family's oddities.

Aqui outlines the challenges that determine the structure of the family depicted in this novel. The novel portrays a type of violent experience that predominantly stems from the father figure and is linked to the possibility of unrestricted speech. As will be shown, the father's violence consists of speaking in a mode of apparent honesty and straightforwardness that goes hand in hand with concealed intentions. Although his true motives are not expressed, there is an absence of deception in the strictest sense. This problem is developed right at the beginning of the novel with the concept of the secret, *el secreto*, which introduces a family figure who also occupies a special position in the family structure: Martina, the adopted daughter. This article will discuss, especially through uncle Óscar, Aqui, and Martina, what family means in this novel and what form it eventually takes. First, the specificity of *this* family – *la familia* – will be described in more detail by analyzing the parents.

2 The Parents. Starting a Family

The novel begins with the statement that there are no secrets in this family: "In this family there are no secrets!" ["¡En esta familia no hay secretos!" (Mesa 2022, 9)] is the title of the first chapter. It is immediately repeated verbatim by Damián senior: "'In this family there are no secrets!,' said Father." The capitalization of the word father, together with the omission of the definite article that precedes it (which should be placed regularly: *dijo el padre*), already emphasizes on a linguistic level the very unusual diction of the characters in this novel. It is a way of speaking that is not fundamentally wrong, but is at least peculiar, strange, and odd.

The omission of the direct article and the capitalization of father here evokes the figure of the priest, who would be addressed in this way in Spanish. A sort of devout atmosphere surrounds the father. It is something that the father constantly stresses by way of his discourse: Do-goodism is an integral part of his discursive horizon. His speech is close to the unctuous, pathetic, and exaggerated. Aquis' comment that he is not to *blame* for his family's peculiarity and that he is therefore allowed to speak openly about it forms the antithesis to this intricate problem of language as a self-expression, on the one hand, and guilt or authority, on the other.

The situation in the chapter "In this family there are no secrets!" presents the following situation: 'Father' finds Martina's diary. It is locked, which prompts the father to question Martina at length about why she does not trust her new family. His insistence causes Martina to become entangled in contradictions, delivering a monologue over the child with moral superiority: "As far as I know, no one has forbidden you to write a diary. What's more, we think it's very good for you to express yourself without restraint. Where does this mistrust come from? Do you really think, Martina, that your mother or I are going to read your diary without permission?" ["Que yo sepa, nadie te ha prohibido escribir un diario [...]. Es más, nos parece muy bien que expreséis sin cortapisas [...]. ¿De verdad crees, Martina, que tu madre o yo vamos a leer tu diario sin permiso?" (Mesa 2022, 9)] Since he straightaway forces Martina not to keep any secrets, she is urged to only write in her diary in the company of family members. One day, when the family gathers around the table for 'individual work in togetherness,' her father urges Martina to write in her diary, and openly reads along as she writes and constantly corrects her: "Dangerously, it was turning into a writing class. Martina froze, she didn't know how to go on. That is what her precious diary had now become, a sad notebook for school essays." ["Peligrosamente, aquello se estaba convirtiendo en una clase de redacción. Martina se quedó paralizada, no supo cómo seguir. En eso se había transformado ahora su preciado diario, [...] en un triste cuaderno para hacer redacciones escolares." (Mesa 2022, 19)]

It is no coincidence that the sentence starts with 'danger' [*peligro*] and ends with 'sadness' [*triste*]. The danger and sadness lie precisely in the situation that was negotiated discursively – in this case respect for Martina's privacy when writing her diary – but then is performatively suspended: one set of facts is turned into another, and diary writing becomes an exercise in style. A change in the quality of a situation takes place, while it is not possible to determine with precision whether the transformation was deliberately brought about and, above all, nor to trace linguistically that this change has occurred. The change in quality takes place tacitly since, nominally, Martina writes in her diary, except that it has become a supervised exercise.

It is remarkable that the tipping point into assault and aggression cannot be traced linguistically but is based on a twisting of the facts that are found within the structure of the family. This reversal has to do with the play of discursive power into which the father forces his counterpart. He acts out his discursive supremacy and creates a violent atmosphere that the children are unable to cope with, either rhetorically or argumentatively. The father's discursive violence is therefore not based on lies, falsehoods, or verbal perfidy as he does not speak untruthfully. The deception lies within the discrepancy of the speech and what is ultimately realized performatively; it is not based on what he explicitly says. The father feigns an exchange on equal footing but does not reveal the actual intention of his speech and counteracts what he communicates through his actions. This is what primarily characterizes the structure of the relationship between the father and the children.

Moreover, said discrepancy is reflected in the content of what the father says and the kind of person he actually is. The father does not hesitate to proclaim his grandiosity – all his speeches center on topics such as trust and convictions, performance and solidarity, and responsibility and community – but he ultimately proves to be a 'heap of misery': "we saw Father sit on the bed, with his head between his legs" ["vimos a Padre sentarse en la cama de espalda hundiendo la cabeza entre las piernas" (Mesa 2022, 222)]. The discrepancy between discursive eloquence and grandiloquence on the one hand, and inner pusillanimity and despondency on the other, is especially shown in two paradigmatic scenes, both of which are set in the parents' bedroom and thus present Damián less in his function as a father and more as a husband. They are particularly significant because – being the family's scenes of origin – they reveal the grammar of the entire family structure, that is, the procreation of the children.

The begetting of the first-born son is simply carried out in a technocratic manner: "He had merely complied with a rigor and a mechanism of a book of mechanics" ["Él se había limitado a cumplir con un rigor y una mecánica de libro de instrucciones" (Mesa 2022, 54)]. This corresponds to the strictly quantitative idea of the family that Damián has: "The more children there are, the more blood ties, the *more family*" ["cuantos más hijos haya, más vínculos de sangre, *más familia*" (Mesa 2022, 52; emphasis in the original)]. After the birth of her eldest son, Laura finds herself in a state of postnatal depression, which is associated with a certain disgust towards her husband: "How should I put this ... After the first child was born, she became disgusted with her husband. This is now called postpartum depression." ["Como diría ... Tras nacer el primero se quedó bloqueada, [...] le cogió asco al marido. [...] | Esto lo llaman ahora depresión posparto." (Mesa 2022, 47)] This constellation leads to a warlike, long-lasting conflict, which is countered accordingly in the mode of 'resistance': "The Resistance, also known as the War, was on the rise. They argued, they screamed, they would have torn each other apart if they weren't so tired of hating each other." ["La Resistencia, también conocida como la Guerra, fue en aumento. [...] | Discutían, gritaban, se habrían despedazado mutuamente si no estuviesen tan cansados de odiarse." (Mesa 2022, 57)] Emotionally, the family's scene of origin is thus initially driven by technocratic pragmatism. Subsequently, it is motivated by Laura's depressive mood, and by the increasing aggression and hateful interaction between the spouses. The blood relationship, which the father of the family cites as a criterion for the essence of a family, is emotionally framed by sobriety, distance, and anger – even to the point that semantically the creation of the family is set in a context of war, mutilation, and hatred.

This aspect is further developed. The first child is born out of a mechanical lack of emotion. As for Rosa, the second child, she enters life in the course of an emotional campaign of revenge, which forms the culmination of the marital warfare. Laura recounts Damián a premarital night of love, which she remembers vividly, in hurtful detail and with the intent to offend him: "She told him that that was the only time in his life she had ever felt *anything*. He, Damián, could never give her anything like it. Not even a glimpse." ["Le dijo que aquella fue la única vez en su vida que había sentido *algo*. [...] Él, Damián, jamás podría darle nada parecido. Ni siquiera un atisbo." (Mesa 2022, 59; emphasis in the original)] Unlike in all the other scenes in the novel, Damián cannot respond discursively and remains silent. Without a word, he throws himself on top of her, from which the second pregnancy emerges.

Intensifying the warlike background, the conception of the second child is placed in the context of rape: "He threw himself on top of her. He crushed her against the sofa. A rape? No, there was no way Laura would have described it that way." ["Él se echó sobre ella. La aplastó contra el sofá. [...] ¿Una violación? No, de ninguna manera Laura la habría calificado de ese modo." (Mesa 2022, 59)] At this point, the narrative voice skillfully imitates the discursive structure of violence: To maintain ambiguity over whether Damián rapes Laura or not, the direct object pronoun *lo* could have been used, which would have left unclear what 'that' refers to. However, the grammatical reference of the feminine object pronoun *la* is undoubtedly the rape, whereby the narrative instance evaluates the scene as such and thus counteracts Laura's assessment of the situation. In this sense, Laura does not call a spade a spade either: According to the narrative instance, it is a rape that is covered up or concealed as such by Laura. This is a noteworthing fact. By continuing the lack of congruence between emotion and sexuality in Damián's conception, by covering up the opposition of the affective and the performative in Rosa's conception, and by not naming the rape as such, Laura duplicates the father's discursive behavior. She appears as an accomplice to this interaction. This parallelism is emphasized by the fact that immediately after this scene the narrator addresses Laura and Damián in the third person plural, whereby the spouses grammatically appear as a couple. Laura therefore takes on the role of a character who carries out Damián's reversal and distortion.

The scene is illustrative of the structure of the family in that it shows that Laura, although far less present in the text than the father figure, agrees to this form of violent and disguising communication and supports it. It should also be emphasized that the 'harmony' of this family is just as discursively structured as it is in the relationship between the father and the children and that it is – typographically marked by the use of capitalization here as well – directly related to war: "From that union Rosa, the second one, was born. With her the War [!] ended and another era began, much more *harmonious*, almost without arguments." ["De esa unión nació Rosa, la segunda. Con ella acabó la Guerra [!] y empezó otra época mucho más *armónica,* casi sin discusiones." (Mesa 2022, 59; emphasis mine)] The fact that the war, but also 'the family project' – "He talked all the time about the Project. The family was that, the Project." ["Hablaba todo el tiempo del Proyecto. La familia era eso, el Proyecto." (Mesa 2022, 48)] – and the parents ("Father and Mother" ["Padre y Madre" (Mesa 2022, 121)]) are written in capital letters not usually used in Spanish indicates their relationship of correspondence. Derived from the harmony of this family, a direct link is established between the Father and the War, a situation that Laura participates in and which thus makes her part of the family violence.

It is difficult to determine whether the description of the foundation of the family is intended to suggest that this way of interacting is 'a family curse or a family destiny' (see Müller-Bochat 1995, 325). It seems more plausible that it is precisely the constellation – discursively dominant father figure versus discursively reticent mother figure – that seals a family fate, which then turns into a family curse. However, this is not an external event, but rather the 'unfortunate' constellation in which both parents – precisely *because* they function *together* in this way – develop said curse. It is for this reason that it is crucial to recognize and name Laura and Damián together as an active force in the structure of this (their) family.

The flip side of the dimension of the wordless, unsaid, and unspoken, represented by Laura, is at the same time a constant, uninterrupted, and excessive act of speaking of the father: "He would talk and talk and talk. Laura wanted to ask him to shut up, to shut up for once in his life, but she would just meekly close her eyes." ["Hablaba y hablaba y hablaba […]. Laura quería pedirle que se callara, que por una vez en su vida se callara, pero se limitaba a cerrar los ojos con mansedumbre" (Mesa 2022, 48)]. Damián's speech is therefore also violent in that it leaves no space for his counterpart. What is a cross-examination in Martina's diary scene is here a one-sided speech, leaving no space for the other to intervene. Damián, the father, does not pose questions. He neither listens to his counterpart nor does he inquire about the other's position.

The inability of the spouses to express their feeling and to communicate is reflected in another scene, which is also set in the parental bedroom. This scene distinctly demonstrates that a lack of emotional correspondence and linguistic expression is at the heart of the problem of speaking in (and about) this family (as it also provides information concerning the narration about this family). Together with the prefatorial chapter "The House" ["La casa" (Mesa 2022, 7], the following scene forms the frame narrative of the novel, insofar as it is the last chapter. At the beginning of the novel the reader is asked to look attentively and in the final scene, "The Gap" ["La Rendijita" (Mesa 2022, 221)] the sons Aqui and Damián see their father in precisely this way: Through the gap in the doors of a cupboard, they secretly spy on him while keeping silent. He sits on the bed and bursts into tears. This display of intense emotion is likewise wordless – "He cried without showing off as we used to cry, without protesting or slurping his snot" ["Lloraba […] sin alardear como solíamos llorar nosotros, sin protestar ni sorberse los mocos" (Mesa 2022, 224)] – and is experienced in loneliness, without support from Laura or any other family member. The father's emotional world receives no feedback from any family member, but it also remains impenetrable: The reason for Damián's tears are not clarified throughout the novel. This is a unique feature compared to all the other characters, whose inner lives are constantly and primarily emphasized as the narrative focuses on the effects the father has on their emotional world. Although Damián is thus at the center of the depiction of a whole series of emotional-affective reactions and developments in his environment, he is oblivious to his own affective disposition. This largely applies to Laura as well, though not to the same extent.

What is noteworthy is that this form of representation imitates Damián-father's manner of speech. The narrator leaves Damián's emotional-affective problem unnamed and bypasses it by only narrating the father's seemingly harmless actions. In accordance with Damián's way of speaking, this novel *appears* to be a narrative about a non-violent family. However, it eventually reveals itself as a narrative about a strange form of violence and malice. The explicit author in the first chapter invites us to look closely (*mirar* is incessantly repeated), and to pay attention: "Do it precisely, it's important." ["Hazlo con precisión, es importante." (Mesa 2022, 7)] He also asks us to draw conclusions from these observations as to what kind of family we are dealing with in *La familia*, since what we read about it is deceptive [*trampa*]: "Words that mean just the opposite of what they appear to be, cheating." ["Palabras que significan justeo lo contrario de lo que aparentan, tramposillas." (Mesa 2022, 7)]

Therefore, we can infer that both the family and the father, are in opposition to each other, just as the emotionality and discursiveness of the father are. The center of the novel, with the father on the one hand and the titular family on the other, is in this respect primarily mediated and thus accessible on a second level. It is fitting that the father is not represented directly; rather, he is depicted through the discourse of the other family members. Their actions and especially the experience of the father's violence allow us to 'observationally read' this novel. The text suggests that *seemingly* non-violent communication is a form of violence.

3 The Power of Language

It is primarily the father who shapes communication in the family. His manner of speech is the reason for the suffering of the other family members. It is not because his words are violent, ruthless, or deliberately hurtful that we can speak of verbal aggression. Just as the parents are unable to resolve conflicts between themselves verbally, and act out a latent aggression, Damián-father interacts with his children in a passive-aggressive manner (it is not accidental that his name etymologically refers to the ancient Greek form of conquering[2]). What exactly does the deception consist of? How can this passive dimension, the unspoken aspect of what is conveyed, be described in more detail?

First of all, Damián is not lying. His words do not betray because they are untrue. To a certain extent, the deception comes from the opposite: The father always calls a spade a spade, unapologetically – and demands the same from his children, precision in expression: "That's the way I like it, Martina, that you

2 *Damazein* means to subdue or to tame/drill an animal, but also to subjugate somebody under the yoke of marriage (Gemoll 2006, 182).

speak, with propriety" ["Así me gusta, Martina, que hables con propiedad" (Mesa 2022, 16)]. It also fits that he rejects idioms and phraseological expressions: "'Stop with the proverbs.' Father hated proverbs." ["–[D]éjate de refranes. –Padre odiaba los refranes." (Mesa 2022, 20)] He rejects the formulaic. His praise of Martina exemplifies that Damián-father is concerned with speech as something real, authentic, something of his own [*lo propio*]. This way he gives the impression that his language is an expression of himself, a genuine self-expression. However, there is the contradiction that his inner self remains hidden, or rather unspoken, throughout the novel. This can be seen in a scene in the opening chapter, which describes the oppositional constellation between the father and uncle Óscar – a person who does not belong to the inner circle of the family but is nevertheless a family member.

Uncle Óscar is Laura's brother and represents the antithesis of Damián-father. Despite this, Damián always behaves politely towards him. One day, however, Óscar accidentally discovers Father's diary, which contains entries concerning him, Óscar. These entries are in complete contrast to Father's usual way of speaking in emphatically complete sentences, his differentiation between idioms and his *propiedad,* his way of speaking aptly, as they are completely incoherent, jumbled, and essentially reveal how much Laura's brother appears to him as a problem, a threat and a belittlement of his person: "*teasing behind my back, he emphasizes that he is taller than me, in love with his own sister?* How much that man suffered, he said to himself" ["*burlas a mis espaldas,* [...] *hace notar que es más alto que yo,* [...] *¿enamorado de su propia hermana?* [...] Cuánto sufría ese hombre, se dijo" (Mesa 2022, 118; emphasis in the original)]. The dissonance between the father's demands regarding a proper way of speaking on the one hand, and his way of formulating when it comes to his emotionality on the other, is the first level of his 'untrue speech' in the sense of discrepancy.

The father's own [*propio*], when articulated in language, is not only incoherent, incongruent and almost linguistically helpless, but on the level of what is actually being said it is interspersed with stereotypes and distortions. These distortions, notably, concern the family and his position in it: Damián's father feels humiliated by his uncle because he is taller than him; it is presumably out of jealousy that Damián reverses the good relationship between siblings into an incestuous one[3] and feels

3 The theme of sibling love, as well as love triangles in general, is of course also part of the literary tradition of the family novel (see Bruss 2016), which the father stereotypically uses here. On the fictional real level of the novel, however, there is no reason to suspect incestuous behaviour. From a family constellation perspective, however, Damián is right that Laura and her brother Óscar form a relationship that is marked sensually (if not sexually, then emphatically). For example, uncle Óscar brings Laura her favorite desserts, which they eat together in secret. Laura finds

betrayed. A further level of discrepancy lies in the fact that, although he condemns inauthentic speech (that which is nos his own [*lo que no es propio de uno*]) Damián-father is unable to create clarity through his words. It remains unclear what he is actually concerned about and what he is suffering from. He is unable to assert himself linguistically when confronted with another family member who is perceived as equal. In this case, the structure of a rhetorically dominant father and an inferior counterpart becomes that of the inferior father and a family member he feels threatened by. Contrary to his objective, his actual speech – i.e., speaking about what is going on inside him – remains largely incomprehensible, and hence needs to be interpreted. However, Damián-father struggles to express his emotions coherently.

It has already been mentioned that the narrator imitates the form of communication between the parents insofar as 'the actual thing' remains unnamed. However, the doubling mechanism of the novel's discursive peculiarity is also present with regard to this peculiar non-descriptiveness of the father's emotionality. While there is no linguistically congruent access to Damián-father's inner life, there are frequent and explicit statements about the inner lives of the other characters. Feelings and inner lives are constantly transformed into, and described as, personality traits. Ad nauseam and in an emphatically annoying way, the narrator explains, determines, and defines exactly how characters feel, what they want, what consequences a certain situation will have for them, what their goals are, and for what reasons they act in this or that way. It is therefore a case of inverted doubling. While nothing coherent can be said about Damián-father and his affective disposition, motivations, it is the opposite for the other characters, especially the children. Here everything is spelled out incessantly and thus psychograms are formulated, which are also presented without any hesitation. This applies only and exclusively to the other family members, but not to the father figure.

The extent of the toxic family communication – especially in regard of the children – can be seen in a scene with Martina. As an adopted child and thus falling outside the biologically defined family circle it is certainly no coincidence that she is the one person who repeatedly raises the question of how openly people can speak within this family. This issue culminates at a later point in time when Martina is sanctioned by her parents for her frankness when talking about what she feels. Martina opens up to a teacher. She confides in her and is happy to be

it difficult to maintain moderation and Óscar encourages her to eat as much as she likes. Here, Damián's asceticism and Óscar's lustfulness are juxtaposed. Food and culinary delights thus form part of the lines of conflict in the marriage (see Adams 2020, 177–230).

able to talk to her without reservations. However, Martina's lack of trust leads to her adoptive parents finding out about her longings. They punish her with disappointment and make her feel that she had betrayed them: "They wore the gleam of disappointment in their eyes. The girl knew then that she had committed the most reprehensible of sins: that of betrayal." ["Ellos llevaban el brillo de la decepción en los ojos. [...] La niña supo entonces que había cometido el más reprochable de los pecados: el de la traición." (Mesa 2022, 189–190)] Here, openness and betrayal are linked. Martina, by saying straightforwardly that what is going on inside her, commits the 'greatest possible sin' (thus revisiting the theme of guilt), adopting the term of her parents.

This scene is so momentous because the connection between betrayal [*traición*] and open speech creates a literal and therefore direct link to the 'cheating' words of the preface: *traición* and *tramposilla* are located in the field of pretense. This applies at least within the family circle. Martina's communicative honesty – which, incidentally, is interspersed with (child-like) untruths – takes place outside the family. This indirect way of expressing herself is, in contrast to her parents' failure, covered by her inner emotion – and therefore appears more truthful than her father's speech. To the extent that Damián-father's seemingly clear and unmediated words ultimately mean the opposite of what they claim to be, Martina's untruthful speech, in turn, becomes true insofar as it is genuine. She lies, but through her speech she defends her interests and her emotions. The father's speech, on the other hand, is hypocritical. However, emotionally truthful speech is punished by the adults. In consequence, the novel is not about a demand for truthful speech, but about inauthentic speech in the sense of an incongruence with the inner self [*lo propio*].

4 Figures of the Third. Alternative Family Constellations

If the father figure is at the center of the novel *La familia*, and the father figure is characterized by deceptive speech and by the fact that his affective dimension remains in the dark, then *La familia* is a family novel insofar as dysfunctional communication is what connects the generations. The novel emphatically presents itself as a family novel insofar as "recurring patterns of behavior – analogies of psychological qualities and transgenerational entanglements" (Eichenberg 2009, 111) are explored. In this sense, the novel deals with how "psychical patterns are perpetuated over generations" (Eichenberg 2009, 124), especially in the area of communication.

How can the idiosyncrasies of this family be understood to define this particular family structure in more detail? A substantial approach to this arises from a combination of the two leading thematic axes: Family constellations on the one hand, and modes of speaking on the other. If modalities of communication are used as a feature of investigation, they rearrange the structure of this family – and new constellations are formed that turn the concept of the familial in a new direction. This relates specifically to Martina and Aquilino, on the one hand, and uncle Óscar, on the other. While the manner of speaking at the level of the children identifies Martina and Aqui separately, this applies to Óscar at the level of the parents.

Martina, Aqui and Óscar additionally form a specific (tripartite) family constellation among themselves: Óscar and Martina correspond recognizably insofar as the motif of the diary connects them to the father; Aqui and Martina, as will be shown below, are the two children who can counter the father's discursive violence. Finally, Óscar and Aqui each belong to a three-sibling constellation within the family: Óscar, Laura, and their deceased sister; the biological children Aqui, Damián, and Rosa. In the succeeding section, these 'figures of the third' ['Figuren des Dritten' (see Eßlinger et al. 2010)] will be used to draw attention to alternative family structures in the novel and to accentuate the understanding of family in a novel way.

4.1 Óscar. Speaking Frankly

Uncle Óscar is the one character who speaks openly and unambiguously. Therefore it makes sense that he speaks of Damián-father's problem in no uncertain terms, when he asks Laura: "Why does he have to talk like that?" ["¿Por qué tiene que hablar así?" (Mesa 2022, 109)]. Óscar not only represents openness but also expresses himself through reasoned arguments. However, this disarms the father: When Óscar suddenly asks him why there is no dishwasher and rejects the father's objections with counterarguments, the latter simply does not know what to do. Damián-father ignores Óscar's reasons, loses himself in bogus arguments, evades them, and ultimately breaks off the conversation in despair. At this point, the father is portrayed regressively: "At that moment, as if on tiptoes, he looked smaller, more fragile." ["En ese momento, [...] como si estuviera de puntillas, se le veía más pequeño, más frágil." (Mesa 2022, 109)] This is accentuated in particular by showing the father as incapable of speaking, with Óscar discovering shortly thereafter that the father is no longer capable of even producing language: "he had incomprehensible notations next to others" ["[h]abía anotaciones incomprensibles junto a otras" (Mesa 2022, 118)].

It is also interesting that uncle Óscar (in the constellation with his sister Laura and her husband Damián) knows how to name the problem of inauthentic speech in this structure: He recognizes Laura as its agent and also names it. Following the uproar over the question of the dishwasher, Óscar turns to his sister and questions her. She defends Damián's position, to which Óscar replies: "'Fuck, Laura,' he said, 'I don't know what you're talking about, are you his manager or what?'" ["–Joder, Laura –dijo–, no sé de qué me estás hablando. ¿Eres su representante o qué?" (Mesa 2022, 112)] Laura speaks by proxy and is a replication of the father and his communicative violence, even if she tends to remain silent.

Óscar, by speaking clearly, addresses his interlocutors directly and wants to untangle problems or misunderstandings. He is evidently different from Damián and Laura. He cannot simply converse with them; this applies to the father, who cannot articulate himself, and to Laura, whom Óscar does not understand in both senses of the word: "I don't know what you're talking about" ["no sé de qué me estás hablando" (Mesa 2022, 112)]. Uncle Óscar is recognizably marked as a 'third figure.'

For a better understanding of this triangulated family constellation, the differentiation of the "triad theorist" (Lachmann 2010, 96) René Guénon is revealing. According to him, "triadic constellations" (Lachmann 2010, 96) can be divided into two groups. He refers to these as *ternaire*: "The first *ternaire* consists of a primary principle from which two opposing or complementary terms are derived. In the first case, the triangle is determined by the primary principle from which the terms are derived" (Lachmann 2010, 96). The three-way constellation between Óscar, Damián, and Laura seems to correspond to this first model, insofar as Óscar is the figure – the primary principle – which reveals the linguistic function of the parents. To the extent that neither Laura nor Damián can assert their position argumentatively or conduct a self-mediated conversation, Óscar appears as the inverted primary principle through which this linguistic inability of 'the two terms' Laura and Damián emanates. They both act in a complementary way. This perspective is important and illuminating because it questions the representational figure of the triangle in terms of its order: "Guénon's relations presented in the *ternaire* types encourage us to ask *how* the three terms relate to each other: whether they are relations of causality or whether hierarchical concepts play a role or ordering factors of other provenance, or whether the ranking as such is the final instance." (Lachmann 2010, 96–97; emphasis mine) Óscar as a *ternaire* shows how much the parents are powerless, unable to represent or assert themselves, even though, seen from a child level, the parents' way of communicating is violent, intimidating, and inhibiting.

4.2 Aquilino. On Consanguinity

Variances in the way of speaking also differentiate the family structure at the level of the children: Rosa and Damián on the one hand, and Martina and Aquilino on the other. Aquilino and Martina are structurally linked in terms of their similar speech patterns and form an additional family constellation with their father, which in turn re-accentuates what is meant by family – via Aqui – and the extent to which communication is the experience of violence which the children suffer – conveyed via Martina.

Damián and Rosa are marked as children, understood as heirs to a family continuity of Damián and Laura: Both of their entries into the family are assigned separate chapters. This is not the case with Aquilino, the youngest son, who is abruptly introduced in the text and who is not seen by the parents as a further descendant. Moreover, he is not assigned a function within the family. The situation is similar for Martina, the adopted child. She is identified as a foreign body from whom the father demands trust and belonging. In this respect, the relationship between the parents and Damián and Rosa is different from that between the parents and Aquilino and Martina. This in turn is reflected in the way they speak: While Damián and Rosa remain silent in their relationship with their father – there is no conversation between Rosa and their father throughout the entire novel and Damián starts to stutter when addressing his father thus being unable to articulate himself – Martina and Aquilino manage to outwit their father at least to some extent linguistically in order to assert themselves.

Aquilino wants to be called by his nickname. He achieves this through a discursive strategy: "He was aware that this, the rejection of his name, Father was not going to approve. To tell him outright would be a frontal attack on himself. He decided to keep quiet, but not out of fear, but out of strategy." ["[E]ra consciente de que eso, el rechazo a su nombre, Padre no iba a aprobarlo. Decírselo a las claras sería un ataque frontal [...] a él mismo. Decidió callarse, pero no por temor, sino por estrategia." (Mesa 2022, 148–150)] Remarkably, Aquilino can assert himself against the violence he encounters at home: "*verbal* aggressions" ["agresiones *verbales*" (Mesa 2022, 150; emphasis in the original)]. Ultimately, he manages to be called the way he wants to. Aquilino's strategy is a rhetorical option that Rosa and Damián do not have. They are trapped in an inability to express what is their own.

It is difficult to answer why Aquilino can assert himself against the 'verbal aggression' at home and why he is not given his own chapter in the family genealogy. What is certain is that, because there is no story about how he enters the family – even Martina's story, that of the adopted child, is being told –, he cannot actually be considered 'a child in this family.' The designation as a child in a structural sense presupposes that he has a particular relationship with his parents. It is essentially defined by its origins (see Müller-Bochat 1995, 310). Moreover, unlike Rosa and Damián, Aquilino is recognizably not infantile (nor is Martina, who comments on Rosa's behavior with analytical acumen from the very beginning). The opposite is the case: "like any other child. No." ["como [...] cualquier otro niño. No." (Mesa 2022, 145)]

In this sense, there are dividing lines running through the family constellation of children on several levels. These are Martina and Aquilino on the one hand (non-childlike, analytical, and discursively partially autonomous) and Rosa and Damián on the other (infantile-regressive, emotionally trapped, and linguistically incapable). They are primarily trying to live up to their father. The fact that Aquilino and Martina are also presented as 'figures of the third' shows that in *La familia,* family cohesion and belonging are not generated through blood relationships, but through emotional dependence and discursive involvement.

However, one important aspect of the family novel remains unanswered: Why is Aquilino different, even though he has the same parents as Rosa and Damián? Goethe's *Elective Affinities* [*Wahlverwandtschaften*] seem to form a helpful intertext. It seems to provide a starting point that Sara Mesa develops further in *La familia* because it highlights the problem of situating Aqui within the family, albeit with a different nuance: What for Goethe is a case of "lack of genetic family resemblance" (Müller-Bochat 1995, 315), is for *La familia* a case of a 'genetic family with an essential heterogeneity,' being Aqui the figuration of this problem. Goethe's novel makes the sexual act and its result (namely the born child) its conceptual center: The child is born out of a broken marriage in "a half-desperate, half-thoughtless frenzy" (Müller-Bochat 1995, 312). These circumstances of conception are also evident in *La familia* – albeit for Rosa and Damián, who resemble their parents. Taking this into account it only makes sense that Aqui's conception is omitted within the narrative. There is no mention of Aqui's conception and birth. He is evidently removed from the hereditary context.

However, it remains unclear *why* Aqui is 'aberrant.' Where does Aqui's affective – and consequently discursive – 'otherness' come from? Martina's 'otherness' is easier to explain, since as an adopted child, she is not blood-related and therefore, arguably, not part of the family in the strictest sense. It seems that it is by establishing a constellation between Aqui *and* Martina that this question is answered.

The closeness between Aqui and Martina is established by Aqui opening the novel (he owns the narrative voice that reports on the observation of the father), and Martina closing it (where her voice reveals that her father only pretended to be a lawyer). This is flanked by the fact that Aqui is assigned the attribute of shrewdness ("the smartest" ["el más listo" (Mesa 2022, 114)]), while Martina in turn is presented primarily as a good observer, and thus both children are presented in analogy. In Spanish, this link is semantically intertwined in *perspicacia* as perspicacity and as a 'watchful eye.' The double semantics are distributed between Aqui and Martina: Martina exposes the father, Aqui exposes him through his observation.

It is by comparing them that the significance of blood relations for this novel's concept of family is questioned: Apparently, with *La familia* one would assume that the question of family affiliation does not arise from the "commonality of experience" (Müller-Bochat 1995, 337) nor from biological descent. Arguably, the omission of Aquilino's conception (and/or birth) makes it undoubtedly clear that although he is part of the family, he was not conceived as a project with a specific purpose. This in turn gives him the space to develop a certain autonomy within the family network. It is noteworthy, then, that the extent to which the child is the parents' project also plays a significant role in family affiliation. Neither Aqui nor Martina were intended as a project.

Aqui and Martina thus appear, in Guénon's sense, as a "second *ternaire*" (Lachmann 2010, 96): "The second *ternaire* is formed by two complementary terms and by their product or resultant. The resultant, which alone gives meaning to this *ternaire*, is of a different order than the complementary terms to which it stands in isolation." (Lachmann 2010, 96) Both Aqui and Martina contribute to an understanding of the father figure: Aqui specifies the concept of the familial in a new way and Martina exposes the father's deceptive speech. Therefore, *both*, when viewed together, form the conceptual framework of the novel, which they also occupy at the plot level. This explains the degree to which both are 'of a different order.' The systematic correlation and intertwining of Aqui and Martina exposes the actual problem surrounding *this family*. It is crucial to understand them as a unit, i.e., Aqui and Martina as a fixed constellation. Only then one can grasp that the foundation of this family is formed by 'communicative unease.'

4.3 Martina. Speaking Authentically

At the end of the novel, Martina finds herself at an airport, which is staged as a place of transit and thus hints at a hopeful ending in the sense of a possibility for change and defense against the experience of violence. This scene again shows the problematic nature of the father's way of speaking, especially concerning the question of truthful speech measured against factual truth or inner correspondence. The scene begins with a factual truth, namely the truth about this family. It exposes the father as a simple legal assistant who insidiously made his family believe that he was a lawyer and ultimately reveals the novel's truth at the plot level. However, a subsequent scene portrays what is truly deceptive about the novel, namely communication as violence.

When Martina reveals that her father had kept quiet about his job, she finds herself at an airport. Air traffic has to be suspended due to the weather and she thus is forced to spend the night there. Throughout the evening and night, a man repeatedly approaches her and engages her in conversation. In an attempt to put an end to it, she finally pretends to be homosexual. The man is offended and feels betrayed: "'You should have told me. I've been after you all night, trying to be nice and get you to like me. It would have been so easy to make me see from the first moment that it wasn't possible!'" ["–Tenías que habérmelo dicho. Llevo toda la noche detrás de ti, intentando ser agradable y gustarte. [...] ¡Con lo fácil que hubiera sido hacerme ver desde el primer momento que no era posible!" (Mesa 2022, 210)] She rejects this and brings the aspect of honesty into play. Had he spoken openly and honestly, she asks silently, referring to a wedding ring on his finger.

What makes this scene intriguing is its parallelism with the father: It creates a new constellation based on ways of speaking: Just like her father, Martina has not lied. However, she has left the other person in the dark about an important fact. And yet this is *not* a repetition of the father's concealed form of communication. The moment of repetition consists in the fact that it is once again the man from whom a communicative distress emanates, whereby another constellation crystallizes under the surface: One between the man at the airport and the family's father.

Martina remains vague due to her intrinsic drive to be polite: "It seems to her that she must be kind to that man because he, in his own way, has tried to be kind to her" ["le parece que debe ser amable con ese hombre porque él, a su modo, ha tratado de serlo con ella" (Mesa 2022, 195)]. To avoid conflict and in order to comply with her father's mannerisms she repeats her childhood mode of speech we had seen in the scene with her journal. This politeness and compliance describe the problem's moment of articulation. Martina genuinely expresses politeness, aiming to avoid causing any offense. The man at the airport represents a contrary position: Demonstrating politeness, he asks if he can sit next to her, but he is actually brash and pushy – just like the father, who is particularly polite towards uncle Óscar, but also towards Martina, by seemingly asking her kindly to stop keeping her diary under lock and key: "Father asked her not to use it [the key] anymore. Please." ["Padre [...] le pidió que no la [la llave – Á.C.] usara más. Por favor." (Mesa 2022, 10)]

When the man sits down next to Martina, he does so under the pretext that the airport restaurant is very busy. However, this is not the truth: "That's not true. It's crowded, even quite crowded, but not *too* crowded." ["No es verdad.

Está lleno, incluso bastante lleno, pero no *muy lleno*." (Mesa 2022, 193; emphasis in the original)] He is persistently intrusive and ignores any attempt by Martina to keep to herself: "He lets out a complicit chuckle. Martina smiles tautly at him, nods so as not to be impolite, and pretends to go back to reading." ["Él suelta una risilla cómplice. | [...] Martina le sonríe con tirantez, asiente para no ser descortés y finge regresar a la lectura." (Mesa 2022, 193)][4] It is noteworthy that is its precisely the man who specifically calls upon the concept of truth in the face of Martina's discomfort: "Although it is also *true* that" ["Aunque también es *verdad* que" (Mesa 2022, 193; emphasis mine)]. This very truth stands on shaky ground. Therefore, Martina is absolutely right when she focuses her attention on the wedding ring.

By naming the chapter at the airport "Buenas personas," the narrative once more underscores the pivotal relationship between this character and the father. The violent and possibly even sinister nature of the communication is not based on whether the truth is being told. Another parallelism is established in the following scene. When Martina becomes resolute, the man, called Bubu, breaks down and reverts to childhood mannerisms: "His lower lip trembles a little, like children about to cry." ["El labio inferior le tremblaba un poco, como a los niños a punto de llorar." (Mesa 2022, 210)] This extends to the point that he no longer thinks he understands her: "'I don't know what you're talking about.'" ["–No sé de qué me estás hablando." (Mesa 2022, 210)] Consequently, this activates the other semantics of Bubu as a form of belittlement to describe infants. Martina's clarity – although a lie – marks a boundary that he cannot overcome and therefore disintegrates into a baby. This specific scene corresponds to two scenes, the one between uncle Óscar and Damián's father on the one hand, who becomes smaller and collapses, and to the one of Óscar and his mother on the other, to whom Óscar says *precisely* this sentence.

It becomes again clear that speaking openly does not equal truth. Speaking openly signifies drawing boundaries that put a stop to this form of invasiveness, regardless of whether it is called by name or not. Consequently, it is only Óscar who can achieve this (or at least he is not a victim figure) as he acts on the adult level and does not belong to the inner family. However, these three characters (Óscar, Martina, Aqui) succeed in defending themselves when they bring up undeniable arguments that cannot be interpreted – be it the advantages of a dishwasher

4 In the Spanish original, it is noticeable that the laughter is set in a diminutive – *la risilla* – which evokes the illusory and deceptive nature of the words ("cheating words" ["[p]alabras [...] tramposillas" (Mesa 2022, 7)]) of the opening prologue, which is also a form of belittlement. It is fitting that the violence is mainly directed at and against the children.

or a divergent sexual orientation.[5] The manipulative and deceptive seep in and twist and turn as long as there is room for it.

5 Conclusion

La familia apparently focuses on trying to get to the bottom of a certain way of speaking that seems to be honest, but reveals to be deceptive. Tightly linked to this supposedly unambiguous way of speaking is a set of nouns that undermine clarity (it is therefore no coincidence that the concept of the passive-aggressive is assigned to this speech as an equally contradictory pair of terms in the field of the affective): The spongy, the nebulous, the diffuse. One of the narrator's comments on Rosa exemplifies this: "There were matters in Rosa's past – problematic things with a glassy texture – that were better not to reveal." ["Había asuntos en el pasado de Rosa – cosas problemáticas de textura vidriosa – que era mejor no revelar." (Mesa 2022, 38)] The novel keeps silent on what exactly the problematic disorder consists of and is noticeably nonspecific: *asuntos, cosas, textura vidriosa.* As the narrative voice says in another passage, we are dealing with 'difficult waters' – in which only Aquilino knows how to move with ease: "Aquilino, the little one, was by far the funniest and the most shameless, also the smartest, he had learned to move with ease in such difficult waters." ["Aquilino, el pequeño, era con diferencia el más gracioso y el más desvergonzado, también el más listo, había aprendido a moverse con soltura en aguas tan difíciles." (Mesa 2022, 114)] *Soltura,* as the detached and relaxed (that only applies to Aqui), refers to the fact that this novel, with its strong narrative voice, is primarily about a mood, forged by tension, latent aggression and lack of freedom.

Since everything that lies beyond the family is not spelled out, the family constellations in this novel remain undefined, insofar as it never explicitly appears

5 The dispute about the necessity (or possibility) of a dishwasher also takes up an aspect of the genre tradition of family narratives: The bourgeois family and the associated question of the relationship between the sphere of gainful employment and the family sphere – and everything that is connected with it. This complex of themes is an important one for the novel's family, as Laura enters into the marriage with Damián also and primarily against the background of being able to lead a symbolically and materially accommodated life with him. Apart from the fact that the tragedy of the family is obviously also due to the fact that Laura is already under the mistaken impression that Damián is a lawyer, the historical dimension of the novel is based on the examination of the possibility of social advancement through material gain as a contemporary diagnosis of a Spanish society that, after the end of the Franco dictatorship, is faced with the possibility of catching up with the emerging prosperity of neighbouring countries. On the intertwining of the family and the sphere of employment, see Hausen 1976.

on the level of plot, but only becomes conceptually tangible. There are no scenes in which recognizable alliances are forged between the family members. The only exceptions are uncle Óscar and Martina: He tries to ally with his sister, while Martina, who covers up Rosa's nocturnal escapades (but these alliances are not developed in any detail with regard to the father figure and are therefore of secondary importance with regard to the family's problems). In fact, the family members only appear as individuals. Although the father is the central source of the violence and undisputedly his figure structures the plot, he is not recognizably staged as the 'pater familias.' On the basis of the plot, it is hardly possible to speak of a dominant figure.

At the same time, the children form different groups, Aqui and Martina, on the one hand, and Rosa and Damián, on the other. In dealing with this 'dominant' father figure, Aqui and Martina show that it is not the blood relationship that is decisive in determining which alliances and constellations can be established. What is, in fact, decisive, if there is a place and a function assigned within the family, or even one's individual character. Ultimately, this means that family is not a biological structure and shows itself to be an interdependent relationship of at least two members, who define the ways in which kinship and connections will be felt.

Bibliography

Adams, Barbara Helena. *Familiendynamiken. Theodor Fontanes* Effi Briest *und* Frau Jenny Treibel. Würzburg: Königshausen und Neumann, 2020.

Bruss, Dagmar. *Zwischen Geschwistern und Geschwisterlichkeit. Giovanni Verga und Robert Walser: Vom Umschlagen des Genealogischen in die Horizontale um 1900*. Heidelberg: Winter, 2016.

Eichenberg, Ariane. *Familie – Ich – Nation. Narrative Analysen zeitgenössischer Generationenromane*. Göttingen: Vandenhoeck & Ruprecht, 2009.

Gemoll, Wilhelm. Ed. *Griechisch-deutsches Schul- und Handwörterbuch*. Coll. Karl Vretska. Intr. Heinz Kronasser. Wien: Oldenbourg, [9]2006.

Hausen, Karin. "Die Polarisierung der Geschlechtscharakter – eine Spiegelung der Dissoziation von Erwerbs- und Familienleben." *Sozialgeschichte der Familie in der Neuzeit Europas*. Ed. Werner Conze. Stuttgart: Klett, 1976. 363–393.

Lachmann, Renate. "Die Rolle der Triaden in sprachbezogenen Disziplinen." *Die Figur des Dritten. Ein kulturwissenschaftliches Paradigma*. Eds. Eva Eßlinger/Tobias Schlechtriemen/Doris Schweitzer/Alexander Zons. Stuttgart: Suhrkamp, 2010. 94–109.

Mesa, Sara. *La familia*. Barcelona: Anagrama, 2020.

Michalski, Anja-Simone. *Die heile Familie. Geschichten vom Mythos in Recht und Literatur*. Berlin/Boston: de Gruyter, 2015.

Müller-Bochat, Eberhard. "Kinder der Kunst – Genetische Fälle in literarischer Behandlung." *Text und Tradition: Gedenkschrift Eberhard Leube*. Ed. Klaus Ley. Frankfurt a.M.: Lang, 1995. 301–339.

Notes on Contributors

Anna Artwińska is a Full Professor of Slavic Literature and Cultural Studies and Chair of the Center for Women and Gender Studies at Leipzig University, Germany. Her main research interests are Polish and Czech Literature, postcatastrophic representations of the Shoah, the concept of generation, memory of the communist past in Slavic literatures and auto/biographical writing. Her current research focuses on family novels in Slavic-Jewish literatures. Recent publications: *Polnische Literatur im langen 19. Jahrhundert. Grundbegriffe – Autor:innen – Textinterpretationen*. Ed. Anna Artwińska (Tübingen, 2024); "'Im Inneren desselben 'Ichs': Karel Čapeks *Hovory s T.G. Masarykem* als kollaboratives Buchprojekt." *Zeitschrift für Slavische Philologie* 80.1 (2024): 79–102; *The Afterlife of the Shoah in Central and Eastern European Cultures. Concepts, Problems, and the Aesthetics of Postcatastrophic Narration*. Eds. Anna Artwińska, and Anja Tippner (London, 2021); "Ołowiane żołnierzyki, cynkowe trumny. Swietłany Aleksijewicz opowieść o wojnie w Afganistanie i granice świadectwa." [Lead Soldiers, Zinc Coffins. Svetlana Alexievich's Afghan Tale and the Limits of Testimony] *Narracje o Zagładzie* (2021; special issue): 255–273.

Anne Brüske is a Full Professor for "Spatial Dimensions of Cultural Processes" at the DIMAS (Department for Interdisciplinary and Multiscalar Area Studies) at the University of Regensburg, Germany. From 2010–2017, she directed the research group "From the Caribbean to North America and Back. Transculturation Processes in Fiction, Popular Culture, and New Media" (Initiative of Excellence, University of Heidelberg, Germany). Her research focuses on Caribbean and Latin American (diaspora) literature, on transregional entanglements between the Americas and Eastern Europe, as well as on Francophone fiction from Enlightenment literature to contemporary texts. Recently, she has published articles on the production of space in Franco-Caribbean and Caribbean diaspora fiction, and on Caribbean graphic novels as well as a monograph with the title *Zwischen De- und Reterritorialisierung. Raumproduktion in US-karibischer Diasporaliteratur* (Boston/Berlin, 2024).

Ángela Calderón is a lecturer and research assistant for Spanish and French literature and cultural studies at Leipzig University, Germany. Her current research project is dedicated to the reflection of history through family narratives in the modern Iberian novel. Her research interests include twentieth century literature and essay writing in Spain, the literature of Galicia, and French literary theory. Further research focuses on French literature of the nineteenth and twentieth centuries, especially Romanticism. In 2022, she published a monograph on the poetological exploration of Gérard de Nerval: *Theorie erzählen. Gérard de Nervals Einleitung zu* Voyage en Orient (Paderborn).

Serena Cianciotto is a Ph.D. candidate in Comparative Literature at the University of Siena, Italy, and Leipzig University, Germany. Her PhD project deals with multi-generational novels at the turn of the nineteenth and twentieth, and twentieth and twenty-first centuries, with a particular focus on Italian, Portuguese, and German literatures. Recent publications are: "O direito ao grito: a rebelião de Macabéa na hora da morte." *Mundos de Língua Portuguesa. Olhares Cruzados*. Vol. IV: *O Brasil em Foco: Perspetivações Literárias e Culturais*. Eds. Valeria Tocco, Filipa Araújo, and Carlos Ascenso André (Coimbra, 2024). 189–204; "*Os Maias* e il romanzo generazionale portoghese contemporâneo." *Il testo e le sue dinamiche nelle culture di lingua portoghese*. Eds. Enrico Martines, and Andrea Ragusa (2023). 251–259; "Adrian Daub. *The Dynastic Imagination: Family and Modernity in Nineteenth-Century Germany* [Review]." *arcadia* 58.2 (2023): 288–292.

https://doi.org/10.1515/9783111208664-016

Matteo Colombi is a literary scholar, comparatist and Slavicist. He is senior researcher at the Department of Slavic Studies at Leipzig University, Germany. His major fields of interest are Czech and Slovene culture and literature and their relations with other Slavic and non-Slavic cultures and literatures (French/German/Italian). Recent publications: Anna Artwińska, and Matteo Colombi "Canons and Their Questioning, Canons and Their Fading: Some Personal Remarks on the Development of the Teaching of Literary History." *Slovo a smysl* 20.2 (2023): 15–48; "Genüssliche Bewegung oder unbehagliche Reibung? Queer(-Theory) im Spannungsfeld: Eve Kosofsky Sedgwick und Sara Ahmed." *Gender Studies im Dialog*. Eds. Anna Artwińska, and Janine Schulze-Fellmann (Bielefeld, 2022). 293–316; "Civil Society and Art/Theory Producers as Parallel Polis? Reflections on the Challenges of Dissident Culture from 1968 to 1989 and Beyond." *Primerjalna književnost* 43.3 (2020): 29–47; Matteo Colombi, and Irene Fantappiè. "Ecletticismo e didattica della letteratura." *Un "osservatore e testimone attento." L'opera di Remo Ceserani nel suo tempo*. Eds. Pierluigi Pellini, and Stefano Lazzarin (Modena, 2018). 463–488.

Anna Gaidash is a literary scholar, Americanist, Ukrainianist and comparatist. She is professor at the Department of Germanic Philology at Borys Grinchenko Kyiv Metropolitan University, Ukraine. Her major fields of academic interest are US-American and Ukrainian culture and literature and communication across languages and nations. Recent publications: *Дискурс старіння у драматургії США: проблемне поле, семантика, поетика* (2019) [The Discourse of Ageing in US Drama: Problematic Field, Semantics, Poetics]; Anna Gaidash, and Inna Red'ka. "Образна гравітація в текстовій модифікації ейджизму: лінгвокогнітивний аспект (на матеріалі вірша Мей Сартон *Old Lovers at the Ballet*)." [Figurative gravity in the textual modification of ageism: a linguistic and cognitive aspect (based on May Sarton's poem *Old Lovers at the Ballet*)] *Science and Education a New Dimension. Philology* 36.136 (2017): 43–46; Anna Gaidash, Olga Bashkyrova, and Mykola Lutsiuk. "The Archetype of the Wise Old Man in Modern Ukrainian Prose: A Diachronic Perspective." *Slavia Centralis* 14.1 (2021): 210–223.

Tamara Hundorova is Chair of the Department of Literary Theory and Comparative Literature at the Institute of Literature, National Academy of Sciences of Ukraine, and an associate of the Harvard Ukrainian Research Institute, USA. Her major fields of academic interest are Ukrainian literature, modernism, postmodernism, gender studies, postcolonial trauma and kitsch. The most important publications: *Кіч і література. Травестії* (2008) [Kitsch and Literature: Travesties]; *Транзитна культура. Симптоми постколоніальної травми* (2013) [Transit Culture: Symptoms of Postcolonial Trauma]; *ПроЯвлення слова. Дискурсія раннього українського модернізму* (1997; 2009) [The Emerging Word: The Discourse of Early Ukrainian Modernism]; *Стать і культура в гендерній утопії Ольги Кобилянської* (2002) [Femina melancholica. Sex and Culture in the Gender Utopia of Olha Kobylianska]; *The Post-Chornobyl Library: Ukrainian Postmodernism of the 1990s* (2019).

Michael Karrer is a lecturer and research assistant at the Institute for Romance Studies at Martin Luther University Halle-Wittenberg, Germany. He holds an M. A. in Cultural and Literary Studies and a B.A. in Political Science and Philosophy from the University of Tübingen, Germany. His doctoral thesis focuses on the political uses of the family archive in contemporary Argentine and Brazilian documentary film. Other research interests include twentieth-century Latin American literature and visual culture. He was visiting scholar at Universidad Nacional Autónoma de México and Universidade Federal Fluminense, Rio de Janeiro, Brazil, and published several book chapters and articles mainly on Latin American film: "Género y temporalidades cotidianas en el cine argentino contemporáneo." *Imagofagia* 16 (2017): 9–28; "Der Mai 68 hat (nicht) stattgefunden. Zum Verhältnis von familiärem und politischem Sonntag in João Moreira Salles' *No intenso agora." Familien-Bilder. Lebensgemeinschaften und Kino*. Eds. Winfried Pauleit, and Angela Rabing (Berlin, 2020). 42–51; "Of Archons and Amateurs. Commissioned Filmmaking in Contemporary Brazilian Cinema." *Ethnographies of 'On Demand' Films: Anthropological Explorations of Commissioned Audiovisual Productions*. Eds. Alex Vailati, and Gabriela Zamorano (London, 2021). 243–265.

Maria de Fátima Marinho is Full Professor in the University of Porto, Portugal. She has been Vice-President of the University of Porto (June 2014–June 2018) and Dean and President of the Scientific Board of the *Faculdade de Letras* [Faculty of Humanities and Social Sciences] (2010–2014). She used to be board member of the IAU (International Association of Universities) (2016–2022), expert of the *Haut Conseil de l'Évaluation de la Recherche et de l'Enseignement Supérieur*, France (2017) and of A3ES [Evaluation and Accreditation Agency for Higher Education, Portugal] (2018). She was decorated by the French Government with the title of 'Officier de l'Ordre des Palmes Académiques' (2015). Her field of interest is Portuguese Literature (Historical Novel and Portuguese Twentieth-Century Poetry). Main Publications: *Camilo Castelo Branco e a Atração dos Abismos* (Vila Nova, 2022); "The Historical Novel." *A Comparative History of Literatures in the Iberian Peninsula.* Vol. II: *A Comparative History of Literatures in European Languages*. Eds. Fernando Cabo Aseguinolaza, Anxo Abuín González, and César Domínguez (Amsterdam, 2016). 206–216; *History and Myth – The Presence of National Myths in Portuguese Literature* (Frankfurt, 2008); *O Romance Histórico em Portugal* (Porto, 1999); papers in many national and international journals and in book chapters.

Adriana Rodríguez-Alfonso holds a Ph.D. and an M.A. in Spanish and Latin American Literature from the University of Salamanca, Spain, as well as a B.A. in Hispanic Philology from the University of Havana, Cuba. Currently, she serves as a teacher and researcher at the Institute of Romance Languages and Literatures at the University of Tübingen, Germany, where she is engaged in her qualification project. Her research interests span across the realms of Portuguese and Spanish literature from the nineteenth and twentieth centuries, material culture, intellectual networks, digital humanities, and the representation of madness. She has published scholarly articles and chapters in various essay collections and refereed journals. De Gruyter will publish her monograph *El grupo Shanghai en Argentina. Redes, estéticas y mercados editoriales latinoamericano*s in 2024. Other main publications are "La estructura del cenáculo: redes intelectuales ante la literatura latinoamericana." *Latin American Research Review* 58.1 (2023): 1–17; "Instrucciones para tornarse literatura mundial: la (inter)nacionalización del grupo *Shanghai*." *Castilla. Estudios de Literatura* 13 (2022): 502–531; "Redes intelectuales y campo literario: *Babel. Revista de Libros*." *Literatura y lingüística* 43 (2021): 101–127.

Karoline Thaidigsmann is a postdoctoral researcher and lecturer of Polish and Russian literature and culture at the Slavic Department of Heidelberg University, Germany. Her research interests include children's and crossover literature, trauma narratives and memory studies as well as transregional entanglements between Cuba and Eastern Europe. She is the co-founder of *Kinderliterarisches Kolloquium*, a research network on Eastern European children's and youth literature. Recently, she has published articles on memory studies and the analysis of crossover literature, the concept of patriotism in Polish literature for young people, imagined communities between Cuba and Eastern Europe in Soviet children's culture [forthcoming] and a monograph with the title *Poetik der Grenzverschiebung. Kinderliterarische Muster, Crosswriting und kulturelles Selbstverständnis in der polnischen Literatur nach 1989* (Heidelberg, 2022).

Anja Tippner is a Full Professor of Slavic Literatures at Hamburg University, Germany. She works on concepts of documentation and life-writing as well as representations of the Shoah and extreme experiences in Russian, Polish, and Czech literature. Her current research focuses on documentary and (collaborative) life-writing after socialism. Recent publications: "Writing a Soviet Holocaust Novel: Traumatic Memory, the Search for Documents, and the Soviet War Narrative in Anatolii Rybakov's *Heavy Sand*." *Growing in the Shadow of Antifascism. Remembering the Holocaust Memory in Communist Eastern Europe*. Eds. Kata Bohus, Peter Hallama, and Stephan Stach (Budapest, 2022). 155–174; *Post-Socialist Cultures of Remembrance*. Eds. Anja Tippner, and Agnieszka Mrozik (2021); *The Afterlife of the Shoah in Central and Eastern European Cultures. Concepts, Problems, and the Aesthetics of Postcatastrophic Narration*. Eds. Anja Tippner, and Anna Artwińska (London, 2021); "Mitteleuropäisch-jüdische Lebensgeschichte als transnationale Verflechtungsgeschichte – Eduard Goldstückers dialogische Erinnerungen." *Zwischen nationalen und transnationalen Erinnerungsnarrativen*. Eds. Lena-Marie Franke, Marek Nekula, and Václav Smyčka (Berlin, 2020). 27–49.

Pablo Valdivia is academic lecturer for Literary Studies at the European University Viadrina in Frankfurt (Oder), Germany. His main research and teaching areas are Latin American and Western European Literature of the early modern/colonial period and twentieth century, critical theory, and the history of modern aesthetics from a decolonial perspective. His publications include *Weltenvielfalt: Eine romantheoretische Studie im Ausgang von Gabriel García Márquez, Roberto Bolaño und Sandra Cisneros* (Berlin, 2013) and *Gegen/Stand der Kritik* (Berlin, 2015; co-editor). He is also first editor of a volume on Paul Valéry (*Paul Valéry: Für eine Epistemologie der Potentialität,* Heidelberg, 2017). In his various publications on Baltasar Gracián he investigates the specificity of early modern aesthetics. As a Latin American Studies scholar, he is one of the PIs of the research project *Perception, Jurisdiction, and Valorization in Colonial Modernity — On the Nexus of Accumulation, Race, and Aesthetics,* funded by the Volkswagen Foundation (https://accumulation-race-aesthetics.org/). His latest work proposes a critical reexamination of Petrarch's *Secretum* as a foundational text of colonial modernity and its cultural politics. He is a regular visiting professor in Bogotá, Colombia.

Jobst Welge is Professor for Romance Literary and Cultural Studies at Leipzig University, Germany, with a specialization on the Ibero-American area. His research interests include the cultural and literary history of the early modern period and the Baroque in Italy, Spain, and Latin America; the history and theory of the novel; literatures of realism, modernism, and the avantgardes in Romance and Ibero-American contexts. He has published the study *Genealogical Fictions: Cultural Periphery and Historical Change in the Modern Novel* (Baltimore, 2015) and has recently co-edited the volumes *Literary Landscapes of Time* (Berlin, 2022), *Armut und Menge* (Paderborn, 2024), and *Unzuverlässiges Erzählen in den romanischen Literaturen* (Berlin, 2024).

Printed in the USA
CPSIA information can be obtained
at www.ICGtesting.com
LVHW021923200924
791668LV00004B/267

9 783111 207766